HAMLYN
MICROWAVE COOKERY

HAMLYN
MICROWAVE COOKERY

Edited by

Bridget Jones

HAMLYN

CONTENTS

USEFUL FACTS AND FIGURES 6

INTRODUCTION 8

MICROWAVE TECHNOLOGY 10

MICROWAVE TIPS AND TRICKS 14

HERBS 16

SPICES 18

SOUPS AND STOCKS 20

FIRST COURSES 30

FISH AND SEAFOOD 42

POULTRY AND GAME 60

MEAT 80

    Beef 82

    Lamb 100

    Pork, bacon and ham 112

EGGS AND CHEESE 126

VEGETABLES 134

RICE, PASTA AND PULSES 150

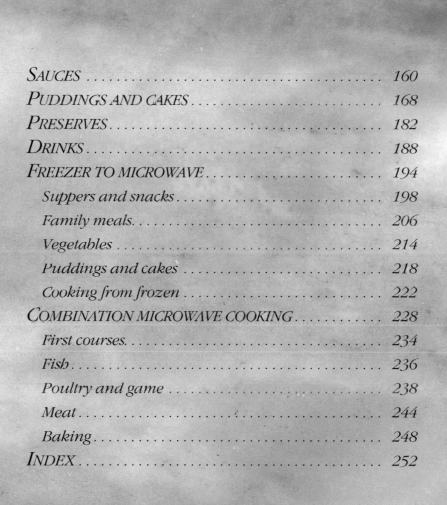

SAUCES 160

PUDDINGS AND CAKES 168

PRESERVES 182

DRINKS 188

FREEZER TO MICROWAVE 194

   Suppers and snacks 198

   Family meals 206

   Vegetables 214

   Puddings and cakes 218

   Cooking from frozen 222

COMBINATION MICROWAVE COOKING 228

   First courses 234

   Fish 236

   Poultry and game 238

   Meat 244

   Baking 248

INDEX 252

USEFUL FACTS
AND FIGURES

Notes on Metrication

In this book quantities are given in metric and Imperial measures. Exact conversion from Imperial to metric measures does not usually give very convenient working quantities and so metric measures have been rounded off into units of 25 grams.

Note: When following any of the recipes in this book, only follow one set of measures as they are not interchangeable.

Ounces	Approx g to nearest whole figure	Recommended conversion to nearest unit of 25	Ounces	Approx g to nearest whole figure	Recommended conversion to nearest unit of 25
1	28	25	11	312	300
2	57	50	12	340	350
3	85	75	13	368	375
4	113	100	14	396	400
5	142	150	15	425	425
6	170	175	16 (1 lb)	454	450
7	198	200	17	482	475
8	227	225	18	510	500
9	255	250	19	539	550
10	283	275	20 (1¼ lb)	567	575

Note: When converting quantities over 20 oz first add the appropriate figures in the centre column, then adjust to the nearest unit of 25. As a general guide, 1 kg (1000 g) equals 2.2 lb or about 2 lb 3 oz. This method of conversion gives good results in nearly all cases, although in certain pastry and cake recipes a more accurate conversion is necessary to produce a balanced recipe.

Liquid measures The millilitre has been used in this book and the following table gives a few examples.

Imperial	Approx ml to nearest whole figure	Recommended ml	Imperial	Approx ml to nearest whole figure	Recommended ml
¼ pint	142	150 ml	1 pint	567	600 ml
½ pint	283	300 ml	1¼ pints	851	900 ml
¾ pint	425	450 ml	1¾ pints	992	1000 ml (1 litre)

Spoon measures All spoon measures given in this book are level unless otherwise stated.

Can sizes At present, cans are marked with the exact (usually to the nearest whole number) metric equivalent of the Imperial weight of the contents, so we have followed this practice when giving can sizes.

Oven temperatures

In the chapter on combinaton microwave cooking oven temperatures are given in °C only as these new appliances do not employ °F. Should you want to convert the temperatures, this chart lists the equivalents.

	°C	°F	Gas Mark		°C	°F	Gas Mark
Very cool	110	225	$\frac{1}{4}$	Moderately hot	190	375	5
	120	250	$\frac{1}{2}$		200	400	6
Cool	140	275	1	Hot	220	425	7
	150	300	2		230	450	8
Moderate	160	325	3	Very hot	240	475	9
	180	350	4				

Comparison of Some Common Different Microwave Oven Settings

Settings	Approx % Power Input	Use

1 Low
  Stay Warm
   Heat and Hold
	25%	To keep cooked dishes hot for comparatively long periods of time.

2-3 Defrost
  Simmer
  Stew
	30–40%	To defrost foods or for lengthy cooking of less tender foods.

4-5 Medium Bake	50%	Reheating foods or cooking delicate foods.
6-8 Medium–High	60–70%	Reheating foods or cooking delicate foods, or simply slowing down the cooking slightly.

9-10 Cook
  – High
  – Roast
  – Maximum
  – Full
	100%	Cooking food.

Microwave Cooking Times
All the recipes and information on cooking times in this book are for a 700 watt microwave cooker.

■ If your microwave has a higher output, then decrease the cooking time, checking two-thirds of the way through the time suggested and continuing to cook as necessary.

■ If your microwave has a lower output, then you will probably have to increase the cooking times slightly. However, there are many factors which influence cooking times, including the actual size of the oven cavity, so always check well-ahead of the maximum time. Remember, you cannot spoil food by removing it halfway through cooking, then putting it back, but once the food is overcooked it is spoilt.

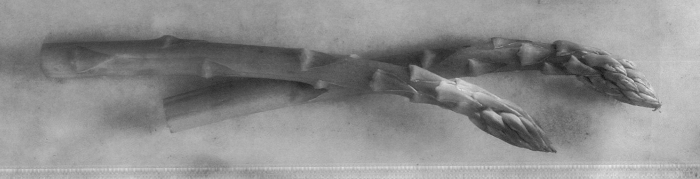

INTRODUCTION

The microwave cooker has introduced a whole new concept to the kitchen; all the traditional methods of cooking rely on the need for an external source of heat to cook the food. Although the older generations may not have understood electricity they certainly accepted the fact that hot grills and radiant hobs would cook the food just as well as an open fire – this was easy, because the effect of the heat on the food was obvious.

By comparison, the microwave does not offer a source of heat in the traditional sense so it is more difficult to appreciate the ins and outs of how this appliance cooks the food and, of more practical relevance, exactly when the food in the oven cavity is cooked, ready to eat. Instead of relying on previous experience, on rule-of-thumb methods and on teachings passed on from mother, with a microwave you have to follow strict guidelines, taking care to be accurate with timings and thinking ahead about cooking utensils as well as preparation techniques.

Before you can realise the full potential of the microwave you will have to get to know it really well. Using your manufacturer's instruction book as a guide, experiment with basic cooking, to discover just how your appliance performs. Note down useful cooking times for the amounts of food that you are likely to cook frequently – vegetables for example. Try different

cooking dishes that you have which are suitable for use in the microwave – you will soon discover which basin or jug is best for a sauce, or which dish is just the right shape and size to cook scrambled eggs. The more you experiment at the beginning, the more you will use the microwave as time goes on.

To help you *Hamlyn Microwave Cookery* offers plenty of guidance on the techniques for preparing and cooking a broad range of foods. At the beginning of each chapter you will find background information, notes and hints on how to achieve the best results. Step-by-step drawings and pictures highlight basic methods and the charts offer a guide to the basic cooking times for a wide variety of foods. When you have mastered all the basic principles of microwave cooking, then you will find the recipes easy to follow. When you are confident about cooking plain foods and are happy to follow microwave recipes, you will find that you can adapt many of your own favourite traditional recipes to this revolutionary new way of cooking. Remember, the key to success is to use the microwave as much as possible – you will soon discover all the advantages and you are sure to decide which foods you prefer to cook by traditional methods, as well as those which you will never dream of boiling or frying again!

ICROWAVE TECHNOLOGY

Before using the microwave read through this chapter and study the manufacturer's instructions. Here you will find all the background information you need to ensure that you make the best and safest use of your microwave cooker.

The concept of cooking food by microwaves has been experimented with by many scientists throughout the world since before the Second World War. The first microwave cooker was manufactured in the United States in the late 1940s, but it was not until 1955 that a domestic model was produced. In those early days the cookers had small cooking cavities but very large cabinets, were expensive to purchase and limited in what they could do.

The modern domestic microwave cooker is small enough to be positioned on a work surface, yet is so well developed technically that it is able to produce a wide variety of cooked foods to suit individual needs.

The benefits of microwave cooking

The microwave cooker is a small appliance which can be accommodated almost anywhere it is required. No special installation is needed as it can be plugged into a 13 or 15 amp socket. It gives fast results in minutes rather than hours. Running costs are low, because the energy concentrates on the food and not on the surrounding areas. It is a safe appliance to use, as it always remains relatively cool, there are no hot parts on which a user can be burnt, and the kitchen is more comfortable to work in.

Almost any utensil can be used, including paper! Depending upon the size of the cooking cavity, almost any quantity of food from a

hamburger to a turkey can be cooked. Since the cooking method retains more nutrients, especially in vegetables, the use of a microwave oven contributes to healthier eating. Foods can also be cooked without fat, so those on a diet can enjoy food without the addition of unwanted calories.

What are microwaves?

Microwaves are a form of the electromagnetic energy which is used every day by all of us in one way or another, for example, when we watch television, listen to the radio, have an X-ray or cook food. It is the frequency at which the energy is used which determines the benefits. The microwave cooker is designed to generate electromagnetic waves and these are contained in the cooking cavity.

How microwaves cook food

To cook raw food conventionally, heat is applied to the outer layer of the food and this gradually penetrates to the centre of the food. Various methods are used to achieve different results. These are known as conduction, convection and radiation. By using one or more of these methods, it is possible to carry out cooking operations, such as boiling, grilling, stewing, frying, baking and roasting. Usually, the heat which cooks the food cannot be seen although the heat source itself can be observed in the form of

electricity, gas or coal.

Microwave cooking is an extension of the three basic principles. The microwaves (short waves) are contained in a cooking cavity and cannot be seen. However, they will act in three different ways:

Absorption Microwaves are attracted to moisture, which is present in all food. Although food looks solid, it is made up of moisture molecules. Once food is placed in the cooking cavity and the microwave energy is switched on, each of the molecules is stimulated and twists back and forth over 2 thousand million times each second. Vibration at such high speed causes the food to heat itself. Unlike conventional cooking, which starts the cooking process on the outer layer of the food, microwaves can penetrate immediately some 4–5 cm ($1\frac{1}{2}$–2 inches) all round. Since all the energy is concentrated on cooking the food, the food cooks more quickly than with conventional methods. As a result there is invariably a reduction in energy costs.

Transmission As microwaves are only attracted to moisture molecules and are absorbed by them, they ignore anything else in the cooking cavity and pass through many other materials as if they were invisible. It is rather like sitting in a car on a warm day, with the sun streaming through the window. The warmth of the sun can be felt but the car windows remain cool. Microwaves act in the

same manner and are not attracted by internal cooker material, only food.

Reflection Although microwaves are absorbed by food and pass through such materials as glass, china, wood, paper and plastic, they are reflected by metal. Since the walls of the cooking cavity are of metal, the microwaves reflect off the walls, creating an invisible energy pattern which contributes to a good energy distribution in the cavity. This also means that if food were to be placed in a metal container it would be screened from the microwaves and would not cook.

It is rather like bouncing a ball against a solid wall – it will always bounce back. If a hole was made in the wall, the ball would continue to travel through it.

The basic controls

Microwave cookers have a variety of controls, in the form of buttons, dials or touch-sensitive pads. However, all models will have a timer and cook control. In addition, many include a defrost control and possibly a variable power control to allow slower cooking.

The timer Timing is an essential part of cooking by microwaves. Once the timer has been set, and the cooking control switched on, cooking will continue until the timer automatically switches off the microwave energy. When it stops, it will indicate completion by a ping, buzz or light. Should you need to get to the food during the cooking, open the door and the timed sequence will halt. Shut the door again and the cooker will continue without needing to be reset.

The cook control This is also sometimes known as the on/off control. It generally works in conjunction with the timer. The majority of cookers have this control but in one or two makes the microwave energy is simply generated by the closing of the cooker door and similarly switches off once the door is opened.

The defrost control This control is for thawing frozen food fast and, once set, will automatically reduce the microwave energy being applied to the food. Depending upon the model selected, it may either reduce the wattage or pulse the energy on and off. It is a particularly useful feature for thawing large items of food as it ensures an even thaw but prevents food from cooking. A further benefit is to use the control for cooking foods slowly; the energy will cycle on and off alternately in accordance with the selected setting, thus slowing the cooking process down. When using this control the timer is set for longer, as directed in specific recipes. For other foods, unless instructions are given in the manufacturer's handbook, the exact timing will have to be judged by experience. The selection of defrost setting is often included as part of a variable power control.

Variable power control This control is simply a method of enabling the user to select more or less microwave energy to suit his or her particular cooking needs. As a dimmer switch for light gives a choice of lighting levels, so the microwave energy can be adjusted. There is no standardisation of settings

between models, but the instruction book supplied with individual cookers gives both recipes and guidance as to which setting is best suited for a specific cooking operation. Like the defrost control, the timer is set and the cooker will automatically adjust to the selected cooking level.

Siting the microwave cooker

The average microwave cooker is about the size of a television and only requires a 13 or 15 amp socket. It can be placed in almost any position and in any room (excluding the bathroom). It may be accommodated on a table top, built in or even placed on a trolley, so that it can be moved at any time to the most convenient working position. Because it is a 'cool' appliance, it is particularly beneficial to the disabled or elderly.

Since air is drawn in by a fan to cool the magnetron, the air inlet grills must not be blocked and the cooker should not be placed near an appliance where this air is likely to be hot, for example near a hob. The magnetron is often referred to as the 'heart' of the cooker, as this component generates the microwave energy.

Safety

Microwave cookers are as safe as any other electrical appliance in the home and must comply with the appropriate government legislation. However, for reassurance, it is worth buying a model which carries the BEAB (British Electrotechnical Approvals Board) label. This confirms that the model meets the requirements of the appropriate British Standard for electrical safety and microwave leakage levels. For safe operation of the appliance, read the manufacturer's instructions and follow them closely.

Cooking containers and utensils

Cooking utensils for the microwave cooker include not only solid shapes like bowls, jugs and casseroles, but also bags, cling film and paper. Practically any material can be used. There are a few exceptions related to metal, and a few plastic materials.

Although microwaves will generally not damage cooking utensils, it is important to remember that the heat of the food may sometimes do so. For example, syrup heated in a glass utensil would reach such a high temperature that the glass could not withstand it.

Metal Unless the cooker manufacturer confirms its use, metal in any form should not be used. China decorated with metal, lead crystal, or any material which contains metal, such as metal ties used for securing roasting bags, are not suitable. Nor are small pieces of foil or shallow foil containers, unless recommended. Metal can cause 'arcing' (i.e. sparking) and may result in the walls inside the cooker becoming pitted.

China, ceramic and oven-to-tableware Make sure that containers do not have metal trim or pattern as this will cause arcing (check for gold or silver printing on the underside) and that any handles have not been glued on. The use of antique china should be avoided. Porous pottery is not really suitable for microwave cooking. Moisture absorbed in the pottery itself will heat up, making the container hot – unlike most microwave containers which remain cool – and this absorption will slow down the cooking of the foods by an unknown and variable amount.

Glass Glass such as tumblers, coupe dishes and small dishes are suitable, but should not be

used in recipes where the food is likely to reach such a high temperature that they may crack. Food containing a high proportion of sugar or fat should not be cooked in glass for this reason. Do not use glass with metal decoration or made of lead crystal. Never leave a thermometer in the bowl while cooking preserves.

Plastic and paper There are several proprietary paper or plastic containers designed for microwave cooking. Providing the plastic can withstand the food temperature it will be satisfactory. This includes boil-in-the-bags, polythene cling film and roasting bags. Thick polythene bags could be used for short-term heating, but preferably not for foods with high fat or sugar content. Avoid melaware (melamine cups, plates, kitchen tools) as these can taint food.

Kitchen paper, greaseproof and cardboard can be used but those which appear to have a wax finish, which could melt from the heat of the food, should not.

Never line a browning dish or skillet with cling film or kitchen paper as they could scorch or burn due to the high temperatures reached by the container.

Wood and baskets Wooden utensils or baskets may be placed in the microwave cooker but only for a short time. Do not use baskets which have been bonded with glue or have wire or staples used in their construction.

Selecting the best utensils Unlike conventional cooking, many utensils can be used, including cups, mugs, tumblers, cardboard boxes lined with microwave-proof cling film or greaseproof paper, bowls, basins and casseroles. Choose the right shape for the cooking operation, remembering that round dishes give better results than square ones. Shallow dishes are better than deep ones.

Avoid cooking cakes in a square or oblong container as the food in the corners may overcook and become dry. Ring-shaped utensils will frequently give a better cooked result with many cake mixtures.

Although not essential, choose a container in which the food may be spread evenly, and be evenly exposed to the action of the microwaves. A utensil which is narrower at one end will cook the food more quickly in the narrow area.

When heating liquids, choose a container large enough to avoid boiling over: glasses should be strong enough to withstand the temperature of the heated liquid. When thawing liquid-based foods, such as soups, place the frozen block in a tight-fitting utensil, so that the thawed liquid is retained close to the frozen block.

Cover foods which need to have the moisture within them to cook the food, for example, stews, soups, fish, peeled fruit, vegetables, steamed puddings, frozen foods. Polythene cling film can be used as a cover, as can plates or casserole lids.

Do not cover foods which are intended to be 'dry', for example, cakes, pastry, fruit and vegetables in skins and bread products.

Cooking instructions

Sometimes instructions are given which may seem unnecessary. As with any cooking operation, the cook is in control, but there are reasons behind instructions.

Stir liquids (such as soups and stews). Some areas of the liquid are getting more exposure to microwave energy. Therefore by stirring, the liquid will heat more evenly. In the case of sauces, stirring will help to avoid lumps.

Rearrange food Unevenly shaped foods, such as chops or fish, may cook more quickly in some parts. By rearranging, for example, turning over the food or changing its position, this can be checked.

Turn food over Large foods like joints and poultry need turning over. As these foods tend to be irregular in shape, the exposure will vary across the food; by turning over, a more even cooking result can be achieved.

Turn containers around This instruction can be particularly beneficial when cooking cakes, as it will contribute to an even rise.

Standing time After cooking, the food is left to stand for a specific number of minutes. This is not done in order to keep food warm but because foods continue to cook by conduction once the microwave energy has been switched off.

Therefore, to avoid dehydration, some foods benefit from being left to stand before serving. This is particularly important with large joints of meat, some cakes and puddings.

Prick or score Any food with a skin or membrane, for example unpeeled apples, jacket potatoes, whole tomatoes, sausages or egg yolks. This simple precaution prevents the food from bursting.

Principles of microwave cooking

By following certain principles when cooking conventionally, a better result will be achieved. The same applies to microwave cooking.

Timing Timing plays a much more important part in the cooked results obtained from a microwave cooker than in conventional cooking. It is wise to undercook, check, and return

Containers for microwave cooking

A wide variety of ordinary kitchen utensils are suitable for use in the microwave oven. Heatproof glass dishes, basins, bowls, jugs and casseroles are ideal for cooking or reheating foods. Plain ovenproof casseroles and classic white gratin dishes that are free of all metal are also useful for microwave cooking. Plain mugs, plates and cereal bowls can be employed for a variety of cooking processes, while loaf dishes and ovenproof glass ring dishes offer variety in shape.

the food to continue cooking. Overcooking or heating will dehydrate the food and render it unpalatably tough or hard.

The quantity of food that can be cooked in one operation relates to the cooking time. For example, one jacket potato may take 5 minutes to cook but two take 8 minutes. This is simply because the level of microwave energy remains the same and has to be distributed amongst an increased quantity of food.

The positioning of food Since the lowest activity of microwave energy is next to the walls, in the corners and absolute centre of the cooking cavity, it is better to place the food off-centre on the floor, unless otherwise directed by the cooker manufacturer.

The more microwave energy exposure the food can get, the more evenly and quickly it is cooked. This is particularly beneficial for small individual items of foods. For example,

items such as small cakes or potatoes should be arranged in a circle with a space between each. For food such as chops, they are best arranged with the thinner areas pointing to the middle of the utensil.

Browning food Microwave energy heats and cooks food but as there is no external application of heat browning in the accepted manner does not occur.

Because large joints of meat and poultry need a longer cooking time, the surface area of fat starts to change colour: it may result in an acceptable colour but it will not be as crisp or as brown as meat cooked conventionally.

There are several methods available which enable the food to benefit from speedy cooking yet retain visual appeal.
● After microwave cooking, brown the food under a pre-heated conventional grill or in a frying pan.

● Use a microwave browning dish. This is specially designed to absorb microwave energy over the base. Once preheated, the base is hot enough to sear food before cooking.
● Should colour be the requirement rather than a crisp skin, the meat can be brushed with a colourful sauce, such as tomato sauce, to liven up its appearance.

Maintenance

Like all appliances, if the manufacturer's instructions are followed, little or no maintenance is required. However, the majority of manufacturers offer a maintenance service, the cost of which can be discussed at the time of purchase. It is important that at no time should anyone but a fully trained microwave service engineer dismantle the cooker or endeavour to carry out a repair.
The manufacturer's instruction

book should always be referred to but in general:
● Any soil or spillage should be wiped clean after use.
● An abrasive cleaning agent must not be used.
● A sharp implement, such as a knife, must never be used to remove hardened food, especially in the area of the door seal.
● A cup of water placed in the cavity will absorb any microwaves if the cooker is turned on accidentally.

Using the recipes

The recipes in this book have been tested in a cooker with a maximum output of 700 watts. Those who have a microwave cooker of a lower output may find it necessary in some instances to increase the cooking time slightly. Before doing so, check the food at the time given in the recipe. Only then should any additional cooking time be considered.

Specialist cookware

There are many different types of specialist cookware available for use in the microwave, from light containers manufactured in plastic, to good looking dishes that are designed for use in the freezer, microwave or conventional oven. One of the great advantages of specialist cookware is that it offers plenty of variety in shape and size, for example bun dishes, cake dishes and ring-shaped containers.

MICROWAVE TIPS & TRICKS

The microwave will save time and effort for a wide variety of cooking processes and minor tasks, from defrosting butter to browning almonds. Here are just a few extra snippets of information that will help you to put the microwave to full use.

Browning almonds

Flaked almonds can be browned in butter. Place the nuts in a basin with a good knob of butter (or margarine) and cook on Maximum (Full), allowing about 4 minutes for 100 g (4 oz), stirring once. Pour the almonds over cooked fish, for example trout, cooked chicken breasts, vegetables or freshly cooked rice.

Crisping bacon

Cook chopped bacon in a basin until the fat runs and the bacon is very well cooked. Stir it halfway through the cooking time to separate the bits, then transfer them to a plate lined with absorbent kitchen paper to cool. When cool they should be crisp and dry.

Defrosting butter

Butter which is taken from the freezer can be defrosted rapidly

Browning almonds

Browning almonds in butter, in a small basin (or try using a jug or mug)

in the microwave for immediate use. Remove the wrapping from the butter, place it on a plate and cook on Medium for 2–3 minutes for 225 g (8 oz).

Dissolving campden tablets

For home wine making: dissolve a campden tablet in just a little water in a mug. Allow about 30 seconds, then stir well to ensure the tablet is completely dissolved, crushing any remaining bits.

Dissolving gelatine

Sprinkle the gelatine over a small amount of cold water and leave for a minute, then heat in the microwave for about 30 seconds or until the water is hot but not boiling. Stir well until the gelatine has dissolved completely, heating it for a few seconds extra if necessary.

Dissolving jelly

Dissolve a tablet of jelly in the microwave. Break the squares apart and place them in a basin with a little water, then heat on Maximum (Full) for about 1–2 minutes. Stir until dissolved, then add cold water to make up the quantity.

Drying biscuits

Biscuits that have been exposed to the air for any length of time absorb moisture and become soft. They can be crisped up by cooking in the microwave on Maximum (Full) for a few seconds. Allow to cool and store in an airtight container.

Crisp bacon bits

1. Place diced bacon, trimmed of rind, in a basin, separating the pieces rather than leaving them in a lump. Cook on Maximum (Full) until all the fat has run from them and they are very well cooked. Stir halfway through cooking to separate the bits.

2. Immediately they are cooked, use a draining spoon to transfer the bacon bits to a plate lined with absorbent kitchen paper.

Drying breadcrumbs

White breadcrumbs can be dried in the microwave. Place them in a dish and cook on Maximum (Full) for 1 minute, or longer if the quantity is large. Stir to rearrange the crumbs and continue to cook, stirring occasionally, until they are fairly dry. Leave to cool completely by which time they should be crisp. Store in an airtight jar. If the crumbs are not dry when cool, then continue to cook them.

Increasing juice yield

Heat whole lemons, oranges or other citrus fruits in the microwave for about 30 seconds each before squeezing their juice. The warmed fruit will yield the maximum juice.

Making croûtons

Make croûtons by drying cubes of bread on absorbent kitchen paper until crisp. Allow 2–3 minutes for 50 g (2 oz) bread cubes. Cool and toss in melted butter.

Melting butter

If you need a small amount of melted butter to fold into a cake or to drizzle over vegetables, then place a knob in a plain mug or small basin and melt it in the microwave.

Melting chocolate

Melt chocolate by breaking the squares in to a basin and heating in the microwave. Allow about 1–1½ minutes for 100 g

(4 oz) on Maximum (Full). Stir halfway through and at the end of the time. If the chocolate is not quite melted, then heat it for a further 30 seconds.

Warming baby's bottle

Warm baby's milk in the microwave. Allow just a few seconds, then shake the milk to distribute the heat evenly and test the milk. The time will depend on the starting temperature of the milk. Once you know the exact timing for your bottle, make a note of it for future reference.

Warming baby food

The microwave is ideal for warming small amounts of puréed foods for baby. Place them in a small basin or dish and heat for a few seconds, then stir well and test before heating further, if necessary, or before using.

Warming bread

Warm a whole loaf, French bread or bread rolls in the microwave. Place on absorbent kitchen paper on the floor or turntable in the cavity and allow just a few seconds or up to 1 minute on Maximum (Full). The bread should feel just slightly warm on the outside when you remove it from the oven. Timing depends on quantity – one or two rolls or French bread heats very rapidly.

Warming cake ingredients

Warm the margarine and sugar for a creamed cake mixture to speed up the preparation. Allow just a few seconds on Maximum (Full) and the ingredients will cream together with ease.

Warming cheese

Bring chilled cheese to room temperature before serving by heating it in the microwave for a few seconds on medium setting (or allow slightly longer on a defrost setting). Unwrap the cheese and place it on absorbent kitchen paper on a plate.

Warming honey

Warm honey which has crystallised slightly, allowing a few seconds on Maximum (Full), then stir well and the crystals should dissolve.

Warming mulled wine

Warm a whole bowl full of mulled wine or heat individual glasses for a few seconds in the microwave. Recipes for mulled wine and other warming drinks are given on pages 188–193.

Warming plates

Warm plates by using them as a cover for the dish in which the food is cooking. Make sure that they do not have any metal trimmings before heating plates in the microwave. Alternatively, if the dish does not need covering, stack the plates underneath the dish to warm them.

Warming sugar for jam

When making jam by conventional methods, warm the sugar in the microwave before adding it to the fruit. Place it in a large microwave-proof bowl and cook on Maximum (Full) for 1–2 minutes, or longer depending on the quantity. The warm sugar dissolves more quickly and lowers the temperature of the preserve less than it would if it is not warmed. Remember that preserving sugar produces less scum on jam.

Making croûtons

1. Cut neat cubes of bread, removing the crusts beforehand if you like. Spread them out on absorbent kitchen paper and cook on Maximum (Full) until firm.

2. The cooled cubes are crisp and they can be tossed in melted butter just before they are to be used.

Melting chocolate

1. Chocolate melts well in the microwave. Break the squares into a small basin.

2. Stir the chocolate halfway through the recommended time; the squares may still retain their shape even when they are soft, so check even if the chocolate looks firm.

HERBS

These are used in microwave cooking in exactly the same way as for conventional methods. The following notes offer general guidance on combining individual herbs with main ingredients and where necessary there are notes on microwave cooking.

DRYING HERBS

The microwave can be utilised to dry herbs. The sprigs of herb should be washed and dried, then laid on a double thickness of absorbent kitchen paper. Place another piece of absorbent kitchen paper loosely over the top. Cook on Maximum (Full) for about 2 minutes, then leave the herbs to cool for 5 minutes. When the herbs have been cooked for long enough they will become crisp and dry when they cool. Continue cooking in bursts of 1 or 2 minutes until the sprigs are properly dried. Cool completely before crumbling and storing in an airtight jar.

The exact timing depends on the type of herbs. If you want to prepare a pot of mixed dried herbs, then dry them individually before mixing.

BASIL

Basil has a unique flavour, closely related to its fragrance. It is lost on prolonged heating, so basil should be used as garnish or added towards the end of cooking. Basil has a special affinity with eggs, pasta, vegetable soups and sauces, but its greatest partner is tomatoes.

BAY

BAY

Bay leaves have a strong flavour and are part of the classic bouquet garni, and are almost always included in stocks, casseroles and pâtés. Make sure they are tucked well between other ingredients, or covered by liquid when cooking in the microwave. They should be removed before serving. They make a good garnish, set in aspic on top of a pâté or terrine.

CHERVIL

Chervil has a light, subtle flavour and forms part of the classic mixture called *fines herbes*, for use in omelettes and sauces. On it own, chervil is good in bland, creamy soups, with baked or scrambled eggs, pounded into butter for serving with grilled fish, or for flavouring a velouté sauce. Wild chervil is also known as sweet cecily.

CHERVIL

CHIVES

CHIVES

Chives are the mildest of the onion family. They are added to dishes just before serving. They make the ideal contrast to pale, creamy dishes like vichyssoise soup and scrambled eggs.

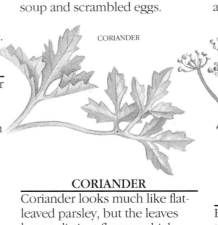

CORIANDER

CORIANDER

Coriander looks much like flat-leaved parsley, but the leaves have a distinct flavour which complements curries and spiced foods.

GARLIC

BASIL

DILL

DILL

Dill resembles fennel, with fethery leaves. Good with fish and as a garnish.

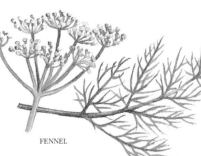

FENNEL

FENNEL

Fennel leaves, with their aniseed taste are chopped and added to sauces and fish dishes.

GARLIC

Garlic is a perennial bulb with extensive uses. In the microwave, like onions, garlic should be cooked first to ensure that it does not overpower the finished dish. A peeled clove will flavour a vinaigrette and it is delicious used to make garlic bread. The flavour becomes milder as it cooks.

HORSERADISH

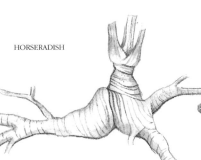

MARJORAM

MARJORAM

MARJORAM

All marjorams dry well and keep their flavour. They give an

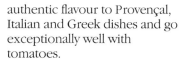

SUMMER SAVOURY

PARSLEY

HORSERADISH

Horseradish has been cultivated in the UK since the sixteenth century, the root is grated and used as a condiment, like mustard, and is the traditional accompaniment to roast beef. When not available fresh, it can be bought ready grated.

authentic flavour to Provençal, Italian and Greek dishes and go exceptionally well with tomatoes.

MINT

PARSLEY

In the UK parsley is used mainly as a garnish, but with its delicious flavour it can be used much more widely in cooking. Parsley forms part of the bouquet garni and *fines herbes* mixtures. Parsley sauce is the traditional accompaniment to boiled bacon and poached fish.

SUMMER SAVORY

Savory has a strong, bitter flavour and should be used in moderation. It dries well and is said to have an affinity with bean dishes.

LEMON BALM

TARRAGON

LEMON BALM

Lemon balm is a perennial, with aromatic leaves which give off a strong lemon fragrance when crushed. The leaves can be chopped and added to stuffings for poultry and game, salads, desserts and fruit cups. They have a flavour somewhat like lemon rind.

MINT

Spearmint is the mint most commonly used in the UK, for making mint sauce and jellies, and cooking with garden peas and new potatoes. Bowles' mint has a superior flavour; do not be put off by its hairy leaves.

Mint is also widely used in both Mediterranean and Middle Eastern cooking. These cuisines particularly favour the spearmint and applemint varieties.

ROSEMARY

Rosemary is a bushy shrub with evergreen needles, dark-green

ROSEMARY

on top and silvery-grey underneath. It has a robust flavour and the sprigs of the herb are removed before serving.

TARRAGON

French tarragon is one of the subtlest of herbs, and goes well with foods of delicate flavour, such as eggs, fish and chicken. It is part of the classic *fines herbes* mixture, and is good in marinades and sauces.

THYME

Both common thyme and lemon thyme are very useful since they keep their flavour when dried or after cooking. Common thyme is good with meat and game. Lemon thyme suits chicken and fish.

LOVAGE

OREGANO

Oregano is the wild marjoram, similar in taste and aroma, but more powerful. It dries

OREGANO

SAGE

Sage has an extremely powerful flavour and can be used fresh or dried. It dries very well in the microwave.

THYME

LOVAGE

Lovage is a hardy perennial growing over 120 cm (4 ft) high, with large, dark green leaves. The chopped leaves are good alone, or combined with other robust herbs, in stuffings, stews and soups, and in fresh tomato sauce for pasta. The flavour is very powerful.

extremely well and is essential in Italian dishes especially Spaghetti Bolognese and pizza. It is also used in commercial chilli powders and is an excellent herb for flavouring stuffings and marinades.

SAGE

SPICES

The art of spicing food has a long and fascinating history, and is one of the most subtle techniques in cooking. When spices are cooked in the microwave, they should be added at an early stage and cooked slightly before the main ingredients are incorporated

ALLSPICE

Allspice berries are similar to large peppercorns with a spicy flavour mingling the tastes of cloves, cinnamon and nutmeg. It is used in smoked and pickled

ALLSPICE

foods and traditional pork or game pies.

ASAFOETIDA

Asafoetida or 'giant fennel' is a huge odiferous member of the parsley family. When used in minute quantities it is a remarkable enhancer of other

ASAFOETIDA

tastes and its frightful smell disappears in cooking. It is used extensively in spicy Middle Eastern dishes.

ANISEED

The small grey-green ribbed seeds of the aromatic anise annual with their spicy/sweet flavour are used in northern and eastern Europe in confectionery, desserts, biscuits, cakes and breads. Anise-flavoured alcoholic drinks are also often used in cookery. In India a small plateful of Aniseed is served with the bill to freshen the mouth and palate.

CARAWAY

CARAWAY SEEDS

Caraway seeds are small oval and ribbed. Strongly aromatic, they have a warming peppery undertone and should be bought as seeds. Breads such as rye and pumpernickel frequently include caraway.

CARDAMOM

Three types of cardamom pods are available, black, green, and

CARDAMOM

white. It is one of the essential spices of Indian cuisine, crucial in biryanis, pilaus, dhals and curries. It is an ingredient of the mixture garam masala and of many Indian dishes.

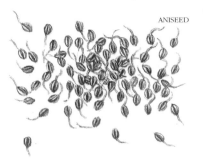

ANISEED

CAYENNE

Cayenne is a very hot pepper which should be used sparingly. It has an affinity with fish and seafood and teams well with cheese and eggs. It is often sprinkled over just before serving.

CAYENNE

CHILLI

Fiery chilli peppers are a very ancient spice, their cultivation stretching back 10,000 years, originating in Latin America.

CHILLI

Chillis vary enormously in size, colour and strength but the ones available in this country generally come from Kenya and are very strong.

CINNAMON

CINNAMON

Cinnamon is a universally popular spice, generally used for sweet dishes in the west and savoury ones in the East. In India it flavours curries and kormas. In Greece it is used in honeyed pastries.

CLOVES

Cloves are both sweet and pungent with an unmistakable aroma, but use them with restraint to avoid swamping other tastes. In British cookery a clove is used to flavour bread

CLOVES

sauce and to stud ham. They blend well with apples in pies and crumbles and should be included in mulled wine mixes.

CUMIN

Cumin's spicy seeds are small, ridged and greenish-brown in colour. They have a strong unmistakable aroma, sweetish and warming. Their flavour is

CUMIN

similarly pungent and penetrating. They should be used in moderation, in seed or powdered form. Always buy whole seeds and grind only when needed.

CORIANDER SEEDS

GINGER

NUTMEG

SAFFRON

CORIANDER SEEDS

Coriander seeds look like tiny ridged brown footballs. They are milder than many other spices so can be used in large quantities. The taste, fresh with a hint of bitterness, improves on keeping.

GINGER

Fresh ginger has a distinctive smell and strong taste, the fieriness of which is diminished in the powdered and crystallised form. Ground ginger is an important and traditional baking spice in the West.

NUTMEG

Nutmeg is milder than mace but has a similar warm sweetish taste. Grate directly over the

mixing bowl or cooking dish to flavour a variety of sauces.

SAFFRON

Saffron is the world's most expensive spice. It imparts a distinctive aroma, a bitter honey-like taste and strong yellow colour to food. It is traditional in Spain's famous Paella and France's Bouillabaisse.

DILL SEEDS

JUNIPER BERRIES

PAPRIKA

SESAME SEEDS

DILL SEEDS

Dill seeds have a fresh sweet aroma but a slightly bitter taste, similar to caraway seeds. They are good in pickled dishes, including the famous dill pickle, vinegars, marinades and dressing.

JUNIPER BERRIES

Juniper berries with their spicy pine aroma and sweet resinous flavour have an affinity with robust meat dishes and are included in marinades and stuffings.

PAPRIKA

Paprika flavours a profusion of savoury foods – from goulashes to vegetables. The mildest kind

is the most widely sold in Britain and imparts a wonderful reddish brown to food.

SESAME SEEDS

Dried sesame seeds have a strong nutty flavour. Dry roast or fry in a little oil before use. They are popular in both Chinese and Japanese cookery and in their ground form make tahini paste.

FENUGREEK

Roast whole fenugreek seeds lightly and grind to a golden powder. It is used most frequently in Indian food, and

FENUGREEK

MACE

PEPPER

STAR ANISE

also in pickles and chutneys and in the Greek sweetmeat, Halva.

MACE

Mace is the crimson, lacy cage enclosing the shell of the nutmeg. It is available both as blades and ready ground. Because of its warm pungency it is best suited to savoury dishes.

PEPPER

Pepper is the most familiar spice of all. Black is stronger than white while green peppercorns have a mild, fresh taste. Peppercorns are added to marinades and stocks and are crushed in French recipes.

STAR ANISE

Star anise is an attractive oriental spice especially associated with Chinese cookery. Red-cooked Chinese dishes frequently include star anise.

FENNEL SEEDS

MUSTARD SEEDS

POPPY SEEDS

Poppy seeds are mild and sweetish and acquire a bitter sweet, nutty flavour when cooked. They are associated with baking and the seeds decorate many types of bread.

POPPY SEEDS

TURMERIC

Turmeric has a distinctive pungent flavour and is best known for its partnership with fish and rice; notably in traditional kedgeree, and pickles such as piccalilli.

TURMERIC

FENNEL SEEDS

Fennel is best known as a vegetable but its seeds are also used in cooking, usually with fish. In the West, they are used in marinades, sauces and stuffing. In India, they are used in fish curries.

MUSTARD SEEDS

Whole mustard seeds are the basis of all prepared mustards and of the pungent mustard oil, beloved in India. They are used primarily in Indian food and to flavour pickles. Cooked, they lose their heat and have a warm nutty flavour.

STOCKS AND SOUPS

Home-made soups can be deliciously simple or delicately sophisticated, from main-meal recipes to smooth and light chilled soups, and they can all be cooked with great success in the microwave. Follow the notes for preparing basic stocks and for adapting your favourite recipes to microwave cooking, then try the range of ideas which follow in the main part of the chapter.

Whether you are preparing a puréed soup or a chunky soup, the microwave can be used to speed up the process considerably given that a few guidelines are followed. When using the microwave for soup-making, the emphasis in the first stage of cooking is on cooking the solid ingredients in the soup and imparting their flavour to a small amount of liquid. Additional liquid is then added to dilute the flavour and to make up the quantity. Soups can be made in advance and reheated in the microwave very successfully.

Cooking utensils

Conventional methods dictate that large saucepans are used to make soup, and when it comes to microwave cooking the same rule applies to the size of the cooking container. You will need a large casserole or bowl in which to cook stocks and soups. This allows plenty of room for rearranging the ingredients and for adding all the liquid. A fairly narrow, deep casserole which has a lid is ideal but a microwave-proof mixing bowl works just as well with a dinner plate as a cover.

Making stock

1. About a third of the water is added at the first stage of cooking.

2. The remaining water is added when the ingredients have yielded their flavour and the stock is cooked briefly, then left to stand.

Cooking utensils

A deep, not too wide, casserole with a lid is ideal for soup-making.

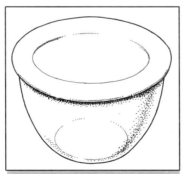

An ovenproof glass mixing bowl is an ideal alternative to a casserole dish. A plain dinner plate makes a good cover.

Home-made stocks give the best flavour to soups, sauces and casseroles. Use leftover meat bones from a roast or from a bacon joint, the carcass of a cooked or boned-out chicken, or use minced beef or chicken joints as the basis for the stock. A vegetable stock should be prepared from a good selection of full-flavoured ingredients. Herbs and onions are essential for flavouring all stocks.

Degreasing stock

Leave the strained stock to cool, then chill it and the fat will set on the surface for easy removal.

Freezing

The cooled stock can be frozen in ice cube trays for later use in small quantities to flavour sauces.

Alternatively, pour all the stock into a rigid container,

leaving head-space for the liquid to expand slightly as it turns to ice. The stock can also be frozen in bags – polythene or boilable bags – in which case they should be supported in a basin or jug until the stock is solid.

Freezing the stock

The stock can be frozen in a concentrated form, in which case add just enough water to cover the ingredients at the second stage, pressing them down into the liquid. You may have to break the chicken into small pieces to immerse it in liquid.

Continue as above but remember that the frozen stock will have a stronger flavour and it will need diluting in soups etc.

Fish Stock

Makes 900 ml (1½ pints)
fish trimmings (heads, tails, fins, bones and skin)
100–175 g (4–6 oz) white fish (the weight depends on the quantity of trimmings used)
1 onion, chopped
1 carrot, thinly sliced
1 bay leaf
2 large parsley sprigs
900 ml (1½ pints) boiling water
salt and pepper

Preparation time: 10 minutes
Cooking time: 25 minutes, plus 30 minutes standing time
Microwave setting: Maximum (Full)

1. Cut up the fish trimmings if necessary, then place them in a large bowl or casserole dish.

Cut the fish into chunks and add it to the trimmings.

2. Add the onion, carrot, bay leaf and parsley, then pour in 300 ml (½ pint) of the water.

3. Cover the dish and cook for 15 minutes. Pour in the remaining water, then continue to cook the stock for a further 10 minutes.

4. Leave the stock to stand for 30 minutes, before straining it through a fine sieve. Press the juices from the flavouring ingredients before discarding them.

5. Season the stock to taste, and use as required.

Vegetable Stock

Makes about 1.15 litres (2 pints)
1 large onion, chopped
1 large carrot, chopped
1 small turnip, chopped
top and root end of 1 head of celery, chopped (include all leaves)
2 tablespoons sunflower oil
3 tomatoes, chopped
1 bay leaf
4 large parsley sprigs
thyme sprig
1.15 litres (2 pints) boiling water
salt and pepper

Preparation time: 15 minutes
Cooking time: 30 minutes, plus 30 minutes standing time
Microwave setting: Maximum (Full)

1. Mix the onion, carrot, turnip and celery in a bowl or large casserole dish. Add the oil and toss the vegetables in it.

2. Cover the dish and cook the vegetables for 5 minutes. Add the tomatoes, herbs and 350 ml (12 fl oz) of the water, then stir.

3. Cover and cook for 15 minutes, stirring once. Add the remaining water and recover the dish, then cook for a further 15 minutes.

4. Leave the stock to stand, still covered, for 30 minutes. Strain it, pressing all the juice out.

5. Season to taste and use the stock as required.

Beef Stock

Makes 900 ml (1½ pints)
225 g (8 oz) lean minced beef
1 large onion, chopped
1 stick celery, sliced
1 carrot, thinly sliced
1 bay leaf
parsley sprig
thyme sprig
blade of mace
900 ml (1½ pints) boiling water
salt and pepper

Preparation time: 10 minutes
Cooking time: 30 minutes, plus 30 minutes standing time
Microwave setting: Maximum (Full)

1. Place the minced beef in a bowl or large casserole dish. Add the vegetables.

2. Tie the bay leaf, parsley, thyme and blade of mace together and add this bouquet garni to the meat.

3. Pour in 350 ml (12 fl oz) of the boiling water, cover the bowl and cook for 15 minutes, stirring once.

4. Pour in the remaining water, stir well, then cover the dish and cook the stock for a further 15 minutes.

5. Leave the stock to stand, covered, for 30 minutes. Remove the bouquet garni, then strain the stock through a fine sieve, pressing all the liquid out of the meat mixture. The stock can be seasoned to taste and used as required.

6. The remaining mince can be used in another dish if you do not want to waste it. Use it with an equal quantity of fresh mince to make a meat sauce, taking care to brown the raw mince first. It should be cooked for the same length of time as the freshly browned meat.

Chicken Stock

Makes 900 ml (1½ pints)
1 chicken carcass or 1 chicken quarter
1 large onion, quartered
1 stick celery, sliced
1 carrot, thinly sliced
1 bay leaf
parsley sprig
thyme sprig
900 ml (1½ pints) boiling water
salt and pepper

Preparation time: 10 minutes
Cooking time: 20 minutes, plus 30 minutes standing time
Microwave setting: Maximum (Full)

1. Break up the carcass and place it in a large bowl. Place the chicken quarter (if used) skin side down in the bowl.

2. Add the vegetables and herbs, putting them round the edges of the chicken and over the top. Pour in 300 ml (½ pint) of the boiling water.

3. Cover and cook for 15 minutes. Pour in the remaining water and re-cover the dish. Cook the stock for a further 5 minutes, then leave it to stand for 30 minutes.

4. If the stock is to be cooled, then leave it until cold before straining. Strain through a fine sieve, pressing all the juice out of the vegetables. Remove and reserve any chicken meat but discard all the flavouring ingredients and bones.

5. Season the stock to taste and use as required. It can be used as the base for soups and sauces, in casseroles or to flavour rice during cooking.

SOUPS

As when cooking stock, the important points to remember are to use hot stock or boiling water and to add only a small amount of liquid with the bulk of the ingredients. If all the liquid is added at the first stage, it takes significantly longer to cook the solid ingredients. If the soup is to be frozen, then it can be left in the concentrated form ready to be thinned when it is defrosted and reheated before serving.

Seasoning

Do not add salt at the first stage of cooking – add it when the bulk of the liquid is stirred in, or taste the soup and adjust the seasoning before serving.

Thickening soup

In all other respects the rules for making soup are the same as for those which can be applied to conventional methods.

Vegetables Potatoes and other vegetables thicken a soup which is puréed.

Flour Flour can be used in the form of a roux (a fat and flour mixture) to thicken soup. Chopped onion, or other ingredients, are cooked with butter or oil first, then flour is stirred in before the first quantity of liquid is added. This is a good method of thickening the liquid in a chunky soup.

Cornflour Used for oriental-style soups, this is mixed with a little cold water and stirred into the full quantity of soup, then cooked for about 3 minutes, until boiling.

Eggs and Cream As with any other cooking method, care should be taken when using eggs or cream as a thickening agent in microwave cooking. Very short heating is required and timings are often measured in seconds rather than minutes. Overheating will result in curdling. When hot liquids are taken from the microwave, they should be stirred well and allowed to cool slightly before eggs or cream are added.

Serving ideas

Simple home-made soups or convenience soups are often made more interesting by the addition of a complementary garnish.

Croûtons Crunchy cubes of bread can be served in a bowl at the table or sprinkled on to the soup just before it is served.

Browned Almonds Browned flaked almonds can be sprinkled over delicate, creamy soups such as chicken, asparagus or spinach soup.

Shredded Orange Rind Finely shredded orange rind adds a tang to tomato or carrot soup. Cook the rind in a little water in a basin for 1–2 minutes, until it is tender, then drain and dry it on absorbent kitchen paper. Sprinkle over individual portions of soup that are swirled with cream.

Herbs Chopped fresh parsley, dill, basil or tarragon are all good on soups.

Cream or Yogurt Swirl single cream, soured cream or natural yogurt into bowls of smooth soups before serving.

Bacon Bits Crunchy bacon bits are delicious in smooth or chunky soups.

Sherry Use good-quality consommé to make a quick starter. Stir in sherry for extra flavour and cream or fromage frais to enrich the soup.

Freezing soups

Many types of soup freeze very well and they can be defrosted and reheated very quickly in the microwave. However, there are one or two points to remember for success.

Fish and seafood soups do not freeze as well as meat and vegetable soups if they contain pieces of fish as the cooked fish tends to break up on defrosting and reheating.

Soups which are thickened with eggs do not freeze well once the eggs are added as they curdle. Similarly, cream should not be added to soup before it is frozen as it will curdle when defrosted and reheated.

Chunky vegetable soups which are prepared for freezing should be slightly under cooked. Pieces of root vegetable in the soup should be firm and slightly crisp when frozen so that they do not break up when they are defrosted and reheated. Cook the soup for a few minutes once it is hot so that the vegetables are tender when served.

If the soup has rice or pasta added, then these ingredients should not be frozen with the soup. Once the soup has defrosted and heated the rice or pasta can be added and cooked before serving.

Packing soup for freezing It is a mistake to pour the soup into large or very tall containers to store in the freezer. Remember that the block of frozen soup will have to fit into a bowl for defrosting. Also, if the block is too tall it may not fit in the microwave.

Convenience foods

Canned soups and consommé can be heated with ease and speed in the microwave. For single portions simply pour the soup into a suitable serving bowl or mug and heat on Maximum (Full) for about 1–2 minutes. Stir well and continue to heat until the soup is heated through. Stir well before eating. Larger portions can be heated in a basin or large jug.

Dried packet soups can also be prepared in the microwave. Turn the mix into a large basin and gradually whisk in the required amount of water. Heat on Maximum (Full), whisking after 1–2 minutes and at intervals until the soup is boiling and thickened. The time depends on the quantity; allow about 4 minutes for 600 ml (1 pint).

Packet cup soups can also be heated in the microwave – slowly stir in the stated quantity of cold water and heat on Maximum (Full) until boiling. Check the soup after 45 seconds.

Stages in soup-making

1. The vegetables and other solid ingredients are cooked first with the minimum of water, until they are almost tender but not completely cooked.

2. Half the quantity of hot stock is added to the vegetables and cooked until all the ingredients are ready for puréeing.

3. The last of the liquid is added as the soup is puréed or afterwards, depending on the thickness. For chunky soups the stock is added with seasoning, then heated briefly and served.

Soup which defrosts best in the microwave is that which is frozen in small containers or blocks. For example, smooth soups can be packed in empty yogurt pots or margarine tubs (put them on a baking tray until frozen). Once the soup is hard it can be removed from the pots and packed in freezer bags for storage. Put the small blocks in a dish to defrost quickly.

Large blocks of soup should be placed in a dish and broken up as they soften to speed up the total defrosting and reheating time.

When the soup is hot, rice or pasta can be added if necessary, before cooking.

Simple Vegetable Soup

Serves 4
1 onion, chopped
1 potato, diced
2 carrots, diced
2 sticks celery, diced
2 tablespoons oil
900 ml (1½ pints) hot chicken stock
100 g (4 oz) frozen peas or cut green beans
3 tablespoons chopped parsley
salt and pepper

Preparation time: 15 minutes
Cooking time: 25 minutes
Microwave setting: Maximum (Full)

1. Mix all the prepared fresh vegetables in a large bowl or casserole dish. Add the oil and toss the vegetables in it to coat them evenly.

2. Cover the dish and cook the vegetables for 5 minutes. Stir in half the stock, re-cover the dish and cook for a further 10 minutes, stirring once.

3. Add the remaining stock, the frozen peas or beans and the parsley. Sprinkle in a little seasoning, then cover the dish and cook the soup for a further 10 minutes.

4. The vegetables should be tender but still whole. Taste the soup and adjust the seasoning, then stir well before serving with crusty bread.

5. If the soup is to be frozen, then cook it for 2–5 minutes after the second batch of stock is added so that the vegetables are still quite firm. Leave the soup to cool before packing and freezing. After it is defrosted the soup should be cooked for a few minutes until the vegetables are tender.

Puréed Potato and Almond Soup

Serves 4
1 onion, chopped
450 g (1 lb) potatoes
100 g (4 oz) blanched almonds
25 g (1 oz) butter
600 ml (1 pint) hot chicken stock
300 ml (½ pint) single cream or milk
1 tablespoon chopped parsley

Preparation time: 10 minutes
Cooking time: 18–19 minutes
Microwave setting: Maximum (Full)

1. Mix the onion, potatoes and almonds in a bowl or casserole dish, and add the butter. Cover and cook for 10 minutes, stirring once.

2. Pour in the stock and recover the dish, then continue to cook for 7 minutes, or until the potatoes are softened but not fallen.

3. Purée the soup in a liquidizer, then pour it back into the bowl and stir in the cream or milk. Heat for 1–2 minutes, taking care not to let the soup boil.

4. Stir and taste for seasoning, then sprinkle with parsley before serving.

5. If the soup is to be frozen, then this should be done when it is puréed but before the cream or milk is added. The cream should be added when the purée has been defrosted and reheated.

Potato and Onion Soup

Serves 4

275 g (10 oz) onions, peeled
   and finely chopped
750 g (1½ lb) potatoes, peeled
   and thinly sliced
1 teaspoon dried mixed herbs
600 ml (1 pint) milk
salt
300 ml (½ pint) hot beef stock
freshly ground black pepper
2 teaspoons chopped chives, to
   garnish

Preparation time: about 10 minutes
Cooking time: about 17½ minutes
Microwave setting: Maximum (Full)

1. Place the onions and potatoes in a large bowl, cover and cook for 13 minutes, stirring halfway through cooking.

2. Stir in the herbs, milk and salt. Cover and cook for 4½ minutes, stirring halfway through cooking.

3. Stir in the hot beef stock,

pepper and more salt, if necessary, to taste. Purée in a blender or food processor.

4. Pour into 4 soup bowls and garnish.

Potato and onion soup; Lentil and orange soup

Lentil and Orange Soup

Serves 4
25 g (1 oz) butter
100 g (4 oz) split red lentils
*1 onion, peeled and finely
  chopped*
1 celery stick, finely sliced
*½ medium carrot, peeled and
  grated*
¼ teaspoon dried thyme
*900 ml (1½ pints) hot chicken
  stock*
150 ml (¼ pint) orange juice
grated rind of ½ orange
bay leaf
salt
freshly ground black pepper
orange rind, to garnish

Preparation time: about 10
minutes
Cooking time: about 27
minutes
Microwave setting: Maximum
(Full)

1. Place the butter and lentils in a large bowl. Cover and cook for 2 minutes, stirring halfway through.

2. Stir in the onion, celery, carrot and thyme. Cover and cook for 7 minutes, stirring halfway through.

3. Stir in 600 ml (1 pint) of the hot stock with the orange juice, rind, bay leaf, salt and pepper. Cover. Cook for 10 minutes, stirring halfway through cooking.

4. Remove the bay leaf and stir in the remaining hot stock. Cool slightly.

5. Pour the soup into a liquidizer and blend.

6. Return to the bowl and reheat for 8 minutes. Adjust the seasoning and garnish with orange.

Mulligatawny Soup

Serves 4
2 tablespoons oil
100 g (4 oz) red lentils
*2 garlic cloves, peeled and
  crushed*
*1 onion, peeled and finely
  chopped*
*1 carrot, peeled and finely
  chopped*
*1 small turnip, peeled and
  finely chopped*
1 teaspoon curry powder
*900 ml (1½ pints) hot chicken
  stock*
salt
freshly ground black pepper
1–2 tablespoons lemon juice

Preparation time: about 10
minutes
Cooking time: about 27
minutes
Microwave setting: Maximum
(Full)

1. Mix the oil, lentils, garlic onion, carrot and turnip in a large bowl. Cover and cook for 9 minutes, stirring twice.

2. Stir in the curry powder and pour in 600 ml (1 pint) of the hot stock, then add seasoning to taste. Stir well, cover and cook for 10 minutes, stirring once.

3. Add the remaining stock, stir well, then blend the soup in a liquidizer. Pour the soup back into the bowl and heat it for 8 minutes.

4. Taste and adjust the seasoning, then sharpen with lemon juice to taste. Serve crisp popadums as an accompaniment.

Sweetcorn and Potato Soup

Serves 4–6
*1 onion, peeled and finely
  chopped*
*450 g (8 oz) potatoes, peeled
  and thinly sliced*
225 g (8 oz) frozen sweetcorn
bay leaf
600 ml (1 pint) milk
salt
*300 ml (½ pint) hot chicken
  stock*
freshly ground black pepper
*2 spring onions, trimmed and
  finely chopped*
*4 tablespoons soured cream, to
  serve*

Preparation time: about 10
minutes
Cooking time: about 19½
minutes
Microwave setting: Maximum
(Full)

1. Mix the onion, potatoes, sweetcorn and bay leaf in a large bowl. Cover and cook for 15 minutes, stirring twice.

2. Pour in the milk and season with a little salt. Cover the bowl and cook for a further 4½ minutes, stirring once.

3. Stir in the hot stock and add some pepper to the soup, then blend it in a liquidizer until smooth.

4. Taste and adjust the seasoning, add the spring onions to the soup and serve. Swirl a little soured cream into each portion.

Cream of Carrot Soup

Serves 6
75 g (3 oz) butter
1 onion, peeled and chopped
*1 rasher back bacon, rind
  removed and chopped*
1 teaspoon salt
1 teaspoon sugar
freshly ground black pepper
*450 g (1 lb) peeled carrots,
  chopped*
1 litre (1¾ pints) chicken stock
To garnish:
150 ml (¼ pint) single cream
croûtons

Preparation time: about 10
minutes
Cooking time: 26 minutes
Microwave setting: Maximum
(Full)

1. Place the butter in a large bowl and cook for 1 minute to melt. Add the onion, bacon, salt, sugar and pepper to taste. Cover and cook for 3 minutes.

2. Stir in the carrots and stock. Cover and cook for 20 minutes.

3. Purée in a blender until smooth or pass through a fine sieve.

4. Turn the soup into a suitable tureen and cook for 2 minutes to reheat. Serve hot, garnished with a swirl of cream and a few croûtons.

Country Vegetable Soup

Serves 4
25 g (1 oz) butter
100 g (4 oz) cabbage, finely
    shredded
100 g (4 oz) potatoes, peeled
    and diced
100 g (4 oz) onions, peeled and
    chopped
100 g (4 oz) carrots, peeled and
    thinly sliced
50 g (2 oz) red pepper, cored,
    seeded and diced
50 g (2 oz) turnip, peeled and
    diced
1 × 400 g (14 oz) can tomatoes
    with juice
salt
freshly ground black pepper
900 ml (1½ pints) hot beef stock

Preparation time: about 15 minutes
Cooking time: about 20 minutes
Microwave setting: Maximum (Full)

1. Place the butter, cabbage, potatoes, onions, carrots, red pepper, turnip, tomatoes, salt and pepper in a large bowl. Cover and cook for 10 minutes, stirring halfway through cooking.

2. Stir in the stock. Cover and cook for 10 minutes or until the vegetables are tender, stirring halfway through cooking.

3. Taste and adjust the seasoning before serving.

Tomato Soup with Rice and Basil

Serves 4
25 g (1 oz) butter
1 large onion, peeled and
    chopped
40 g (1½ oz) plain flour
2 tablespoons tomato purée
750 g (1½ lb) ripe tomatoes, cut
    into quarters
¼ teaspoon celery salt
1 teaspoon caster sugar
1 teaspoon dried basil
salt
freshly ground black pepper
300 ml (½ pint) milk
450 ml (¾ pint) hot chicken
    stock
4 tablespoons cooked rice
2 tablespoons single cream, to
    serve (optional)

Preparation time: about 5 minutes
Cooking time: about 18 minutes
Microwave setting: Maximum (Full)

1. Place the butter and onion in a large bowl. Cover and cook for 4 minutes.

2. Stir in the flour, tomato purée, tomatoes, celery salt, sugar, basil, salt and pepper. Add the milk. Cover and cook for 10 minutes, stirring halfway through cooking.

3. Add the hot stock and allow to cool slightly.

4. Pour the soup into a liquidizer and blend until smooth.

5. Sieve the liquidized soup to remove the tomato skins and pips. Stir in the cooked rice.

6. Return the soup to the bowl and reheat uncovered for 3–4 minutes. Adjust the seasoning.

7. Serve the soup with a swirl of cream floating on the top, if liked.

Country vegetable soup; Tomato soup with rice and basil

Fish Soup

Serves 4–6

1 onion, peeled and finely chopped
1 small green pepper, cored, seeded and finely diced
225 g (8 oz) potatoes, peeled and finely diced
1 tablespoon oil
1 garlic clove, peeled and crushed
½ teaspoon dried rosemary
1 teaspoon chopped fresh parsley
salt
2 bay leaves
600 ml (1 pint) cold water
750 g (1½ lb) filleted white fish, cut into small pieces
450 ml (¾ pint) hot water
freshly ground black pepper

Preparation time: about 20 minutes
Cooking time: about 17½ minutes
Microwave setting: Maximum (Full)

1. Place the onion, green pepper, potatoes, oil, garlic, rosemary, parsley and salt in a large bowl. Cover and cook for 7½ minutes or until the vegetables are tender.

2. Stir in the bay leaves, cold water and fish. Cover and cook for 10 minutes, stirring halfway through.

3. Stir the hot water gently into the fish mixture.

4. Remove the bay leaves. Taste and adjust the seasoning, then serve in individual soup bowls.

Pea and Mint Soup

Serves 4–5

25 g (1 oz) butter
1 medium onion, peeled and finely chopped
450 g (1 lb) frozen peas
1 tablespoon chopped fresh mint
600 ml (1 pint) hot chicken stock
salt
freshly ground black pepper
25 g (1 oz) plain flour
450 ml (¾ pint) milk
4 mint sprigs, to garnish

Preparation time: about 5 minutes
Cooking time: about 19 minutes
Microwave setting: Maximum (Full)

1. Place the butter, onion, peas and mint in a large bowl. Cover and cook for 8 minutes, stirring halfway through cooking.

2. Add the hot chicken stock, salt and pepper. Cover and cook for 5 minutes.

3. Place the flour in a small bowl and gradually blend in the milk. Stir the milk into the soup.

4. Pour the soup into a liquidizer and blend until smooth.

5. Return the soup to the bowl, cover and cook for 6 minutes, stirring halfway through cooking.

6. Taste and adjust the seasoning, then serve garnished with sprigs of mint.

Fish soup, Pea and mint soup

Lettuce Soup with Croûtons

Serves 4

1 medium onion, peeled and
finely chopped
50 g (2 oz) butter
25 g (1 oz) plain flour
450 ml (¾ pint) hot chicken
stock
300 ml (½ pint) milk
225 g (8 oz) lettuce leaves,
washed and chopped
¼ teaspoon grated nutmeg
¼ teaspoon caster sugar
salt
freshly ground black pepper
1 egg yolk
Croûtons:
2 slices fresh white bread, cut
into cubes
4 tablespoons oil

Preparation time: about 5
minutes
Cooking time: about 19
minutes
Microwave setting: Maximum
(Full)

1. Place the onion and butter in
a large bowl. Cover and cook
for 4 minutes.

2. Stir in the flour, hot stock,
milk, lettuce, nutmeg, sugar, salt
and pepper. Cover and cook for
9 minutes. Cool slightly.

3. Pour the soup and the egg
yolk into a liquidizer and blend
until smooth.

4. Return soup to the bowl.
Reheat for 2 minutes.

5. Taste and adjust the
seasoning, then serve garnished
with croûtons.

6. To make the croûtons, toss
the cubes of bread in the oil.
Spread the cubes over a plate.
Cook for 2 minutes. Stir and
cook for a further 2 minutes,
checking and stirring the
croûtons frequently until
browned. Drain on paper
towels.

Chicken and Vegetable Soup

Serves 4

1 carrot, peeled and finely
sliced
1 medium potato, peeled and
diced
2 button mushrooms, sliced
1 small red pepper, cored,
seeded and diced
1 small turnip, peeled and
diced
½ leek, trimmed and finely
sliced
1 small onion, peeled and
chopped
600 g (1¼ lb) chicken pieces
1 litre (1¾ pints) hot chicken
stock
salt
freshly ground black pepper
bouquet garni

Preparation time: about 15
minutes
Cooking time: about 26
minutes
Microwave setting: Maximum
(Full)

1. Place the carrot, potato,
mushrooms, red pepper, turnip,
leek and onion in a large bowl.
Place the chicken pieces on top
of the vegetables. Cover and
cook for 15 minutes, stirring
halfway through.

2. Add the hot chicken stock,
salt, pepper and bouquet garni.
Cover and cook for 8 minutes.

3. Take out the chicken. Remove
and discard the skin, then cut
the flesh from the bones. Chop
the chicken flesh and return it to
the soup.

4. Remove the bouquet garni.
Reheat for 3 minutes. Taste and
adjust the seasoning, before
serving.

Lettuce soup with croûtons; Chicken
and vegetable soup

Vichyssoise

Serves 4–5

350 g (12 oz) potatoes, peeled and thinly sliced
750 g (1½ lb) leeks, trimmed and thinly sliced
1 celery stick, finely chopped
50 g (2 oz) butter
4 tablespoons water
900 ml (1½ pints) hot chicken stock
salt
freshly ground black pepper
150–300 ml (¼–½ pint) double cream
1 tablespoon chopped fresh chives, to garnish

Preparation time: about 10 minutes, plus chilling
Cooking time: about 14 minutes
Microwave setting: Maximum (Full)

1. Place the potatoes, leeks, celery, butter and water in a large bowl. Cover and cook for 8 minutes, stirring halfway through cooking.

2. Add half the stock, salt and pepper. Cover and cook for 6 minutes. Add the remaining stock.

3. Pour the soup into a liquidizer and blend.

4. Sieve the liquidized soup. Taste and adjust the seasoning.

5. Allow to cool completely, then chill for 2 hours.

6. Before serving, stir in the cream and garnish with chopped chives.

Mushroom Soup

Serves 4

25 g (1 oz) butter
1 medium onion, peeled and finely chopped
225 g (8 oz) flat mushrooms, chopped
25 g (1 oz) plain flour
300 ml (½ pint) milk
salt
freshly ground black pepper
600 ml (1 pint) hot chicken stock
4 tablespoons single cream
2 button mushrooms, thinly sliced, to garnish

Preparation time: 5–10 minutes
Cooking time: about 13½ minutes
Microwave setting: Maximum (Full)

1. Place the butter and chopped onion in a large bowl. Cover it and cook for 5 minutes. Stir in the chopped mushrooms, cover again and cook for a further 3 minutes.

2. Stir in the flour, then gradually blend in the milk. Season to taste with salt and pepper. Cover and cook for 2½ minutes.

3. Stir in the hot chicken stock. Purée in a blender or food processor, then pour the soup back into the bowl.

4. Taste and adjust the seasoning, if necessary. Stir in the cream. Reheat, uncovered, for 3 minutes, if required.

5. Pour into 4 individual soup bowls and garnish with the thinly sliced button mushrooms.

Vichyssoise; Mushroom soup

FIRST COURSES

The microwave really does take the trouble out of preparing first courses. Speedy pâtés can be prepared and cooked in advance or mouth-watering hot appetisers can be organised ahead ready for cooking in minutes just before you sit at the table to dine.

The key to success when it comes to serving the perfect first course is good planning. Either have the starter ready in advance or have it prepared to the stage at which it can be put in the microwave to be quickly cooked or heated just before it is served.

Plan the first course along with the rest of the menu, making sure that there is plenty of contrast in textures and that the flavours are complementary. Before filling main courses serve light starters, or if you particularly want to serve a splendid first course, then make sure that the main course is simple. If the first course and main courses are both hot, then the dessert can be a cool one.

The accompaniments which go with the starter are also important. Crusty French bread, thinly sliced bread and butter or crisp toast are often served but you may like to try microwave-cooked jug bread for a change.

Lastly, the garnish is important – this opening dish of the meal should catch the eye as well as tempt the palate, so add a few sprigs of fresh herbs, shredded lettuce, twists of lemon or other simple garnishing ingredients.

Fruit starters

Fruit starters are not always cold and the microwave can be used to prepare quick 'baked' grapefruit or light fruit compôtes that arouse the appetite. These should be ready prepared, in suitable dishes, to be warmed in the microwave just before you sit to eat.

Vegetable starters

Many classic first courses rely on the simple preparation of perfect vegetables – asparagus with butter, or artichokes with vinaigrette dressing – and the microwave is ideal for this purpose. If you are serving asparagus, have it ready in its cooking container so that it can be cooked just before it is served. To one side have some butter ready to melt as you transfer the cooked asparagus to the plates. Lemon wedges will provide garnish and a refreshing contrast in taste.

Corn-on-the-cob is less expensive and equally easy. The cobs can be cooked in one large roasting bag or they look good when individually wrapped in greaseproof paper and served in their paper cases. Think ahead and have the cobs all ready to go into the microwave well in advance. Remember that you may have to check and rearrange them halfway through the cooking time to move any from the middle of the dish to the outside.

Pâtés

The microwave is excellent for cooking all types of pâtés. Use the microwave to melt butter for simple fish pâtés which are puréed and chilled, or substitute microwave-cooked smoked haddock instead of smoked mackerel for a change. Chicken or turkey liver pâté can be cooked very successfully in the microwave or you can cook heavier, loaf or dish pâtés in the same way. For example, try

serving the Picnic Ham Pâté on page 124 as a first course, offering hot toast as an accompaniment. Many of your favourite meat pâtés can be cooked in the microwave but remember that a dense mixture takes time to cook through. It is a good idea to roughly chop and part-cook liver or meat before it is puréed or minced and mixed with the other pâté ingredients. The pâté should be covered to prevent drying out as it cooks. Make sure the mixture is cooked right through by cutting out a tiny sample from the middle of it.

Seafood starters

Ready-cooked shellfish can be heated rapidly in the microwave and coated in a well-flavoured

sauce to make an impressive starter. As a change from prawn cocktails why not sample the Hot Seafood Cocktail on page 35, or cook delicate scallops in a creamy sauce? When cooking delicate fresh shellfish, like scallops or mussels, it is important to remember that they require very little cooking and that they will toughen and lose flavour if they are overcooked. So the rule of thumb for these ingredients is to check in advance rather than cooking the food for the full length of time suggested.

Cook corn-on-the-cob

1. Individual cobs of corn are generously brushed with melted butter and wrapped in greaseproof paper before cooking. (They can be served in the paper wrappings.)

2. Arrange four cobs in a shallow dish, placing them as near to the outside of the dish as possible. Rearrange them halfway through cooking, turning the ends from the middle towards the outside.

Quick Jug Bread

Sliced into small circles, this quick-to-make bread is the ideal accompaniment for light first courses or it can be used as a base for serving rolls of smoked salmon.

Makes 2 loaves

1 × 280 g (10 oz) packet bread mix
300 ml (½ pint) hand-hot water
oil for greasing
3–4 tablespoons sesame seeds, roasted

Preparation time: about 15 minutes, plus about 40 minutes proving time
Cooking time: 4 minutes, plus standing, for each loaf
Microwave setting: Maximum (Full)

1. Place the bread mix in a bowl and gradually beat in the water to make a thick, smooth batter. Continue to beat until the batter is smooth and elastic; this takes about 10 minutes.

2. Grease 2 × 600 ml (1 pint) ovenproof glass measuring jugs (or use a jug and a basin). Sprinkle the insides with sesame seeds, then divide the batter between the jugs.

3. Cover loosely with microwave-proof cling film and leave in a warm place until the batter has doubled in size.

4. Cook for 3½–4 minutes, until the dough is firm, then leave to

stand in the jug for 2 minutes. Turn out onto a wire rack to cool. Cut the bread into round slices to serve.

5. The bread keeps successfully for 24 hours but it should be wrapped in plastic film or placed in a plastic bag to prevent it from drying out.

1. A packet of bread mix is beaten into a smooth, elastic batter: it will cook well to yield small, soft loaves. Alternatively a batter can be prepared from strong-flow, easy-blend yeast and lukewarm water.

2. The batter is divided between jugs or a jug and basin and left in a warm place until well risen, as here.

3. The cooked loaves are left to stand in the jugs for 2 minutes, then turned out to cool. They are sliced into attractive, delicate slices.

Globe Artichokes with French Dressing

Serves 4
4 globe artichokes
300 ml (½ pint) water
1 tablespoon lemon juice
French dressing:
salt
freshly ground black pepper
1 teaspoon dry mustard
6 tablespoons wine vinegar
175 ml (6 fl oz) olive oil

Preparation time: about 10 minutes, plus cooling
Cooking time: about 20 minutes
Microwave setting: Maximum (Full)

1. Using a pair of scissors, snip off the point from each of the outer leaves of the artichokes. Cut the stalks from the bases. Rinse the artichokes and turn upside down to drain.

2. Pour the water and lemon juice into a large shallow dish. Cook for 4 minutes.

3. Stand the artichokes in the water and cover the dish with cling film. Cook for 10 minutes.

4. Rearrange the artichokes, so the front ones are at the back, and cook, covered, for a further 10 minutes, or until the bases are tender when pricked with a fork.

5. Leave to stand, covered, for 10 minutes. Drain off the water and leave to cool.

6. While the artichokes are cooling, make the dressing. Place the salt, pepper and mustard in a small basin. Stir in the vinegar. Whisk in the oil a little at a time, until smooth.

7. To serve, pour a little French dressing over each artichoke. Hand the remaining dressing separately.

Mushrooms in Garlic Butter

Serves 4
450 g (1 lb) button mushrooms
1 teaspoon dried mixed herbs
2 garlic cloves, peeled and crushed
1 tablespoon lemon juice
100 g (4 oz) butter, cut into pieces
1 tablespoon double cream
salt
freshly ground black pepper

Preparation time: about 7 minutes
Cooking time: about 8½ minutes
Microwave setting: Maximum (Full)

1. Place the mushrooms, herbs, garlic and lemon juice in a large bowl. Cover and cook for 6 minutes. Pour off any excess liquid.

2. Stir in the butter, cream and salt and pepper to taste. Cook, uncovered, for 2½ minutes, stirring every minute. Serve with crusty French bread.

Globe artichokes with French dressing;
Mushrooms in garlic butter

Hot Crab

Serves 4
*50 g (2 oz) fresh white
    breadcrumbs*
2 teaspoons oil
1 tablespoon anchovy essence
1 tablespoon lemon juice
*1 tablespoon Worcestershire
    sauce*
150 ml (¼ pint) double cream
175 g (6 oz) crab meat
salt
freshly ground black pepper
4 pieces fried bread
To garnish:
mild paprika
parsley sprigs

Preparation time: about 10
minutes
Cooking time: about 3 minutes
Microwave setting: Maximum
(Full)

1. Place the breadcrumbs, oil, anchovy essence, lemon juice, Worcestershire sauce, cream, crab meat, salt and pepper in a bowl and mix them all together.

2. Cook for 3 minutes, stirring every minute. Taste and adjust the seasoning.

3. Spoon on to the fried bread and serve garnished with paprika and a sprig of parsley.

Rollmops

Serves 4
4 medium herrings, filleted
*1 large onion, peeled and finely
    sliced*
300 ml (½ pint) cider vinegar
1 teaspoon caster sugar
salt
freshly ground black pepper
1 teaspoon mixed spice
2 teaspoons pickling spice
4 bay leaves

Preparation time: about 5
minutes, plus cooling
Cooking time: about 9 minutes
Microwave setting: Maximum
(Full)

1. Roll up each herring fillet with the skin to the outside and place in a shallow dish. Scatter the onion over the top of the herrings.

2. Mix together the vinegar, sugar, salt, pepper, mixed spice, pickling spice and bay leaves. Pour the mixture over the herrings and onion.

3. Cover and cook for 5 minutes. Turn the plate round and cook for a further 4 minutes.

4. Leave to cool before serving.

Coquilles St Jacques

Serves 4
*450 g (1 lb) potatoes, peeled
    and roughly diced into
    2.5 cm (1 inch) cubes*
3 tablespoons water
salt
*100 g (4 oz) button mushrooms,
    sliced*
*1 garlic clove, peeled and
    crushed*
50 g (2 oz) butter
25 g (1 oz) plain flour
150 ml (¼ pint) dry white wine
1 egg yolk
*4 large scallops, sliced, with
    shells*
2 tablespoons double cream
freshly ground black pepper
1 tablespoon milk
To garnish:
4 parsley sprigs
1 scallop, cooked and sliced

Preparation time: about 17
minutes
Cooking time: about 15
minutes
Microwave setting: Maximum
(Full)

1. Place the potatoes in a medium bowl with the water and a pinch of salt. Cover and cook for 8 minutes, stirring halfway through cooking. Leave to stand, covered.

2. Place the mushrooms, garlic and 25 g (1 oz) of the butter in a medium bowl. Cover, cook for 3 minutes.

3. Stir in the flour and wine. Cook, uncovered, for 2 minutes.

4. Beat in the egg yolk, then stir in the scallops, cream and salt and pepper to taste. Cook, uncovered, for 2 minutes.

5. Meanwhile, mash the potatoes with the remaining butter, the milk and salt and pepper to taste. Place in a piping bag filled with a large star nozzle and pipe around the edges of 4 scallop shells.

6. Spoon the sauce into the centre. Reheat if necessary. Serve garnished with parsley and scallop slices.

Hot Seafood Cocktail

Serves 4
50 g (2 oz) butter
50 g (2 oz) plain flour
600 ml (1 pint) milk
salt
freshly ground black pepper
1 teaspoon tomato purée
75 g (3 oz) cooked cockles
75 g (3 oz) cooked mussels
*75 g (3 oz) cooked, peeled
    prawns*
To garnish:
mild paprika
whole cooked prawns
4 lemon slices

Preparation time: about 5
minutes
Cooking time: about 10
minutes
Microwave setting: Maximum
(Full)

1. Place the butter in a bowl and cook for 1½ minutes.

2. Stir in the flour, then gradually blend in the milk. Stir in the salt and pepper. Cook for 4 minutes, stirring every minute. Taste and adjust the seasoning.

3. Add the tomato purée to colour the sauce pink. Stir in the cockles, mussels and prawns. Cook for 4½ minutes, stirring halfway through cooking.

4. Place the mixture in a large dish. Garnish with a sprinkling of paprika, whole prawns and lemon slices. Serve immediately

*Clockwise: Coquilles St Jacques; Hot
seafood cocktail; Rollmops; Hot crab*

Ratatouille

Serves 4

1 small courgette, sliced
1 medium aubergine, sliced
6 tomatoes, skinned and chopped
½ green pepper, cored, seeded and finely sliced
½ red pepper, cored, seeded and finely sliced
1 onion, peeled and sliced
1 tablespoon tomato purée
2 garlic cloves, peeled and crushed
6 tablespoons olive oil
1 teaspoon dried mixed herbs
salt
freshly ground black pepper

Preparation time: about 15 minutes, plus cooling
Cooking time: about 15 minutes
Microwave setting: Maximum (Full)

1. Place the courgette, aubergine, tomatoes, green and red peppers, onion, tomato purée, garlic, oil, herbs, salt and pepper in a large bowl. Cover and cook for 5 minutes.

2. Stir, then cook for 5 minutes. Stir again and cook for a further 5 minutes.

3. Taste and adjust the seasoning, then allow to cool before serving.

Honeyed Grapefruit and Orange

Serves 4

2 large grapefruit, halved, segmented, drained, with shells reserved
1 large orange, pith and skin removed, segmented and drained
1 tablespoon clear honey
1 tablespoon multicoloured sugar crystals or demerara sugar

Preparation time: about 15 minutes
Cooking time: about 3½ minutes
Microwave setting: Maximum (Full)

1. Place the grapefruit segments and the orange segments in a bowl. Add the honey. Cook for 1½ minutes.

2. Divide the mixture between the grapefruit shells. Sprinkle the sugar crystals or the demerara sugar over each.

3. Stand the halves on a plate or in individual sundae dishes or bowls. Cook for 2 minutes.

Ratatouille; Honeyed grapefruit and orange

Jellied Ham and Chicken

Serves 4

*100 g (4 oz) cooked chicken
  meat, finely diced*
*100 g (4 oz) cooked ham, finely
  chopped*
15 g (½ oz) powdered gelatine
*450 ml (¾ pint) well-flavoured
  chicken stock*
½ teaspoon meat extract
*2 teaspoons chopped fresh
  parsley*
freshly ground black pepper
4 cucumber slices, to garnish

Preparation time: about 8
minutes
Cooking time: about 2½
minutes, plus setting
Microwave setting: Maximum
(Full)

1. Mix together the chicken and
ham and divide between 4 pots.

*Jellied ham and chicken; Corn-on-the-
cob with parsley butter*

2. Place the gelatine in a jug and
slowly stir in half the stock.
Cook for 2½ minutes or until the
gelatine has dissolved, stirring
after each minute.

3. Stir in the meat extract,
parsley and remaining chicken
stock. Season to taste with
pepper. Cool, then pour over
the chicken and ham. Chill until
set.

4. Garnish each pot with a slice
of cucumber.

Corn-on-the-cob with Parsley Butter

Serves 4

75 g (3 oz) butter
*4 corn-on-the-cob, fresh or
  frozen*
*2 tablespoons finely chopped
  fresh parsley*

Preparation time: about 5
minutes
Cooking time: about 14
minutes
Microwave setting: Maximum
(Full)

1. Cut the butter into pieces and
place in a small dish. Heat for 1½
minutes or until melted.

2. Brush the corn with melted
butter and wrap each one in
greaseproof paper.

3. Arrange the corn in a shallow
container. Cover and cook for
10 minutes, if using fresh corn,
or 12 minutes, if using frozen,
until the corn is tender when

pricked with a fork or skewer.

4. Remove the corn from the
greaseproof paper and put into
individual dishes.

5. Stir the parsley into the
remaining butter and reheat for
45 seconds. Pour the hot
parsley butter over the corn.

Prawns with Garlic and Tomatoes

Serves 4
25 g (1 oz) butter
½ onion, peeled and grated
225 g (8 oz) cooked, peeled
prawns
4 tomatoes, skinned and finely
chopped
2 garlic cloves, peeled and
crushed
1 tablespoon tomato purée
½ teaspoon ground mace
salt
freshly ground black pepper

Preparation time: about 20
minutes
Cooking time: about 7 minutes
Microwave setting: Maximum
(Full)

Prawns with garlic and tomatoes;
Scampi in brandy sauce

1. Place the butter and onion in
a large bowl, cover and cook for
2 minutes.

2. Stir in the prawns, tomatoes,
garlic, tomato purée, mace, salt
and pepper. Cover and cook for
5 minutes, stirring halfway
through cooking.

3. Taste and adjust the
seasoning.

Scampi in Brandy Sauce

Serves 4
2 garlic cloves, peeled and
crushed
1 medium onion, peeled and
finely chopped
25 g (1 oz) butter
25 g (1 oz) cornflour
scant 300 ml (½ pint) milk
2 teaspoons tomato purée
2 tablespoons brandy
1 tablespoon double cream
450 g (1 lb) peeled scampi
salt
freshly ground black pepper
***To garnish**:*
1 tablespoon chopped fresh
parsley
lemon wedges

Preparation time: about 8
minutes
Cooking time: about 12
minutes
Microwave setting: Maximum
(Full)

1. Place the garlic, onion and
butter in a large bowl. Cover
and cook for 4 minutes.

2. Stir in the cornflour, then
blend in the milk, tomato purée,
brandy, cream and scampi.
Season to taste with salt and
pepper. Cook, uncovered, for 8
minutes, stirring halfway
through cooking.

3. Sprinkle with parsley and
serve with lemon.

Prawn and Lemon Pancakes

Serves 4
1 egg (sizes 1, 2)
1 egg yolk
300 ml (½ pint) milk
pinch of salt
100 g (4 oz) plain flour
oil, for frying
Filling:
40 g (1½ oz) butter
40 g (1½ oz) plain flour
300 ml (½ pint) milk
salt
freshly ground black pepper
1 teaspoon anchovy essence
grated rind of 1 small lemon
175 g (6 oz) cooked, peeled
prawns

Preparation time: about 25 minutes, including pancakes
Cooking time: about 6 minutes plus 15 minutes to make pancakes
Microwave setting: Maximum (Full)

1. Beat together the egg, egg yolk and milk. Place the salt and flour into a mixing bowl and whisk in the egg mixture.

2. Make 8 pancakes using the conventional hob. Set aside and keep warm while making the filling.

3. Place the butter in a bowl. Cook for 45 seconds or until melted.

4. Stir in the flour. Gradually blend in the milk and add salt and pepper. Cook for 2½ minutes, stirring every minute.

5. Add the anchovy essence. Taste and adjust the seasoning. Stir in the lemon rind and prawns.

6. Spread the mixture in a line down the centre of each pancake. Fold each edge of the pancake over the mixture.

7. Divide the pancakes between 2 plates. Cook each plate of pancakes for 1½ minutes.

Prawn and lemon pancakes; Tomato pasta bows

Tomato Pasta Bows

Serves 4
1.8 litres (3 pints) boiling water
1 tablespoon oil
salt
225 g (8 oz) pasta bows
Sauce:
1 medium onion, peeled and
finely chopped
2 garlic cloves, peeled and
crushed
1 teaspoon cornflour
1 × 225 g (8 oz) can tomatoes,
chopped with their juice
1 teaspoon dried mixed herbs
2 tablespoons tomato purée
salt
freshly ground black pepper
15 g (½ oz) butter
2 tablespoons grated Parmesan
cheese

Preparation time: about 10 minutes, plus standing
Cooking time: about 14 minutes
Microwave setting: Maximum (Full)

1. Place the boiling water, oil, salt and pasta in a large bowl. Cover and cook for 8 minutes. Leave to stand, covered, for 10 minutes.

2. Place the onion and garlic in a small bowl, cover and cook for 3 minutes.

3. Stir in the cornflour, undrained tomatoes, herbs, tomato purée and salt and pepper to taste. Cook, uncovered, for 3 minutes, stirring halfway through.

4. Drain the pasta and stir in the sauce and butter. Serve sprinkled with Parmesan cheese.

Liver Pâté

Serves 4
2 bacon rashers, rinds removed
*   and chopped*
225 g (8 oz) chicken livers
1 garlic clove, peeled and
*   crushed*
150 g (5 oz) butter
1 tablespoon dried mixed herbs
freshly ground black pepper
1 tablespoon dry sherry
1 tablespoon cream

Preparation time: about 10
minutes, plus chilling
Cooking time: about 6½ minutes
Microwave setting: Maximum
(Full)

1. Place the bacon in a medium
bowl. Cook for 1 minute.

2. Add the livers, garlic, 100 g
(4 oz) of the butter, herbs and
pepper. Cover and cook for 5
minutes, stirring halfway
through cooking.

3. Add the sherry and cream.
Place the mixture in a liquidizer
and blend until smooth. Divide
the pâté between 4 ramekin
dishes or put in 1 large dish.

4. Place the remaining butter in
a bowl. Cook for 30 seconds or
until melted. Pour a little butter
over each serving of the pâté.

5. Allow to cool completely,
then chill for 2 hours.

Kipper Pâté

Serves 4
225 g (8 oz) frozen kipper fillets
1 small onion, peeled and
*   chopped*
50 g (2 oz) butter
75 g (3 oz) full fat soft cheese
¼ teaspoon ground mace
1 tablespoon lemon juice
salt
freshly ground black pepper
parsley sprigs, to garnish

Preparation time: about 10
minutes, plus chilling
Cooking time: about 9 minutes
Microwave setting: Maximum
(Full)

1. Place the kippers in a shallow
dish. Cover and cook for 2½
minutes.

2. Separate the fillets. Cook for a
further 2½ minutes. Set aside.

3. Place the onion and butter in
a bowl, cover and cook for 4
minutes.

4. Chop the kippers and add to
the onion and butter. Stir in the
cheese, mace, lemon juice, salt
and pepper.

5. Place the mixture in a
liquidizer and blend.

6. Divide the pâté between 4
ramekin dishes. Allow to cool
completely and chill for 2 hours.
Garnish with parsley sprigs.

Liver pâté; Kipper pâté

Stuffed Tomatoes

Serves 4
*4 large tomatoes, about 750 g
  (1½ lb)*
*40 g (1½ oz) fresh brown
  breadcrumbs*
*15 g (½ oz) Cheddar cheese,
  finely grated*
25 g (1 oz) chopped ham
1 teaspoon dried mixed herbs
*1 teaspoon made English
  mustard*
*2 tablespoons plain
  unsweetened yogurt*
salt
freshly ground black pepper
4 parsley sprigs, to garnish

Preparation time: about 10
minutes
Cooking time: about 5½ minutes
Microwave setting: Maximum
(Full)

1. Slice the top off each of the
tomatoes and reserve, then,
using a grapefruit knife, scoop
out the centres. Chop the flesh
and seeds, then mix with the
breadcrumbs, cheese, ham,
herbs, mustard, yogurt and salt
and pepper to taste.

2. Fill each tomato with the
stuffing and replace the 'lids' on
top of the tomatoes.

3. Place the tomatoes in 4 small
dishes and arrange in a circle in
the cooker. Cook, uncovered,
for 5½ minutes or until soft,
rearranging halfway through
cooking. Remove any which
may be cooked before the total
cooking time.

4. Garnish each tomato with a
sprig of parsley.

Stuffed Baked Avocado with Shrimps

Serves 4
25 g (1 oz) butter
*50 g (2 oz) fresh brown
  breadcrumbs*
1 tablespoon grated lemon rind
100 g (4 oz) peeled shrimps
5 tablespoons single cream
salt
freshly ground black pepper
2 large ripe avocados
1 tablespoon lemon juice
To garnish:
lettuce leaves
lemon twists

Preparation time: about 10
minutes
Cooking time: about 5 minutes
Microwave setting: Maximum
(Full)

1. Place the butter in a bowl.
Cook for 30 seconds or until
melted.

2. Stir in the breadcrumbs.
Cook for 1 minute. Stir in lemon
rind, shrimps, cream, salt and
pepper.

3. Cut the avocados in half.
Remove and discard the stones,
then sprinkle the flesh with
lemon juice.

4. Pile the shrimp mixture into
each of the avocado halves.
Arrange on a plate. Cook for 3½
minutes.

5. Serve on lettuce garnished
with lemon.

*Stuffed tomatoes; Stuffed baked avocado
with shrimps*

ISH AND SEAFOOD

Tender, light fish and seafood cook very successfully in the microwave. Prepared simply, with butter and herbs, or combined with complementary ingredients, the range of dishes which can be created is broad, from traditional favourites like fish pie to exotic specialities such as Spiced Haddock

Most fish and seafood is very light, tender and ideally suited to microwave cooking. Whole fish, fillets, steaks or cubes of fish all cook speedily. Uncooked Mediterranean prawns, scallops and mussels are also good candidates for cooking in the microwave. Ready-cooked shellfish can be reheated in sauced dishes in seconds. Since these foods cook so quickly, the rule to follow is to take great care not to overcook them.

Until you are certain of the cooking times for particular foods or recipes in your own microwave, then check the fish ahead of the suggested cooking times given in charts and recipes. If the fish is not quite ready it can be cooked for a while longer but once it is overcooked, then it will be dry and lacking flavour. Follow the guidelines given here and you will discover that microwave-cooked fish is succulent, flavoursome and particularly easy to prepare.

Cooking containers

Generally, fish and seafood should be covered when cooked in the microwave. Ovenproof glassware is ideal – for example, casseroles with lids or pie dishes which can be covered with plates or microwave-proof cling film. Large shallow dishes are useful for cooking whole fish – flan dishes can be covered with upturned plates or film – and sauced fish dishes can be contained in casseroles, bowls or basins. Fillets and steaks are best in shallow dishes.

Roasting bags or boil-in-the-bags are also useful to hold steaks or small whole fish. The bag can be placed on a large, plain dinner plate and the fish arranged inside it. This is particularly useful for small neat steaks which do not need re-arranging halfway through cooking. Remember to use a special microwave tie to close the bag (leaving room for the steam to escape).

Arranging the ingredients

It is important that the fish or seafood is arranged to the best advantage in the cooking container to ensure even cooking. Whole fish – for example, mackerel, trout or mullet – should be placed head to tail in the cooking container. Halfway through the cooking time the whole fish should be rearranged, moving any from the middle of the dish towards the outside and turning each fish over and around. If two fish are being cooked, then they simply need turning but if three or four are closely packed into one dish, then those from the middle will need moving towards the outside.

Fillets need particular attention to ensure that the thin ends do not dry out before the thicker parts are cooked. When one fillet is cooked in the middle of a shallow dish or on a plate, then simply ensure that the cooking time is not overlong. When ready, the thicker part of the fillet will still be slightly translucent between the flakes but by the time the fish is removed from the oven,

uncovered and transferred to a serving plate it will be cooked.

If a number of fillets are cooked together, then they should be arranged with the thin tails towards the middle of the dish. If the fillets are large ones, tuck the tail of one under the thick part of another to prevent overcooking.

Alternatively, the tail ends of the fillets can be folded under – this is useful when cooking several plaice or whiting fillets. Fish steaks and cutlets cook very well if they are evenly thick. Tuck the thin flaps of fish neatly into the cavity in the middle of the steaks and secure them with wooden cocktail sticks.

Large whole fish

A small whole salmon or medium-sized salmon trout will cook well in the microwave. If it is too large for the oven cavity, then curl it into a large flan dish and use special microwave-proof cling film to keep it in

place, covering it twice. Remember to pierce the skin of the fish.

Piercing fish skin

When cooking whole fish, it is important to pierce the skin in one or two places to prevent it from bursting.

Covering during cooking

Most fish and seafood do need covering during cooking, the only exception being when the bulk of the dish is a sauce and the seafood is well coated.

Shielding with foil

Lastly, remember that small pieces of foil can be used to protect areas which are likely to overcook. This is a useful method of protecting the heads and tails of whole fish. If the fish are quite large, by the time the main part of each is cooked, the heads and tails may be rather

Cooking a whole salmon

1. Curve a small whole salmon into a flan dish.

2. Use microwave-proof cling film to keep the fish in place.

shrivelled, so use small pieces of foil to shield them.

Seasoning

Do not sprinkle salt on fish before cooking as this results in dried patches. Sauces can be lightly seasoned in advance but check the cooked seafood and add salt to taste before serving.

Shellfish

Delicate items like scallops or prawns cook very quickly so check them in good time. Scallops should be sliced or cut to prevent them from 'bursting' during cooking. They should be cooked with a little liquid if they are not in a sauce. Remember that they will continue to cook slightly after they are removed from the microwave.

Mediterranean prawns should be arranged round the edge of a shallow dish, a little water added and the dish covered.

Mussels cook particularly well in a large casserole or mixing bowl with a little cooking liquid and covered with a plate or lid. A good shake halfway through the time will ensure even cooking. Any unopened shellfish should be discarded.

Preparing mussels

The mussels should be left in cold water overnight, with a handful of oatmeal sprinkled into the bucket. This process of purging the shellfish rids them of sand. Scrub the shells and scrape off the black hairy beards. Discard any open shellfish which do not close when tapped sharply.

The mussels are cooked in a large container with the minimum of liquid. Any shellfish which are still closed at the end of cooking, when most are open, should be discarded.

Arranging and shielding fish

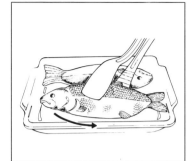

Arrange whole fish head to tail in the dish.

Arrange fillets with the thin tails tucked under.

Use wooden cocktail sticks to neaten steaks

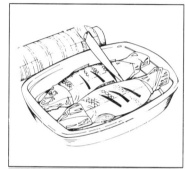

Tails and heads can be shielded with foil.

Cooking mussels

1. The mussels are cooked in a large container with the minimum of liquid – here 150 ml ($\frac{1}{4}$ pint) warmed dry white wine is added. A mixing bowl is ideal and a plate can be used to cover the bowl. A small chopped onion, a small finely diced carrot, ground pepper, a bay leaf and chopped parsley are added for flavour but do not add salt at this stage. A finely chopped clove of garlic can also be added to the mussels.

2. Halfway through cooking the bowl is given a good shake. The mussels open when cooked as shown above; any which do not open are discarded. To cook 1 kg (2 lb) mussels allow 5–7 minutes on Maximum (Full). The mussels are ready for seasoning and ladling into individual bowls.

PREPARATION

There are many basic preparation techniques that apply to fish cookery that are useful for microwave cooking. The aim when cooking food in the microwave is to make individual food items as even in shape and size as possible. Boned fish, skinned fillets which can be rolled and even-sized chunks of fish all cook well. Often a good fishmonger will bone or skin fish but it you have to tackle the task, then follow these guidelines.

Boning round fish

Whole mackerel and trout cook quite successfully in the microwave; however, there are advantages to cutting the heads off and boning these fish if you are cooking more than two at a time. The boned fish take up less space in the dish and they cook quickly and evenly. The fish should be folded back into shape and a little butter, herbs or other flavouring ingredients can be placed in the body cavity.

Alternatively, the fish can be cut in half lengthways to yield two fillets which can be rolled and secured with wooden cocktail sticks before cooking.

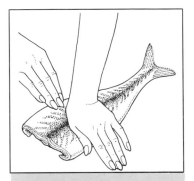

1. Clean the fish and remove the heads. Cut off the fins and lay the fish, flesh down on a clean surface. Using the heel of your hand or your thumbs, press along the centre back of the fish.

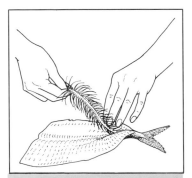

2. Turn the fish over and the bone should be loose. Carefully lift the bone away from the flesh, working from head end to tail. Snip the bone free at the tail end, then lightly run your finger over the flesh and pick out any stray bones.

Skinning fish fillets

Skinned plaice or sole fillets can be rolled and secured with cocktail sticks, then arranged in a shallow dish or casserole for even cooking in the microwave. The fillets can be sprinkled with lemon rind or chopped herbs before rolling but they must not be seasoned with salt. Larger fish fillets should be skinned if they are cut into chunks for cooking in casseroles or sauces.

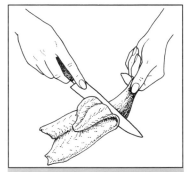

Place the fish fillet on a clean surface, skin side down. Rub your fingertips in a little salt and hold the tail firmly. Using a sharp knife and holding it at an acute angle to the skin of the fish, cut between the skin and the flesh. Use a sawing action and avoid breaking the skin of the fish. Roll back the fish flesh as you cut it free of the skin.

Rolling fish fillets

Thin fish fillets cook best if they are rolled. The skinned fillets can be dotted with butter and sprinkled with chopped herbs or grated lemon rind. They should be rolled from head end to tail, then the rolls secured with wooden cocktail sticks.

Arrange the rolls as far apart as possible for even cooking, ideally round the edge of a round dish. A little liquid is added – water, wine or lemon juice – and the dish is covered before cooking. Pierce the rolls to ensure they are cooked through. Remember that they are ready when still very slightly translucent in the middle. The middle will finish cooking by the time the fish is served.

1. The skinned fish fillets are rolled neatly from head end to tail, with the skinned side inwards.

2. The rolls are secured with wooden cocktail sticks and arranged as far apart as possible in the cooking dish.

Cutting fillets and arranging small portions

Even-sized chunks of fish cook very well in the microwave. Fish which is to be cooked with other ingredients in sauces is best skinned first. The skinned fillets can be cut into even-sized portions or into neat chunks. These can be added to a sauce for cooking, or they can be cooked with vegetables and liquid, casserole-style.

If the chunks are cooked alone, they should be arranged round the outside of a dish, or placed in a large basin and rearranged halfway through cooking.

Even-sized pieces of shellfish can be cooked in the same way, for example scallops or Mediterranean prawns.

Basic preparation methods for fish

These are the essentials which the fishmonger will usually carry out as they are necessary for all fish, regardless of the cooking method. However, if you buy from a busy market stall or if you have freshly caught fish to prepare, then you may find that you have to clean and scale fish once you have brought it home.

Scaling fish

Scaly fish – salmon or mullet, for example – should have the scales removed before cooking. This is a messy job and no matter how well organized you are in your approach a few scales always manage to escape and make a mess.

The best place to scale fish is in the sink, with the cold tap running slowly to wash all the scales away. Using a sharp cook's knife, hold the fish head upwards and at an angle, scrape off the scales working from head to tail. The more vigorously you scrape the fish the farther the scales wll fly, so it is best to scrape them off fairly gently to avoid making a mess.

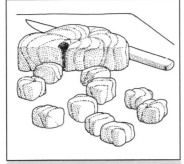

Fillets which are cut into even-sized chunks or portions will cook evenly.

Once all the scales have been completely removed, rinse the fish under cold running water and pat it dry on absorbent kitchen paper. Even if the fish-monger scales the fish for you it is often as well to check and remove any scales that remain before you cook the fish.

Gutting fish

The easiest and most common method of removing the innards from round fish (for example trout or mackerel) is by slitting the fish down the belly, from head to tail. The innards can then be scraped out easily with a knife. The fish should be gutted as soon as possible – do not leave it in the refrigerator overnight before cleaning.

It is best to gut the fish near the sink. Have ready two or three layers of newspaper. Holding the fish firmly in one hand, slit it with a sharp knife, then scrape out all the innards on to the paper. Rinse the fish under cold water, rubbing away any membranes. Pat the fish dry on absorbent kitchen paper.

Cleaning scallops

Use an oyster knife or stout, short-bladed kitchen knife to

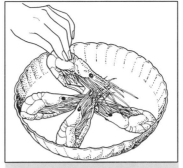

Arrange small portions of fish or seafood round the edge of a dish for even cooking. Tail ends of large prawns should be pointed towards the middle of the dish.

open the shells. The shells open more easily if the scallops are warmed for about half a minute in a hot grill compartment. As you open the shell, cut the membrane which attaches the scallop to the top part of the shell. The round white flesh and the pink coral are the main edible parts. The membrane, small intestine and dark grey, soft area should be discarded. Carefully cut the flesh and coral away from the shell and trim off all membranes, then rinse it briefly under cold water. Do not soak the scallops in water or hold them under the tap for too long as they have a delicate flavour and texture. The rounded shells can be thoroughly scrubbed and washed for serving the cooked scallops.

Peeling prawns

Peeled cooked prawns are readily available, both fresh and frozen but you may prefer to buy the whole prawns and peel them yourself. Uncooked Mediterranean prawns are sold with shells on or frozen ready peeled. You can use prawn shells to flavour stock.

First remove the head of the prawn. To do this, grip the tail

Convenience foods

Frozen fish can be first defrosted, then cooked in the microwave in one operation.

Canned fish can be turned into tempting supper dishes in minutes – try adding canned tuna to a cheese or mushroom sauce and serving it with cooked rice or pasta. Canned prawns, shrimps, crab meat or mussels can be added to sauces and briefly reheated. Remember that these foods are already cooked and that they simply require heating through.

Frozen prawns can be defrosted quickly and used in a variety of ways but again it is important to heat them briefly as they can easily be overcooked and become tough.

firmly and pull off the head where it joins the back. Next the shell must be removed from the body of the prawn. Hold the prawn with both hands, using your thumbs and index fingers only. Have the under side of the prawn facing upwards, then use your thumbs to push the shell off from the sides. It will slide off easily leaving the middle of the prawn free of shell. Lastly pull off the tail unless it is to be left in place for serving.

DEFROSTING AND COOKING CHARTS

The following charts provide a guide to the methods and timings for defrosting and cooking a selection of fish and shellfish, and reheating cooked shellfish. Make use of this information to prepare plain cooked fish and seafood or when you are pre-cooking these foods for use in another recipe, for example to make fish cakes.

GUIDE TO COOKING FISH

Fish		Quantity	Time in minutes on Maximum (Full)	Method
Bass	whole	450 g (1 lb)	5–7	Shield the head and tail with foil. Cut the skin in two or three places to prevent it from bursting.
Cod	fillets	450 g (1 lb)	5–7	Place the fillet tails to the centre of the dish or shield with foil. Cut the skin in two or three places to prevent it from bursting.
	steaks	450 g (1 lb)	4–5	Cover with greaseproof paper before cooking.
Haddock	fillets	450 g (1 lb)	5–7	Place the fillet tails to the centre of the dish or shield with foil. Cut the skin in two or three places to prevent it from bursting.
	steaks	450 g (1 lb)	4–5	Cover with greaseproof paper before cooking.
Halibut	steaks	450 g (1 lb)	4–5	Cover with greaseproof paper before cooking.
Kippers	whole	1	1–2	Cover before cooking.
Red mullet and red snapper	whole	450 g (1 lb)	5–7	Shield the head and tail with foil. Cut the skin in two or three places to prevent it from bursting.
Salmon	steaks	450 g (1 lb)	4–5	Cover with greaseproof paper before cooking.
Salmon trout	whole	450 g (1 lb)	7–8	Shield the head and tail with foil. Cut the skin in two or three places to prevent it from bursting.
Scallops		450 g (1 lb)	5–7	Cover with dampened absorbent kitchen paper
Smoked haddock	whole	450 g (1 lb)	4–5	Cover before cooking.
Trout	whole	450 g (1 lb)	8–9	Shield the head and tail with foil, cut the skin in two or three places to prevent it from bursting.

GUIDE TO REHEATING BOILED SHELLFISH

Fish		Quantity	Time in minutes on Maximum (Full)	Method
Lobster	tails	450 g (1 lb)	5–6	Turn tails over halfway through the cooking time.
	whole	450 g (1 lb)	6–8	Allow to stand for 5 minutes before serving. Turn over halfway through the cooking time.
Prawns and scampi		450 g (1 lb)	5–6	Arrange the peeled shellfish in a ring in a shallow dish and cover.
Shrimps		450 g (1 lb)	5–6	Arrange the peeled shrimps in a ring in a shallow dish and cover.

GUIDE TO DEFROSTING FISH AND SHELLFISH

Fish	Quantity	Time in minutes on defrost	Method
Fish fillets	225 g (8 oz) 450 g (1 lb)	5–7 7–9	Place in a shallow dish. Cover. Separate and rearrange when partially thawed.
Fish cutlets	2, 100 g (4-oz) 4, 100-g (4-oz)	4–5 6–8	Arrange thickest part to outer edge. Cover. Turn or rearrange once. Thickness varies so watch timing.
Fish steaks	2, 100-g (4-oz) 4, 100-g (4-oz)	5–7 10–12	As above.
Whole gutted fish (herring, trout, mackerel)	450 g (1 lb)	4–8	Arrange head to tail. Cover. Rearrange and stand halfway through thawing. Shield tails if necessary.
Prawns, shrimps, scampi, scallops	225 g (8 oz) 450 g (1 lb)	3–5 6–8	Turn into shallow dish. Stir once or twice. Drain. Use as soon as possible.
Smoked salmon	100 g (4 oz)	1–1½	Unwrap and arrange slices on a plate. Cover.

Serving Suggestions

Fish which is cooked very simply can be turned into a tempting meal by adding a complementary sauce, an interesting topping or an edible garnish. The following suggestions are all fairly simple, they do not take long to prepare or cook and there is no need to follow a complicated recipe. Remember that the fish will cook very quickly in the microwave, so have the sauce made in advance, ready to heat for a minute before serving; the topping should be prepared or any garnishing ingredients should be ready to add to the cooked fish.

Sauced Fish

Parsley sauce A traditional accompaniment, pour the sauce over fish fillets or steaks and serve with creamy mashed or baked potatoes.

Egg sauce Egg sauce is delicious with white or smoked fish. Spoon the sauce over fillets and serve at once. Good with cooked rice and peas.

Cheese sauce Make a tasty supper dish by coating white fish fillets with cheese sauce, then browning them under the grill. Serve with mashed potatoes or pasta. This is very good with cod or haddock.

Tomato sauce Serve cooked white fish on a bed of pasta, breaking the fillets into chunks. Top with hot tomato sauce, plenty of chopped parsley or basil and serve at once. Grated Parmesan cheese can be offered with the fish. Strongly flavoured fish fillets, such as coley, can be served in this way.

Savoury Butters

Butter can be creamed with a variety of different flavouring ingredients. The butter should be formed into a roll and wrapped in plastic film or foil, then chilled until it is firm. Cut the roll into neat slices. The slices of butter should be brought to room temperature before they are used and they should be placed on the fish when it is freshly cooked and very hot.

Maître d'hôtel butter Cream butter with a little lemon juice, seasoning and chopped fresh parsley. Good with all delicately flavoured fish.

Herb butter Chopped fresh tarragon, chives, basil or dill can be creamed with butter. Alternatively a mixture of herbs can be used but do not use too much of any one strong herb. Serve with plaice or sole.

Lemon butter Beat grated lemon rind and a little juice into butter. The zesty lemon is particularly good with mackerel or smoked fish and helps counteract oiliness.

Walnut and orange butter An unusual combination but one that complements chunky fish steaks. Beat grated orange rind and finely chopped walnuts into butter. Do not add too many walnuts as they can spoil the texture of the butter.

Anchovy butter A rich butter to accentuate the natural flavour of fish. Beat a can of mashed anchovy fillets into butter, adding the oil if you like. Beat in a dash of lemon juice and some freshly ground black pepper. Good with cod steaks, haddock fillet or rolled whiting fillets which can taste rather bland.

Topping combinations

Buttered crumbs Toss fresh white or wholemeal breadcrumbs in hot melted butter and cook on Maximum (Full) briefly (about 30–60 seconds) until they are piping hot. Mix in some chopped parsley and spoon a little on fish steaks.

Nutty topping Chop some roasted peanuts and mix them with some chopped spring onion. Sprinkle a little on fish fillets or steaks and add lemon wedges so that the juice can be squeezed over.

Tomato and chive topping Mix peeled chopped tomatoes with some chopped chives and seasoning. Spoon a little on fillets or steaks before serving.

Steamed Fish

Serves 3–4
450 g (1 lb) fresh white fish (e.g. haddock, cod)
To garnish:
lemon twists
parsley sprigs

Preparation time: about 3 minutes
Cooking time: about 6 minutes, plus standing
Microwave setting: Maximum (Full)

1. Place the fish in a shallow dish. Cover and cook for 6 minutes.

2. Leave to stand, covered, for 3–4 minutes or until the fish is opaque and the flesh flakes easily when tested with a fork. Serve garnished with lemon twists and parsley sprigs.

Cook's Tip

The addition of water is unnecessary in this recipe as the fish itself is moist and succulent, and cooked very simply without extra ingredients.

Cod with Herbs

Serves 4
1 small onion, peeled and chopped
½ teaspoon dried thyme
½ teaspoon dried parsley
½ teaspoon dried rosemary
½ teaspoon dried sage
50 g (2 oz) fresh white breadcrumbs
3 tablespoons water
salt
freshly ground black pepper
4 cod steaks, total weight 750 g (1½ lb)
25 g (1 oz) butter, cut into pieces

Preparation time: about 10 minutes
Cooking time: about 9½ minutes, plus standing
Microwave setting: Maximum (Full)

1. Place the onion in a medium bowl, cover and cook for 2½ minutes. Stir in the thyme, parsley, rosemary, sage, breadcrumbs, water, and salt and pepper to taste. Set aside.

2. Place the cod steaks, thin ends to the centre, in a shallow casserole. Cover and cook for 4 minutes.

3. Stuff each steak with the herb mixture. Sprinkle with pepper, and dot with the butter. Cover and cook for 3 minutes. Leave to stand, covered, for 3 minutes before serving.

4. Serve with green noodles and Cauliflower cheese (page 143).

Steamed fish; Cod with herbs

Stuffed Trout

Serves 4

25 g (1 oz) flaked almonds
100 g (4 oz) cooked, peeled
  prawns
4 tablespoons fresh white
  breadcrumbs
2 tablespoons lemon juice
salt
freshly ground black pepper
4 trout, total weight 1 kg (2 lb),
  cleaned, with heads left on
To garnish:
parsley sprigs
lemon slices

Preparation time: about 15
minutes
Cooking time: about 12
minutes, plus standing
Microwave setting: Maximum
(Full)

1. Mix together the almonds,
prawns, breadcrumbs, lemon
juice, and plenty of salt and
pepper to taste.

2. Fill each trout with the
stuffing. Cover and cook for 12
minutes, rearranging halfway
through cooking. Leave to
stand, covered, for 5 minutes
before serving.

3. Garnish with parsley and
lemon.

Mackerel Roll-ups

Serves 4

75 g (3 oz) fresh brown
  breadcrumbs
½ teaspoon dried marjoram
½ teaspoon dried thyme
½ teaspoon dried parsley
½ teaspoon dried sage
grated rind of 1 lemon
2 tablespoons lemon juice
1 teaspoon anchovy essence
6 tablespoons hot water
salt
freshly ground black pepper
4 mackerel, about 350 g
  (12 oz) each, cleaned and
  filleted
To garnish:
lemon slices
flat-leaved parsley

Preparation time: about 15
minutes
Cooking time: about 11
minutes, plus standing
Microwave setting: Maximum
(Full)

1. Mix together the
breadcrumbs, marjoram, thyme,
parsley, sage, lemon rind, lemon
juice, anchovy essence, water,
and salt and pepper to taste.

2. Spread the stuffing over the
fish. Roll up from the head to
the tail. Secure with wooden
cocktail sticks. Cover and cook
for 11 minutes, rearranging
halfway through cooking.

3. Leave to stand, covered, for 5
minutes before serving,
garnished with lemon slices and
parsley.

Stuffed trout; Mackerel roll-ups

Herrings with Mustard Sauce

Serves 4
1 small onion, peeled and
   chopped
½ teaspoon dried thyme
½ teaspoon dried marjoram
grated rind of ½ lemon
50 g (2 oz) fresh brown
   breadcrumbs
salt
freshly ground black pepper
1 egg (size 4)
4 herrings, total weight 350 g
   (12 oz), cleaned and gutted
Sauce:
40 g (1½ oz) butter
25 g (1 oz) plain flour
450 ml (¾ pint) milk
1 tablespoon dry English
   mustard
1 tablespoon white wine
   vinegar
1 teaspoon caster sugar
salt
freshly ground black pepper

Preparation time: about 15
minutes
Cooking time: about 12–14
minutes
Microwave setting: Maximum
(Full)

1. Place the onion in a small bowl, cover and cook for 3 minutes. Stir in the thyme, marjoram, lemon rind, breadcrumbs, salt and pepper and bind with egg.

2. Fill the herrings with the stuffing. Close and secure with wooden cocktail sticks. Place the herrings in a shallow casserole dish, cover and cook for 5 minutes, rearranging halfway through cooking. Set aside, covered, whilst making the sauce.

3. Place the butter in a large jug and cook for 1 minute or until melted. Stir in the flour. Gradually blend in the milk, mustard, vinegar, sugar and salt and pepper to taste. Cook for 4–6 minutes, stirring every minute.

4. Remove the cocktail sticks from the herrings and pour over the sauce. Sprinkle with chopped parsley to garnish and serve with new potatoes.

Cheesy Smoked Haddock

Serves 4
4 smoked haddock fillets, about
   150 g (5 oz) each
25 g (1 oz) butter, cut into
   pieces
Cheese sauce:
25 g (1 oz) butter
25 g (1 oz) plain flour
300 ml (½ pint) milk
1 teaspoon prepared mustard
salt
freshly ground black pepper
50 g (2 oz) Cheddar cheese,
   grated
flat-leaved parsley, to garnish

Preparation time: about 5
minutes
Cooking time: about 11
minutes
Microwave setting: Maximum
(Full)

1. Place the fillets in a shallow casserole dish. Dot with the butter. Cover and cook for 6 minutes, rearranging halfway through cooking. Set aside, covered, whilst making the sauce.

2. Place the butter in a large jug and cook for 1 minute or until melted. Blend in the flour. Stir in the milk, mustard and salt and pepper. Cook, uncovered, for 3 minutes, stirring every minute.

3. Stir in the cheese and cook, uncovered, for 1 minute.

4. Drain the fish and arrange on a serving dish. Pour over the sauce. Garnish with sprigs of parsley.

Baked Haddock Cutlets with Capers

Serves 4
25 g (1 oz) butter
4 haddock cutlets
Sauce:
25 g (1 oz) butter
25 g (1 oz) cornflour
300 ml (½ pint) milk
salt
freshly ground black pepper
2 tablespoons capers, drained
   and chopped
1 tablespoon caper juice
dill sprigs, to garnish

Preparation time: about 10
minutes
Cooking time: about 16
minutes
Microwave setting: Maximum
(Full)

1. Place the butter in a small dish. Cook for 1 minute or until melted.

2. Brush the haddock with the butter. Arrange the haddock in a shallow casserole, cover and cook for 4 minutes.

3. Turn the casserole round and cook for a further 4 minutes. Set aside, covered.

4. To make the sauce, place the butter in a 600 ml (1 pint) jug. Cook for 1 minute or until melted. Stir in the cornflour, and blend in the milk, salt and pepper. Cook for 4 minutes, stirring every minute.

5. Stir in the capers and their juice and pour the sauce over the fish. Cook for 2 minutes. Garnish with dill and serve.

Fillets of Plaice in White Wine

Serves 4
50 g (2 oz) button mushrooms,
   finely sliced
1 medium onion, peeled and
   finely chopped
100 g (4 oz) butter
300 ml (½ pint) dry white wine
1 kg (2 lb) plaice fillets
50 g (2 oz) plain flour
300 ml (½ pint) milk
salt
freshly ground black pepper
100 g (4 oz) white grapes,
   peeled, halved and seeded
To garnish:
4 lemon slices

Preparation time: about 15
minutes
Cooking time: about 21
minutes
Microwave setting: Maximum
(Full)

1. Place the mushrooms, onion, 50 g (2 oz) of the butter and wine into a shallow casserole. Cover and cook for 4 minutes or until the onion is translucent.

2. Roll up the plaice fillets and place them in the casserole. Cover and cook for 4 minutes. Turn the casserole round and cook for a further 5 minutes.

3. Drain the fish, reserving the liquid and keep hot.

4. Place the remaining butter in 1 litre (1¾ pint) jug. Cook for 1 minute or until the butter has melted.

5. Blend in the flour, fish liquid, milk, salt and pepper. Cook for 7½ minutes, stirring every minute.

6. Stir in the grapes. Pour the sauce over the fish, cover and cook for 1 minute. Garnish with lemon.

Clockwise: Herrings with mustard sauce; Baked haddock cutlets with capers; Fillets of plaice in white wine; Cheesy smoked haddock

Cod with Anchovies

Serves 4

*4 cod steaks, total weight 750 g
    (1½ lb)*
salt
freshly ground black pepper
*25 g (1 oz) butter, cut into 4
    pieces*
*1 × 40 g (1½ oz) can anchovy
    fillets, drained*
16 capers
To garnish:
lemon twists
parsley sprigs

Preparation time: about 5
minutes
Cooking time: about 7 minutes
Microwave setting: Maximum
(Full)

1. Place the cod steaks, with the thin ends to the centre, in a dish. Cover and cook for 4 minutes.

2. Season the steaks with salt and pepper and turn over. Place a piece of butter on each. Cover and cook for 1½ minutes.

3. Baste the fish with the melted butter. Arrange a cross of 2 anchovies on each steak with a caper in between. Cook, uncovered, for 1½ minutes. Garnish with lemon twists and parsley.

Plaice Fillets with Sweetcorn

Serves 4

*12 skinned plaice fillets, total
    weight 600 g (1¼ lb)*
*75 g (3 oz) butter, cut into
    pieces*
*1 × 350 g (12 oz) can
    sweetcorn with sweet peppers,
    drained*
salt
freshly ground black pepper
parsley sprigs, to garnish

Preparation time: about 10
minutes
Cooking time: about 8½ minutes
Microwave setting: Maximum
(Full)

1. Roll up the plaice fillets and arrange them in a shallow ovenproof casserole dish. Cover and cook for 3½ minutes. Set aside, covered.

2. Place the butter in a jug and cook, uncovered, for 1 minute or until it has melted.

3. Place the butter, sweetcorn, and salt and pepper to taste in a blender. Blend until smooth.

4. Rearrange the fillets. Sprinkle with salt and pepper to taste, and spoon the sweetcorn mixture over the top.

5. Cook, uncovered, for 4 minutes.

6. Garnish with sprigs of parsley and serve immediately.

*Cod with anchovies; Plaice fillets with
sweetcorn*

Sole and Shrimp Rolls

Serves 4–6
*1 × 200 g (7 oz) can shrimps,
 drained or frozen shrimps,
 thawed*
juice of ½ lemon
*12–16 skinned sole fillets, total
 weight 750 g (1½ lb)*
2 tablespoons dried parsley
salt
freshly ground black pepper
*50 g (2 oz) butter, cut into
 pieces*
chopped parsley, to garnish

Preparation time: about 16
minutes
Cooking time: about 6 minutes
Microwave setting: Maximum
(Full)

1. Sprinkle the shrimps with
lemon juice, then spread over
the fillets. Sprinkle over the
dried parsley, salt and pepper.
Roll up and secure with wooden
cocktail sticks.

2. Place the fish rolls in a
shallow casserole dish. Cover
and cook for 4 minutes.

3. Rearrange. Dot the fish rolls
with the butter. Cover and cook
for 2 minutes.

4. Remove the cocktail sticks.
Garnish with chopped parsley,
and serve with duchesse
potatoes and fried courgettes or
green beans.

Spiced Haddock

Serves 4
*1 small onion, peeled and
 chopped*
*600 g (1¼ lb) skinned haddock
 fillet, cut into pieces*
*50 g (2 oz) button mushrooms,
 sliced*
*1 garlic clove, peeled and
 crushed*
*2 tablespoons Worcestershire
 sauce*
1 teaspoon dried mixed herbs
½ teaspoon curry powder
1 teaspoon soy sauce
*1 × 400 g (14 oz) can tomatoes,
 chopped with their juice*
salt
freshly ground black pepper

Preparation time: about 10
minutes
Cooking time: about 10
minutes
Microwave setting: Maximum
(Full)

1. Place the onion in a large
bowl, cover and cook for 2½
minutes.

2. Stir in the haddock,
mushrooms, garlic,
Worcestershire sauce, herbs,
curry powder and soy sauce.
Cover and cook for 3½–4
minutes, stirring halfway
through cooking.

3. Stir in the tomatoes, and salt
and pepper to taste. Cook,
uncovered, for 3½ minutes.

4. Serve surrounded by boiled
rice with peas.

Sole and shrimp rolls; Spiced haddock

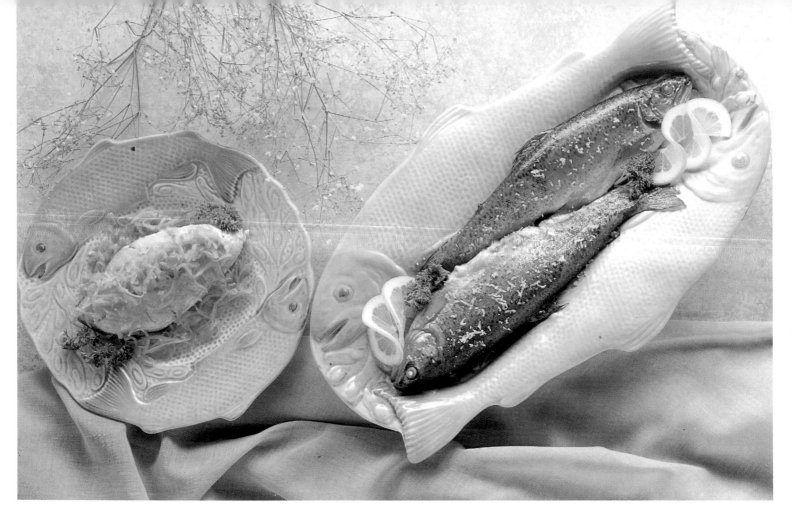

Haddock Steaks with Carrots

Serves 4
1 medium onion, peeled and
*   finely chopped*
225 g (8 oz) carrots, peeled and
*   finely grated*
4 haddock steaks, total weight
*   750 g (1½ lb)*
50 g (2 oz) butter
salt
freshly ground black pepper
parsley sprigs, to garnish

Preparation time: about 15
minutes
Cooking time: about 17
minutes
Microwave setting: Maximum
(Full)

1. Place the onion in a medium bowl, cover and cook for 2 minutes. Stir in the carrots, cover and cook for 5 minutes. Set aside, covered.

2. Place the haddock steaks, with the thin ends to the centre, in a shallow casserole dish, cover and cook for 6 minutes. Set aside.

3. Place the butter in a small jug and cook, uncovered, for 1 minute or until melted. Stir the butter into the vegetables, and season to taste with salt and pepper. Stir in the liquid from the fish.

4. Top the fish steaks with the carrot mixture and pour over any juice. Cook, uncovered, for 3 minutes.

5. Garnish with the parsley sprigs.

Lemon Trout

Serves 4
1 lemon, cut into 8 wedges
4 trout, total weight 1 kg (2 lb),
*   cleaned, with heads left on*
grated rind of 2 lemons
50 g (2 oz) butter, cut into 8
*   pieces*
To garnish:
lemon twists
parsley sprigs

Preparation time: about 10
minutes
Cooking time: about 9 minutes,
plus standing
Microwave setting: Maximum
(Full)

1. Place 2 wedges of lemon inside each trout. Place in a shallow casserole dish. Cover and cook for 4 minutes.

2. Rearrange the trout. Sprinkle with the lemon rind and dot with the butter. Cover and cook for 5 minutes. Halfway through cooking, baste the trout with the melted butter.

3. Leave to stand, covered, for 3 minutes.

4. Garnish with lemon twists and parsley, and serve with a mixed green salad.

Haddock steaks with carrots; Lemon trout

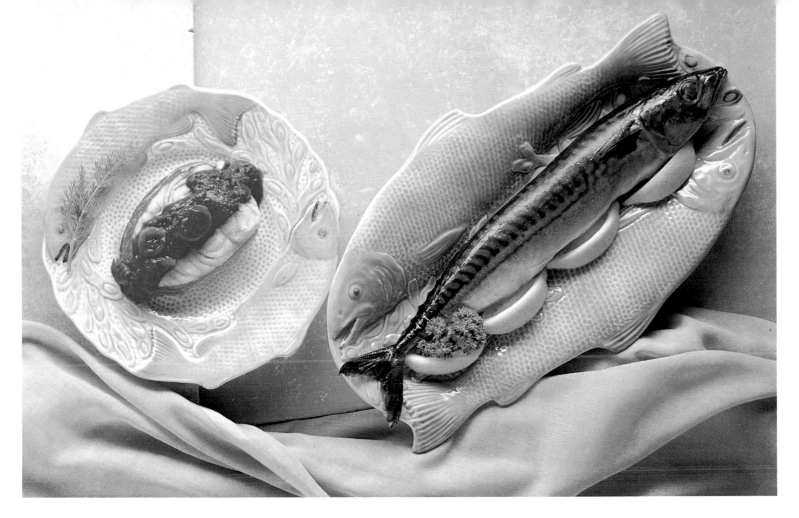

Cod in Tomato and Onion Sauce

Serves 4

*1 medium onion, peeled and
  finely sliced*
*4 tomatoes, skinned and
  chopped*
1 tablespoon tomato purée
½ teaspoon dried thyme
*1 teaspoon chopped fresh
  parsley*
½ teaspoon dried marjoram
½ teaspoon dried rosemary
*1 garlic clove, peeled and
  crushed*
25 g (1 oz) butter
salt
freshly ground black pepper
4 cod steaks
fresh dill, to garnish

Preparation time: about 10
minutes
Cooking time: about 14
minutes
Microwave setting: Maximum
(Full)

*Cod in tomato and onion sauce;
Mackerel in a bag*

1. Place the onion, tomatoes,
tomato purée, thyme, parsley,
marjoram, rosemary, garlic,
butter, salt and pepper in a large
bowl. Cover and cook for 6
minutes, stirring halfway
through cooking. Set aside,
covered while cooking the fish.

2. Place the fish in a shallow
dish. Cover and cook for 3
minutes. Turn the dish round
and cook for a further 3
minutes.

3. Pour the sauce over the fish.
Cover and cook for 2 minutes,
then garnish with dill.

4. Serve with creamed potatoes
and green beans.

Mackerel in a Bag

Serves 4

50 g (2 oz) butter
*4 mackerel, total weight 1.5 kg
  (3 lb), gutted*
*1 tablespoon chopped fresh
  parsley*
salt
freshly ground black pepper
To garnish:
lemon quarters
parsley sprigs

Preparation time: about 10
minutes
Cooking time: about 12
minutes, plus standing
Microwave setting: Maximum
(Full)

1. Spread the butter inside each
of the fish. Sprinkle the parsley
over the butter in the fish.
Season with salt and pepper. If
the mackerel are too big to fit
inside the cooker, remove the
heads.

2. Place each mackerel in a
roasting bag and secure the end
with a non-metallic tie. Prick
each bag.

3. Place the mackerel side by
side on a large plate, cut side up.
Cook for 4 minutes.

4. Turn the mackerel over and
turn the plate round. Cook for a
further 4 minutes. Turn the
mackerel again and turn the
plate round. Cook for 4
minutes.

5. Leave to stand in the bags for
4 minutes. Remove from bags
and serve garnished with lemon
quarters and parsley.

Fish Pie

Serves 4
450 g (1 lb) smoked haddock
  fillets
3 tablespoons water
salt
750 g (1½ lb) potatoes, peeled
  and cubed
about 4 tablespoons milk
15 g (½ oz) butter
freshly ground black pepper
Sauce:
300 ml (½ pint) milk
25 g (1 oz) butter
25 g (1 oz) plain flour
salt
freshly ground black pepper
1 hard-boiled egg, finely
  chopped
parsley sprigs, to garnish

Preparation time: about 10
minutes
Cooking time: about 23½
minutes
Microwave setting: Maximum
(Full)

1. Place the fish in a large bowl.
Cover and cook for 6 minutes,
rearranging halfway through
cooking. Set aside, covered.

2. Place the water, salt and
potatoes in a large bowl. Cover
and cook for 10 minutes. Set
aside, covered.

3. Drain the liquid from the fish
and add the milk for the sauce.

4. To make the sauce, place the
butter in a large jug and cook
for 30 seconds. Stir in the flour,
milk/fish liquid, and salt and
pepper to taste. Cook for 3
minutes, stirring every minute.

5. Flake the smoked haddock,
removing any skin and
remaining bones. Fold into the
sauce with the chopped egg.

6. Mash the potatoes with the

remaining milk and butter, and
add pepper to taste.

7. Pour the fish mixture into a
1.2 litre (2 pint) casserole dish.
Pipe the potatoes over the fish.
Cook, uncovered, for 4 minutes.
Garnish with sprigs of parsley,
and serve with peas.

Cook's Tip

If using frozen haddock fillets,
cook for a further 3 minutes at
step 1 to ensure that the fish has
time to defrost, then cook
through.

Fish Risotto

Serves 4
50 g (2 oz) butter
1 large onion, peeled and finely
  chopped
½ green pepper, cored, seeded
  and finely diced
½ red pepper, cored, seeded and
  finely diced
2 tablespoons tomato purée
1 garlic clove, peeled and
  crushed
1 teaspoon dried mixed herbs
50 g (2 oz) mushrooms, finely
  chopped
350 g (12 oz) long-grain rice
750 ml (1¼ pints) hot chicken
  stock
salt
¼ teaspoon oil
750 g (1½ lb) cod fillets, rinsed
  in cold water
freshly ground black pepper

Fish pie; Fish risotto

Preparation time: about 15
minutes
Cooking time: about 30
minutes, plus standing
Microwave setting: Maximum
(Full)

1. Place the butter, onion, green
and red peppers, tomato purée,
garlic, herbs and mushrooms
in a large bowl. Cover and
cook for 10 minutes, stirring
halfway through the cooking
process.

2. Stir in the rice, hot chicken
stock, salt and oil. Cover and
cook for 13 minutes. Stir
halfway through cooking. Set
aside, covered.

3. Place the fish fillets in a
shallow ovenproof dish. Cover
and cook for 7 minutes,
rearranging halfway through
cooking. Leave to stand for 4
minutes, covered.

4. Flake the fish, removing any
skin. Stir the fish into the rice
mixture and season to taste with
pepper.

Tuna Mousse

Serves 4–6
25 g (1 oz) butter
25 g (1 oz) plain flour
300 ml (½ pint) cold chicken
    stock
¼ teaspoon ground mace
15 g (½ oz) powdered gelatine
1 tablespoons dry sherry
300 ml (½ pint) mayonnaise
2 teaspoons anchovy essence
2 × 200 g (7 oz) cans tuna fish,
    drained and chopped
salt
freshly ground black pepper
150 ml (¼ pint) double or
    whipping cream, whipped
To garnish:
slices of lemon
parsley sprigs

Preparation time: 10 minutes,
plus setting
Cooking time: 5 minutes
Microwave setting: Maximum
(Full)

1. Place the butter in a 600 ml
(1 pint) jug and cook for 1
minute or until melted.

2. Blend in the flour, stock and
mace. Cook for a further 3½
minutes, stirring every minute,
and set aside.

3. Place the gelatine in a small
bowl and stir in the sherry.
Cook for 30 seconds, or until
dissolved. Stir again, the liquid
should be clear.

4. Whisk the sherry gelatine
liquid into the sauce. Set aside
to cool slightly.

5. Stir the mayonnaise, anchovy
essence, tuna fish, salt and
pepper into the sauce. Fold in
the cream.

6. Gently pour the mixture into
a 1.2 litre (2 pint) prepared
soufflé dish. Place in the
refrigerator and chill for at least
4 hours or until set.

7. Turn out and garnish with
lemon and parsley.

Haddock Mousse

Serves 4
450 g (1 lb) haddock fillets, cut
    into pieces
25 g (1 oz) aspic jelly powder
300 ml (½ pint) hot water
1 teaspoon dried parsley
salt
freshly ground black pepper
3 tablespoons double cream
2 egg whites
To garnish:
cucumber slices
watercress sprigs

Preparation time: about 10
minutes, plus chilling
Cooking time: 6½–7½ minutes
Microwave setting: Maximum
(Full)

1. Place the fillets in a medium
bowl, cover and cook for 6–7
minutes. Rearrange halfway
through. Set aside, covered.

2. Stir the aspic jelly into the hot
water. Cook, uncovered, for 30
seconds. Stir well to dissolve.

3. Drain, skin and flake the fish.
Stir in the aspic, parsley, salt and
pepper to taste. Set aside until
cold. Stir in the cream.

4. Whisk the egg whites until
stiff. Gently fold into the fish
mixture. Spoon into a 750 ml (1¼
pint) ring mould. Chill until set.
Serve with a garnish of
cucumber and watercress.

Tuna mousse; Haddock mousse

MENU PLANNER

The illustration shows a typical menu which can be cooked in advance in the microwave – ideal for entertaining.

Cook the Vichyssoise the day before, then cool and chill it. Cook the salmon early on the day, leaving it to cool and allowing time for garnishing it. The syrup and some of the fruit for the dessert can be prepared early on the day of serving but prepare fruits that discolour just an hour ahead. The potato salad can be prepared a few hours in advance, allowing time for the flavours to mingle. Alternatively, have new potatoes ready to cook when you serve the first course so that they can be served hot with the salmon.

Poached Salmon

Serves 6–8
1 × 1.5 kg (3 lb) salmon
mayonnaise, to serve

Preparation time: about 3 minutes, plus cooling
Cooking time: about 12 minutes, plus standing
Microwave setting: Maximum (Full)

1. Cover a large plate with cling film and place the salmon on the plate. Cover and cook for 12 minutes, rearranging halfway through cooking. Leave to stand, covered, for 5 minutes. Remove cover and leave to cool.

2. Pipe mayonnaise along length of salmon and serve with mixed green salad and potato salad.

Poached salmon;
Fruit salad; Vichyssoise;
Mixed green salad and potato salad

POULTRY AND GAME

Tender chicken, turkey and duck cook with great success in the microwave, yielding moist results in minutes. The broad variety of recipes which follow highlight the versatile nature of poultry and its compatability with microwave cooking. This chapter also offers a selection of delicious game recipes.

Poultry and many types of game are tender, with little tough connective tissue and require fairly quick cooking, making them ideally suited to microwave cooking. Most supermarkets now offer a wide variety of different poultry products, from quarter portions of chicken to boneless cuts and fillets, all of which can be cooked in the microwave. The cooking times vary according to the type of portion as well as for different poultry and game.

Regardless of the particular product, there are some general guidelines which can be applied to the microwave method of cooking poultry and game.

Cooking utensils

There is no need to acquire any special utensils or containers for cooking poultry. Sauced dishes can be cooked in microwave-proof casseroles, portions can be cooked in shallow containers or large plates can be useful for single portions. However, there are special microwave roasting racks which allow the poultry to be raised above the cooking juices and avoid the need for frequent draining off of excess fat. This type of specialist cookware is useful but it is certainly not essential. As an alternative to a rack, whole birds can be positioned on an upturned saucer in a dish, so allowing the fat to drain away.

Covering

In most cases poultry and game should be covered during cooking. Casseroles with lids

are ideal, microwave-proof cling film can be used or dinner plates can be useful for covering dishes which do not have lids. Roasting bags with special microwave ties are ideal for cooking whole poultry and game. They retain all the moisture and flavour and can be placed in a flan dish or other shallow dish in case of any spillage of juices. Roasting racks can be completely enclosed within large bags.

Shielding

Any protruding parts of a whole bird or of joints can be protected from overcooking by covering with small pieces of foil. The wing and leg tips or the highest point of the breast may benefit from being covered with small pieces of foil.

Protruding bones and thin areas can be protected by covering with small pieces of foil.

Seasoning

Poultry and game should not be sprinkled with salt before cooking as this will result in dried patches. Pepper, herbs, spices and other flavouring

ingredients can be added to the poultry, and stuffings can be seasoned with salt. Casseroles and sauces can be seasoned before cooking.

Cooking whole birds

Whole, unboned birds are very irregular in shape, with wing tips and legs that protrude. Whole birds should be covered during cooking to keep them moist and they should be turned over to ensure that the meat on the underside is cooked through.

The delicate meat on the breast of the bird cooks particularly quickly so it should be placed downwards for at least half the cooking time. It is a good idea to start cooking the bird with the breast uppermost, then turn it so that the breast is down and turn it over again for a short period at the end of the cooking time.

Covering the breast with rashers of bacon helps to protect against overcooking as well as providing flavour.

Cooking joints

Portions of poultry can be just as uneven in shape and size as whole birds, and the ins and outs of arranging these cuts for successful cooking are discussed overleaf. In the same way that turning is necessary when cooking a whole bird, the portions should be covered and turned at least once during cooking. Portions do not have as thick an area for the microwaves to penetrate, so they take proportionally less

Whole poultry can be cooked on a microwave roasting rack, allowing cooking juices to drain away. Here the bird and rack are completely enclosed in a roasting bag.

cooking time than a whole bird, depending on the number which are cooked and on the shape and size of the cooking container.

Trussing and boning

Whole birds should be trussed as neatly as possible, with the wing ends tied as close as possible to the body and the legs tied tightly together.

Boned whole poultry cooks particularly well in the microwave. The preparation of the stuffing is important to ensure even cooking. If bacon, ham, sausagemeat or other raw ingredients which require lengthy cooking are included they should be cooked before being combined with the other stuffing ingredients. This way there is no danger of any dense stuffing being undercooked.

The stuffed bird should be moulded into as even a shape as possible for cooking and it should be turned halfway through the time.

A comparison of joints on the bone and boneless cuts is given on page 62.

Cooking preformed joints

The evenly shaped, preformed joints of chicken or turkey can be defrosted and cooked in the microwave but they are very dense and have a greater depth of meat to cook. These do need a short resting time during cooking as well as at the end of the cooking time.

Browning

There are a number of seasonings and browning agents which are sold specifically for use on poultry which is to be cooked in the microwave. Other means of giving whole birds and joints extra colour include brushing with dark sauces, such as soy sauce, or sprinkling with paprika. However there is one very successful, and highly preferable, method of browning poultry and game which has been cooked in the microwave, and that is by placing it briefly under a hot conventional grill.

When the poultry is casseroled with vegetables and sauce there is not as great a need to brown the outside, because the cooked bird will be coated in sauce. Since the skin does not crisp it is a good idea to remove it before adding joints to a casserole.

Whole birds – chicken, duck or pheasant – can be quickly browned under a hot grill when they are cooked. Any suggested standing time can be accounted for as the bird browns and the result is an excellent 'roast'.

For fatty poultry like duck this browning is essential for a palatable result – either brown and crisp both sides of the cooked duck under a hot grill or put the bird in a very hot oven for about 10–15 minutes before it is served. Before the poultry is browned under the grill it should be basted with cooking juices and it can be sprinkled with a little salt.

Alternatively, joints or whole birds can be browned before microwaving by cooking them very briefly in hot fat on the conventional hob.

Browning dishes which are manufactured for use in the microwave can also be used to brown poultry and game before cooking. Follow the manufacturer's instructions for preheating the browning dish before using.

Grilling to brown

1. The microwave-cooked bird is pale and the skin is not crisp.

2. The skin is basted and seasoned, then the bird is browned for a few minutes under a hot grill to give the best results.

Testing the cooked bird

Before serving, all poultry should be checked to make sure that it is properly cooked by piercing the meat at the thickest part. This should be done when the bird has been allowed to stand for the recommended standing time. A large bird which is covered by a good

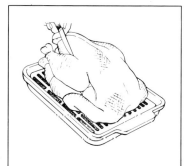

To check that the bird is cooked through, the thick flesh behind the thigh joint is pierced: when the bird is cooked there should be no trace of blood in the juices.

depth of meat requires longer standing than small birds or joints. For small portions the standing time is often accounted for by the time the food is transferred to serving dishes.

Pierce the meat on whole birds at the thickest part which is just behind the thigh. When cooked, the juices should run clear of blood. If there is any sign of pink meat or blood in the juices, then the bird is not well cooked and, in the case of chicken and turkey, it must be returned to the microwave and cooked for extra time.

Game

When selecting game for microwave cooking, remember that it is only the tender birds that can be cooked successfully by this method.

Young hen pheasants can be cooked in the microwave but older birds, or cocks which tend to be tougher, are best casseroled or braised by traditional methods. As a general guide, for microwave cooking use the birds which are suitable for roasting by conventional methods.

Small game birds can be treated in much the same way as chicken quarters and they need to be turned over and around once or twice during cooking for best results.

Boning a chicken

This method can be used for other game and poultry – pheasant, duck or turkey are boned in the same way.

For success do not try to rush this task – allow plenty of time and you will not have problems. Chicken is easier to bone out than pheasant or duck as the bones are larger and the process is less fiddly.

You will need a sharp, pointed knife and a pair of kitchen scissors are useful. Place the bird breast side down on a clean surface with the head end away from you. Cut down the back, from head to tail, then start by working the meat off one side of the carcass.

Cut between the meat and the bones, working as closely as possible to the bones and scraping off all the meat.

Snip the meat and tendons from the wing and leg joints, then scrape the meat off the bones. Chop off the ends of the joints and peel back the meat and skin (in the same way as you would turn the sleeves of a jumper inside out).

When you have boned one side, turn the bird round and work all the meat off the other side. You will be left with the carcass and the meat attached to it along the breast bone. It is important to avoid cutting the skin at all, so turn the bird on its side and carefully cut the meat off the breast bone, taking the slightest sliver of soft bone off with the meat.

COOKING TECHNIQUES FOR POULTRY

One of the key factors which influences the result when cooking poultry and game in the microwave is the shape of the piece of food. Apply the comparison of different portions and the suggestions for arranging them to chicken, duck, turkey, rabbit and pheasant as appropriate. Note the cooking stages for a casserole and use them for all similar recipes. Remember that only tender game microwaves well.

Quarters

Quarter joints of poultry are usually quite irregular in shape, with protruding leg or wing bones and areas of meat of different thickness.

The rule to apply is that thinner parts should be positioned towards the middle of the cooking container.

The joints should be turned halfway through cooking, and possibly rearranged in the container, depending on the number which are being cooked. It is a good idea to start cooking the joints with the skin side down, then turn them over so that the bone side is on top for the second part of the time.

Before cooking you may prefer to brown the joints or remove the skin.

The joints should be covered during cooking and the result is more even if the quarters are cooked in a sauce. The ends of the joints can be shielded with foil, although this should not be necessary as the cooking time is short.

Drumsticks

The thin and thick ends of drumsticks will cook at quite different rates. For small drumsticks off a chicken this does not create a problem, since the main area of meat is at the thick end. Placing the thin bone ends to the middle of the cooking container is usually enough to prevent overcooking.

Turkey drumsticks do have meat at the thinner end and this is likely to overcook if it is not shielded by a small piece of foil.

If the drumsticks are cooked with vegetables or other ingredients, then simply cover the thin end of the meat with food to help prevent overcooking.

Drumsticks are best skinned before cooking and they can be coated in a variety of tasty sauces and herbs to avoid the necessity for browning them separately.

Thighs

Small neat thigh joints, on the bone, are excellent portions for cooking in the microwave. They have a regular shape and cook evenly. They can be cooked with herbs and butter or they can be prepared in a sauce or casserole.

Fold any meat and skin ends neatly underneath and keep them in shape with wooden cocktail sticks, if necessary.

Arrange the portions round the outside of the dish if they are cooked on their own and turn them over halfway through cooking.

Boneless breasts

Both fully boned and part-boned breasts cook well in the microwave. The skin may be removed or browned before cooking and the meat can be cooked on its own or with other ingredients in a sauced dish.

The portions should be arranged as far apart as possible during cooking and turned halfway through the time. It is best to start cooking with the skin side down.

This meat can be cut into chunks for casseroles, or into strips to make oriental-style recipes. The boneless meat can be flattened, then stuffed and rolled. Fillets of breast meat can be sprinkled with chopped herbs and rolled before cooking.

Casseroles

Poultry and game casseroles cook very well in the microwave. The liquid content of these dishes helps to prevent thin areas of meat from overcooking. Tougher cuts of game are not suitable for microwave cooking and they are best casseroled slowly by conventional methods.

When preparing casseroles there are a few basic guidelines to follow. Because the microwave cooks the poultry or game very quickly, it is essential that any strongly flavoured ingredients, or vegetables that will require fairly lengthy cooking, are cooked for a short time before the liquid and main food is added. Onions, garlic and peppers should be cooked first in a little oil, butter or water. If carrots are added, then they too should be par-cooked before the main ingredients are added, depending on the type of dish. Not only does this method ensure that all the ingredients are evenly cooked but it also avoids any likelihood of the finished dish being dominated by the flavour of raw onion.

The choice of casserole dish also plays a part in determining the result. Ideally, there should be plenty of room in the dish to spread the food out slightly and to allow for easy turning and rearranging of the ingredients halfway through the cooking time. During cooking the dish should be covered.

The liquid which is added should be hot or boiling. The greater the quantity of liquid,

Different-shaped portions

Drumsticks and quarters are uneven in shape and thickness.

Thighs and boned breasts are neatly shaped and they cook particularly well in the microwave.

then the more important it is to follow this rule. Small quantities – for example a can of tomatoes – will heat quickly in the casserole but significant amounts of stock, water or wine should be heated before they are added to the casserole. Stock cubes should be diluted with boiling water from the kettle, home-made stock can be heated in the microwave first, similarly wine.

Although the portions of poultry or game should not be individually sprinkled with salt, the sauce in which they are cooked can be seasoned to taste. If the quantity of sauce is very small, then it should be lightly seasoned first, then tasted and the seasoning adjusted at the end of the cooking time.

Duck

Before cooking, prick the skin of the duck all over to allow the fat to drain away. During cooking drain away the fat once or twice. Season the bird after cooking and brown it under a hot grill or in a very hot oven.

The result is a bird which is tender, moist and well flavoured. Unlike duck cooked by conventional methods, microwaved duck is succulent and excellent when browned.

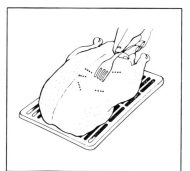

Prick the duck all over before cooking to encourage the fat to drain away.

Stages for casseroles

1. Strongly flavoured ingredients or those that require fairly lengthy cooking are par-cooked before the poultry and liquid are added. Here chopped onion, diced carrot and crushed garlic are first par-cooked in a little oil.

2. The portions are arranged in the dish with the thinner parts towards the middle.

3. The remaining ingredients which will cook in the same time required for the poultry or game are added, then hot liquid is poured in. Sliced mushrooms, quartered peeled and deseeded tomatoes and a bay leaf are added above. Boiling stock moistens the dish.

Preparing thigh joints and fillets for cooking

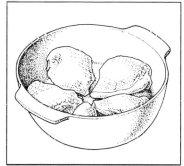

1. Neatly shaped thigh joints are arranged around the outside of a casserole dish so that they will all cook evenly.

2. Fillets of turkey breast are rolled into neat shapes so that they will cook evenly.

3. The rolls are secured with wooden cocktail sticks and they are arranged round the outside of the cooking dish, here a flan dish is used. The dish is covered with an upturned plate or microwave-proof cling film before cooking.

GUIDE TO COOKING POULTRY AND GAME

Poultry/Game	Cooking time in minutes on Maximum (Full) per 450 g (1 lb)	Cooking time in minutes on Medium per 450 g (1 lb)	Method
Chicken whole	6–8	9–10	Shield the tips of the wings and legs with foil. Place in a roasting bag in a dish with 2–3 tablespoons stock. Turn the chicken over halfway through cooking.
pieces 1 2 3 4 5 6	2–4 4–6 5–7 6½–10 7½–12 8–14		Place the meatiest part of the chicken piece to the outside of the dish. Cover and turn the pieces over halfway through the cooking time.
Duck whole	7–8	9–11	Shield the tips of the wings, tail end and legs with foil. Prick the skin thoroughly to help release the fat. Place on a roasting rack or upturned saucer and turn over halfway through the cooking time.
Grouse, guinea fowl, partridge, pheasant, pigeon, poussin, quail and woodcock	6–8	9–11	Shield the tips of the wings and legs with foil. Smear the breast with a little butter and place in a roasting bag in a dish. Turn over halfway through the cooking time.
Turkey	9–11	11–13	Shield the tips of the wings and legs with foil. Place in a roasting bag in a dish with 2–3 tablespoons stock. Turn over at least twice during the cooking time.

STUFFINGS AND ACCOMPANIMENTS

Stuffings for roast poultry

Sage and Onion Finely chop 1 large onion and place in a basin with a knob of butter. Cook on Maximum (Full) for 3 minutes. Mix with 225 g (8 oz) fresh breadcrumbs, 1 tablespoon finely chopped fresh sage or rubbed sage, plenty of seasoning and enough milk to bind the ingredients.

Parsley and Thyme Make the stuffing as above, substituting 4 tablespoons chopped fresh parsley and 1 tablespoon chopped fresh or dried thyme for the sage.

Fresh Herb and Walnut Prepare the stuffing as for sage and onion, using 175 g (6 oz) fresh breadcrumbs and 2 tablespoons chopped fresh herbs, such as parsley, basil and tarragon. Add 100 g (4 oz) finely chopped walnuts before mixing in the milk.

Serving suggestions

Plain cooked chicken, duck or turkey can be served with a variety of simple accompaniments to make deliciously quick meals. If the poultry is skinned before cooking, then the following complementary ingredients can be poured or sprinkled straight over them and served. If the skin is left on, then you may like to brown the joint briefly under a hot grill before adding the accompaniments.

Herb butter Cream chopped fresh herbs into butter with a little seasoning. Try chopped parsley, dill, tarragon, basil or a mixture of herbs. Shape the butter into a roll on a piece of cling film, wrap it tightly and chill until firm, then cut the roll into slices. Top each poultry portion with a slice of butter just before it is served. Add a lemon wedge for garnish, and so that the juice can be squeezed over.

Walnut cream Mix finely chopped walnuts into fromage frais or soured cream. Add snipped chives and seasoning to taste. Top each portion with a spoonful of the mixture just before serving and garnish with sprigs of parsley.

Spicy peanut sauce Mix a little crunchy peanut butter to a cream with fromage frais or soured cream. Season with garlic salt and add a few drops of sesame oil. Serve with chicken or duck, offering thinly sliced onion rings, cucumber slices and shredded lettuce as garnish and decorating with lemon wedges.

Buttered almonds Brown flaked almonds in butter following the instructions on page 14. Pour over the portions just before serving.

Peach garnish Garnish each portion with thin slices of fresh, peeled peach. Sprinkle the fruit with a little lime juice to prevent discoloration.

DEFROSTING POULTRY AND GAME

One of the great advantages of owning a microwave is the facility for rapidly defrosting food. It is important to ensure that poultry is thoroughly defrosted before it is cooked. Check the manufacturer's instructions which come with your oven for suggested timings and follow these guidelines to ensure success. When they are removed from the microwave, the birds should still be very slightly icy before standing.

Defrosting whole birds

Leave the bird in its bag and remove any metal clips or ties. Cook for half the recommended time, then unwrap the bird and place it in a dish. If any protruding areas are warm or look as if they are beginning to cook, then cover them with small pieces of foil. Cook for the remaining time and observe the standing time. Place the bird under cold running water to remove the giblets from the inside. When the bird is defrosted it should be soft but still very slightly icy in the cavity. If you are filling the body cavity with a stuffing, then scald it first with plenty of boiling water and cut away any lumps of fat.

Large birds, like turkey, will need frequent turning during defrosting to ensure that each part defrosts evenly.

Defrosting portions

If the pieces are in a block, then wrap them in greaseproof paper or place in a covered dish. Arrange individual pieces with meatier parts towards the middle of the dish. Cook for half the recommended defrosting time, uncover and turn a block, or turn individual portions. Cook for the remaining time, then separate the pieces from the block. Leave to stand as recommended or cook for a further 1–2 minutes if necessary. When defrosted the meat should be soft, moist and very cold. Small game birds should be treated as for chicken quarters.

GUIDE TO DEFROSTING POULTRY AND GAME

Poultry/Game		Cooking time in minutes on Defrost per 450 g (1 lb)	Method
Chicken	whole	6	Shield the wing tips with foil. Give the dish a quarter turn every 1½ minutes. Remove the giblets at the end of the defrosting time.
	pieces	5	Place the meatiest part of the chicken pieces to the outside of the dish. Turn over halfway through the defrosting time.
Duck		4–6	Shield the wings, tail end and legs with foil. Give the dish a quarter turn every 1½ minutes. Remove the giblets at the end of the defrosting time.
Grouse, guinea fowl, partridge, pheasant, pigeon, poussin, quail and woodcock		5–6	Shield the tips of the wings and legs with foil. Turn over halfway through the defrosting time and give the dish a quarter turn every 1½ minutes.
Turkey		10–12	Shield the tips of the wings and legs with foil. Turn over twice during the defrosting time and give the dish a quarter turn every 6 minutes. Shield any warm spots with foil during defrosting. Remove the giblets at the end of the defrosting time.

Note To defrost poultry and game on Maximum (Full), cook for 1 minute per 450 g (1 lb), allow to stand for 10 minutes then continue cooking in bursts of 1 minute per 450 g (1 lb) until the poultry or game is thawed.

Devilled Chicken Drumsticks

Serves 4

*8 chicken drumsticks, total
weight 750 g (1½ lb)*
1 teaspoon curry powder
1 tablespoon soy sauce
8 tablespoons tomato purée
*3 tablespoons soft dark brown
sugar*
*25 g (1 oz) butter, cut into
pieces*
spring onions, to garnish

Preparation time: about 5
minutes
Cooking time: about 12½
minutes
Microwave setting: Maximum
(Full)

1. Place the drumsticks in the bottom of a shallow oblong casserole dish. Cook, uncovered, for 4½ minutes. Set aside.

2. Place the curry powder, soy sauce, tomato purée, sugar and butter in a jug. Cook, uncovered for 1½ minutes.

3. Rearrange the drumsticks and brush with the sauce. Cook, uncovered, for 4½ minutes.

4. Brush the remaining sauce over the drumsticks and cook for 2 minutes. Garnish with the spring onions.

5. Serve with boiled rice and a green salad or with a beansprout salad.

Turkey Breasts Cordon Bleu

Serves 4

*4 turkey breasts, total weight
750 g (1½ lb)*
freshly ground black pepper
50 g (2 oz) butter, diced
4 slices cooked ham
4 slices Gruyère cheese
parsley sprigs, to garnish

Preparation time: about 3
minutes
Cooking time: about 7½–9
minutes, plus grilling
Microwave setting: Maximum
(Full)

1. Place the turkey breasts in a shallow casserole dish. Sprinkle with pepper and dot with the butter. Cover and cook for 6 minutes, turning over and rearranging the meat halfway through cooking.

2. Transfer to a serving plate. Place a slice of ham and then a slice of cheese on top of each breast. Cook, uncovered, for 3 minutes until the cheese has melted. Brown under a preheated conventional grill, if preferred.

3. Garnish with the parsley sprigs. Serve with sauté potatoes and broccoli.

*Devilled chicken drumsticks; Turkey
breasts cordon bleu*

Chicken and Peppers

Serves 4
4 chicken pieces, total weight
1.25 kg (2½ lb)
1 carrot, peeled and sliced
1 onion, peeled and sliced
1 small red pepper, cored,
seeded and sliced
1 small green pepper, cored,
seeded and sliced
1 garlic clove, peeled and
crushed
1 teaspoon dried sage
1 teaspoon dried parsley
2 tablespoons tomato purée
25 g (1 oz) butter, cut up
25 g (1 oz) plain flour
about 450 ml (¾ pint) hot
chicken stock
salt
freshly ground black pepper

Preparation time: about 20 minutes
Cooking time: about 26½–29½ minutes
Microwave setting: Maximum (Full)

1. Place the chicken pieces in a large bowl. Cover and cook for 9–12 minutes, rearranging halfway through cooking. Set aside, covered.

2. Place the carrot, onion, peppers, garlic, sage, parsley and tomato purée in a large bowl. Cover and cook for 10 minutes, stirring halfway through.

3. Stir in the butter until melted, then stir in the flour. Make up the chicken juices to 450 ml (¾ pint) with stock, then stir in with salt and pepper. Cook, uncovered, for 3½ minutes, stirring every minute.

4. Stir in the chicken and, cook, uncovered, for 4 minutes.

Chicken Livers and Grapes

Serves 4
100 g (4 oz) butter
1 garlic clove, peeled and
crushed
2 tablespoons tomato purée
1 tablespoon chopped fresh
parsley
25 g (1 oz) mushrooms, finely
sliced
750 g (1½ lb) chicken livers,
chopped
350 g (12 oz) black grapes,
halved and seeded
salt
freshly ground black pepper
25 g (1 oz) cornflour
125 ml (4 fl oz) red wine
chopped fresh parsley, to
garnish

Preparation time: about 20 minutes
Cooking time: about 16½ minutes
Microwave setting: Maximum (Full)

1. Place the butter, garlic, tomato purée, parsley and mushrooms in a large bowl. Cover and cook for 3 minutes.

2. Stir in the livers. Cover and cook for 6 minutes. Stir in the grapes, salt and pepper. Cover and cook for 5 minutes.

3. Blend together the cornflour and wine, then stir into the livers. Cook, uncovered, for 2½ minutes, stirring halfway through cooking.

4. Garnish with the chopped parsley and serve with rice and courgettes.

Coq au Vin

Serves 4–6
1 medium onion, peeled and
finely chopped
100 g (4 oz) streaky bacon,
rinds removed and chopped
100 g (4 oz) button mushrooms
1 × 1.5 kg (3 lb) chicken, cut
into 8 pieces
150 ml (¼ pint) chicken stock
600 ml (1 pint) red wine
2 garlic cloves, peeled and
crushed
25 g (1 oz) butter, cut into
pieces
1 bouquet garni
salt
freshly ground black pepper

Preparation time: about 20 minutes
Cooking time: about 50 minutes
Microwave setting: Maximum (Full) and Defrost

1. Place the onion in a large bowl, cover and cook on Maximum for 4 minutes. Stir in the bacon and cook, uncovered, for 1 minute. Stir in the mushrooms and cook for 1 minute.

2. Stir in the chicken pieces and cook on Maximum, uncovered, for 8 minutes, stirring halfway through.

3. Stir in the stock, wine, garlic, butter, bouquet garni and salt and pepper to taste. Cook, covered, on Maximum for 6 minutes.

4. Cook on Defrost, covered, for 30 minutes, stirring halfway through. Before serving, remove the bouquet garni.

Chicken Marengo

Serves 4
1 onion, peeled and finely
chopped
4 chicken portions, total weight
1 kg (2 lb)
6 tomatoes, skinned and
chopped
175 g (6 oz) button mushrooms
2 tablespoons tomato purée
1 garlic clove, peeled and
crushed
½ teaspoon dried rosemary
½ teaspoon dried sage
25 g (1 oz) butter, cut into
pieces
25 g (1 oz) plain flour
about 150 ml (¼ pint) hot
chicken stock
150 ml (¼ pint) Marsala
salt
freshly ground black pepper
fresh sage, to garnish

Preparation time: about 15 minutes
Cooking time: about 28 minutes
Microwave setting: Maximum (Full)

1. Place the onion in a large bowl, cover and cook for 2 minutes. Add the chicken pieces, cover and cook for 10 minutes, rearranging halfway through cooking. Set aside, covered.

2. Place the tomatoes, mushrooms, tomato purée, garlic, rosemary and sage in a large bowl. Cover and cook for 8 minutes, stirring halfway through.

3. Stir in the butter until melted. Stir in the flour. Make up the chicken juices to 150 ml (¼ pint) with stock, then stir in with the Marsala, and salt and pepper. Cover and cook for 4 minutes, stirring halfway through.

4. Stir in the chicken and onions. Cook, uncovered, for 4 minutes. Garnish with sage.

Clockwise: Chicken marengo; Coq au vin; Chicken livers and grapes; Chicken and peppers

Sherry Chicken

Serves 4

*4 chicken legs, total weight 1 kg
(2 lb)*
1 courgette, sliced
1 onion, peeled and sliced
½ teaspoon dried rosemary
*1 teaspoon chopped fresh
parsley*
½ teaspoon dried tarragon
*1 garlic clove, peeled and
crushed*
25 g (1 oz) butter, diced
25 g (1 oz) cornflour
*about 300 ml (½ pint) hot
chicken stock*
150 ml (¼ pint) dry sherry
1 tablespoon tomato purée
50 g (2 oz) flaked almonds
salt
freshly ground black pepper
2 tablespoons double cream

Preparation time: about 10
minutes
Cooking time: about 22–25
minutes
Microwave setting: Maximum
(Full)

1. Place the chicken legs in an
oblong casserole. Cover and
cook for 9–12 minutes,
rearranging halfway through
cooking. Set aside, covered.

2. Place the courgette, onion,
rosemary, parsley, tarragon and
garlic in a large bowl. Cover and
cook for 5 minutes.

3. Stir in the butter until melted.
Stir in the cornflour. Make up
the chicken juices to 300 ml
(½ pint) with the stock, then stir
in with the sherry, tomato
purée, almonds, salt and
pepper. Cook, uncovered, for 4
minutes, stirring every minute.
Stir in the cream.

4. Pour over the chicken. Cook
for 4 minutes.

Turkey with Orange and Almonds

Serves 4

*4 turkey breasts, total weight
750 g (1½ lb)*
freshly ground black pepper
grated rind of 1 orange
*50 g (2 oz) flaked almonds,
toasted*
50 g (2 oz) butter
125 ml (4 fl oz) orange juice
1 tablespoon Grand Marnier
*25 g (1 oz) soft dark brown
sugar*
*1 orange, peeled and sliced, to
garnish*

Preparation time: about 10
minutes
Cooking time: about 10
minutes
Microwave setting: Maximum
(Full)

1. Place the turkey breasts in a
shallow casserole dish and
sprinkle with pepper. Cover and
cook for 6 minutes. Rearrange
and turn over halfway through
cooking. Set aside, covered.

2. Place the orange rind,
almonds, butter, orange juice,
Grand Marnier and sugar in a
jug. Cook, uncovered, for 2
minutes.

3. Drain the juice off the breasts.
Pour over the hot sauce. Cook,
uncovered, for 2 minutes.
Garnish with orange slices.

Stuffed Roast Chicken

Serves 4–6
1 celery stick, finely chopped
1 medium onion, peeled and
  finely chopped
1 eating apple, peeled, cored
  and chopped
175 g (6 oz) dried prunes,
  soaked in 125 ml (4 fl oz)
  port overnight, and chopped
1 × 1.5 kg (3 lb) roasting
  chicken
2 tablespoons clear honey
1 teaspoon Worcestershire
  sauce
1 teaspoon soy sauce
parsley sprigs, to garnish

Preparation time: about 20
minutes, plus soaking
Cooking time: about 27½
minutes, plus standing
Microwave setting: Maximum
(Full)

1. Place the celery, onion and apple in a medium bowl. Cover. Cook for 3½ minutes. Stir in prunes.

2. Spoon stuffing into the chicken, and secure the opening and the legs with trussing thread.

3. Mix the honey, Worcestershire sauce and soy sauce together. Brush the chicken with the sauce.

4. Place the bird in a roasting bag. Secure with a non-metallic tie and prick the bag. Place the bird breast side down in a shallow dish. Cook for 12 minutes. Turn over and cook for a further 12 minutes.

5. Remove the chicken from the bag and wrap tightly in foil. Leave to stand for 15 minutes. Garnish with parsley sprigs.

Turkey Legs Casserole

Serves 4
4 turkey legs, total weight
  1.25 kg (2½ lb)
1 celery stick, chopped
1 small turnip, peeled and
  diced
1 medium onion, peeled and
  chopped
1 carrot, peeled and sliced
1 tablespoon tomato purée
½ teaspoon dried marjoram
½ teaspoon dried thyme
1 teaspoon dried parsley
25 g (1 oz) butter, cut into
  pieces
25 g (1 oz) plain flour
about 450 ml (¾ pint) chicken
  stock
salt
freshly ground black pepper
chopped fresh parsley to garnish

Preparation time: about 20
minutes
Cooking time: about 29
minutes
Microwave setting: Maximum
(Full)

1. Place the turkey legs in a large bowl. Cover and cook for 12 minutes, rearranging halfway through cooking. Set aside, covered.

2. Place the celery, turnip, onion, carrot, tomato purée, marjoram, thyme and parsley in a large bowl. Cover and cook for 10 minutes, stirring halfway through cooking.

3. Stir in the butter until melted. Stir in the flour. Make up turkey juices to 450 ml (¾ pint) with stock, then stir in with salt and pepper. Cook, uncovered, for 3 minutes, stirring every minute.

4. Pour the vegetable sauce over the turkey. Cook, uncovered, for 4 minutes. Garnish with parsley.

From left to right: Sherry chicken;
Turkey with orange and almonds;
Stuffed roast chicken; Turkey legs
casserole

Turkey Casserole

Serves 4

4 turkey fillets
1 carrot, peeled and finely sliced
1 celery stick, finely sliced
1 medium onion, peeled and finely chopped
50 g (2 oz) button mushrooms, finely sliced
40 g (1½ oz) butter
40 g (1½ oz) plain flour
150 ml (¼ pint) sherry
450 ml (¾ pint) hot chicken stock
salt
freshly ground black pepper

Preparation time: about 15 minutes
Cooking time: about 18½ minutes
Microwave setting: Maximum (Full)

1. Place the turkey fillets in a large shallow casserole. Cover and cook for 2 minutes.

2. Turn the casserole round and cook for a further 2 minutes. Turn the casserole round again and cook for 1½ minutes. Set aside.

3. Place the carrot, celery, chopped onion, sliced mushrooms and butter in a medium bowl. Cover and cook for 6 minutes, stirring halfway through cooking.

4. Stir in the flour, sherry, hot stock, salt and pepper. Cover and cook for 2 minutes, stirring halfway through.

5. Pour over the turkey. Cover. Cook for 5 minutes.

Glazed Poussins

Serves 4

75 g (3 oz) butter
1 tablespoon soft dark brown sugar
1 tablespoon Worcestershire sauce
4 bacon rashers, rinds removed
4 poussins, total weight 1.5 kg (3 lb), trussed
watercress sprigs to garnish

Preparation time: about 10 minutes
Cooking time: about 23 minutes, plus standing
Microwave setting: Maximum (Full)

1. Place 25 g (1 oz) of the butter, the sugar and Worcestershire sauce in a small jug. Cook, uncovered, for 1 minute. Set aside.

2. Push a rasher of bacon into each chicken. Place the chickens, breast side down, in a shallow casserole. Cook, uncovered, for 12 minutes. Turn the chickens over and brush with the sugar glaze. Cook, uncovered, for 10 minutes. Wrap the casserole in foil and leave to stand, covered, for 10 minutes. Garnish with watercress.

Chicken in Vermouth

Serves 4

*1 medium onion, peeled and
  finely chopped
½ green pepper, cored, seeded
  and finely chopped
100 g (4 oz) mushrooms, sliced
1 teaspoon dried basil
50 g (2 oz) butter
salt
freshly ground black pepper
4 chicken quarters
50 g (2 oz) cornflour
150 ml (¼ pint) dry white
  vermouth
300 ml (½ pint) milk
300 ml (½ pint) hot chicken
  stock
flat-leaved parsley sprigs, to
  garnish*

*From left to right: Turkey casserole;
Chicken in vermouth; Glazed poussins*

Preparation time: about 15
minutes
Cooking time: about 26
minutes
Microwave setting: Maximum
(Full)

1. Place the onion and green
pepper in a large bowl. Cover
and cook for 4 minutes. Stir in
the mushrooms, basil, butter,
salt and pepper.

2. Arrange the chicken around
the sides of the bowl, cover and
cook for 8 minutes.

3. Stir the chicken and
vegetables together and turn the
bowl round. Cook for a further
7 minutes. Remove the chicken
from the bowl and set aside.

4. Blend the cornflour and

vermouth together, then
gradually stir in the milk. Add to
the vegetables. Stir in the hot
stock. Cool slightly.

5. Pour into a liquidizer and
blend until smooth. Pour the
sauce back into the bowl, cover
and cook for 2 minutes.

6. Return the chicken to the
bowl, cover and cook for 5
minutes. Garnish with sprigs of
parsley.

Cook's Tip

Crisp potato slices are an
excellent accompaniment for
poultry. Speed up the cooking
time by par-cooking the
potatoes in the microwave
before shallow frying them or
browning them under a hot
grill. Peel and slice the potatoes,
then place them in a dish with 2
tablespoons water. Cover and
cook on Maximum (Full),
allowing about 10 minutes for
675 g (1½ lb) of potatoes and
rearranging them halfway
through cooking. Lay the slices
on a baking tray, brush with oil
and grill to brown.

Rabbit in White Wine

Serves 4
1 medium onion, peeled and
    finely chopped
1 celery stick, finely sliced
1 carrot, peeled and finely
    diced
½ green pepper, cored, seeded
    and finely sliced
1 garlic clove, peeled and
    crushed
½ teaspoon dried rosemary
1 teaspoon chopped fresh
    parsley
50 g (2 oz) butter
4 rabbit joints
50 g (2 oz) cornflour
300 ml (½ pint) hot chicken
    stock
150 ml (¼ pint) milk
150 ml (¼ pint) white wine
salt
freshly ground black pepper
rosemary sprigs, to garnish

Preparation time: about 20
minutes
Cooking time: about 19
minutes, plus standing
Microwave setting: Maximum
(Full)

1. Place the onion, celery,
carrot, green pepper, garlic,
rosemary, parsley and butter in
a large bowl. Cover and cook
for 9 minutes, stirring halfway
through cooking.

2. Place the rabbit around the
sides of the bowl. Cover and
cook for 3 minutes.

3. Stir the rabbit and vegetables
together and turn the bowl
round. Cook for a further 3
minutes.

4. Remove the rabbit. Stir in the
cornflour, then blend in the hot
stock, milk, wine, salt and
pepper.

5. Return the rabbit to the bowl,
cover and cook for 4 minutes.
Leave to stand, covered, for 5
minutes before serving,
garnished with rosemary.

Duck with Red Wine Sauce

Serves 4
4 duck joints
3 tomatoes
1 medium onion, peeled and
    finely chopped
50 g (2 oz) butter
2 tablespoons tomato purée
2 garlic cloves, peeled and
    crushed
½ teaspoon dried rosemary
½ teaspoon dried basil
salt
freshly ground black pepper
50 g (2 oz) cornflour
150 ml (¼ pint) dry red wine
450 ml (¾ pint) hot chicken
    stock

Preparation time: about 20
minutes
Cooking time: 32 minutes, plus
grilling
Microwave setting: Maximum
(Full)

1. Place the pieces of duck in a
large bowl. Cover and cook for
8 minutes. Turn the bowl round
and cook for a further 7
minutes.

2. Place the joints in a grill pan
and brown under a preheated
conventional grill. Keep hot.

3. Meanwhile, skin the tomatoes
by pricking them with a fork
and placing in a large bowl.
Cover with 600 ml (1 pint) cold
water and cook for 6 minutes.
Drain immediately to prevent
the tomatoes cooking and
remove the skins with a knife.
Chop the flesh.

4. Place the onion, butter,
tomatoes, tomato purée, garlic,
rosemary, basil, salt and pepper
in a large bowl. Cover and cook
for 8 minutes.

5. Blend the cornflour and wine
together. Stir the cornflour
mixture into the vegetables,
then stir in the hot stock. Cool
slightly.

6. Pour into a liquidizer and
blend until smooth.

7. Pour into a large bowl and
cook for 3 minutes or until
thickened and hot, stirring
halfway through.

Roast Pheasant with Bread Sauce

Serves 4
1 medium onion, peeled
6 cloves
150 ml (¼ pint) milk
150 ml (¼ pint) cold chicken
    stock
100 g (4 oz) fresh white
    breadcrumbs
75 g (3 oz) butter
salt
freshly ground black pepper
1 × 1 kg (2 lb) pheasant
3 streaky bacon rashers, rinds
    removed
1 tablespoon plain flour
watercress sprigs to garnish

Preparation time: about 15
minutes
Cooking time: about 23
minutes, plus standing and
grilling
Microwave setting: Maximum
(Full)

1. To make the sauce, stud the
onion with the cloves and place
in a medium bowl. Add the milk,
chicken stock, breadcrumbs, 50 g
(2 oz) of the butter, salt and
pepper. Cook for 5½ minutes,
stirring halfway through.

2. Place the remaining butter
inside the cavity of the pheasant
and secure the opening with
trussing thread. Lay the bacon

rashers over the breast of the
pheasant and secure.

3. Place the pheasant in a
roasting bag, and secure with a
non-metallic tie. Prick the bag
and place in a shallow casserole.
Cook for 7 minutes. Turn the
pheasant over and cook for a
further 7 minutes.

4. Remove the pheasant from
the bag and discard the bacon.
Wrap in foil. Stand for 10
minutes.

5. Place the pheasant in a grill
pan. Sprinkle with flour and
brown under a preheated
conventional grill.

6. Meanwhile, remove and
discard the onion from the
sauce. Cook for 3½ minutes,
stirring halfway through.

7. Serve the pheasant
garnished with watercress and
hand the sauce separately.

Braised Pigeons

Serves 4

4 bacon rashers, rinds
  removed, then rolled
4 pigeons, drawn and trussed,
  total weight 1.25 kg (2½ lb)
2 small onions, peeled and
  sliced
50 g (2 oz) mushrooms, sliced
1 tablespoon tomato purée
¼ teaspoon dried thyme
¼ teaspoon dried parsley
¼ teaspoon dried rosemary
¼ teaspoon dried marjoram
1 garlic clove, peeled and
  crushed

25 g (1 oz) butter, diced
25 g (1 oz) plain flour
300 ml (½ pint) hot chicken
  stock
300 ml (½ pint) red wine
salt
freshly ground black pepper
flat-leaved parsley to garnish

Preparation time: about 10
minutes
Cooking time: about 29
minutes, plus standing
Microwave setting: Maximum
(Full)

1. Place a bacon rasher inside
each pigeon. Place the pigeons
in a 23 cm (9 inch) round,
shallow casserole dish, breast
side down. Cover and cook for
8 minutes. Turn pigeons over
and cook, uncovered, for 5
minutes. Set aside, covered.

2. Place the onions,
mushrooms, tomato purée,
herbs and garlic in a medium
bowl. Cover and cook for 6
minutes, stirring halfway
through cooking.

3. Stir in the butter until melted.
Stir in the flour, stock, wine, and
salt and pepper to taste. Cook,
uncovered, for 4 minutes,
stirring every minute.

4. Pour the sauce over the
pigeons. Cover and cook for 6
minutes. Stand, covered, for 5
minutes before serving
garnished with parsley.

*Clockwise: Rabbit in white wine; Duck
with red wine sauce; Roast pheasant
with bread sauce; Braised pigeons*

Roast duck; Spiced duck

Roast Duck

Serves 6–8

1 × 2.75 kg (6 lb) duck, washed
*   and cleaned*
1 orange, cut into 8 pieces

Preparation time: about 5
minutes
Cooking time: about 40
minutes, plus standing and
grilling
Microwave setting: Maximum
(Full)

1. Stuff the duck with the orange
pieces. Truss with string. Place
in a roasting bag and tie the
opening with string. Pierce the
bag.

2. Place the bird, breast side
down, on a trivet in a shallow
container. Cook for 20 minutes.

3. Drain off the fat and juices.
Remove the bag and return to
the cooker with the breast side
up. Cook uncovered for 20
minutes.

4. Wrap the bird in foil and
stand for 15 minutes.

5. Brown under a preheated
conventional grill, cut in to
portions if necessary.

Spiced Duck

Serves 4

1 large onion, peeled and
*   chopped*
3 tablespoons soft dark brown
*   sugar*
1½ teaspoons salt
2 tablespoons paprika
2 tablespoons tomato purée
2 tablespoons Worcestershire
*   sauce*
4 tablespoons white wine
*   vinegar*
4 tablespoons lemon juice
½ teaspoon dried rosemary
½ teaspoon dried chives
½ teaspoon grated nutmeg
900 ml (1½ pints) cold water
freshly ground black pepper
1 × 2 kg (4½ lb) duck, quartered
25 g (1 oz) butter
25 g (1 oz) plain flour
spring onions, to garnish

Preparation time: about 5
minutes, plus marinating
Cooking time: about 23½
minutes, plus standing and
grilling
Microwave setting: Maximum
(Full)

1. Place the onion, sugar, salt,
paprika, tomato purée,

Worcestershire sauce, vinegar,
lemon juice, rosemary, chives,
nutmeg, water, and pepper to
taste in a large bowl. Add the
duck and marinate overnight.

2. Drain the duck, reserving the
marinade. Place in a large bowl,
cover and cook for 10 minutes.
Halfway through cooking, drain
off the juice, then rearrange the
duck pieces.

3. Leave the duck to stand,
covered, for 10 minutes. Drain
off the juices and cook, covered,
for a further 8 minutes.

4. Place the duck on a grill pan
and grill under a preheated
conventional grill until the skin
is crisp.

5. Meanwhile, place the butter
in a large jug and cook,
uncovered, for 30 seconds or
until melted. Stir in the flour.
Measure out 600 ml (1 pint) of
the strained reserved marinade.
Blend into the butter and flour
mixture. Cook, uncovered, for 5
minutes, stirring every minute.

6. Serve the duck with the sauce,
garnished with spring onions.

MENU PLANNER

Stuffed Roast Turkey

Christmas is the time of year to make the very most of all your cook's gadgets, and your microwave can be put to full use to cut down on time spent working in the kitchen.

Mix the Christmas Pudding (page 173) the day before, then cover it and leave overnight.

Make the Cranberry Sauce (page 164) the day before. Prepare the stuffing the day before but do not put it in the bird until Christmas morning.

Before the meal, cook the Bread Sauce (page 165) first. Cook the turkey next, then while it stands halfway through cooking, cook the potatoes. Finish cooking the turkey, then make the gravy. Put the potatoes under a slow grill to brown, heat the starter and have the vegetables ready to cook.

Cook the vegetables while the starter is served. Heat the sauces and serve the main course. Cook the pudding while the main course is served. Make any sweet sauces just before serving the pudding.

Serves 6–8
25 g (1 oz) butter
1 large onion, peeled and finely chopped
50 g (2 oz) fresh white breadcrumbs
50 g (2 oz) fresh brown breadcrumbs
150 ml (¼ pint) hot chicken stock
¼ teaspoon dried thyme
¼ teaspoon dried rosemary
¼ teaspoon dried marjoram
1 teaspoon dried parsley
¼ teaspoon dried sage
1 orange, peeled and chopped
grated rind of 1 orange
25 g (1 oz) sultanas
salt
freshly ground black pepper
1 × 3 kg (7 lb) turkey, thawed if frozen and at room temperature
watercress, to garnish
Glaze:
50 g (2 oz) butter
2 tablespoons soft dark brown sugar
½ tablespoon sherry
2 teaspoons soy sauce

Preparation time: about 15 minutes
Cooking time: about 58 minutes, plus standing
Microwave setting: Maximum (Full)

1. Place the butter and onion in a medium bowl, cover and cook for 4 minutes. Stir in the breadcrumbs, stock, thyme, rosemary, marjoram, parsley, sage, orange, orange rind, sultanas, and salt and pepper to taste. Stuff the turkey.

2. Truss the turkey. Mask the wings and legs with pieces of foil. Place the turkey, breast side down, on an inverted plate or trivet in a shallow dish. Cover with a paper towel. Cook for 26¼ minutes. Set aside.

3. Place the butter, sugar, sherry and soy sauce in a small jug. Cook for 1½ minutes.

4. Remove the foil pieces from the turkey, turn over and brush with the glaze. Cook for 26¼ minutes.

5. Wrap in foil and stand for 30 minutes.

6. Garnish with watercress and serve with sauces, gravy and vegetables.

Cook's Tip

If using a different size of turkey, allow 7½ minutes to each 450 g (1 lb) for turkeys under 4.5 kg (10 lb) in weight.

Honeyed grapefruit and orange; Christmas pudding; Bread sauce; Peas; Roast turkey; Potatoes; Cranberry sauce

MEAT

Microwave cooking times for meat are a fraction of those needed for conventional methods but for true success select the tender cuts to prepare by this method. Remember that you can always use the microwave to part-cook joints before they are roasted in the conventional oven.

The rule for cooking meat in the microwave is to select the tender cuts which require shorter traditional cooking. Chops, roasts, tender steaks and mince recipes will all cook well. However, microwave cooking is a moist method so the result will be the same as if the meat were steamed. The meat will not be browned at the end of the cooking but this can be remedied by placing joints under a grill or by using a browning dish. For sauced dishes the lack of browning is not as important.

To achieve success with traditional roasts, it is a good idea to start the cooking process in the microwave, then to finish the joint in the conventional oven. This way the overall cooking time is greatly reduced and the result is as good as that expected of conventional methods.

The cuts which do not cook as successfully are the tougher ones which require long, moist stewing and braising to tenderise them. These can be cooked on Low power for a longer time and the finished dish will be acceptable but it is not possible to produce 'melt-in-the-mouth' casseroles in the microwave. Really it is a question of taste – if you favour slightly chewy casseroles and stews then you will find microwave cooking perfectly good enough; if you like your meat really tender, then it is best to use traditional methods for stewing and long braising.

Cooking joints

Medium power often gives better results for large joints, allowing time for the meat to cook through evenly. The meat should be covered with greaseproof paper or it can be placed in a roasting bag. Plastic ties or elastic bands should be used to close the bag. Do not season meat before cooking – it can be flavoured by sticking with herb sprigs or by topping with bay leaves.

Using a microwave-proof meat thermometer

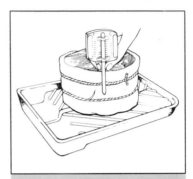

1. Use a special microwave-proof thermometer. Before inserting it into the meat mark the distance with your finger from the outside of the joint into the thickest part.

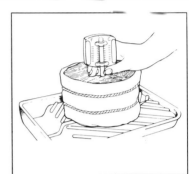

2. Insert the thermometer to the depth marked by your finger, choosing a point at the centre of the meat and avoiding contact with bone or fat.

During cooking the joint should be checked frequently and turned over at least twice, if not more. The larger the joint the more attention it needs.

Observe the suggested standing times as a joint of meat will continue to cook by means of the residual heat.

Shielding

Shield areas that look as if they are going to overcook by covering them with small pieces of foil.

Using a meat thermometer

Do not use an ordinary meat thermometer. Special thermometers are manufactured for use in the microwave. Insert the thermometer into the thickest part of the joint, pushing it into the centre of the meat. Make sure that the

thermometer does not touch fat or bone.

Cooking meat portions

Small portions of meat – chops, steaks, burgers or meatballs – can all be cooked in the microwave.

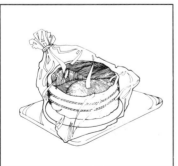

Joints can be cooked in a roasting bag which should be loosely closed with an elastic band or a special microwave tie which is free of metal.

Areas that cook more rapidly than others should be protected with small pieces of smooth foil to prevent them from overcooking.

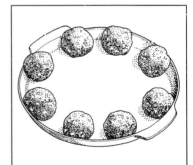

Small portions of meat should be arranged round the edge of a dish for even cooking. Here meatballs are positioned round the edge of a flan dish.

Turning

The portions should be turned over and around halfway through the cooking time.

Arranging meat portions

As for other foods, small portions of meat should be arranged round the outside of the dish to promote even cooking. Thin parts should be pointed towards the middle of the dish where they are less likely to overcook. Chops, small steaks, burgers and meatballs should be arranged in this way.

Browning

The meat will not brown in the microwave. A browning dish is useful for chops, burgers or meatballs and the manufacturer's instructions should be followed closely. If the pieces are cooked in a sauce, then the fact that they do not brown is less noticeable. If you like crisp, well browned portions, then you will find traditional cooking methods or combination cooking more acceptable.

Cutting meat

For moist, casserole-style or braised dishes the result is best if the meat is cut across the grain as this method gives the most tender results. Frying

Halfway through cooking the portions of meat should be turned over and around. Here burgers are being cooked in a browning dish.

steak, pork and lamb are all tender and they can be cooked with vegetables and other flavouring ingredients in sauced recipes with great success.

There are two methods of cutting the meat for best results. It can be cut across the grain into small thin slices which can then be cooked in a sauce or they can be flattened and filled with a stuffing. The slices are rolled round the filling and secured with thread or wooden cocktail sticks. They should be arranged round the edge of a dish for cooking.

Thin strips of meat cook well by this method. The meat should first be cut across the grain into thin slices. The slices are then cut into fine strips. These can be cooked with vegetables, stir-fry style or they can be braised in a sauce.

Defrosting meat

The microwave can be used for defrosting all cuts of meat, whether they are to be cooked by this method or by traditional means. There are a few points which apply to all defrosting methods for meat.

When defrosting large joints it is necessary to turn or rearrange the meat several times during cooking. About halfway through the cooking time check for any areas that are likely to start cooking and shield these with small pieces of foil. Do observe standing times to ensure that the meat is thoroughly defrosted.

To defrost chunks of meat, place them in a dish and rearrange them once or twice during the recommended time. If the chunks are frozen together in a block, then break them away as soon as they can be loosened and remove any from the microwave if they are likely to start cooking.

Mince defrosts particularly speedily. Place a block of mince in a dish and cook for a third of the time, then break up the block and continue to cook

Cutting meat for microwaving

1. The meat is cut across the grain into thin slices to give tender results.

2. The thin slices can be cut into fine strips for cooking with vegetables or moist ingredients.

until completely defrosted. Break up the pieces several times during defrosting and remove any that is likely to start cooking. It is not necessary to defrost 'free-flow' frozen mince before cooking.

Chops and steaks should be arranged round the edge of a dish for even defrosting. If they are in one block, then cook them for part of the time until they can be separated and arranged. Turn them once or twice to prevent any areas from cooking and observe the suggested standing times.

Break mince down as it defrosts and remove any which is starting to cook.

BEEF

Lean, tender beef steaks cook well in the microwave but the result is not browned as by conventional methods. Frying or braising steak can be cut into thin slices or strips to be cooked successfully. Tender joints cook well and they can be browned under the grill before serving. Tough stewing cuts do not give the best results, so they are better cooked by conventional methods; mince cooks very well, with significant savings on time.

Marinating beef

Marinating not only contributes to the flavour of the finished dish but it is also a means of tenderising the meat before cooking. Thin strips or slices of beef can be marinated for several hours or overnight before cooking. The marinade can be a spicy one, consisting of garlic, grated fresh root ginger, sesame oil and lime or lemon juice. Alternatively try soaking the meat in a combination of chopped thyme and parsley, a little walnut oil and some dry sherry.

Red wine marinade

Mix 1 crushed clove of garlic with 2 tablespoons sunflower oil and 1 teaspoon concentrated tomato purée. Add 300 ml ($\frac{1}{2}$ pint) red wine and plenty of freshly ground black pepper. Stir in a bay leaf, 1 teaspoon chopped fresh thyme or $\frac{1}{2}$ teaspoon dried thyme, then add the meat strips or slices. Mix really well, press the meat down into the marinade and cover the dish. Leave for several hours or overnight; ideally, turn the meat several times.

The meat should be drained of the marinade for the first stages of cooking. The marinade should be added when the meat is par-cooked to make a delicious sauce.

The marinade can be varied by using different herbs, lightly crushed juniper berries or a blade of mace. The tomato can be omitted and hazelnut or walnut oil can be used instead of the sunflower oil. Both these oils are strongly flavoured and they should be used with care.

Cooking mince

Minced beef is the most common form of minced meat but the notes given here can also be applied to minced pork, lamb or veal.

Before the mince is cooked any onions, garlic, peppers or other ingredients which require lengthy cooking, or have strong flavours, should be par-cooked with a little oil, butter or liquid.

The mince is added to the flavouring ingredients and stirred well. The dish should be covered and the mince is cooked for half the recommended time. The meat from the outside of the dish must be stirred into the middle to promote even cooking. When the meat is partly cooked any other ingredients are added – mushrooms or other quick-cooking vegetables and the liquid.

Unless the quantity is small, the liquid should be heated before mixing into the mince. Stock cubes should be dissolved in boiling water. If the dish contains plenty of liquid, then it can be seasoned. If the quantity of liquid is small only a little of the seasoning should be added at this stage and the balance should be stirred in at the end of the cooking time. Once all the ingredients are added, the dish is covered and the meat sauce is stirred at least once during cooking. It should be left to stand for a few minutes at the end of the cooking time to allow the temperature to equalise, then it should be stirred before serving.

Versatile meat sauce

The basic bolognese-style meat sauce can be served in many ways or it can form the base for a variety of dishes. In its simplest form it can be ladled over cooked pasta or rice. It can be served in a ring of piped mashed potatoes and sprinkled with a little grated cheese, then browned under the grill or used to make a lasagne.

Cooking mince

1. The onion, peppers and garlic are cooked first with a little oil until they are just softened.

2. The mince is added and part cooked, then the meat from the outside of the dish is stirred with that in the middle to ensure even cooking.

3. The remaining ingredients are added; here a bolognese sauce is prepared. Hot stock is stirred in and, since the mixture is quite moist, the seasoning is added at this stage. The meat sauce is now ready for cooking to completion and it will need stirring once.

GUIDE TO DEFROSTING BEEF

Type of Meat	Defrosting time in minutes on Defrost 450 g (1 lb)	
joints	9	Turn over at least once during the defrosting time.
steaks (large)	8	
steaks (small)	4	
minced beef	10	Break up during defrosting.

GUIDE TO COOKING BEEF

Type and cut of meat	Cooking time in minutes on Medium per 450 g (1 lb) or for quantity given	Cooking time in minutes on Maximum (Full) per 450 g (1 lb) or for quantity given	Method
topside			Choose a good quality joint with an even covering of fat and a neat shape. Allow to stand for 15–20 minutes, wrapped in foil, before carving.
rare	12	5–6	
medium	14	$6\frac{1}{2}$–$7\frac{1}{2}$	
well done	16	$8\frac{1}{2}$–$9\frac{1}{2}$	
sirloin			As above.
rare	12	5–6	
medium	14	$6\frac{1}{2}$–$7\frac{1}{2}$	
well done	16	$8\frac{1}{2}$–$9\frac{1}{2}$	
rib			Ideally, bone and roll the joint before cooking. Allow to stand for 15–30 minutes, wrapped in foil, before carving.
rare	12–13	$5\frac{1}{2}$–$6\frac{1}{2}$	
medium	14–15	7–8	
well done	16–17	8–10	
minced beef	14–16	10–12	Cover during cooking. Stir once or twice.
rump steak			Preheat a browning dish according to the manufacturer's instructions. Add the meat and brown. Turn over and cook for the recommended time.
rare	—	2	
medium		3–4	
well done		4	
fillet steak			As above.
rare	—	2	
medium		2–3	
well done		3	
braising steak	16–17	10	Ideally, cook on Medium. If using Maximum (Full), leave to stand for 10 minutes halfway through cooking time.
hamburgers			Preheat a browning dish. Add the hamburgers and cook for the recommended time, turning the 100-g (4-oz) burgers over halfway through the cooking time, and turning the 225-g (8-oz) burgers over twice during the cooking time.
1 100-g (4-oz)	—	2–3	
2 100-g (4-oz)		3–4	
4 100-g (4-oz)		5–6	
1 225-g (8-oz)		$2\frac{1}{2}$–$3\frac{1}{2}$	
2 225-g (8-oz)		6–7	

Beef Tournedos with Pâté

Serves 4

1 medium onion, peeled and chopped
50 g (2 oz) button mushrooms, peeled and sliced
1 garlic clove, peeled and crushed
½ teaspoon dried tarragon
¼ teaspoon dried oregano
1 teaspoon dried rosemary
25 g (1 oz) butter, cut into pieces
25 g (1 oz) plain flour
3 tablespoons tomato purée
300 ml (½ pint) hot beef stock
salt
freshly ground black pepper
4 fillet steaks, 2.5 cm (1 inch) thick, 7.5–10 cm (3–4 inches) wide, total weight 600 g (1¼ lb)
4 slices fried bread, 5 mm (¼ inch) thick
225 g (8 oz) chicken liver pâté

Preparation time: about 20 minutes
Cooking time: about 12–14 minutes
Microwave setting: Maximum (Full)

1. Place the onion, mushrooms, garlic, tarragon, oregano and rosemary in a large jug. Cover and cook for 3 minutes.

2. Stir in the butter until melted. Stir in the flour. Blend in the tomato purée, stock, and salt and pepper to taste. Cook uncovered for 3 minutes, stirring every minute. Set aside, covered.

3. Place the steaks in a shallow 1.5 litre (2½ pint) casserole dish. Cook, uncovered, for 3–5 minutes, depending on how rare you like your steak, and turning over and rearranging halfway through cooking. Pour the steak juices into the sauce.

4. Cut the fried bread to fit the steaks. Spread each piece of bread with pâté. Place steak on the top. Cook, uncovered, for 3 minutes.

5. Pour over the sauce and serve, with a mixed green salad.

Cook's Tip

This recipe shows how to make the best of microwave-cooked food by adding ingredients or side dishes which offer a contrast in texture. The fillet steaks are cooked in the microwave, then heated on rounds of crunchy fried bread which are cooked conventionally. Pour the sauce over the steak just before it is served to keep the bread as crisp as possible.

As well as the button mushrooms in the sauce you may like to add chanterelles. Add about 50–75 g (2–3 oz) to the sauce 1 minute before the end of its cooking time. The sauce and mushrooms may need to be heated for 1 minute before serving.

Beef tournedos with pâté

Garlic Roast Beef

Serves 4

1.5 kg (3 lb) topside of beef
oil, to coat
3 garlic cloves, peeled
salt
freshly ground black pepper

Preparation time: about 10 minutes
Cooking time: about 20 minutes, plus standing and grilling
Microwave setting: Maximum (Full)

1. Rub the beef with the oil, 1 of the garlic cloves, and salt and pepper.

2. Stand the beef on an upturned saucer in a shallow container and cook for 10 minutes.

3. With a sharp knife, cut the remaining garlic cloves into slivers. Make incisions in the meat and insert the slivers of garlic.

4. Cook for 10 minutes.

5. Remove the meat and wrap tightly in foil, with the shiny side inside. Leave the meat to stand for 20 minutes. Brown under a preheated conventional grill then carve.

Beef Olives

Serves 4

50 g (2 oz) mushrooms
1 onion, peeled and quartered
1 tablespoon orange juice
3 tablespoons beef stock
grated rind of 1 lemon
⅓ teaspoon dried mixed herbs
salt
freshly ground pepper
25 g (1 oz) fresh white breadcrumbs
450 g (1 lb) topside of beef, cut into 4 thin slices and lightly beaten
½ green pepper, cored, seeded and chopped
100 g (4 oz) mushrooms, chopped
40 g (1½ oz) butter, diced
2 tablespoons plain flour
150 ml (¼ pint) white wine
1 teaspoon soy sauce
chopped parsley, to garnish

Preparation time: about 20 minutes
Cooking time: about 13 minutes
Microwave setting: Maximum (Full)

1. Purée the whole mushrooms, onion, orange juice, stock, lemon rind, herbs and salt and pepper. Stir in the crumbs.

2. Divide the mixture between the slices of beef and roll up. Cook, uncovered for 6 minutes, turning over halfway through.

3. Place the green pepper and chopped mushrooms in a large jug. Cover and cook for 4 minutes. Stir in the butter until melted. Stir in the flour, wine, soy sauce and meat juices. Season. Pour over the beef. Cook for 3 minutes. Garnish with parsley.

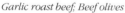

Garlic roast beef; Beef olives

Tarragon Beef

Serves 4

3 tablespoons fresh tarragon
4 fillet steaks, total weight 750 g
(1½ lb), lightly beaten
25 g (1 oz) butter
about 150 ml (¼ pint) hot beef
stock
15 g (½ oz) cornflour
salt
freshly ground black pepper
6 tablespoons double cream
fresh tarragon, to garnish

Preparation time: about 6 minutes
Cooking time: about 10 minutes
Microwave setting: Maximum (Full)

1. Sprinkle 2 tablespoons of the tarragon over both sides of the steaks and rub in well. Place the steaks in a shallow dish and cook, uncovered, for 7 minutes, turning over and rearranging halfway through cooking. Pour off and reserve the juices.

2. Place the butter in a large jug and cook, uncovered, for 30 seconds or until melted. Make up the meat juices to 150 ml (¼ pint) with the stock, then stir in with the cornflour, remaining tarragon, and salt and pepper to taste. Cook, uncovered, for 2½ minutes, stirring every minute.

3. Stir in the cream and pour over the steaks and reheat for 1 minute if necessary. Garnish with tarragon and serve with a mixed green salad.

Tarragon beef

Beef, Mushroom and Onion Suet Pudding

Serves 4

Pastry:

225 g (8 oz) self-raising flour

½ teaspoon salt

100 g (4 oz) shredded suet

175–200 ml (6–7 fl oz) water

Filling:

25 g (1 oz) butter

*2 medium onions, peeled and
  sliced*

*100 g (4 oz) mushrooms,
  chopped*

*1 garlic clove, peeled and
  crushed*

¼ teaspoon dried parsley

¼ teaspoon dried rosemary

¼ teaspoon dried oregano

¼ teaspoon dried marjoram

salt

freshly ground black pepper

350 g (12 oz) minced beef

½ teaspoon meat extract

parsley sprig, to garnish

Preparation time: about 30 minutes

Cooking time: about 18 minutes

Microwave setting: Maximum (Full)

1. Mix together the flour, salt, suet and enough water to form a smooth dough. Roll out two-thirds of the pastry and use to line a greased 1.2 litre (2 pint) pudding basin. Roll out the remainder for a lid and set aside.

2. Place the butter, onions, mushrooms, garlic, parsley, rosemary, oregano, marjoram and salt and pepper to taste in a medium bowl. Cover and cook for 5 minutes.

3. Stir in the beef and meat extract. Cover and cook for 4 minutes, stirring halfway through cooking. Drain off the excess liquid.

4. Fill the basin with the mixture. Place the pastry lid in position and seal. Cover loosely with cling film and cook for 9 minutes, turning round halfway through cooking.

5. Serve immediately, garnished with the parsley and accompanied by creamed potatoes and carrots.

Beef, mushroom and onion suet pudding

Chilli con Carne

Serves 4

1 large onion, peeled and finely
  chopped
1 garlic clove, peeled and
  crushed
2 teaspoons tomato purée
25 g (1 oz) butter, cut into
  pieces
25 g (1 oz) plain flour
½ teaspoon dried oregano
½ teaspoon ground cumin
1 tablespoon chilli powder
1 × 400 g (14 oz) can tomatoes,
  chopped with their juice
450 g (1 lb) minced beef
1 × 425 g (15 oz) can red
  kidney beans, drained
salt
freshly ground black pepper

Preparation time: about 10
minutes
Cooking time: about 17
minutes
Microwave setting: Maximum
(Full)

1. Place the onion, garlic and
tomato purée in a large bowl.
Cover and cook for 5 minutes.

2. Stir in the butter until melted.
Stir in the flour, oregano, cumin,
chilli powder, undrained
tomatoes and beef. Cook,
uncovered, for 8 minutes. Stir
and break up with a fork
halfway through cooking.

3. Stir in the beans and cook,
uncovered, for 4 minutes,
stirring halfway through
cooking.

4. Season to taste with salt and
pepper. Serve with boiled rice
and peas.

Beef Bourguignon

Serves 4–6

2 medium onions, peeled and
  chopped
2 bacon rashers, rinds removed
  and chopped
175 g (6 oz) mushrooms, sliced
750 g (1½ lb) topside of beef,
  cubed
25 g (1 oz) plain flour
225 ml (7½ fl oz) red wine
65 ml (2½ fl oz) hot beef stock
2 garlic cloves, peeled and
  crushed
1 teaspoon dried mixed herbs
salt
freshly ground black pepper

Preparation time: about 15
minutes
Cooking time: about 56
minutes, plus standing
Microwave setting: Maximum
(Full) and Defrost

1. Place the onions and bacon
in a large bowl, cover and cook
on Maximum for 5 minutes

2. Stir in the mushrooms and
beef, cover and cook on
Maximum for 7 minutes, stirring
halfway through.

3. Stir in the flour, red wine,
stock, garlic, herbs and salt and
pepper to taste. Cover and cook
on Maximum for 4 minutes,
stirring halfway through
cooking, then reduce to Defrost
and cook for 40 minutes.

4. Leave to stand, covered, for
10 minutes before serving.

Chilli con carne; Beef bourguignon

Chinese Style Beef

Serves 4–6
1 tablespoon sesame oil
2 medium onions, peeled and
    sliced
1 red pepper, cored, seeded and
    thinly sliced
1 garlic clove, peeled and
    crushed
600 g (1¼ lb) fillet steak, cut into
    strips, 7.5 cm × 1 cm (3
    inches × ½ inch)
100 g (4 oz) button mushrooms,
    sliced
1 teaspoon ground ginger
¼ teaspoon ground cumin
¼ teaspoon grated nutmeg
1 teaspoon dried mixed herbs
15 g (½ oz) cornflour
1 tablespoon lemon juice
50 ml (2 fl oz) dry sherry
175 ml (6 fl oz) hot beef stock
1 tablespoon Worcestershire
    sauce
1 tablespoon soy sauce
salt
freshly ground black pepper
1 × 275 g (10 oz) can bean
    sprouts, drained

Preparation time: about 15
minutes
Cooking time: about 12
minutes, plus standing
Microwave setting: Maximum
(Full)

1. Place the oil, onions, red
pepper and garlic in a large
bowl. Cover and cook for 5
minutes, stirring halfway
through cooking.

2. Stir in the beef, mushrooms,
ginger, cumin, nutmeg, and
herbs. Cover and cook for 3
minutes.

3. Stir in the cornflour, lemon
juice, sherry, stock,
Worcestershire sauce, soy sauce
and salt and pepper to taste.
Fold in the bean sprouts. Cover
and cook for 4 minutes, stirring
halfway through.

4. Leave to stand, covered, for 4
minutes before serving. Serve
with boiled rice.

Mexican Beef

Serves 4–6
1 medium onion, peeled and
    sliced
1 small carrot, peeled and
    sliced
1 green pepper, cored, seeded
    and chopped
1 red pepper, cored, seeded and
    chopped
1 medium potato, peeled and
    diced
50 g (2 oz) butter, cut into
    pieces
1 teaspoon dried mixed herbs
½ teaspoon chilli powder
½ teaspoon Worcestershire sauce
1 teaspoon dried parsley
1 garlic clove, peeled and
    crushed
600 g (1¼ lb) topside beef, cut
    into strips
salt
freshly ground black pepper
2 tablespoons plain flour
1 × 400 g (14 oz) can tomatoes,
    chopped with their juice
150 ml (¼ pint) hot beef stock

Preparation time: about 20
minutes
Cooking time: about 15½
minutes, plus standing
Microwave setting: Maximum
(Full)

1. Place the onion, carrot,
peppers and potato in a large
bowl. Cover and cook for 6½
minutes.

2. Stir in the butter until melted.
Stir in the herbs, chilli powder,
Worcestershire sauce, parsley,
garlic, beef, and salt and pepper
to taste. Cover and cook for 4
minutes, stirring halfway
through.

3. Stir in the flour, undrained
tomatoes and stock. Cover and
cook for 5 minutes, stirring
halfway through cooking.

4. Leave to stand, covered, for 5
minutes before serving.

Chinese style beef; Mexican beef

Beef with Cheese Sauce

Serves 4

1 onion, peeled and thinly
  sliced
1 medium carrot, peeled and
  sliced
100 g (4 oz) potato, peeled and
  sliced
100 g (4 oz) mushrooms,
  chopped
1 tablespoon tomato purée
350 g (12 oz) minced beef
1 teaspoon dried mixed herbs
salt
freshly ground black pepper
40 g (1½ oz) butter
40 g (1½ oz) plain flour
600 ml (1 pint) milk
100 g (4 oz) Cheddar cheese,
  finely grated
1 tablespoon chopped fresh
  parsley, to garnish

Preparation time: about 20
minutes
Cooking time: 22 minutes, plus
grilling
Microwave setting: Maximum
(Full)

1. Place the onion, carrot and
potato in a 1.5 litre (2½ pint)
soufflé dish. Cover and cook for
4½ minutes, stirring halfway
through cooking.

2. Stir in the mushrooms,
tomato purée, beef, herbs, and
salt and pepper to taste. Cover
and cook for 8 minutes. Break
up and stir with a fork halfway
through cooking. Set aside.

3. Place the butter in a large jug
and cook, uncovered, for 30
seconds or until melted. Stir in
the flour, then gradually blend
in the milk, with salt and pepper
to taste. Cook, uncovered, for 7
minutes or until thick, stirring
every 2 minutes.

4. Stir in the cheese until melted.
Pour the sauce over the beef
mixture. Cook, uncovered, for 2
minutes. Brown under a
preheated conventional grill, if
preferred.

5. Sprinkle with parsley to
garnish. Serve with sauté
potatoes and peas.

Beef with cheese sauce

Steak with Chestnuts

Serves 4
*4 fillet steaks, 2.5 cm (1 inch)
  thick, total weight 450 g
  (1 lb), lightly beaten*
1 small celery stick, chopped
*½ green pepper, cored, seeded
  and chopped*
*½ red pepper, cored, seeded and
  chopped*
*1 garlic clove, peeled and
  crushed*
2 tablespoons tomato purée
15 g (½ oz) cornflour
3 tablespoons dry sherry
2 tablespoons soy sauce
*6 canned water chestnuts,
  drained and sliced*
salt
freshly ground black pepper

Preparation time: about 15
minutes
Cooking time: about 12–14
minutes
Microwave setting: Maximum
(Full)

1. Place the steaks in a casserole
dish. Cook, uncovered, for 3–5
minutes, depending on how
rare you like your steak, and
turning over and rearranging
halfway through cooking. Set
aside, covered, while making
sauce.

2. Place the celery, peppers,
garlic and tomato purée in a
medium bowl. Cover and cook
for 5 minutes, stirring halfway
through cooking.

3. Stir in the cornflour, sherry,
soy sauce, water chestnuts, and
salt and pepper to taste. Add any
juice from the cooked steaks.

4. Pour the mixture over the
steaks. Cover and cook for 4
minutes. Serve with croquette
potatoes.

Steak in Pepper Sauce

Serves 4
*1 medium onion, peeled and
  finely chopped*
50 g (2 oz) butter
*1 garlic clove, peeled and
  crushed*
40 g (1½ oz) cornflour
300 ml (½ pint) hot beef stock
150 ml (¼ pint) milk
*½ teaspoon freshly ground black
  pepper*
16 whole black peppercorns
salt
4 sirloin steaks
parsley sprig, to garnish

Preparation time: about 10
minutes
Cooking time: about 13½
minutes, plus standing
Microwave setting: Maximum
(Full)

1. Place the onion, butter and
garlic in a medium bowl. Cover
and cook for 4 minutes.

2. Stir in the cornflour, hot
stock, milk and ground pepper.

Crush 6 of the peppercorns and
add them to the sauce with the
remaining peppercorns and the
salt.

3. Cover and cook for 2
minutes, stirring halfway
through cooking. Leave covered
and set aside.

4. Place the steaks in a large
shallow casserole. Cook for 3
minutes. Turn the steaks over
and turn the casserole round.
Cook for a further 2½ minutes.

5. Stir any meat juices into the
sauce. Pour the sauce over the
steaks, cover and cook for 2
minutes.

6. Leave to stand, covered, for 3
minutes before serving
garnished with parsley. Serve
with a mixed salad.

*Steak with chestnuts; Steak in pepper
sauce*

Whisky Steak

Serves 4

4 rump steaks, total weight
 750 g (1½ lb), lightly beaten
2 tablespoons whisky
1 garlic clove, peeled and
 crushed
1 medium onion, peeled and
 finely chopped
50 g (2 oz) butter
½ teaspoon Worcestershire sauce
freshly ground black pepper
spring onion, to garnish

Preparation time: about 7
minutes, plus marinating
Cooking time: about 14
minutes
Microwave setting: Maximum
(Full)

1. Marinate the steaks in the
whisky for 2 hours.

2. Place the garlic and onion in a
large jug. Cook, covered, for 4
minutes. Stir in the butter and
cook, uncovered, for 30
seconds. Set aside while
cooking the steaks.

3. Drain the steaks, reserving the
marinade. Place the steaks in a
shallow casserole dish. Cook,
uncovered, for 7 minutes,
turning over and rearranging
halfway through cooking.

4. Pour the juice from the steaks
into the butter mixture. Stir in
the Worcestershire sauce,
whisky from the marinade and
pepper to taste.

5. Pour the sauce over the
steaks and cook, uncovered, for
2½ minutes.

6. Garnish with spring onion
and serve with boiled rice.

Whisky steak; Steak with mushroom
sauce

Steak with Mushroom Sauce

Serves 4

1 celery stick, chopped
1 onion, peeled and studded
 with 6 cloves
1 carrot, peeled and sliced
450 ml (¾ pint) milk
4 thin sirloin steaks, total weight
 750 g (1½ lb)
175 g (6 oz) mushrooms, sliced
50 g (2 oz) butter, cut into
 pieces
about 150 ml (¼ pint) hot
 chicken stock
50 g (2 oz) plain flour
salt
freshly ground black pepper
parsley sprig, to garnish

Preparation time: about 15
minutes, plus infusing
Cooking time: about 20
minutes
Microwave setting: Maximum
(Full)

1. Place the celery, onion, carrot
and milk in a large jug. Cook,
uncovered, for 3 minutes. Set
aside to infuse for 15 minutes.
Strain and discard vegetables.

2. Place the steaks in a casserole
dish and cook uncovered for 6
minutes, turning over and
rearranging halfway through
cooking. Set aside, covered,
while making the sauce.

3. Place the mushrooms in a
medium bowl, cover and cook
for 3 minutes. Stir in the butter
until melted. Make up the meat
juices to 150 ml (¼ pint) with the
stock, then stir in with the flour,
strained milk, and salt and
pepper to taste. Cook,
uncovered for 5 minutes,
stirring every minute.

4. Pour the sauce over the
steaks. Cook, uncovered, for 3
minutes. Garnish with the
parsley.

Meatballs in Mushroom and Tomato Sauce

Serves 4
450 g (1 lb) minced beef
25 g (1 oz) fresh brown
*   breadcrumbs*
1 onion, peeled and grated
1 teaspoon dried mixed herbs
1 tablespoon tomato purée
salt
freshly ground black pepper
1 egg
Sauce:
40 g (1½ oz) butter
100 g (4 oz) mushrooms, finely
*   chopped*
350 g (12 oz) tomatoes,
*   skinned and chopped*
1 tablespoon tomato purée
40 g (1½ oz) plain flour
450 ml (¾ pint) hot beef stock
salt
freshly ground black pepper

Preparation time: about 15 minutes
Cooking time: about 20 minutes
Microwave setting: Maximum (Full)

1. Mix the beef, breadcrumbs, onion, herbs, tomato purée, salt and pepper together. Add the egg and mix well. Form the mixture into 16 balls.

2. Place the meatballs on a plate and cook for 2 minutes. Turn the meatballs over and turn the plate round. Cook for a further 2 minutes.

3. To make the sauce, place the butter, mushrooms, tomatoes and tomato purée in a medium bowl. Cover and cook for 5 minutes. Stir in the flour, then gradually add the hot stock. Cook for 2 minutes. Cool slightly.

4. Pour into a liquidizer and blend until smooth. Stir in salt and pepper to taste.

5. Place the meatballs in a bowl. Pour over the sauce. Cook for 5 minutes. Serve with noodles and grated Parmesan cheese.

Beefburger and Onion Rolls

Serves 4
1 medium onion, peeled and
*   sliced*
1 medium onion, peeled and
*   grated*
225 g (8 oz) minced beef
1 garlic clove, peeled and
*   crushed*
1 teaspoon dried mixed herbs
salt
freshly ground black pepper
25 g (1 oz) plain flour
4 soft rolls, cut in half
lettuce and tomatoes, to garnish

Preparation time: about 10 minutes
Cooking time: about 12¾ minutes
Microwave setting: Maximum (Full)

Meatballs in mushroom and tomato sauce; Beefburger and onion rolls.

1. Place the sliced onion in a medium bowl. Cover and cook for 4 minutes. Set aside.

2. Place the grated onion in another medium bowl. Cover and cook for 3 minutes.

3. Stir in the minced beef, garlic, herbs, salt, pepper and flour. Shape into 4 patties.

4. Place on a plate and cook for 3 minutes. Turn the beefburgers over and turn the plate round. Cook for a further 2 minutes.

5. Place a few cooked onion slices on 4 of the roll halves. Place a beefburger on top and top with the remaining half roll. Place on a plate and cook for 45 seconds. Garnish with lettuce and tomatoes.

Savoury Mince with Mixed Vegetables

Serves 4

1 large potato, peeled and diced
1 turnip, peeled and diced
1 carrot, peeled and sliced
1 medium onion, peeled and sliced
1 celery stick, chopped
450 g (1 lb) minced beef
1 teaspoon dried mixed herbs
1 tablespoon tomato purée
150 ml (¼ pint) hot beef stock
salt
freshly ground black pepper

Preparation time: about 20 minutes
Cooking time: about 17 minutes
Microwave setting: Maximum (Full)

1. Place the potato, turnip, carrot, onion and celery in a large bowl. Cover and cook for 10 minutes.

2. Stir in the beef, herbs, tomato purée, stock, and salt and pepper to taste. Cover and cook for 7 minutes, stirring halfway through cooking.

3. Serve with creamed potatoes.

Savoury mince with mixed vegetables;
Tomato cottage pie

Tomato Cottage Pie

Serves 4

750 g (1½ lb) potatoes, peeled and cut into 1 cm (½ inch) cubes
3 tablespoons water
1 medium onion, peeled and chopped
4 tablespoons tomato purée
2 tomatoes, skinned and chopped
450 g (1 lb) cooked beef, finely chopped
1 teaspoon dried mixed herbs
40 g (1½ oz) butter
½ teaspoon celery salt
150 ml (¼ pint) hot beef stock
freshly ground black pepper
2–3 tablespoons milk
salt
parsley sprigs, to garnish (optional)

Preparation time: about 15 minutes
Cooking time: about 23½ minutes
Microwave setting: Maximum (Full)

1. Place the potatoes in a large bowl with the water. Cover and cook for 12 minutes, stirring halfway through cooking. Leave to stand, covered.

2. Place the onion in a round 1.2 litre (2 pint) casserole dish, cover and cook for 3½ minutes. Stir in the tomato purée, the chopped tomatoes, the beef, herbs, 25 g (1 oz) of the butter, the celery salt, stock and pepper to taste. Cover and cook for 4 minutes. Stir.

3. Meanwhile, mash the potatoes with the milk, remaining butter and season with salt and pepper to taste. Using a piping bag filled with a large star nozzle, pipe rosettes of the potato mixture over the meat. Cook, uncovered, for 4 minutes.

4. Garnish with parsley and serve with creamed swedes.

Meat Loaf

Serves 4
15 g (½ oz) butter
1 medium onion, peeled and
  finely chopped
225 g (8 oz) minced pork
225 g (8 oz) minced beef
1 garlic clove, peeled and
  crushed
/ tablespoons fresh white
  breadcrumbs
1 tablespoon tomato purée
¼ teaspoon celery salt
1 teaspoon dried mixed herbs
¼ teaspoon dried thyme
salt
freshly ground black pepper
1 egg, beaten

Preparation time: about 10
minutes, plus chilling
Cooking time: 12–14 minutes
Microwave setting: Maximum
(Full)

1. Place the butter and onion in
a 900 ml (1½ pint) soufflé dish.
Cover and cook for 4 minutes.

2. Mix together the pork, beef,
garlic, breadcrumbs, tomato
purée, celery salt, herbs, thyme,
salt and pepper to taste. Stir in
the onion and beaten egg.

3. Place in the soufflé dish.
Cook, uncovered, for 4 minutes.
Break up and stir with a fork.
Cook uncovered, for a further
4–6 minutes. Allow to cool.

4. Chill until cold. Turn out,
slice and serve with a mixed
green salad and sliced tomatoes.

Shepherd's Pie

Serves 6
1 kg (2 lb) potatoes, peeled and
  roughly diced into 2.5 cm (1
  inch) cubes
3 tablespoons water
1 medium onion, peeled and
  thinly sliced
600 g (1¼ lb) minced beef
2 tablespoons tomato purée
½ teaspoon beef extract
¼ teaspoon chopped fresh parsley
¼ teaspoon dried oregano
¼ teaspoon dried marjoram
¼ teaspoon chopped fresh sage
1 teaspoon Worcestershire
  sauce
salt
freshly ground black pepper
4 tablespoons milk
25 g (1 oz) butter
parsley sprig, to garnish
gravy (page 99), to serve

Preparation time: 15 minutes
Cooking time: 26 minutes, plus
grilling
Microwave setting: Maximum
(Full)

1. Place the potatoes and water
in a large bowl, cover and cook
for 12 minutes. Stir once during
cooking. Set aside, covered.

2. Place the onion in a large
dish. Cover and cook for 4
minutes or until translucent.

3. Stir in the beef, tomato purée,
beef extract, parsley, oregano,
marjoram, sage, Worcestershire
sauce and salt and pepper to
taste. Cover and cook for 6
minutes. Stir to break up the
mince with a fork halfway
through cooking. Drain off the
excess liquid.

4. Mash the potatoes with the
milk, butter and salt and pepper
to taste. Spread over the beef
mixture and cook for 4 minutes.
Brown under a preheated
conventional grill, if preferred.

5. Garnish with parsley and
serve with gravy.

Meat loaf; Shepherd's pie

MENU PLANNER

A traditional meal can be the most difficult to plan, so use your microwave to ease the load. Make a Trifle (page 177) the day before. Prepare the Rollmops (page 35) a few hours in advance; leave them to cool.

Time the meat and vegetables well: cook the meat before serving the starter, then leave it to stand and make the gravy. Cook the potatoes. Cook the vegetables while eating the starter.

When ready to serve the main course, heat the gravy and potatoes if necessary.

Alternatively the vegetables can be three-quarters cooked well in advance, then finish the cooking just before they are served. This works well if you have a divided dish to hold all

the vegetables, so that they can be put together for the final cooking.

Roast beef with Gravy

Serves 6–8
1 × 1.5 kg (3 lb) joint of topside beef
Gravy:
2 tablespoons cold water
2 tablespoons meat sediment (from the roasting bag)
1 tablespoon plain flour
300 ml (½ pint) hot beef stock
¼ teaspoon gravy browning

Preparation time: about 6 minutes
Cooking time: about 23 minutes, plus standing
Microwave setting: Maximum (Full)

1. Place the beef in a roasting bag. Pierce the bag and tie with a non-metal tie.

2. Place the meat on a trivet or

upturned saucer in a shallow dish. Cook for 21 minutes, turning over halfway through cooking.

3. Remove the bag, wrap the meat tightly in foil, shiny side inwards, and stand for 20 minutes.

4. For the gravy, place the water in a jug. Stir in the meat sediment and flour. Add the stock and gravy browning.

5. Cook, uncovered, for 2 minutes, stirring twice.

*Gravy Roast beef;
Boiled potatoes; Green
beans; Trifle; Rollmops*

LAMB

Most cuts of lamb which can be grilled or roasted by traditional methods can be cooked to give tender results in the microwave. The majority of cuts are tender, the only exception being the neck of lamb. The guidelines at the beginning of the meat chapter apply to this section and the following notes relate to specific cuts of lamb and the techniques which should be applied when cooking them in the microwave.

Lamb cooks very well in the microwave but it is important to observe all the basic preparation rules. The size and shape of the meat affects not only the cooking time but also the result.

Boned joints

Boned joints cook more evenly than meat on the bone. The bone in a joint becomes very hot during cooking and overcooking can occur at the point where the meat on the bone is thinnest. If meat on the bone is cooked, then it is necessary to shield areas that

Arranging cutlets

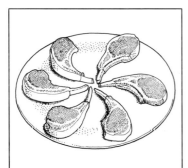

Lamb cutlets should be trimmed of excess fat before cooking and they should be arranged in a shallow dish with the bones pointing in towards the middle. They can be covered with absorbent kitchen paper. If a little liquid is added, or flavouring ingredients are included, then it is best to cover the dish with a lid, upturned plate or microwave-proof cling film.

might overcook with small pieces of securely fixed foil.

Boned lamb not only cooks better but it is easier to carve and serve. Most butchers will oblige by boning out a leg or shoulder of lamb. If you want to bone the meat yourself then the following tips may be of some help in ensuring success.

Use a fairly small, sharp kitchen knife. Work from the widest end at which the bone is exposed. Make small cuts as close as possible to the bone cutting the meat away from it. Work inwards, easing the meat away from the bone with your fingers and cutting carefully round the shape of the bone. A leg joint is easier to bone than the shoulder because the bone is straight. When you reach any joints in the bone you will find that a pair of kitchen scissors are useful to snip any sinews. Leave all the gristly bits attached to the meat until you have removed the bone, then trim them off. When you are almost through to the far end of the bone you may find it easier to work inwards from the thin end. It is important to allow enough time to bone out the joint – you will probably find the task far easier if you do not have to rush.

Once the joint is boned it can be stuffed, flavoured with chopped fresh herbs or garlic, then tied into a neat shape. If you have a trussing needle, then the opening in a shoulder joint can be sewn into shape. Mould a boned shoulder of lamb into a neat shape, tucking in small protruding pieces of meat, and it will cook particularly well.

Boneless cuts cook best

1. A boned shoulder of lamb can be tied or sewn into a neat, rounded shape. Before cooking the thin skin round the joint should be pierced to prevent bursting, here the slits in the skin have been studded with sprigs of rosemary.

2. Neat noisettes of lamb are prepared from boned cutlets. They cook particularly successfully either brushed with a little oil or melted butter, or prepared in a sauce.

Piercing the skin

Joints of lamb are covered by a thin skin as well as some fat. This should be pierced before cooking to prevent it from bursting. Small slits can be cut into the meat and these studded with sprigs of rosemary or cloves of garlic. The meat should not be seasoned before cooking.

Small cuts

Cutlets and chops can be microwaved successfully. They should be trimmed of excess fat which will be pale and soft when cooked. A browning dish can be used to brown the fat first. Alternatively, the edges of chops can be browned by rolling the fat on the surface of a very hot frying pan on the conventional hob before placing them in the dish for microwave cooking.

The chops should be arranged in the dish, as far apart as possible, with thin areas or bone ends towards the middle of the dish.

As with large joints, boned small cuts cook better than those on the bone, so noisettes of lamb are ideal candidates for microwave cooking.

Covering during cooking

Large joints should be covered during cooking – they can be placed on a microwave roasting rack inside a roasting bag, alternatively they can be cooked in a large casserole dish.

Small cuts should be arranged in a shallow dish or on

GUIDE TO COOKING LAMB

Cut of meat		Cooking time in minutes on Medium per 450 g (1 lb) or for quantity given	Cooking time in minutes on Maximum (Full) per 450 g (1 lb) or for quantity given	Method
leg	on bone	11–13	8–10	Choose a good quality joint. Roll the meat into a neat shape if it is off the bone. Cover the pointed end with foil to protect it if on the bone. Allow to stand for 25–30 minutes, wrapped in foil, before carving.
	off bone	12–13	9–10	
breast		14–16	12	Roll and stuff, if liked, before cooking. Allow to stand for 30 minutes, wrapped in foil, before carving.
crown roast		—	5	Cover tips of bone with foil during cooking.
loin		11–13	8–10	Choose a good quality joint. Roll into a neat shape if off the bone. Allow to stand for 25–30 minutes, wrapped in foil, before carving.
chops, loin or chump	2	—	6–7	Preheat the browning dish according to the manufacturer's instructions. Add the chops and cook for the recommended time, turning over halfway through the cooking time.
	4	—	7–9	
	6	—	15–17	
liver		—	5–6	
kidney		—	7–8	

a roasting rack. They can be covered with absorbent kitchen paper, with a lid or, microwave-proof cling film.

Turning and rearranging

Joints should be turned at least twice during cooking and it is a good idea to allow a period of standing time when they are turned, particularly if the joint is fairly large and filled with a stuffing.

Small pieces of meat should be turned over halfway through cooking and rearranged in the dish.

Cutting slices and strips

Since lamb is a tender meat it can be braised or cooked with vegetables, stir-fry style. Rather than cutting the meat into chunks, it is better to cut thin slices across the grain or fine strips for tender results when cooked. See pages 80 and 81 for general advice on cutting and preparing meat.

Marinating

Before cooking, lamb benefits from marinating. Whole joints can be rubbed with spices or herbs and marinated in wine, oil or citrus juices to give tender, full-flavoured results. The joint should be turned frequently in the marinade and the liquid can be cooked in a sauce to serve with the meat.

Small cuts – chops, noisettes or lamb steaks off the leg – and slices or strips of meat can be thoroughly coated in marinade and left in the refrigerator, covered, for several hours or overnight. For certain spicy lamb recipes the meat can be marinated for up to 2 days but it must be purchased fresh.

Ingredients that are particularly complementary to the flavour of lamb include garlic, rosemary, grated fresh root ginger, orange (rind and juice), apricots (puréed), olive oil, ground coriander or crushed coriander seeds, ground cumin and red wine.

GUIDE TO DEFROSTING LAMB

Type of meat	Defrosting time in minutes on Defrost per 450 g (1 lb)	Method
joints	10	Turn over at least once during the defrosting time.
chops	5	
kidney	4	Turn over at least once during the defrosting time.
liver	4	Turn over at least once during the defrosting time.

Roast Leg of Lamb

Serves 6–8
1 × 1.5 kg (3 lb) leg of lamb,
lightly beaten

Preparation time: about 5
minutes
Cooking time: about 21
minutes, plus standing and
grilling
Microwave setting: Maximum
(Full)

1. Wrap a small piece of foil
around the thin end of the lamb.
Place the lamb in a roasting bag.
Pierce the bag and tie with a
non-metallic tie.

2. Place the lamb on a trivet or
upturned saucer in a shallow
dish. Cook for 21 minutes,
turning over halfway through
cooking.

3. Remove the lamb from the
bag and wrap tightly in foil,
shiny side inwards. Leave to
stand for 20 minutes before
carving. Brown under a
preheated conventional grill, if
preferred.

4. Serve with mint sauce,
potatoes and vegetables.

Accompaniments for lamb

Mint sauce The traditional
accompaniment to roast
lamb. Chop a handful of
mint with a sprinkling of
sugar. Place in a basin and
pour in just enough boiling
water to cover the mint.
Add 2 teaspoons sugar and
stir until it has dissolved.
Stir in enough vinegar to
make a small amount of
thin sauce. Cider vinegar is
excellent as it is not as
harsh as others.

Mint cream Stir a little
chopped mint into soured
cream, then season lightly
with garlic salt. Good with
noisettes of lamb and
courgettes.

Rich redcurrant cream
Melt 2 tablespoons
redcurrant jelly in a small
basin on Maximum (Full) –
it will take about 30
seconds. Stir in 1

tablespoon port, 1
teaspoon grated orange
rind and a little garlic salt
and pepper. Lightly stir in
150 ml ($\frac{1}{4}$ pint) thick Greek-
style yogurt or whipped
double cream. Good with
cutlets.

Quick tomato relish Peel,
deseed and finely chop 4
tomatoes and mix them
with a finely chopped,
deseeded fresh green chilli.
Add 4 finely chopped
spring onions, plenty of
seasoning and 1 teaspoon
sugar. Stir in 1 finely
chopped clove of garlic and
a little chopped fresh mint
when in season. Dress with
2 tablespoons sunflower oil
and sharpen with 2
teaspoons cider vinegar.
Stir well, crushing the
tomatoes slightly. Best left
to stand for 1–2 hours
before serving.

Roast leg of lamb

French-style Lamb

Serves 4
550 g (1$\frac{1}{4}$ lb) lamb fillet, cubed
40 g (1$\frac{1}{2}$ oz) butter
1 tablespoon plain flour
Marinade:
250 ml (8 fl oz) red wine
2 carrots, peeled and sliced
2 onions, peeled and roughly
*   cut into chunks*
1 teaspoon dried thyme
1 bay leaf
small piece of orange rind
salt
freshly ground black pepper
40 g (1$\frac{1}{2}$ oz) butter
1 tablespoon plain flour

Preparation time: about 15
minutes, plus marinating
Cooking time: 26$\frac{1}{2}$ minutes
Microwave settings: Maximum
(Full) and Defrost

1. Place the lamb and marinade
ingredients in a bowl. Cover and
leave to marinate for 3 hours.

2. Drain the wine from the meat
mixture and set aside.

3. Place the butter in a casserole
and cook on Maximum (Full)
for $\frac{1}{2}$ minute to melt. Blend in
the flour and cook on Maximum
(Full) for 1 minute. Gradually
add the reserved wine, blending
well. Stir in the meat mixture.
Cover tightly and cook on
Maximum (Full) power for 15
minutes, stirring twice.

4. Reduce the power setting to
defrost and cook for a further
10 minutes. Remove and discard
the bay leaf and orange rind.

Lemon and Herb Marinated Lamb Chops

Serves 4
4 large 'butterfly' or double-loin
*   lamb chops*
Marinade:
4 tablespoons olive oil
grated rind of 1 lemon
3 tablespoons lemon juice
1 tablespoon chopped fresh
*   parsley*
1 tablespoon dried herbes de
*   Provence*
1 garlic clove, crushed
4 bay leaves
salt
freshly ground black pepper
Vegetables:
1 head celery, trimmed and
*   sliced*
1 onion, peeled and chopped
25 g (1 oz) butter
5 teaspoons water
$\frac{1}{2}$ teaspoon salt
350 g (12 oz) frozen peas
To garnish:
celery leaves

Preparation time: about 10
minutes, plus marinating
Cooking time: 24–25$\frac{1}{2}$ minutes
Microwave settings: Maximum
(Full) and Medium

1. Mix the marinade ingredients
together and pour over the
chops; cover and leave to
marinate for 4–5 hours.

2. Place the celery, onion,
butter, water and salt in a large
dish. Cover and cook on full/
maximum power for 6 minutes.
Add the peas, cover and cook,
on maximum (full) for 7–8
minutes, stirring once. Cover
and leave to stand while
cooking the chops.

3. Preheat a browning dish on
Maximum (Full) for 8 minutes
(or according to the
manufacturer's instructions).
Drain the chops and add to the
browning dish, turning quickly
on all sides to brown evenly.
Cook on Maximum (Full) for 1$\frac{1}{2}$
minutes. Turn over and cook on
Medium for 1$\frac{1}{2}$–2 minutes.

4. To serve, place the cooked
vegetables on a preheated
serving dish and top with the
cooked lamb chops. Garnish
with celery leaves.

Noisettes of Lamb

Serves 4

8 lamb noisettes
1 small carrot, peeled and
   thinly sliced
1 medium onion, peeled and
   chopped
1 celery stick, chopped
25 g (1 oz) button mushrooms,
   sliced
1 teaspoon dried mixed herbs
1 teaspoon dried rosemary
25 g (1 oz) butter, diced
25 g (1 oz) plain flour
about 300 ml ($\frac{1}{2}$ pint) hot
   chicken stock
2 tablespoons tomato purée
150 ml ($\frac{1}{4}$ pint) red wine
salt
freshly ground black pepper
parsley sprigs, to garnish

Preparation time: about 15
minutes
Cooking time: about 21–22
minutes
Microwave setting: Maximum
(Full)

1. Place the noisettes in a
shallow 1.5 litre (2$\frac{1}{2}$ pint)
casserole dish. Cover with a
piece of paper towel and cook
for 7–8 minutes, turning over
and rearranging halfway
through cooking. Set aside,
covered.

2. Place the carrot, onion,
celery, mushrooms and herbs in
a medium bowl. Cover and
cook for 7 minutes, stirring
halfway through cooking.

3. Stir in the butter until melted,
then stir in the flour. Make up
the meat juices to 300 ml
($\frac{1}{2}$ pint) with the stock, then stir
in with the tomato purée, wine,
and salt and pepper to taste.
Cook, uncovered, for 4 minutes,
stirring every minute.

4. Pour over the meat and cook
for 3 minutes.

5. Garnish with the parsley and
serve with boiled potatoes and
broccoli.

Lambs' Kidney Casserole

Serves 4

1 medium onion, peeled and
   finely sliced
1 carrot, peeled and finely
   sliced
25 g (1 oz) butter
8 lambs' kidneys, halved, cores
   removed
50 g (2 oz) mushrooms, sliced
50 g (2 oz) frozen peas
2 tablespoons chopped fresh
   parsley
1 garlic clove, peeled and
   crushed
25 g (1 oz) cornflour
150 ml ($\frac{1}{4}$ pint) dry sherry
300 ml ($\frac{1}{2}$ pint) hot beef stock
1 tablespoon tomato purée
4 small frankfurter sausages,
   sliced
salt
freshly ground black pepper

Preparation time: about 25
minutes
Cooking time: about 14$\frac{1}{2}$
minutes, plus standing
Microwave setting: Maximum
(Full)

1. Place the onion, carrot and
butter in a large bowl. Cover
and cook for 4 minutes.

2. Stir in the kidneys,
mushrooms, peas, half the
parsley and the garlic. Cover and
cook for 5$\frac{1}{2}$ minutes, stirring
halfway through cooking.

3. Stir in the cornflour, sherry,
hot stock, tomato purée,
sausages, salt and pepper. Cover
and cook for 5 minutes, stirring
halfway through cooking.

4. Leave to stand, covered, for 3
minutes before serving,
sprinkled with the remaining
parsley.

*Noisettes of lamb; Lambs' kidney
casserole*

Liver and Bacon Casserole

Serves 4
4 streaky bacon rashers, rinds
   removed, chopped
25 g (1 oz) butter
1 carrot, peeled and thinly
   sliced
$\frac{1}{2}$ celery stick, finely chopped
1 medium onion, peeled and
   finely chopped
25 g (1 oz) cornflour
300 ml ($\frac{1}{2}$ pint) hot beef stock
225 g (8 oz) tomatoes, skinned
   and chopped
3 tablespoons tomato purée
1 teaspoon Worcestershire
   sauce
50 g (2 oz) mushrooms,
   chopped
1 teaspoon dried mixed herbs
2 bay leaves
salt
freshly ground black pepper
450 g (1 lb) lambs' liver, thinly
   sliced
bay leaves to garnish

Preparation time: about 20
minutes
Cooking time: about $16\frac{1}{2}$
minutes, plus standing
Microwave setting: Maximum
(Full)

1. Place the bacon, butter,
carrot, celery and onion in a
large bowl. Cover and cook for
$6\frac{1}{2}$ minutes, stirring halfway
through cooking.

2. Stir in the cornflour, then
blend in the hot stock.

3. Add the tomatoes, tomato
purée, Worcestershire sauce,
mushrooms, herbs, bay leaves,
salt, pepper and liver. Cover.
Cook for 10 minutes, stirring
halfway through cooking time.

4. Leave to stand, covered, for 5
minutes. Garnish with bay
leaves.

Lamb Chop Casserole

Serves 4
8 lamb loin chops, total weight
   1 kg (2 lb)
225 g (8 oz) potatoes, peeled
   and diced
1 large onion, peeled and
   chopped
2 large carrots, peeled and
   thinly sliced
1 small turnip, peeled and
   diced
2 courgettes, sliced
3 tablespoons cold water
25 g (1 oz) butter, cut into
   pieces
25 g (1 oz) plain flour
about 450 ml ($\frac{3}{4}$ pint) hot
   chicken stock
$\frac{1}{2}$ teaspoon dried thyme
$\frac{1}{4}$ teaspoon gravy browning
salt
freshly ground black pepper

Preparation time: about 18
minutes
Cooking time: about 28–31
minutes
Microwave setting: Maximum
(Full)

1. Place the chops over the
bottom and sides of a large
bowl. Cover and cook for $6\frac{1}{2}$–$9\frac{1}{2}$
minutes, rearranging halfway
through cooking. Set aside,
covered.

2. Place the potatoes, onion,
carrots, turnip, courgettes and
water in another large bowl.
Cover and cook for 13 minutes
or until tender, stirring halfway
through.

3. Stir in the butter until melted.
Stir in the flour. Make up the
meat juices to 450 ml ($\frac{3}{4}$ pint)
with the stock, then stir in with
the thyme, gravy browning, and
salt and pepper. Cover and
cook for 4 minutes, stirring
halfway through cooking.

4. Stir in the chops. Cook,
uncovered, for 4 minutes.

*Liver and bacon casserole; Lamb chop
casserole*

Lamb with Mozzarella Cheese

Serves 4
8 lamb cutlets
100 g (4 oz) Mozzarella cheese,
*   thinly sliced*
Marinade:
2 tablespoons white wine
*   vinegar*
150 ml (¼ pint) dry sherry
2 teaspoons dark brown sugar
1 tablespoon orange juice
¼ teaspoon Worcestershire sauce
salt
freshly ground black pepper
Garnish:
1 tablespoon chopped parsley
1 tomato

Preparation time: about 5
minutes, plus marinating
overnight
Cooking time: about 6–7
minutes
Microwave setting: Maximum
(Full)

1. Mix together the vinegar,
sherry, sugar, orange juice,
Worcestershire sauce, and salt
and pepper.

2. Arrange the cutlets in a
shallow dish. Pour over the
marinade and add sufficient
cold water to cover the cutlets.
Leave to marinate for about 24
hours.

3. Drain the marinade off the
cutlets. Cover the cutlets with a
piece of paper towel. Cook for
4–5 minutes, rearranging
halfway through cooking.

4. Pour off the juice and overlap
the cutlets to look attractive.
Cover the cutlets with the
cheese. Cook, uncovered, for 2
minutes.

5. Sprinkle with chopped
parsley and garnish with the
tomato.

Sweet and Sour Lamb

Serves 4
4 lamb loin chops, total weight
*   600 g (1¼ lb)*
1 medium onion, peeled and
*   chopped*
½ green pepper, cored, seeded
*   and finely chopped*
½ red pepper, cored, seeded and
*   finely chopped*
½ teaspoon dried rosemary
½ teaspoon dried marjoram
½ teaspoon dried parsley
1 garlic clove, peeled and
*   crushed*
25 g (1 oz) butter, cut into
*   pieces*
25 g (1 oz) plain flour
300 ml (½ pint) hot chicken
*   stock*
2 tablespoons white wine
*   vinegar*
1 tablespoon light soy
*   sauce*
50 g (2 oz) brown sugar
salt
freshly ground black pepper

Preparation time: about 18
minutes
Cooking time: about 18
minutes
Microwave setting: Maximum
(Full)

1. Place the chops in a shallow
1.5 litre (2½ pint) casserole dish,
cover with a piece of paper
towel and cook for 7 minutes,
turning over and rearranging
halfway through cooking. Set
aside, covered.

2. Place the onion, peppers,
rosemary, marjoram, parsley
and garlic in a medium bowl.
Cover and cook for 5 minutes,
stirring halfway through.

3. Stir in the butter until melted.
Stir in the flour. Make up the
meat juices to 300 ml (½ pint)
with the stock, then blend into
the vegetables with the vinegar,
soy sauce, sugar, and salt and
pepper to taste. Cook,
uncovered, for 3 minutes,
stirring every minute.

4. Pour the sauce over the
chops and cook, uncovered, for
3 minutes.

5. Serve with buttered noodles.

Lamb with Cherries

Serves 4
4 lamb fillets, total weight 750 g
*   (1½ lb), lightly beaten*
1 medium onion, peeled and
*   chopped*
25 g (1 oz) butter, cut into
*   pieces*
450 g (1 lb) frozen black pitted
*   cherries, thawed and*
*   drained (no sugar added)*
1 teaspoon dried marjoram
salt
about 300 ml (½ pint) hot
*   chicken stock*
25 g (1 oz) cornflour

Preparation time: about 10
minutes
Cooking time: about 20½
minutes
Microwave setting: Maximum
(Full)

1. Place the fillets over the
bottom and sides of a large
bowl. Cover and cook for 6½
minutes, rearranging halfway
through cooking. Set aside,
covered.

2. Place the onion in a medium
bowl, cover and cook for 3
minutes. Stir in the butter until
melted. Stir in the cherries,
marjoram and a little salt, cover
and cook for 3 minutes.

3. Make up the meat juices to
300 ml (½ pint) with the stock,
then stir into the onion and
cherries with the cornflour.
Cook, uncovered, for 5 minutes,
stirring occasionally.

4. Arrange the fillets in a shallow
serving dish and pour over the
sauce. Cook, uncovered, for 3
minutes. Serve with piped
creamed potatoes.

Clockwise: Lamb with Mozzarella
cheese; Sweet and sour lamb; Lamb with
cherries; Lamb chops with spicy sauce

Lamb Chops with Spicy Sauce

Serves 4

*1 small onion, peeled and finely
    sliced*
50 g (2 oz) butter
4 chump lamb chops
1 tablespoon molasses sugar
*1 teaspoon Worcestershire
    sauce*
1 teaspoon soy sauce
*1 garlic clove, peeled and
    crushed*
4 tablespoons tomato purée
salt
freshly ground black pepper

Preparation time: about 10
minutes
Cooking time: about 11½
minutes
Microwave setting: Maximum
(Full)

1. Place the sliced onion and
butter in a small ovenproof
bowl. Cover and cook for 3½
minutes or until translucent.

2. Place the chops in a shallow
casserole. Cover with a piece of
paper towel and cook for 5
minutes. Check if cooked to
taste. Cook for 1 more minute if
necessary.

3. Pour off the fat collected in
the casserole.

4. While the chops are cooking,
mix the onion and butter with
the sugar, Worcestershire sauce,
soy sauce, garlic, tomato purée,
salt and pepper.

5. Spoon the sauce over the
chops in the casserole, cover
and cook for a further 3
minutes.

6. Serve with boiled rice and
sweetcorn.

Crown Roast of Lamb

Serves 4

*1 medium onion, peeled and
  finely chopped*
*50 g (2 oz) butter, cut into
  pieces*
*1 garlic clove, peeled and
  crushed*
*meat trimmings (from
  preparing crown roast),
  finely chopped*
*100 g (4 oz) fresh white
  breadcrumbs*
¼ teaspoon dried marjoram
¼ teaspoon dried basil
¼ teaspoon dried parsley
¼ teaspoon celery salt
freshly ground black pepper
1 egg, lightly beaten
*1 crown roast of lamb,
  prepared weight 1.1 kg
  (2¼ lb), comprising 12 chops*
12 glacé cherries, to garnish

Preparation time: about 10
minutes
Cooking time: about 29
minutes, plus standing
Microwave setting: Maximum
(Full)

1. Place the onion, butter, garlic
and meat trimmings in a
medium bowl. Cover and cook
for 4 minutes.

2. Stir in the breadcrumbs,
marjoram, basil, parsley, celery
salt, and pepper to taste. Bind
with the egg.

3. Stuff the centre of the roast
and stand on a trivet or
upturned saucer. Cook,
uncovered, for 25 minutes,
turning round halfway through
cooking.

4. Wrap tightly in foil and stand
for 20–25 minutes.

5. Place a cherry on top of each
bone to garnish. Serve with
mashed potatoes and French
beans.

Cook's Tip

To prepare the crown roast
bend each rack into a semi-
circle, fat inwards, cutting
between, but not dividing
chops, if necessary. Sew ends
together to form a circle.

Lamb in Cream and Cider

Serves 4

*8 lamb loin chops, total weight
  1 kg (2 lb)*
*1 medium onion, peeled and
  chopped*
*½ green pepper, cored, seeded
  and chopped*
225 g (8 oz) mushrooms, sliced
1 teaspoon dried rosemary
*25 g (1 oz) butter, cut into
  pieces*
*about 65 ml (2½ fl oz) hot
  chicken stock*
25 g (1 oz) plain flour
225 ml (7½ fl oz) dry cider
salt
freshly ground black pepper
4 tablespoons double cream
chopped parsley, to garnish

Preparation time: about 20
minutes
Cooking time: about 17½
minutes
Microwave setting: Maximum
(Full)

1. Place the chops around the
bottom and sides of a large
bowl, cover and cook for 6½
minutes, rearranging them
halfway through. Set them aside,
covered.

2. Place the onion and green
pepper in a large bowl, cover
and cook for 4 minutes. Stir in
the mushrooms, rosemary and
butter. Cover and cook for 3
minutes.

3. Make up the meat juices to
65 ml (2½ fl oz) with the stock,
then stir in with the flour, cider,
and salt and pepper to taste.
Add the chops. Cover and cook
for 4 minutes, stirring halfway
through.

4. Skim if necessary, then stir in
the cream and reheat for 1
minute if necessary. Sprinkle
with chopped fresh parsley, to
garnish.

*Crown roast of lamb; Lamb in cream
and cider*

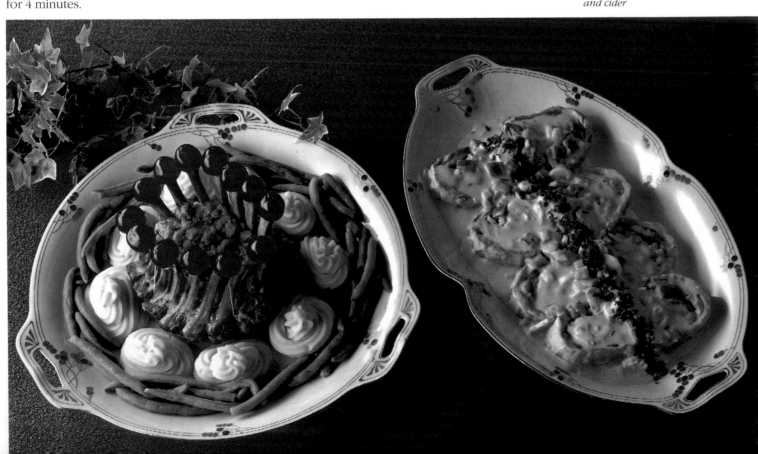

Lamb Curry

Serves 4

1 onion, peeled and chopped
1 garlic clove, peeled and
  crushed
1 tablespoon ground coriander
1 teaspoon turmeric
½ teaspoon ground cumin
¼ teaspoon chilli powder
¼ teaspoon ground ginger
¼ teaspoon grated nutmeg
1 tablespoon plain flour
1 tablespoon tomato purée
1 teaspoon lemon juice
1 tablespoon desiccated coconut
¼ teaspoon meat extract
25 g (1 oz) sultanas
450 ml (¾ pint) chicken stock
2 teaspoons curry paste
750 g (1½ lb) boneless cooked
  lamb, finely chopped
salt

Preparation time: about 15 minutes
Cooking time: 14 minutes
Microwave setting: Maximum (Full)

1. Place the onion, garlic, coriander, turmeric, cumin, chilli powder, ginger and nutmeg in a large bowl. Cover and cook for 4 minutes.

2. Stir in the flour, tomato purée, lemon juice, coconut, meat extract, sultanas, stock, curry paste and lamb. Season. Cover and cook for 10 minutes, stirring twice.

3. Serve with rice, sliced tomatoes and mango chutney.

Moussaka

Serves 4

1 large aubergine, cut into
  5 mm (¼ inch) slices
salt
25 g (1 oz) butter
2 medium onions, peeled and
  finely sliced
2 garlic cloves, peeled and
  crushed
450 g (1 lb) lean lamb,
  minced
3 tablespoons tomato purée
1 teaspoon dried mixed herbs
25 g (1 oz) plain flour
150 ml (¼ pint) hot beef
  stock
freshly ground black pepper
Sauce:
25 g (1 oz) butter
25 g (1 oz) plain flour
300 ml (½ pint) milk
50 g (2 oz) Cheddar cheese,
  grated
1 teaspoon dry mustard
1 egg, beaten

Preparation time: about 20 minutes, plus standing
Cooking time: about 29 minutes
Microwave setting: Maximum (Full)

1. Place the aubergine slices in a colander and sprinkle with salt. Leave for 30 minutes, rinse and drain.

2. Place the aubergine slices in a medium bowl, cover and cook for 3 minutes. Set aside.

3. Place the butter, onions and garlic in a large bowl. Cover and cook for 3 minutes. Stir in the lamb, cover and cook for 4 minutes.

4. Stir in the remaining ingredients. Cover. Cook for 12 minutes. Set aside.

5. To make the sauce, place the butter in a 600 ml (1 pint) jug. Cook for 45 seconds. Blend in the flour and milk. Cook for 2½ minutes, stirring twice. Stir in the cheese, mustard and egg.

6. Make alternate layers of lamb and aubergine in a large shallow casserole. Pour over the sauce and cook for 5 minutes.

Lamb curry; Moussaka

Stuffed Leg of Lamb

Serves 4–6
*1 small onion, peeled and finely
  chopped*
25 g (1 oz) butter
*75 g (3 oz) fresh white
  breadcrumbs*
*1 tablespoon dried mint or 2
  tablespoons chopped fresh
  mint*
salt
freshly ground black pepper
1 egg, beaten
1 kg (2 lb) boned leg of lamb

Preparation time: about 15
minutes
Cooking time: about 18
minutes, plus standing
Microwave setting: Maximum
(Full)

1. Place the onion and butter in
a large bowl. Cover and cook
for 2 minutes.

2. Stir in the breadcrumbs, mint,
salt and pepper. Add the egg
and mix well.

3. Lay the boned leg of lamb out
flat. Spread the stuffing over the
meat, roll up and secure.

4. Wrap in cling film and place
on an upturned saucer in a large
dish. Cook for 16 minutes.

5. Remove cling film and wrap
the meat in foil, then leave for
15 minutes before carving.

Stuffed Breast of Lamb

Serves 3–4
*1 medium onion, peeled and
  chopped*
25 g (1 oz) butter
*100 g (4 oz) fresh white
  breadcrumbs*
1 teaspoon dried mixed herbs
1 teaspoon dried rosemary
grated rind of 1 orange
1 tablespoon orange juice
salt
freshly ground pepper
*1 × 450 g (1 lb) boned breast of
  lamb*

Preparation time: about 20
minutes
Cooking time: about 11
minutes, plus standing and
grilling
Microwave setting: Maximum
(Full)

1. Place the onion and butter in
a medium bowl, cover and cook
for 3 minutes. Stir in the
breadcrumbs, herbs, orange
rind and juice, and salt and
pepper to taste.

2. Spread the stuffing over the
breast, roll up and secure with
string. Stand in a shallow dish
and cook, uncovered, for 8
minutes, turning over halfway
through cooking.

3. Wrap in foil and stand for 10
minutes before serving, with
new potatoes and peas. For a
crispy finish, brown under a
preheated conventional grill.

*Stuffed leg of lamb;
Stuffed breast of lamb*

MENU PLANNER

The most successful dinner parties are those that are well planned. Impressive meals do not mean spending time in a hot kitchen while your guests sit waiting expectantly.

The menu suggestion illustrated here is ideal for a formal dinner party. Make a rich, creamy Liver Pâté (page 40) the day before and chill it overnight.

Prepare the lamb in advance – order the guard from your butcher or, if you have to prepare it yourself, then buy two racks of lamb with six cutlets each. Trim the bone

Vichy carrots;
Guard of honour; Sweetcorn;
Cold strawberry soufflé; Liver pâté

ends, then place the racks of lamb together with the fat on the outside and interlock the bones. Sew or tie the guard together. Do this the day before or well ahead.

Make a Cold Strawberry Soufflé (page 172) the evening before or early on the day and set it to chill. Prepare the carrots for Vichy Carrots in advance.

Decorate the soufflé a couple of hours before the meal. Cook the lamb just before you serve the starter, then leave it to stand.

While the starter is served cook the Vichy Carrots. Next cook the sweetcorn (see page 141) – this can be done as you take the lamb to the table and serve the carrots.

Guard of Honour

Serves 4
25 g (1 oz) butter
1 small onion, peeled and chopped
¼ teaspoon chopped fresh marjoram
¼ teaspoon chopped fresh rosemary
¼ teaspoon chopped fresh sage
1 tablespoon chopped fresh parsley
75 g (3 oz) fresh white breadcrumbs
salt
freshly ground black pepper
1 egg, beaten
1 guard of honour, prepared weight 750 g (1½ lb), each rack comprising 6 chops

Preparation time: about 20 minutes
Cooking time: about 25 minutes, plus standing
Microwave setting: Maximum (Full)

1. Place the butter, onion and herbs in a small bowl. Cover and cook for 3 minutes. Stir in the breadcrumbs, and salt and pepper to taste. Bind with the egg.

2. Stuff the guard and place in a shallow dish. Cook for 22 minutes, turning round halfway through.

3. Wrap tightly in foil and stand for 15–20 minutes.

PORK, BACON AND HAM

Pork, ham and bacon are all tender meats and they cook well in the microwave. Careful preparation is required for some cuts to ensure the best results and it is essential that these meats are thoroughly cooked before they are served, so standing times should be rigidly observed and the middle of a large joint should be pierced to make sure that the centre is cooked – this can be done from the underside.

Tender pork cooks very successfully in the microwave but those cuts with large quantities of fat on them, or portions which are marbled with fat, should be trimmed and prepared with care. Since unbrowned, soft, cooked fat is not palatable the outside of chops or joints benefit from being browned under a grill before serving.

Alternatively, in the case of chops, the fat can be rolled on the surface of a very hot frying pan to thoroughly brown it before the chops are arranged in a dish for microwave cooking.

Boneless joints

As for lamb, those joints which are boned and neatly tied into shapes cook better than meat on the bone. A special microwave-proof thermometer is useful for making sure that the middle of the joint is cooked. Alternatively, remember that you can combine microwave cooking with a final short period of traditional roasting.

Stuffing

If the joint is to be stuffed, then it is important to weigh it when it is ready for cooking. The cooking time should be calculated with the weight of stuffing included.

Seasoning

As for other meats, pork meat should not be seasoned before cooking; however the crackling should be rubbed with salt as this produces a crisp result.

Crackling

Pork crackling is very good when cooked in the microwave and combined with conventional methods for browning – the result is particularly crunchy. The rind should be well scored before cooking and rubbed with salt, avoiding seasoning the meat. At the end of the cooking time the crackling should be well basted with the juices and browned under a conventional grill.

Small cuts

Follow the instructions on pages 80 and 81 for the most tender results.

Pork chops should be trimmed of excess fat before cooking and they can be cooked with vegetables and liquid to make a delicious casserole. If the chops are cooked on their own, they should be covered with absorbent kitchen paper to prevent spattering during cooking and they should be turned and rearranged in the dish halfway through the cooking time.

Trimming fatty cuts

Hand and knuckle of pork are both inexpensive cuts of meat which yield tender and deliciously flavoured meat once they are well trimmed. The outer rind and fat should be removed and the meat cut off the bone. All sinews and membranes should be removed, then the meat can be cut into thin strips or small slices for cooking with vegetables in a casserole.

Spare rib pork chops can be cooked in the microwave as well as loin chops. Care should be taken to remove excess fat from the sparerib cut as the meat itself is usually marbled with fat.

When prepared in the microwave it benefits from the addition of a spicy coating or sauce.

Spare ribs can be cooked with liquid before they are browned under the grill, or they can be trimmed well before cooking and coated in a rich barbecue sauce to be served unbrowned.

Arranging pork chops

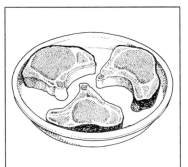

Before cooking the chops are trimmed of excess fat and the edge of fat which remains is quickly browned on the surface of a hot conventional frying pan. The thickest parts of the chops are placed towards the outside of the dish. Halfway through cooking the chops are turned and rearranged.

Casseroled chops

Pork chops make excellent casseroles. First the chopped onion is cooked with a little oil, then the chops are arranged in the dish and part-cooked. They are turned and, above, the remaining ingredients are added and boiling stock or heated cider or wine is poured in before the dish is covered for the last part of the cooking time.

GUIDE TO COOKING PORK, GAMMON AND BACON

Type of meat		Cooking time in minutes on Medium per 450 g (1 lb) or for quantity given	Cooking time in minutes on Maximum (Full) per 450 g (1 lb) or for quantity given	Method
Pork				
leg		13–15	10	Choose a good quality joint. Cover the pointed end with foil to protect from overcooking. Score fat with a sharp knife and sprinkle liberally with salt to get a crisp crackling. Allow to stand for 20 minutes, wrapped in foil, before carving. Brown under a hot grill if liked.
loin		14–16	10–13	Roll into a neat shape before cooking. Allow to stand for 20 minutes, wrapped in foil, before carving.
fillet		—	7	Preheat the browning dish according to the manufacturer's instructions. Add the fillet and cook for the recommended time, turning over halfway through the cooking time.
chops, loin or chump	2 3 4 6	14–18 19–24 26–32 33–37	—	Preheat the browning dish according to the manufacturer's instructions. Add the chops and cook for the recommended time, turning over halfway through the cooking time.
Bacon or Gammon				
joint		11–12	—	
gammon steaks (each)		—	14	Place in a large covered dish with 4–6 tablespoons water. Turn at least twice during cooking. Allow to stand for 10–20 minutes, wrapped in foil, before carving. Cook in a browning dish if liked (observing preheating times) or cover with cling film. Turn halfway through the cooking time.
Bacon	4 rashers 450 g (1 lb)	—	$3\frac{1}{2}$–4 12–14	Place on a plate or roasting rack and cover with absorbent kitchen paper. Turn rashers over halfway through cooking.
Sausages	2 4	—	$1\frac{1}{2}$–2 3–$3\frac{1}{2}$	Prick thoroughly and arrange on a rack or plate. Cover with absorbent kitchen paper and turn the sausages halfway through the cooking time.

GUIDE TO DEFROSTING PORK

Cut	Defrosting time per 450 g (1 lb) in minutes on Defrost	Method
joints	$8\frac{1}{2}$	Turn over at least once during the defrosting time.
chops	5	Turn over at least once during the defrosting time.

Gammon

Gammon steaks or joints of gammon both cook well in the microwave. Thick chunks of gammon can be cut into small cubes, or strips, to make good casseroles.

Large steaks are best cooked no more than two at a time for reasons of space and they should be turned over halfway through cooking.

Large joints of gammon require frequent turning and they are best cooked in a large, covered casserole with water or cider added. The joint should be soaked in water for several hours before cooking to ensure that it is not too salty.

Bacon

Lay bacon rashers on a microwave roasting rack or on a large plate and cover them with a piece of absorbent kitchen paper before cooking.

The rashers can be rolled and secured with wooden cocktail sticks or threaded onto wooden skewers before cooking.

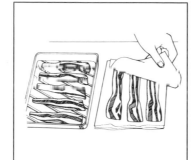

Bacon rashers are laid on a microwave roasting rack or on a double thickness of absorbent kitchen paper. They are covered with a piece of absorbent kitchen paper to prevent spattering during cooking.

Chopped bacon can be cooked until quite dry and used as a crunchy garnish (see page 14).

Cooking sausages

Sausages can be cooked in the microwave but the result is unbrowned and not crisp. A browning dish can be used to brown the skins. Skinless sausages can be cooked and cut into chunks for adding to casseroles (for example with kidneys or to make a mock cassoulet) or for slicing and adding to heated baked beans for a quick snack on toast. The cold sliced sausages also make good sandwiches with crisp lettuce and pickle.

The microwave is good for cooking frankfurters and similar smoked and unsmoked continental sausages (prick the skins first).

Not only is the microwave as speedy and convenient way of cooking smoked continental sausages, it is also ideal for those like the French *andouillettes*, which need to be boiled before they are cooled and grilled. It is also excellent for preparing combination dishes in which the sausages are poached in stock or wine (again in the French manner) and not intended to be brown or crisp.

Roast Pork

Serves 6–8
1 tablespoon oil
1 × 1.5 kg (3 lb) fillet half leg of pork, scored
½ teaspoon salt

Preparation time: about 4 minutes
Cooking time: about 30 minutes, plus standing and grilling
Microwave setting: Maximum (Full)

1. Rub the oil into the fat on the meat, then rub in the salt. Place the meat in a shallow dish with the fat uppermost. Cover with a paper towel. Cook for 30 minutes. Remove the towel after 15 minutes.

2. Wrap the meat in foil, shiny side inwards, and leave for 15–20 minutes before carving. If desired brown under a preheated conventional grill.

3. Serve with potatoes, peas, carrots, stuffing, apple sauce (page 166) and gravy.

Accompaniments for pork

Apple sauce A traditional English accompaniment for roast pork; recipe on page 166.
Cumberland sauce Mix the grated rind and juice of 1 orange, 4 tablespoons redcurrant jelly and 150 ml (¼ pint) dry red wine in a basin. Cook on Maximum (Full) for about 3 minutes, until the jelly has dissolved. Blend 2 teaspoons cornflour or arrowroot with a little cold water and add to the sauce, then cook for a further 1–2 minutes, until boiling and thickened. Good with gammon steaks or chops.
Mustard cream Mix 2 tablespoons wholegrain mustard, 1 teaspoon grated orange rind and ½ teaspoon chopped sage into 150 ml (¼ pint) soured cream or fromage frais. Good with gammon, chops or stirred into strips of pork cooked with mushrooms.

Cook's Tip

If an exact 1.5 kg (3 lb) fillet is not available, check the chart on page 113 for cooking times per 450 g (1 lb) and adjust the time accordingly.

Pork Chops with Apple

Serves 4

2 teaspoons soy sauce
2 teaspoons Worcestershire
  sauce
50 g (2 oz) butter
25 g (1 oz) soft dark brown
  sugar
salt
freshly ground black pepper
4 pork chops
1 large eating apple, peeled,
  cored and cut into 4 slices

Preparation time: about 10
minutes
Cooking time: about 9 minutes,
plus standing
Microwave setting: Maximum
(Full)

1. Place the soy sauce,
Worcestershire sauce, butter,
sugar, salt and pepper in a
300 ml (½ pint) jug. Cook for 1
minute. Stir the sauce.

2. Brush both sides of the chops
and apple slices with the sauce.

3. Arrange the pork chops in a
shallow casserole. Cover and
cook for 4 minutes. Turn the
chops over and turn the
casserole round.

4. Brush the chops with any
remaining sauce and place a
slice of apple on each one.
Cover and cook for 4 minutes.

5. Leave to stand, covered, for 3
minutes.

Pork Casserole

Serves 4

450 g (1 lb) pork fillet, cut into
  2.5 cm (1 inch) cubes
1 onion, peeled and chopped
2 carrots, peeled and thinly
  sliced
1 red pepper, cored, seeded and
  chopped
1 garlic clove, peeled and
  crushed
¼ teaspoon ground mace
¼ teaspoon dried thyme
¼ teaspoon dried sage
¼ teaspoon dried parsley
2 tablespoons tomato purée
25 g (1 oz) butter, cut up
25 g (1 oz) plain flour
300 ml (½ pint) chicken stock
1 × 200 g (7 oz) can sweetcorn
  kernels, drained
salt
freshly ground black pepper

Preparation time: about 10
minutes
Cooking time: about 16–18
minutes
Microwave setting: Maximum
(Full)

1. Place the pork in a shallow
dish, cover and cook for 4–6
minutes, stirring halfway
through cooking. Set aside
covered.

2. Place the onion, carrots, red
pepper, garlic, mace, thyme,
sage, parsley and tomato purée
in a medium bowl. Cover and
cook for 8 minutes, stirring
halfway through cooking.

3. Stir in the butter until melted.
Stir in the flour. Make up the

Pork Chops with Oregano and Tomato Sauce

meat juices to 300 ml (½ pint) with stock, then stir in with the sweetcorn, pork and salt and pepper. Cook, uncovered, for 4 minutes, stirring every minute.

4. Serve with creamed potatoes and mange-touts.

Serves 4
4 pork loin chops, total weight 750 g (1½ lb)
1 medium onion, peeled and finely chopped
1 teaspoon dried oregano
25 g (1 oz) butter, cut into pieces
25 g (1 oz) cornflour
1 × 400 g (14 oz) can tomatoes, chopped with their juice
1 tablespoon tomato purée
1 tablespoon chopped fresh parsley
200 ml (7 fl oz) hot chicken stock
salt
freshly ground pepper

Preparation time: about 7 minutes
Cooking time: about 17–19 minutes
Microwave setting: Maximum (Full)

1. Place the chops around a medium bowl, cover and cook for 7 minutes, rearranging halfway through cooking. Set aside, covered.

2. Place the onion and oregano in a large bowl, cover and cook for 4 minutes, stirring halfway through.

3. Stir in the butter until melted. Stir in the cornflour, undrained tomatoes, tomato purée, parsley, stock, and salt and

pepper to taste. Cover and cook for 3–5 minutes, stirring halfway through cooking.

4. Add drained chops. Cook, uncovered, for 3 minutes.

From left to right: Pork casserole; Pork chops with apple, Pork chops with oregano and tomato sauce

Glazed Bacon Joint

Serves 6–8
*1.5 kg (3 lb) unsmoked fore end
bacon joint, soaked overnight
and drained
2 tablespoons marmalade*

Preparation time: about 5
minutes
Cooking time: about 27½
minutes, plus standing and
grilling
Microwave setting: Maximum
(Full)

1. Place the bacon joint in a
roasting bag and secure with a
non-metallic tie. Prick the bag
and place the bacon in a
shallow dish. Cook for 13½
minutes. Turn the bacon over
and cook for a further 13½
minutes.

2. Remove the bacon joint from
the bag and wrap tightly in foil.
Leave to stand for 15 minutes.

3. Place the marmalade in a
small bowl and heat for 30
seconds.

4. Place the bacon in a grill pan
and spread the marmalade over
the top of the joint. Cook under
a preheated conventional grill
until bubbling.

Garlic Bacon Sticks

Makes 8
*1 garlic clove
8 streaky bacon rashers, rinds
removed and stretched
8 grissini (bread sticks)
25 g (1 oz) Cheddar cheese,
finely grated*

Preparation time: about 10
minutes
Cooking time: about 5½ minutes
Microwave setting: Maximum
(Full)

1. Rub the garlic over each
rasher of bacon.

2. Twist a rasher of bacon
around the top half of each
bread stick. Place the sticks on a
piece of paper towel on a plate.
Cook, uncovered, for 5½ minutes
or until the bacon is cooked.

3. Twirl the hot bacon in the
cheese to coat on all sides.

4. Serve hot or cold with drinks.

Glazed bacon joint; Garlic bacon sticks

Pork with Orange and Cranberries

Serves 4
*4 pork fillets, total weight 750 g
 (1½ lb)
grated rind of 1 orange
125 ml (4 fl oz) orange juice
25 g (1 oz) caster sugar
225 g (8 oz) fresh cranberries
4 orange slices, to garnish*

Preparation time: about 10
minutes
Cooking time: about 17
minutes
Microwave setting: Maximum
(Full) and Defrost

1. Place the fillets in a shallow
dish, cover and cook on
Maximum for 6 minutes,
rearranging them halfway
through cooking. Set aside,
covered.

2. Place the orange rind and
juice, sugar and cranberries in a
medium bowl. Cover and cook
on Maximum for 2½ minutes.
Stir, re-cover and cook for 5½
minutes on Defrost.

3. Drain the fillets and spoon
the cranberry mixture over
them. Cook, uncovered, for 3
minutes on Maximum.

4. Cut into slices and garnish
with orange.

*Pork with orange and cranberries;
Pork fillets in wine sauce*

Pork Fillets in Wine Sauce

Serves 4
*4 pork fillets, total weight 750 g
 (1½ lb)
1 medium onion, peeled and
 chopped
100 g (4 oz) button mushrooms,
 sliced
1 celery stick, sliced
¼ teaspoon dried parsley
¼ teaspoon dried sage
¼ teaspoon dried tarragon
25 g (1 oz) butter, diced
25 g (1 oz) plain flour
about 150 ml (¼ pint) hot
 chicken stock
150 ml (¼ pint) rosé wine
salt
freshly ground black pepper
fried apple rings, to garnish*

Preparation time: about 10
minutes
Cooking time: about 16½–19½
minutes
Microwave setting: Maximum
(Full)

1. Place the pork fillets in a
shallow dish, cover and cook for
6–9 minutes, turning over and
rearranging halfway through
cooking. Set aside, covered.

2. Place the onion, mushrooms,
celery, parsley, sage and
tarragon in a medium bowl.
Cover and cook for 5½ minutes.

3. Stir in the butter until melted.
Stir in the flour. Make up the
meat juices to 150 ml (¼ pint)
with stock, then stir in with the
wine and salt and pepper. Cook,
covered, for 2 minutes, stirring
after 1 minute.

4. Add the fillets and turn to
coat with the sauce. Cook,
covered, for 3 minutes.

5. Garnish with the apple rings.
Serve with new potatoes and
fried courgettes.

Gammon Steaks with Pineapple

Serves 4
4 gammon slices, total weight
  1 kg (2 lb)
4 slices of canned pineapple,
  drained and cut in half
parsley sprig, to garnish

Preparation time: about 5
minutes
Cooking time: about 13
minutes, plus standing
Microwave setting: Maximum
(Full)

1. Arrange the gammon slices over the bottom and sides of a large bowl. Cover and cook for 10 minutes, rearranging halfway through cooking.

2. Pour off the juice and arrange the gammon in a serving dish. Arrange the pineapple halves over the gammon. Cook, uncovered, for 3 minutes.

3. Cover the dish with foil and stand for 4 minutes before serving. Garnish with parsley sprig and serve with sauté potatoes.

Bacon and Vegetable Casserole

Serves 3–4
½ green pepper, cored, seeded
  and thinly sliced
225 g (8 oz) onion, peeled and
  thinly sliced into rings
275 g (10 oz) potato, peeled
  and diced
1 celery stick, chopped
100 g (4 oz) carrot, peeled and
  thinly sliced
100 g (4 oz) frozen cauliflower
  florets
12 streaky bacon rashers, rinds
  removed, stretched, rolled
  and secured with wooden
  cocktail sticks
25 g (1 oz) plain flour
450 ml (¾ pint) hot chicken
  stock
1 teaspoon dried mixed herbs
salt
freshly ground black pepper

Preparation time: about 15
minutes
Cooking time: about 20
minutes
Microwave setting: Maximum
(Full)

1. Place the green pepper, onion, potato, celery, carrot and cauliflower in a large bowl. Cover and cook for 10 minutes, stirring twice during cooking.

2. Place the bacon rolls on the top of the vegetables, cover and cook for 5 minutes.

3. Remove the bacon and keep warm. Stir in the flour, stock, herbs, and salt and pepper to taste. Cook, uncovered, for 3 minutes.

Bacon and vegetable casserole;
Gammon steaks with pineapple

Gammon in Cider

4. Remove the sticks from the bacon rolls. Stir the bacon into the vegetables. Cook, uncovered, for 2 minutes. Serve immediately as a complete supper dish.

Cook's Tip

Use red or yellow peppers in place of the green pepper, and swedes or turnips in place of the carrots.

Homemade chicken stock will give the casserole a richer flavour.

Serves 4

600 g (1¼ lb) gammon, cubed
1 medium onion, peeled and chopped
1 celery stick, chopped
1 teaspoon dried marjoram
2 red eating apples, cored and sliced
25 g (1 oz) butter, cut into pieces
25 g (1 oz) cornflour
150 ml (¼ pint) hot chicken stock
300 ml (½ pint) dry cider
freshly ground black pepper

Preparation time: about 10 minutes
Cooking time: about 15 minutes
Microwave setting: Maximum (Full)

1. Place the gammon in a shallow dish, cover and cook for 4 minutes, stirring halfway through cooking. Remove the gammon with its juices and set aside, covered.

2. Add the onion, celery and marjoram to the dish, cover and cook for 3 minutes.

3. Stir in the apples, cover and cook for 2 minutes.

4. Stir in the butter until melted. Stir in the cornflour, stock, cider and pepper to taste. Cook, uncovered, for 3 minutes, until thickened, stirring every minute.

5. Replace the gammon and its juices and heat through for about 3 minutes.

6. Serve with boiled potatoes and broccoli.

Gammon in cider

Paprika Pork Chops

Serves 4
*4 pork spare rib chops, total
    weight 750 g (1½ lb)*
*½ green pepper, cored, seeded
    and sliced*
*½ red pepper, cored, seeded and
    sliced*
1 celery stick, chopped
¼ teaspoon Worcestershire sauce
2 tablespoons tomato purée
1 tablespoon paprika
¼ teaspoon dried oregano
¼ teaspoon dried basil
*25 g (1 oz) butter, cut into
    pieces*
25 g (1 oz) cornflour
*about 450 ml (¾ pint) hot
    chicken stock*
salt
freshly ground black pepper
2 tablespoons soured cream

Preparation time: about 10
minutes
Cooking time: about 16–19
minutes
Microwave setting: Maximum
(Full)

1. Place the chops in a shallow
dish, cover and cook for 6–9
minutes, turning over and
rearranging halfway through
cooking. Set aside, covered.

2. Place the peppers, celery,
Worcestershire sauce, tomato
purée, paprika, oregano and
basil in a medium bowl. Cover
and cook for 5 minutes, stirring
halfway through cooking.

3. Stir in the butter until melted.
Stir in the cornflour. Make up
the meat juices to 450 ml (¾
pint) with stock, then stir in
with salt and pepper to taste.
Cook, uncovered for 2 minutes,
stirring after 1 minute.

4. Add the chops and cook,
uncovered, for 3 minutes. Stir in
the soured cream.

5. Serve with plain boiled rice
and sweetcorn.

Spare Ribs with Barbecue Sauce

Serves 4
15 g (½ oz) butter
*1 garlic clove, peeled and
    crushed*
*1 medium onion, peeled and
    finely chopped*
*1 × 400 g (14 oz) can tomatoes,
    drained*
1 tablespoon dried mixed herbs
*2 tablespoons Worcestershire
    sauce*
1 tablespoon clear honey
1 tablespoon soy sauce
1 tablespoon dark brown sugar
salt
freshly ground black pepper
750 g (1½ lb) pork spare ribs

Preparation time: about 5
minutes
Cooking time: about 28½
minutes
Microwave setting: Maximum
(Full)

1. Place the butter, garlic and
onion in a large shallow bowl.
Cover and cook for 3½ minutes.

2. Stir in the tomatoes, herbs,
Worcestershire sauce, honey,
soy sauce, sugar, salt and
pepper. Cover and cook for 5
minutes.

3. Add spare ribs. Cover and
cook for 10 minutes.

4. Rearrange the spare ribs and
baste with the sauce. Cook for a
further 10 minutes or to taste.

Pork Kebabs

Serves 4
Marinade:
3 tablespoons olive oil
150 ml (¼ pint) water
*2 tablespoons Worcestershire
    sauce*
1 small onion, peeled and sliced
1 tablespoon wine vinegar
1 teaspoon dried mixed herbs
1 tablespoon redcurrant jelly
salt
freshly ground black pepper
Kebabs:
*450 g (1 lb) pork fillet, cut into
    4 cm (1½ inch) cubes*
*½ red pepper, cored, seeded and
    cut into 8 pieces*
*½ green pepper, cored, seeded
    and cut into 8 pieces*
2 tomatoes, halved
Sauce:
25 g (1 oz) butter
25 g (1 oz) plain flour
150 ml (¼ pint) chicken stock
2 tablespoons tomato purée

Preparation time: about 15
minutes, plus marinating
Cooking time: about 13
minutes
Microwave setting: Maximum
(Full)

1. Mix together the marinade
ingredients, with salt and
pepper to taste, in a shallow
dish. Add the pork cubes and
turn to coat. Leave for 2 hours.

2. Place the peppers in a
medium bowl, cover and cook
for 2 minutes.

3. Drain the pork cubes,
reserving the marinade. Thread
the pork cubes and pepper
pieces alternately on to 4
wooden skewers. Place on a
plate and cover with paper
towels. Cook for 3 minutes.

4. Place half a tomato on each
skewer, cover again and cook
for 4 minutes. Set aside.

5. Place the butter in a large jug
and cook, uncovered, for 1
minute or until melted. Stir in

the flour. Blend in the strained,
reserved marinade, hot chicken
stock and tomato purée. Cook
for 3 minutes, stirring every
minute.

*Clockwise: Spare ribs with barbecue
sauce; Pork kebabs; Cold curried pork;
Paprika pork chops*

Cold Curried Pork

Serves 4

450 g (1 lb) pork fillet, cubed
2 eating apples, cored and diced
2 spring onions, trimmed and chopped
½ red pepper, cored, seeded and chopped
½ small cucumber, peeled and diced
1 carrot, peeled and grated
25 g (1 oz) sultanas
25 g (1 oz) roasted peanuts

1 celery stick, chopped
1 tablespoon mild curry powder
225 ml (8 fl oz) mayonnaise
salt
freshly ground black pepper
spring onions, to garnish

Preparation time: about 20 minutes, plus cooling and chilling

Cooking time: about 5–7 minutes

Microwave setting: Maximum (Full)

1. Place the pork in a large bowl, cover and cook for 5–7 minutes, stirring halfway through cooking. Leave to stand, covered, until cold. Drain.

2. Mix together the apples, spring onions, red pepper, cucumber, carrot, sultanas, peanuts and celery.

3. Mix together the curry powder, mayonnaise, and salt and pepper to taste. Stir in the pork and the fruit and vegetable mixture. Chill. Garnish with spring onions.

Cook's Tip

The way in which meat is cut before cooking affects the result achieved in the microwave oven. Cut across the grain into small slices rather than chopped into chunks, the meat will be tender and will cook more quickly.

Picnic Ham Pâté

Serves 4
50 g (2 oz) mushrooms
*100 g (4 oz) onions, peeled and
    quartered*
*350 g (12 oz) lean ham,
    roughly chopped*
1 garlic clove, peeled
¼ teaspoon dried sage
¼ teaspoon dried parsley
¼ teaspoon dried rosemary
¼ teaspoon dried marjoram
freshly ground black pepper
2 eggs, lightly beaten
To garnish:
lettuce
tomato slices

Preparation time: about 6
minutes, plus cooling
Cooking time: about 7½ minutes
Microwave setting: Maximum
(Full)

1. Process or finely mince the
mushrooms, onions, ham,
garlic, sage, parsley, rosemary,
marjoram and pepper to taste.
Bind the mixture with the eggs.

2. Line a 16 cm (6½ inch)
diameter soufflé dish with cling
film and place an inexpensive
tumbler upside-down in the
centre. Spread the ham mixture
evenly over the bottom.

3. Cover and cook for 7½
minutes, turning round halfway
through cooking. Leave to cool
before turning out.

4. Garnish with lettuce and
sliced tomatoes and serve with
potato salad.

Frankfurters Wrapped in Bacon

Makes 8
*8 streaky bacon rashers, rinds
    removed*
8 large frankfurters
parsley sprigs, to garnish

Preparation time: about 5
minutes
Cooking time: about 4 minutes
Microwave setting: Maximum
(Full)

1. Wind the bacon around the
frankfurters. Place in a circle on
a plate. Cover with a paper
towel and cook for 4 minutes.

2. Garnish with parsley and
serve with potato salad.

*Picnic ham pâté; Frankfurters
wrapped in bacon*

MENU PLANNER

It is a mistake to leave all the cooking until the last minute when using the microwave to make a meal. The picture below illustrates a well planned, microwave menu: Jellied Ham and Chicken (page 37) is cooked in advance to serve cold for the first course; this can be done the day before.

Prepare the Croquette Potato (page 142) and Apple Sauce (page 166) early on the day, then set them aside ready to reheat before serving.

Prepare the pork, trimming, stuffing and tying it in a neat joint. Have the broccoli ready to

cook and make the cheese sauce in advance (page 144), covering it with a piece of greaseproof paper to prevent a skin forming.

Prepare the ingredients for Baked Bananas (page 178) but do not peel the fruit.

Cook the pork and leave it to stand while the starter is served. Cook the broccoli while the starter is served. Heat the sauce and pour it over. Heat the potatoes and apple sauce just before serving. They will take 3 minutes each or 4–6 minutes together by standing a suitable jug for the sauce in the middle of the dish of croquettes. Remove the sauce as soon as it is hot.

Prepare and cook the bananas just before they are to be served.

Clockwise: Jellied ham and chicken; Baked bananas; Stuffed loin of pork; Croquette potatoes; Apple sauce; Broccoli with cheese sauce

Stuffed Pork Loin

Serves 6

1 small onion, peeled and finely chopped
1 garlic clove, peeled and crushed
25 g (1 oz) butter
25 g (1 oz) fresh white breadcrumbs
grated rind of 1 lemon
¼ teaspoon dried rosemary
¼ teaspoon dried thyme
salt
freshly ground black pepper
1 × 1 kg (2 lb) boned loin of pork, skin scored

Preparation time: about 20 minutes
Cooking time: about 14–17 minutes, plus standing and grilling
Microwave setting: Maximum (Full)

1. Place the onion, garlic and butter in a bowl. Cover and cook for 3 minutes. Stir in the breadcrumbs, lemon rind, rosemary, thyme, and salt and pepper to taste.

2. Spread the stuffing over the loin, close up and secure with string. Place in a shallow dish, skin uppermost, and cook, uncovered, for 11–14 minutes, turning round halfway through cooking.

3. Wrap tightly in foil and stand for 10 minutes before carving. If desired, brown the loin under a preheated conventional grill.

# EGGS AND CHEESE

Quick to cook and easy to prepare, both eggs and cheese form the base for a wide variety of tasty supper dishes. Many of your favourite egg and cheese recipes can be cooked with great success in the microwave, as you will discover in this chapter, but do not cook eggs in their shells.

Both eggs and cheese cook very quickly by conventional methods and in the microwave they can be prepared with even greater speed. Because they cook so quickly, great care has to be taken to ensure that they cook evenly and that they do not overcook. If you are cooking just one or two eggs then you will have to time them in seconds and check their cooking progress frequently otherwise they may become overcooked and leathery.

The yolk and white of the egg cook at different rates. Conventionally, the white tends to cook before the yolk but in the microwave the yolk cooks faster than the white. So for plain cooked eggs you may prefer to use conventional cooking methods to achieve a perfectly cooked egg with a firmly set white and runny yolk. However, do try scrambled eggs in the microwave as they are very smooth and creamy.

There are one or two tips that must be remembered for

Before cooking, the yolks of eggs should be pierced to prevent them from bursting. Here a cocktail stick is used.

success when microwaving eggs. A thin membrane surrounds the yolk of an egg and this should always be pricked before the egg is cooked in the microwave (unless, of course, it is beaten). Use a wooden cocktail stick or meat skewer to prick the yolk otherwise it will burst and spatter yolk everywhere during cooking.

The eggs are ready when they are very slightly undercooked – the residual heat which remains in the food is sufficient to complete the cooking process.

Plain cooked eggs

Whichever way eggs are cooked, they are not the easiest of ingredients to present as perfect. Individual tastes vary enormously, so it is difficult to advise people how best to cook eggs in the microwave.

The way in which microwave ovens cook food means that the eggs do not cook in quite the same way as normal. Usually, as the eggs simmer in, or over, the water, or as they bake in the oven, they are cooked from the white inwards. In the microwave oven the yolks cook at the same rate as the whites, if not slightly faster. So if you like eggs with firm whites and soft yolks then you are unlikely to achieve this in the microwave.

If you are not too fussy about small areas of floppy egg white, then microwaved eggs are fine. They are easy to prepare when you are in a dreadful hurry.

A bun dish (or muffin dish) specially designed for the microwave oven is the best

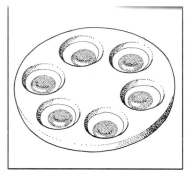

A special microwave bun dish is ideal for cooking several eggs at once. Microwave-proof cling film can be used as a cover, enabling you to see just when the eggs are ready.

container to use, otherwise the eggs can be cooked in individual ramekin dishes. Crack the eggs into the containers and prick the yolk of each one with a small cocktail stick. Top each egg with a small knob of butter and cover with microwave-proof cling film, then cook for the times given below.

2 eggs — 1 to $1\frac{1}{4}$ minutes
3 eggs — $1\frac{1}{2}$ to $1\frac{3}{4}$ minutes
4 eggs — $1\frac{3}{4}$ to 2 minutes

Scrambled eggs

Opinion seems to be very divided about whether scrambled eggs cooked in the microwave are successful or not. Cooking scrambled eggs on the top of the hob means standing over the pan every second if you want a creamy result; however you cannot go away and leave the eggs to cook in the microwave oven either because they do need regular

whisking, but you can actually spend time buttering the toast or making the tea during the 2 minute intervals when you are not whisking the eggs. So don't let anyone put you off by saying it's more work cooking eggs in the microwave, it's not but you've got to get used to the frequent whisking.

Another plus to microwave scrambled eggs is found when it comes to clearing up – washing up a basin in which the eggs were cooked is far easier than cleaning a dirty saucepan.

Another advantage is that as the eggs are cooking you can stop the process if needs be. For example, you can leave the eggs at the stage when they just need another half a minute or so, make and butter your toast, and still go back to finish cooking them without having a ruined breakfast or supper. Obviously this would not be the case if the eggs were virtually cooked, but at the half-set stage they can be left for a while.

Timing scrambled eggs

The timing is fairly crucial and 30 seconds can mean rubbery eggs, so until you know your own particular oven, keep an eye on the eggs to see how they are setting. Once you have cooked your usual two or four eggs you will become used to the time it takes and know how careless you can be with them. Follow the instructions and times below, keeping a close eye on the eggs until you know *exactly* how long it takes to scramble a certain number of eggs in your oven.

Preparing scrambled eggs

1. Beat the eggs thoroughly and add a generous knob of butter or margarine. The eggs should be seasoned at this stage.

2. The eggs should be whisked as soon as they have a set rim round the inside of the basin.

3. As the eggs set round the side of the basin, they should be whisked again. Here the scrambled eggs are half set.

4. The eggs are ready when they are still very slightly runny. By the time the eggs shown above are whisked and served they will be perfectly creamy. If the eggs are cooked for a longer period, until they are firmly set, by the time they are whisked or stirred and served, they will have started to separate out slightly.

Cooking instructions

2 eggs whisk the eggs thoroughly with 1 tablespoon milk and seasoning to taste. Add about 15 g (½ oz) (a good knob) of butter or margarine and cook on Maximum (Full) power for 1 minute. Whisk thoroughly, then cook for another minute and whisk again. Cook for a final 30 seconds and whisk before serving.

4 eggs whisk the eggs thoroughly with 2 tablespoons milk, seasoning to taste and 25 g (1 oz) butter or margarine. Cook on Maximum (Full) power for 2 minutes, then whisk the eggs thoroughly. Cook for a further 1 minute and whisk again; cook for a final 1 minute, then whisk before serving.

6 eggs whisk the eggs thoroughly with 3 tablespoons milk and seasoning to taste. Add 1 large knob of butter or margarine (don't be mean, because the butter or margarine give the eggs a good flavour) and cook on Maximum (Full) power for 2 minutes. Whisk the eggs thoroughly, cook for a further 2 minutes and whisk again. Cook for a final 2 to 2½ minutes, then whisk the eggs until smooth and serve.

Variations

Creamy eggs Scrambled eggs are delicious made with single or double cream instead of milk. Cook them as in the instructions, using cream in place of the suggested quantities of milk.

Scrambled eggs with cheese Allow 50 g (2 oz) finely grated cheese to every 2 eggs. Add the cheese to the eggs when they are half set and stir in a pinch of mustard powder if you like. Continue cooking until the eggs are set, then serve on toast or use to fill a baked potato. The addition of cheese makes the eggs more substantial.

Scrambled eggs with herbs A pinch of thyme, lots of chopped parsley and chives go very well with scrambled eggs. This is particularly tasty if you are serving the eggs with grilled sausages.

Eggs with prawns For a rather special supper dish, add 100 g (4 oz) peeled cooked prawns to every 2 eggs when they are half set. Serve in small bowls with hot French bread. This also makes a good starter.

Smoked salmon special A good one for a very special breakfast treat (try serving this on Christmas morning with a bottle of champagne or buck's fizz). Add 25–50 g (1–2 oz) chopped smoked salmon to every 2 eggs (depending on how many you are cooking; if it is only two then use the greater quantity). Stir the smoked salmon into the eggs when they are almost set – the salmon should be warmed through but not cooked. This recipe can also be served as an elegant starter, on small circles of buttered toast or with very thin brown bread and butter.

Bacon eggs Finely chop 50 g (2 oz) lean rindless bacon for every 2 eggs and cook it in the basin for 2 minutes before adding the eggs. Add chopped spring onions to the cooked eggs if you like.

Eggs with tomatoes Peel, deseed and chop 2 ripe but firm tomatoes for every 2 eggs. Add these to the half set eggs and continue cooking until the eggs are set. Stir the eggs rather than whisking them, but do make sure you thoroughly break up the set bits otherwise they will become leathery.

Ham and eggs Add 50 g (2 oz) chopped cooked ham to every 2 eggs when almost set. Then continue cooking.

Cooking cheese

Cheese also cooks very quickly in the microwave and it too can be overcooked all too easily.

Combined with sauces, melted into a fondue or used in stuffings for tomatoes and other vegetables, the cheese will melt quickly and evenly if it is cut into small, even-sized pieces or grated. When cheese is used as a topping for other foods, then care must be taken and the main food should be cooked first so that the cheese can be melted in just a few seconds. If the top of the food to be sprinkled with cheese covers a large area, then it is often better to melt the cheese on a medium setting instead of Maximum (Full) power. This ensures that the cheese will be evenly melted and not overcooked in some areas before other parts are melted – a problem which can occur when cooking it in a large shallow dish.

Fried Eggs

Serves 2
20 g (¾ oz) butter
2 eggs (size 3), taken from
*   refrigerator*
freshly ground black pepper
*   (optional)*

Preparation time: about 2
minutes
Cooking time: about 1¾
minutes, plus standing
Microwave setting: Maximum
(Full)

1. Divide the butter between
two 12.5 cm (5 inch) top
diameter saucers. Cook for 30
seconds or until melted.

2. Break an egg into each saucer
and pierce the yolk with a
cocktail stick. Sprinkle with
pepper, if desired. Cover tightly
with cling film.

3. Cook for 1¼ minutes, turning
round halfway through cooking.
Leave to stand, covered, for 1
minute before serving. If the egg
is not cooked, return to the
cooker for 15 seconds.

Baked Eggs

Serves 4
15 g (½ oz) butter
2 small mushrooms, finely
*   chopped*
50 g (2 oz) ham, finely chopped
4 teaspoons tomato purée
4 eggs (sizes 1, 2)
salt
freshly ground black pepper
4 tablespoons double cream

Preparation time: about 5
minutes
Cooking time: about 4½ minutes
Microwave setting: Maximum
(Full)

1. Divide the butter and the
chopped mushrooms between
4 cocotte dishes. Cook for
1½ minutes.

2. Place the ham on the
mushrooms and 1 teaspoon of
the tomato purée on the ham in
each dish.

3. Break the eggs on to the ham
and pierce the yolks with a
needle. Season with salt and
pepper.

4. Pour 1 tablespoon cream
over each of the eggs. Cook for
1½ minutes.

5. Rearrange the dishes, so the
front ones are at the back, and
cook for a further 1½ minutes.
Serve the eggs at once.

Fried eggs; Baked eggs

Omelette

Serves 2
4 eggs (size 2)
4 tablespoons milk
salt
freshly ground black pepper
20 g (¾ oz) butter
1 tablespoon chopped fresh parsley, to garnish

Preparation time: about 3 minutes
Cooking time: 3¾ minutes
Microwave setting: Maximum (Full)

1. Beat together the eggs, milk and salt and pepper to taste.

2. Place the butter in a 23 cm (9 inch) round shallow casserole. Cook, uncovered, for 30 seconds.

3. Tilt the casserole to be sure the bottom is evenly coated with melted butter, then pour in the egg mixture. Cover and cook for 2 minutes.

4. Using a fork, draw the edges of the egg to the centre. Cover and cook for a further 1¼ minutes. If not quite cooked, stand for 1 minute before serving.

5. Serve sprinkled with chopped parsley.

Cook's Tip

Chopped ham could be added at step 4 after the cooking is completed.

Poached Eggs

Serves 2
125 ml (4 fl oz) water
2 tablespoons white vinegar
2 eggs (size 2)
hot buttered toast, to serve

Preparation time: about 2 minutes
Cooking time: about 3 minutes, plus standing
Microwave setting: Maximum (Full)

1. Divide the water and vinegar equally between 2 ramekin dishes. Cook, uncovered, for 2 minutes or until boiling.

2. Break the eggs into the water and pierce the yolks with a needle. Cook, uncovered, for 1 minute. Leave to stand for 1 minute.

3. Drain off the water and vinegar, then serve on hot buttered toast.

Boiled Eggs

Eggs must **never** be cooked in their shells in a microwave cooker as there is a build-up of pressure within the egg which causes the shell to 'explode' or burst. As a result, the cooker interior would have to be cleaned which is a nuisance, more important, the impact could cause damage to the components of the cooker. Piercing the shell does not prevent it exploding.

Omelette, Poached eggs

Eggs Benedict

Serves 4
4 slices of cooked ham
4 thick slices of buttered white
toast, cut to the size of the
ham
Poached eggs:
250 ml (8 fl oz) water
4 tablespoons white vinegar
4 eggs (size 3)
Hollandaise sauce:
2 egg yolks (size 3)
1 tablespoon lemon juice
100 g (4 oz) butter, cut into 8
pieces
pinch of cayenne pepper
½ teaspoon dry mustard

Preparation time: about 10 minutes
Cooking time: about 4½ minutes
Microwave setting: Maximum (Full)

1. Place a piece of ham on each slice of toast. Keep warm.

2. Divide the water and vinegar equally between 4 ramekin dishes. Cook, uncovered, for 2 minutes or until boiling. Break an egg into each dish and pierce its yolk.

3. To make the sauce, prick the egg yolks and place with the lemon juice in a small bowl. Cook, uncovered, for 30 seconds. Beat hard until smooth.

4. Place the eggs for poaching into the microwave and cook for 2 minutes. Stand for 1 minute before draining.

5. Meanwhile, beat one piece of butter at a time into the sauce, until all 8 pieces are incorporated. Beat in the cayenne pepper and mustard.

6. Place the poached eggs on the ham and toast and top with a large spoonful of sauce. Serve at once.

Eggs Florentine

Serves 4
1 × 225 g (8 oz) can chopped
spinach, drained or frozen
spinach, thawed and drained
salt
freshly ground black pepper
¼ teaspoon grated nutmeg
4 eggs (size 2), from
refrigerator

Preparation time: about 4 minutes
Cooking time: about 3¾ minutes, plus standing
Microwave setting: Maximum (Full)

1. Divide the spinach between 4 ramekin dishes. Cook, uncovered, for 1½ minutes.

2. Sprinkle the spinach with a little salt, pepper and nutmeg. Break the eggs on to the spinach. Prick the yolks and cover dishes with cling film. Arrange in a circle in the cooker.

3. Cook for 2¼ minutes, rearranging the dishes halfway through cooking. If the eggs are not quite cooked, allow to stand, covered, for 1 minute.

4. Serve with hot buttered toast.

Eggs benedict; Eggs Florentine

Welsh Rarebit

Serves 4

*225 g (8 oz) Cheddar cheese,
    finely grated*
4 tablespoons milk
salt
freshly ground black pepper
1 teaspoon French mustard
4 slices toast
parsley sprigs, to garnish

Preparation time: about 5
minutes
Cooking time: about 1½ minutes
plus grilling
Microwave setting: Maximum
(Full)

1. Place the cheese and milk in a medium bowl and cook for 1 minute.

2. Stir in the salt, pepper and mustard and cook for 30 seconds.

3. Spread the cheese mixture over the toast.

4. If desired, place the Welsh rarebit under a preheated conventional grill, to brown the top. Garnish with the parsley.

Cheese and Ham Pudding

Serves 4

*225 g (8 oz) fresh brown
    breadcrumbs*
*50 g (2 oz) cooked ham, finely
    chopped*
pinch of dry mustard
1 teaspoon dried mixed herbs
*175 g (6 oz) mild Cheddar
    cheese, finely grated*
salt
freshly ground black pepper
3 eggs, lightly beaten
600 ml (1 pint) milk
*1 tablespoon chopped fresh
    parsley, to garnish*

Preparation time: about 10
minutes
Cooking time: about 10–12
minutes, plus standing
Microwave setting: Maximum
(Full)

1. Mix together the breadcrumbs, ham, mustard, herbs, cheese and salt and pepper to taste. Lightly beat in the eggs and milk. Pour into a 1.75 litre (3 pint) soufflé dish. Allow to stand for 10 minutes.

2. Cook, uncovered, for 10–12 minutes, stirring halfway through cooking.

3. Sprinkle with parsley and serve with a green vegetable.

Welsh rarebit; Cheese and ham pudding

Salami and Cheese Flan

Serves 4

175 g (6 oz) prepared
  shortcrust pastry
125 ml (4 fl oz) milk
3 eggs
75 g (3 oz) salami, finely diced
salt
freshly ground black pepper
50 g (2 oz) Samsoe or Cheddar
  cheese, finely grated
parsley sprig, to garnish

Preparation time: about 15 minutes
Cooking time: about 9 minutes, plus grilling
Microwave setting: Maximum (Full)

1. Roll out the pastry and line a 17 cm (6½ inch) base diameter, 22 cm (8½ inch) top diameter plate tart dish. Prick the sides and base with a fork. Cook for 3½ minutes or until the pastry looks dry. Set aside.

2. Place the milk, eggs, salami, salt and pepper in a jug, lightly beat together. Cook for 2 minutes, beating with a fork every 30 seconds.

3. Pour the mixture into the pastry case and cook for 3 minutes, stirring gently after 1 and 2 minutes.

4. Sprinkle the cheese over the egg and brown under a preheated conventional grill for about 5 minutes. Serve garnished with a sprig of parsley.

Salami and cheese flan; Smoked haddock with egg sauce

Smoked Haddock with Egg Sauce

Serves 4

300 ml (½ pint) milk
1 bay leaf
1 onion slice
8 smoked haddock fillets
50 g (2 oz) butter
25 g (1 oz) plain flour
salt
freshly ground black pepper
2 hard-boiled eggs, finely
  chopped
2 tablespoons chopped fresh
  chives

Preparation time: about 10 minutes, plus infusing
Cooking time: about 11 minutes
Microwave setting: Maximum (Full)

1. Place the milk in a jug with the bay leaf and onion slice and cook for 2 minutes. Leave for 15 minutes.

2. Place the haddock fillets in a shallow dish and dot with 25 g (1 oz) of the butter. Cover and cook for 2 minutes. Turn the dish round and cook for a further 2 minutes. Keep warm while making the sauce.

3. Place the remaining butter in a 600 ml (1 pint) jug. Cook for 1 minute or until melted. Blend in the flour.

4. Strain the hot milk, discarding the bay leaf and onion, and stir it into the flour mixture. Add salt and pepper. Cook for 2 minutes, stirring every minute.

5. Stir in the chopped hard-boiled eggs and chives.

6. Pour the sauce over the fish and reheat for 2 minutes before serving.

Scrambled eggs; Kidneys, mushrooms and bacon

MENU PLANNER

Breakfast time in most homes is not the time to experiment with the newest appliance, so it is well worth getting to know how to use your microwave for this meal.

Most of us tend to cook the same breakfast on weekdays so it is as well to note the microwave timing for the number of eggs, or rashers of bacon, which you cook daily.

If the members of the household appear at different times all making different demands, then put the microwave to full use for cooking individual breakfasts. Remember you can cook a single portion of porridge with ease or Baked Eggs (page 128) can be served with hot buttered toast.

If unbuttered toast has long since cooled, then place it on absorbent kitchen paper to heat for 30 seconds in the microwave. Also, croissants, buns or rolls can be heated in a few seconds to make a delicious breakfast.

Remember, too, that you can make a jug of coffee in the microwave and use it for heating up individual cups. It is also excellent for heating milk to serve with coffee or with breakfast cereals.

Scrambled Egg Breakfast

Serves 2
Kidneys, mushrooms and
  bacon:
4 rashers streaky bacon, rinds
4 flat mushrooms
2 lambs' kidneys, membrane
  and core removed, halved
Scrambled eggs:
4 eggs (size 2)
1 tablespoon milk
salt
freshly ground black pepper
15 g (½ oz) butter
parsley sprigs to garnish
  (optional)

Preparation time: about 5 minutes
Cooking time: about 8½ minutes
Microwave setting: Maximum (Full)

1. Place a piece of absorbent paper towel on a plate. Lay the bacon on one side, cover with another piece of paper and cook for 1 minute.

2. Uncover. Place the mushrooms in the centre of the plate, cover and cook for 1½ minutes, then put the kidneys round the outside of the plate. Re-cover and cook for 2 minutes, turning the kidneys over and rearranging the mushrooms if necessary. Re-cover and cook for 1 minute.

3. While the kidneys are cooking whisk the eggs, milk, salt and pepper to taste in a large jug and add the butter.

4. Remove the paper towel from the kidneys and bacon, then cover with a warmed plate.

5. Cook the eggs for 3 minutes. Break up the mixture and beat gently once a minute.

6. Serve the scrambled eggs with the bacon, kidneys and mushrooms.

VEGETABLES

Vegetables are among the foods which cook with most success in the microwave. They can be prepared to perfection – no more soggy, overcooked cabbage or broken, watery potatoes. Whether cooking from frozen, serving them plain, or creating a colourful accompaniment, you'll find plenty of vegetable variety in the pages which follow.

Almost all vegetables cook well in the microwave, retaining their maximum flavour and nutrients. The colour of microwave-cooked vegetables is excellent and their texture is good and firm rather than soft or soggy. Both fresh and frozen vegetables can be cooked, whole or cut into evenly sized pieces as appropriate. Older root vegetables, such as carrots, do not improve with microwave cooking as their own lack of moisture can produce a rather tough, slightly dehydrated result.

Cooking liquid

Very little water or other liquid is added when cooking vegetables in the microwave. The moisture which is present in the vegetables produces a certain amount of steam in which to cook the food. Usually a few tablespoons of water are added to increase the moisture content.

If you do cook old, slightly tough, root vegetables in the microwave, then add extra water to help to tenderise them and remember to lengthen the cooking time slightly.

Cutting vegetables

As with other ingredients which are to be cooked in the microwave, when preparing vegetables it is best to cut them as evenly as possible both in terms of size and shape.

Cut slices of the same thickness; prepare dice or chunks which are of similar size and fingers that are of roughly the same length and thickness.

Break a cauliflower into florets of similar size unless you plan to cook the vegetable whole. Trim off any very thick pieces of the stalk end before cooking. Trim broccoli florets in the same way.

Before cooking, those vegetables which are not left whole should be cut into chunks, slices or fingers which are as even in shape and size as possible.

If vegetables are cooked whole in their skins, then it is important that the skins are pricked to prevent them from bursting during cooking; for example, potatoes, aubergines or tomatoes should be pricked with a fork before they are cooked if they are to be left whole.

Arranging and rearranging

The whole vegetables, such as potatoes in their jackets, may be cooked in a container or straight on the turntable or floor of the microwave, depending on their type. Regardless of whether they are in a dish or not, the individual vegetables should be placed as far apart as possible for the quickest and most even results.

Vegetables which have stalks that are tougher than their heads – for example broccoli – should be arranged with the tougher stalks towards the outside of the dish and the heads as close together as possible in the centre. Short asparagus spears can be arranged in this way. Alternatively, long asparagus can be cooked in a roasting bag or large shallow dish, placing the tender tips very closely together and overlapping each other at one end, with the tougher stalks which require extra cooking separated as far apart as possible at the other end.

Halfway through the cooking time the whole vegetables should be turned over or around so that they cook evenly.

If the vegetables are cut they should be stirred to rearrange them halfway through the cooking time.

Seasoning

Vegetables should not be seasoned with salt before cooking as this results in a dehydrated surface caused by the fact that the liquid content of the vegetables is attracted by the salt and drawn out during cooking. Seasoning should be added along with a knob of butter or margarine after the vegetables are drained of any cooking liquid and before they are served.

Covering

It is important to cover the dish in which the vegetables are cooked so that the steam produced by the small amount of cooking liquid is contained within the vessel. It is this steam which tenderises the vegetables.

Covered dishes – a casserole, basin or mixing bowl topped with a plate – are ideal for cooking most vegetables.

Stirring vegetables

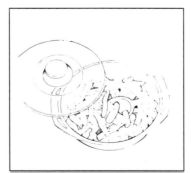

Small vegetables or those which are cut up should be stirred halfway through

cooking to rearrange the pieces and to ensure that they are all evenly cooked.

Roasting bags or boilable bags are also useful and frozen vegetables can be stored in these, ready to be transferred straight to the microwave for cooking. Large vegetables, like globe artichokes, or a small whole cauliflower, cook very well in bags and they can be easily turned or rearranged during cooking.

Small amounts of small vegetables, such as peas or sweetcorn kernels, cook very well in a suitable measuring jug which can be covered with microwave-proof cling film or a saucer.

Reheating vegetables

One of the great advantages of microwave cooking is that foods can be successfully reheated without spoiling their texture and without tasting inferior. This is a particularly useful facility when cooking the vegetables for a meal especially when you are entertaining dinner guests. They can be prepared and part cooked some time in advance, then kept closely covered right up until they are to be served at which time the cooking can be completed quickly. The liquid should be drained off (it can be saved for use in stocks or sauces) and butter tossed into the vegetables.

If you use the facility often then it may be worth investing in some practical cooking dishes for the purpose. Divided dishes can be used to contain two or three different types of vegetable which can be reheated together. This is sensible if you often reheat portions to serve two or three but it is not practical for larger quantities.

Alternatively, special microwave plate stackers can also be used for two dishes.

Cooking potatoes

 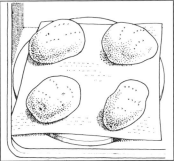

1. Before cooking potatoes in their jackets, the skins should be thoroughly scrubbed and dried, then pricked all over to prevent them bursting.

2. The potatoes are arranged as far apart as possible on the turntable or on a plate. Here they are arranged on a piece of absorbent kitchen paper on the turntable; the paper prevents the turntable from being soiled by juices which escape from the potatoes as they cook. Halfway through cooking the potatoes are turned over and their positions may be swapped if they are not cooking at quite the same rate.

Cooking broccoli and aubergines

Broccoli spears or cauliflower florets should be arranged with the tender heads towards the centre of the dish, pushed closely together, and the stalks round the outside. The individual pieces may need turning over halfway through cooking.

Before cooking, the skins should be pricked and the vegetables arranged as far apart as possible on a plate or on absorbent kitchen paper on the floor or turntable in the microwave. The cooked vegetables should be allowed to stand for several minutes before they are ready to be sliced or cut up. To obtain the flesh only (for a purée or to use in a dip), cut the aubergines in half and scoop or cut out the tender middle.

Blanching vegetables for the freezer

The chances are, if you're a keen gardener, pick-your-own fanatic, or simply someone who likes to enjoy fresh vegetables while they are low in price and high in quality, then you probably like to freeze vegetables for year-round eating.

A main advantage of having a microwave is that minutes after the vegetables are picked you can have them blanched and ready to freeze, without spending all day in the kitchen with a bubbling saucepan and a stop watch.

Prepare the vegetables as you would for normal cooking and place them in a covered dish, then add water as given in the chart. Cook for half the time given in the chart and stir, re-cover and cook for the remaining time, then stir again. Plunge the vegetables into iced water immediately to prevent further cooking. Drain the blanched vegetables and spread them out on absorbent kitchen paper to absorb excess moisture. Pack in freezer containers or boil-in-the-bag pouches, seal and label, then freeze.

Vegetables may be blanched in boil-in-the-bags and then, still in their bags, plunged into iced water up to their necks to cool. This chills the vegetables and expels the air in the bag at the same time, automatically creating a vacuum pack ready for freezing. Seal and label in the usual way.

Cooking frozen vegetables

Most commercially packaged frozen vegetables offer microwave cooking instructions on the outside of the carton or packet. It is best to follow these manufacturer's instructions as far as possible.

However if you have frozen your own vegetables you may find the times given on the chart a useful guide when it comes to cooking them.

When you pack vegetables for the freezer it is a good idea to pack them as flat as possible in a bag, with all air excluded, then seal them so that they fall apart easily into individual pieces when you transfer them to the cooking container. Alternatively, they can be packed 'free-flow' style, or open frozen.

If you are cooking a block of frozen vegetables, then you will have to break them apart as they cook.

Since most frozen vegetables are surrounded by a certain amount of ice, there is no need to add extra liquid, the only exception being whole or cut French beans which may need an extra spoonful or so of water added to the cooking container. Plain cooked vegetables can be coated with a sauce, served with a gratin topping, tossed in a flavoured butter or complemented by the addition of chopped fresh herbs. These ideas are intended to inspire you to turn some plain cooked vegetables into a tempting first course, clever side dish or tasty supper dish. Some crusty bread or nutty Granary bread makes an ideal accompaniment to supper dishes and crisp melba toast complements a vegetable first course.

Buttered vegetables

Use either butter or margarine for all the following ideas.

Lemon parsley butter Cream chopped fresh parsley and a little grated lemon rind into

Defrosting frozen spinach

Remove the spinach from its packet if possible and transfer it to a suitable dish. If the frozen spinach cannot be removed from the carton, then cook the whole packet on Maximum (Full) power for 1 minute, or until the contents can be released into a dish. Cover and cook on Maximum (Full) power for 2 minutes. Break a block of spinach into chunks or rearrange free-flow chunks of spinach. Continue cooking until all the spinach is separate and quite watery but still icy. For 225 g (8 oz) frozen block spinach allow approximately 3–4 minutes, for 450 g (1 lb) frozen block spinach allow approximately 6–7 minutes. Drain the water from the spinach and use as required – it should still be icy.

softened butter or margarine. Add a dash of lemon juice and seasoning to taste. Serve with freshly cooked asparagus, button mushrooms, or globe artichokes to make a delicious first course. Offer crusty rolls or curly melba toast as an accompaniment. Toss Jerusalem artichokes, French beans, new potatoes or diced celeriac in the butter to make a delicious side dish.

Basil and garlic butter Cream chopped fresh basil, a crushed clove of garlic and seasoning into softened butter. For a delicious supper dish use the butter to top cooked quartered tomatoes or button mushrooms and serve them on thick slices of hot buttered toast. Toss cooked cubed aubergines, sliced courgettes or cooked chicory in the butter to make a full-flavoured accompaniment for poultry, lamb or veal.

Almond and orange butter Beat a little grated orange rind and some chopped toasted almonds into softened butter with seasoning to taste. This butter is good with cobs of corn for a first course or light lunch dish. Tossed into cooked carrots, button onions (pickling onions) or cooked shredded spinach it flavours a delicious side dish for pork or ham.

Parmesan herb butter Beat some grated Parmesan cheese – preferably fresh – and chopped fresh parsley, tarragon or marjoram into softened butter with plenty of freshly ground black pepper. Serve this butter with large open mushrooms or halved tomatoes as a first course, or spoon the mushrooms or tomatoes on toast as a light lunch. For a more substantial meal serve the vegetables with plain cooked rice or pasta. Present a tempting side dish by tossing cooked cubed potatoes in the butter – it will enliven simple fish steaks, plain cooked mackerel or trout as well as poultry or meat.

Sauced vegetables

Cheese sauce Prepare a cheese sauce, following the recipe on page 162. Pour it over cooked cauliflower, broccoli, wedges of cabbage, chicory or a dish of mixed vegetables.

Egg sauce Prepare an egg sauce following the recipe on page 162. Serve as a topping for asparagus, broccoli, French beans or courgettes and serve the vegetables in small portions as a starter or as a side dish.

Mushroom sauce Prepare a mushroom sauce following the instructions on page 163. Toss small cooked new potatoes or diced old potatoes into the sauce to make a delicious side dish.

Tomato sauce Prepare a tomato sauce, following the recipe on page 165. Toss cooked courgettes, aubergines or cauliflower florets into the sauce and serve topped with chopped parsley and grated Parmesan cheese.

Simple serving suggestions

Buttered crumbs Toss browned breadcrumbs in melted butter. Add seasoning and some chopped fresh parsley or other herbs. Heat on Maximum (Full) power for about $\frac{1}{2}$–1 minute, or longer depending on the quantity, then sprinkle over cooked cauliflower, carrots, brussels sprouts, mushrooms or spinach.

Boiled egg Hard-boiled egg makes an excellent topping for vegetables. Cook the eggs conventionally, then cool them immediately in cold water. Separate the white and yolk: chop the white and sieve the yolk. Top cooked asparagus, French beans, courgettes, shredded cabbage or spinach with first the white, then the yolk.

Simple serving suggestions

Toss cooked potatoes in Parmesan herb butter to make a delicious side dish. Use cubed old potatoes, as here, or scrubbed new potatoes.

Top cooked broccoli with an egg sauce. Prepare the sauce before cooking the broccoli, cover and set aside. Heat the sauce on Maximum (Full) for $\frac{1}{2}$–1 minute, then pour over broccoli and serve. Garnish with hard-boiled egg.

GUIDE TO BLANCHING VEGETABLES

Vegetable	Quantity	Water (tablespoons)	Time in minutes on Maximum (Full)
Asparagus	450 g (1 lb)	3	3–4
Beans	450 g (1 lb)	6	5–6
Broccoli	450 g (1 lb)	6	5–6
Brussels sprouts	450 g (1 lb)	6	5–6
Cabbage, shredded	450 g (1 lb)	3	4–4$\frac{1}{2}$
Carrots, sliced	450 g (1 lb)	3	3–4
whole	450 g (1 lb)	3	6–7
Cauliflower florets	450 g (1 lb)	6	4$\frac{1}{2}$–5
Corn on the cob	4	3	5–6
Courgettes, sliced	450 g (1 lb)	3	3–3$\frac{1}{2}$
Leeks, sliced	450 g (1 lb)	3	5–6
Marrow, sliced or cubed	450 g (1 lb)	3	4–4$\frac{1}{2}$
Onions, quartered	4 medium	6	4–4$\frac{1}{2}$
Parsnips, cubed	450 g (1 lb)	3	3–4
Peas	450 g (1 lb)	3	4–4$\frac{1}{2}$
	1 kg (2 lb)	3	6–7
Spinach	450 g (1 lb)	—	3–3$\frac{1}{2}$
Turnips, cubed	450 g (1 lb)	3	3–4

GUIDE TO COOKING FROZEN VEGETABLES

Vegetable	Quantity	Cooking time in minutes on Maximum (Full)
Asparagus	225 g (8 oz)	6–7
	450 g (1 lb)	11
Beans, broad	225 g (8 oz)	8
	450 g (1 lb)	10
Beans, French or runner	225 g (8 oz)	7
	450 g (1 lb)	10
Broccoli	225 g (8 oz)	6–8
	450 g (1 lb)	8–10
Cabbage	225 g (8 oz)	6–7
	450 g (1 lb)	10–11
Carrots	225 g (8 oz)	7
	450 g (1 lb)	10
Cauliflower florets	225 g (8 oz)	5
	450 g (1 lb)	8
Corn kernels	225 g (8 oz)	4
	450 g (1 lb)	7 8
Corn on the cob	1	4–5
	2	7–8
Courgettes	225 g (8 oz)	4
	450 g (1 lb)	7
Diced mixed vegetables	225 g (8 oz)	5–6
	450 g (1 lb)	7–9
Peas	225 g (8 oz)	4
	450 g (1 lb)	8
Spinach, chopped, or leaf	225 g (8 oz)	7–8
	450 g (1 lb)	10–11
Root vegetable stewpack (mixed)	225 g (8 oz)	7
	450 g (1 lb)	10
Swedes	225 g (8 oz)	7
	450 g (1 lb)	11
Turnips	225 g (8 oz)	8
	450 g (1 lb)	12

GUIDE TO COOKING FRESH VEGETABLES

Vegetable	Quantity	Water	Preparation	Cooking time in minutes on Maximum (Full)	Method
Artichokes, globe	1 2 4	8 tablespoons 8 tablespoons 250 ml (8 fl oz)	Discard the tough, outer leaves. Snip the tips off the remaining leaves and cut off the stems. Cover to cook.	5–6 7–8 14–15	To test if cooked, at the minimum time, try to pull a leaf from the whole artichoke. If it comes away freely, the artichoke is cooked. Drain upside down before serving.
Asparagus	450 g (1lb)	6 tablespoons	Place in a dish, arranging any thicker stems to the outside of the dish and tender tips to the centre. Cover to cook.	12–14	Give the dish a half turn after 6 minutes cooking time.
Aubergines	2 medium, halved	2 tablespoons	Cover to cook.	7–9	Scoop out the cooked flesh from the halved aubergines and use as required.
	1 whole, peeled and cubed	2 tablespoons		5–6	Stir the cubed aubergine after 3 minutes cooking time.
Beans, all except thin French beans	450 g (1 lb)	8 tablespoons	Cover to cook.	14–16	Stir the beans twice during cooking. Test after the minimum time to see if cooked.
French beans	450 g (1 lb)	8 tablespoons	Cover to cook.	5–7	
Beetroot	2 medium 5 medium	8 tablespoons 8 tablespoons	Cover to cook.	12–16 22–25	Stir or rearrange halfway through the cooking time. Allow to stand for 10 minutes before peeling.
Broccoli	450 g (1 lb)	8 tablespoons	Place in a dish arranging the stalks to the outside and florets in the centre. Cover to cook.	10–12	Rearrange after 6 minutes.
Brussels sprouts	450 g (1 lb)	4 tablespoons	Trim away any damaged or coarse leaves and cut large sprouts in half. Cover to cook.	7–9	Stir the sprouts after 4 minutes cooking time.
Cabbage, shredded	450 g (1 lb)	8 tablespoons	Use a large dish and ensure that the cabbage fits loosely. Cover to cook.	8–9	Stir or rearrange halfway through the cooking time.
Carrots, whole sliced	450 g (1 lb) 1 kg (2 lb) 450 g (1 lb)	8 tablespoons 8 tablespoons	Cut carrots into 1-cm/$\frac{1}{2}$-in thick slices. Slicing carrots diagonally reduces the cooking time by 2 minutes. Cover to cook.	12–14 18–20 12–14	Stir or rearrange halfway through the cooking time.
Cauliflower, whole	1 medium about 675 g (1$\frac{1}{2}$ lb)	8 tablespoons	Cook whole cauliflower on Medium.	13–17	Turn a whole cauliflower or florets halfway through the cooking time. Allow whole cauliflower to stand for 5 minutes after cooking.
florets	450 g (1 lb)	8 tablespoons	Cover to cook.	10–12	

GUIDE TO COOKING FRESH VEGETABLES

Vegetable	Quantity	Water	Preparation	Cooking time in minutes on Maximum (Full)	Method
Celery, whole or sliced	450 g (1 lb)	4 tablespoons	Cover to cook.	14–16	Turn or stir halfway through the cooking time.
Chicory, whole	4 medium	4 tablespoons	Cover to cook.	5–8	Rearrange halfway through the cooking time.
Corn on the cob	1 2 4 6	3 tablespoons 3 tablespoons 5 tablespoons 5 tablespoons	Cover to cook.	4–5 7–8 13–15 17–20	Cook the corn in the husk, if liked, with no extra water. Rearrange halfway through the cooking time if cooking 4–6.
Courgettes, sliced whole	450 g (1 lb) 6 small	— —	Cover to cook.	5–6 7	Dot lightly with 25 g (1 oz) butter before cooking. Stir or rearrange halfway through the cooking time.
Leeks, sliced	450 g (1 lb)	4 tablespoons	Cover to cook.	10–12	Stir halfway through cooking.
Marrow, sliced	450 g (1 lb)	—	Cover with greaseproof paper before cooking. Add salt after cooking.	8–10	Stir halfway through the cooking time.
Mushrooms, whole or sliced	225 g (8 oz) 450 g (1 lb)	2 tablespoons water or butter	Cover to cook.	2–4 4–6	Stir halfway through the cooking time.
Onions, whole or quartered	4 medium 8 medium	4 tablespoons	Cover to cook.	10–12 14–16	Stir halfway through the cooking time.
Parsnips, cubed	450 g (1 lb)	8 tablespoons	Cover to cook.	8–10	Stir halfway through cooking.
Peas, shelled	450 g (1 lb) 1 kg (2 lb)	8 tablespoons	Cover to cook.	9–11 12–14	Stir halfway through the cooking time. Add 15–25 g ($\frac{1}{2}$–1 oz) butter after cooking and allow to stand for 5 minutes before serving.
Potatoes, peeled and quartered baked in skins	450 g (1 lb) 1 2 3 4	8 tablespoons — — — —	Cover to cook. Prick thoroughly and cook on absorbent kitchen paper.	10–14 4–6 6–8 8–12 12–16	Stir twice during cooking. Potatoes may still feel firm when cooked. Leave to stand for 3–4 minutes to soften.
Spinach	450 g (1 lb)	—	Wash but do not dry before cooking. Place in a roasting bag and secure loosely with string.	6–8	Drain well before serving.
Tomatoes, halved	2	—	Add a knob of butter and a little pepper to each half before cooking. Cover to cook.	1–1$\frac{1}{2}$	
Turnips, cubed	450 g (1 lb) (2–3 medium)	8 tablespoons	Cover to cook.	12–14	Stir twice during cooking.

Cabbage with Caraway

Serves 4
3 tablespoons water
salt
350 g (12 oz) cabbage, stalk
  removed and finely shredded
1 tablespoon caraway seeds
15 g (½ oz) butter

Preparation time: about 5
minutes
Cooking time: about 8 minutes
Microwave setting: Maximum
(Full)

1. Place the water and salt in a
large bowl. Place the cabbage
on top. Cover and cook for 8
minutes. Halfway through
cooking, stir in the caraway
seeds.

2. Stir the butter into the
cabbage until melted.

Parsnips with Parsley

Serves 4–6
3 tablespoons water
salt
1 tablespoon chopped fresh
  parsley
750 g (1½ lb) parsnips, peeled
  and quartered
15 g (½ oz) butter

Preparation time: about 8
minutes
Cooking time: about 8 minutes,
plus standing
Microwave setting: Maximum
(Full)

1. Place the water, salt and
parsley in a large bowl. Place the
parsnips on top. Cover and
cook for 8 minutes, stirring
halfway through cooking.

2. Leave to stand, covered, for 5
minutes. Strain, then stir in the
butter until melted.

Vichy Carrots

Serves 4
3 tablespoons cold water
1 teaspoon caster sugar
450 g (1 lb) carrots, peeled and
  thinly sliced
25 g (1 oz) butter, cut into
  pieces
1 tablespoon chopped fresh
  parsley

Preparation time: about 10
minutes
Cooking time: about 6–9
minutes
Microwave setting: Maximum
(Full)

1. Place the water, sugar and
carrots in a medium bowl.
Cover and cook for 6–9 minutes
or until tender, stirring halfway
through cooking.

2. Drain and stir in the butter
until melted. Fold in the parsley.
Serve hot. If serving with the
Guard of Honour (page 111),
stand covered until the corn has
heated and then drain, and
complete the recipe.

Braised Celery

Serves 4
3 tablespoons water
salt
450 g (1 lb) head of celery,
  trimmed and stalks halved
1 medium onion, peeled and
  thinly sliced
150 ml (¼ pint) hot chicken
  stock
25 g (1 oz) butter, cut into
  pieces
1 teaspoon chopped fresh
  parsley
freshly ground pepper

Preparation time: about 5
minutes
Cooking time: about 11
minutes, plus standing
Microwave setting: Maximum
(Full)

1. Place the water and salt in an
oblong or oval casserole dish.
Place half the celery in the dish
and spread over the onion.
Cover the onion with the
remaining celery. Cover and
cook for 8 minutes. After 5
minutes of cooking, rearrange
the vegetables.

2. Mix together the hot stock,
butter, parsley, and seasoning.
Pour over the celery, cover and
cook for 3 minutes. Leave to
stand, covered, for 3–4 minutes
before serving.

Minted Peas

Serves 4
3 tablespoons water
1 teaspoon chopped fresh mint
salt
450 g (1 lb) frozen peas
25 g (1 oz) butter, diced

Preparation time: about 3
minutes
Cooking time: about 7–9
minutes
Microwave setting: Maximum
(Full)

1. Place the water, mint, salt and
peas in a medium bowl. Cover
and cook for 7–9 minutes,
stirring halfway through
cooking.

2. Drain the peas and toss in the
butter.

Green Beans

Serves 4
450 g (1 lb) frozen whole green
  beans
salt

Preparation time: about 2
minutes
Cooking time: about 9 minutes,
plus standing
Microwave setting: Maximum
(Full)

1. Place the beans in a medium
bowl. Cover and cook for 9
minutes, stirring halfway
through cooking. Leave to
stand, covered, for 2 minutes.
Drain off all excess water.

2. Sprinkle with salt and toss
before serving.

Boiled Potatoes

Serves 4
3 tablespoons cold water
pinch of salt
4 potatoes, total weight 750 g
  (1½ lb), peeled and cut in half
25 g (1 oz) butter, cut into
  pieces
1 tablespoon chopped fresh
  parsley

Preparation time: about 10
minutes
Cooking time: about 9 minutes,
plus standing
Microwave setting: Maximum
(Full)

1. Place the water and salt in a
large bowl. Add the potatoes,
cover and cook for 9 minutes,
stirring halfway through
cooking. Leave to stand,
covered, for 8–10 minutes.

Sweetcorn

Serves 4–6
2 × 300 g (11½ oz) cans
   sweetcorn kernels, drained
25 g (1 oz) butter, cut into
   pieces

Preparation time: about 3
minutes
Cooking time: about 6 minutes
Microwave setting: Maximum
(Full)

1. Place the sweetcorn in a
casserole dish, cover and cook
for 6 minutes, stirring halfway
through.

2. Stir in the butter until melted,
then serve at once.

*Clockwise: Braised celery; Sweetcorn;
Minted peas; Parsnips with parsley;
Green beans; Vichy carrots; Boiled
potatoes; Cabbage with caraway*

Buttered Jerusalem Artichokes

Serves 4
3 tablespoons water
salt
450 g (1 lb) Jerusalem
*   artichokes, peeled and sliced*
40 g (1½ oz) butter, cut into
*   pieces*
1 tablespoon chopped fresh
*   parsley, to garnish*

Preparation time: about 10
minutes
Cooking time: about 9 minutes,
plus standing
Microwave setting: Maximum
(Full)

1. Place the water, salt and
artichokes in a large bowl.
Cover and cook for 9 minutes,
stirring halfway through
cooking.

2. Leave to stand, covered, for 5
minutes.

3. Drain and toss in the butter.
Garnish with parsley.

Croquette Potatoes

Serves 4
3 tablespoons water
salt
600 g (1¼ lb) potatoes, peeled
*   and chopped*
25 g (1 oz) butter
½ tablespoon milk
freshly ground pepper
1 egg, lightly beaten
75 g (3 oz) toasted
*   breadcrumbs*

Preparation time: about 10
minutes, plus chilling
Cooking time: 11½–13 minutes,
plus standing
Microwave setting: Maximum
(Full)

1. Place the water and salt in a
large bowl. Add the potatoes,
cover and cook for 9 minutes.
Leave to stand, covered, for 5
minutes.

2. Beat the butter, milk and salt
and pepper to taste into the
potatoes. Roll the mixture into

Cauliflower Cheese

16 cork shapes. Chill for 30 minutes for a firmer texture.

3. Coat the croquettes with egg and roll in breadcrumbs. Place on a piece of paper towel, in a circle. Prick with a fork. Cook, uncovered, for 2½–4 minutes, turning over halfway through cooking.

Serves 4
*1 cauliflower, prepared weight
    750 g (1½ lb)*
Sauce:
25 g (1 oz) butter
25 g (1 oz) plain flour
300 ml (½ pint) milk
salt
freshly ground black pepper
*1 teaspoon made English
    mustard*
*50 g (2 oz) Cheddar cheese,
    grated*
*chopped fresh parsley, to
    garnish*

Preparation time: about 10 minutes
Cooking time: about 15 minutes
Microwave setting: Maximum (Full)

1. Rinse the cauliflower in water and place in a medium bowl. Cover and cook for 10 minutes, turning the cauliflower over halfway through cooking. Keep hot while making the sauce.

2. Place the butter in a 600 ml (1 pint) jug. Cook for 1 minute or

until the butter has melted.

3. Blend in the flour, milk, salt, pepper and mustard. Cook for 3 minutes, stirring every minute.

4. Stir in the cheese and cook for 1 minute.

5. Pour the sauce over the cauliflower and garnish with the parsley.

*From left to right: Buttered Jerusalem
artichokes; Croquette potatoes;
Cauliflower cheese*

Cabbage Parcels

Serves 4

1 small, tight green cabbage,
stalk removed
1 medium onion, peeled and
finely chopped
225 g (8 oz) tomatoes, skinned
and chopped
15 g (½ oz) butter
4 tablespoons plain flour
300 ml (½ pint) hot beef stock
½ teaspoon Worcestershire sauce
½ teaspoon dried mixed herbs
salt
freshly ground pepper
4 tablespoons cooked rice

Preparation time: about 15
minutes
Cooking time: about 13
minutes, plus standing
Microwave setting: Maximum
(Full)

1. Cook the whole cabbage
conventionally for 4 minutes in
boiling salted water. Drain.

2. Gently peel off 8 leaves. Use
the remaining cabbage in a
vegetable soup.

3. Place the onion, tomatoes
and butter in a medium bowl.
Cover and cook for 4 minutes.

4. Stir in the flour, stock,
Worcestershire sauce, herbs,
salt, pepper and rice. Cook
uncovered for 2 minutes.

5. Place a little of the mixture on
each of the cabbage leaves. Fold
the cabbage leaves over to make
a parcel and tie with string.

6. Arrange the cabbage parcels
in a shallow dish, cover and
cook for 7 minutes, turning the
dish round halfway through
cooking.

7. Leave the cabbage parcels to
stand for 5 minutes.

Broccoli with Cheese Sauce

Serves 4

3 tablespoons water
salt
450 g (1 lb) fresh broccoli, stalks
halved lengthways
chopped fresh parsley, to
garnish (optional)
Sauce:
25 g (1 oz) butter
25 g (1 oz) plain flour
300 ml (½ pint) milk
1 teaspoon made English
mustard
salt
freshly ground black pepper
50 g (2 oz) Cheddar cheese,
grated

Preparation time: about 10
minutes
Cooking time: about 11
minutes, plus standing
Microwave setting: Maximum
(Full)

1. Place the water and salt in a
large bowl. Arrange the broccoli
in the bowl with stalks standing
upwards. Cover with cling film
and cook for 7 minutes. Set
aside, covered.

2. Place the butter in a jug. Cook
for 1 minute or until melted.
Blend in the flour, milk, mustard
and salt and pepper to taste.
Cook for 3 minutes, stirring
every minute. Stir in the cheese.
Cook for 1 minute.

3. Drain the broccoli. Pour over
the sauce and garnish with
parsley (if using).

Cook's Tip

Frozen broccoli may be used
instead of fresh.

Cabbage parcels; Broccoli with cheese sauce

Stuffed Onions

Serves 4
*4 large onions, total weight 1 kg
(2 lb), peeled*
*25 g (1 oz) fresh white
breadcrumbs*
¼ teaspoon dried sage
¼ teaspoon dried tarragon
¼ teaspoon dried parsley
*1 teaspoon Worcestershire
sauce*
½ egg, lightly beaten
salt
freshly ground black pepper
15 g (½ oz) butter

Preparation time: about 25
minutes
Cooking time: about 14–16
minutes, plus standing
Microwave setting: Maximum
(Full)

1. Remove the centres from the onions, using a grapefruit knife, leaving shells about 2–3 layers deep. Set the shells aside, and chop the centres.

2. Mix the chopped onion with the breadcrumbs, sage, tarragon, parsley, Worcestershire sauce, egg, and salt and pepper to taste.

3. Stuff each onion with the breadcrumb mixture and top with a small knob of butter.

4. Arrange the onions in a circle on a plate and cook, uncovered, for 14–16 minutes, rearranging halfway through cooking. Leave to stand for 3 minutes before serving.

Stuffed Jacket Potatoes

Serves 4
*4 medium potatoes, washed
and dried*
*75 g (3 oz) Cheddar cheese,
grated*
1 tablespoon tomato purée
*1 tablespoon Worcestershire
sauce*
15 g (½ oz) butter
salt
freshly ground black pepper
*chopped fresh parsley, to
garnish*

Preparation time: about 10
minutes
Cooking time: about 16
minutes, plus standing
Microwave setting: Maximum
(Full)

1. Place the potatoes on a paper towel, prick them and cook for 6 minutes.

2. Turn the potatoes over and turn the paper towel round. Cook for a further 7 minutes.

3. Wrap each potato tightly in foil and leave to stand for 5 minutes.

4. Cut a lengthways slice off the top of each potato. Scoop out the flesh, leaving the potato shell intact.

5. Mix the potato flesh with the cheese, tomato purée, Worcestershire sauce, butter, salt and pepper.

6. Pile the mixture back into the potato jackets and reheat for 3 minutes. Serve garnished with parsley.

Stuffed onions; Stuffed jacket potatoes

Courgette Shells with Bacon

Serves 4

4 courgettes, halved lengthways
1 bacon rasher, rinds removed and chopped
1 small onion, peeled and finely chopped
1 teaspoon dried mixed herbs
25–50 g (1–2 oz) fresh white breadcrumbs
1 egg yolk
4 tablespoons stock
salt
freshly ground black pepper

Preparation time: about 10 minutes
Cooking time: about 12 minutes, plus standing
Microwave setting: Maximum (Full)

Courgette shells with bacon; Peppers with savoury rice

1. Using a teaspoon, scoop the centres from the courgette halves. Set the shells aside, and chop the scooped-out flesh; there should be about 25 g (1 oz).

2. Place the courgette flesh, bacon, onion and herbs in a small bowl. Cover and cook for 3 minutes. Stir in the breadcrumbs, egg yolk, stock, and salt and pepper to taste.

3. Fill one half of each courgette shell with the stuffing. Replace the other half and secure with wooden cocktail sticks.

4. Place in a shallow dish, cover and cook for 9 minutes, rearranging halfway through cooking. Leave to stand for 3–4 minutes before serving.

Peppers with Savoury Rice

Serves 4

1 onion, peeled and finely chopped
25 g (1 oz) butter
50 g (2 oz) ham, finely chopped
1 garlic clove, peeled and crushed
1 tablespoon tomato purée
1 teaspoon dried mixed herbs
salt
freshly ground pepper
100 g (4 oz) long-grain rice
450 ml (¾ pint) hot beef stock
4 green peppers, cored, seeded and blanched

Preparation time: about 10 minutes
Cooking time: about 23 minutes, plus standing
Microwave setting: Maximum (Full)

1. Place the onion, butter, ham, garlic, tomato purée, herbs, salt and pepper in a large bowl. Cover and cook for 4 minutes.

2. Stir in the rice and hot stock, cover and cook for 9 minutes.

3. Leave to stand, covered, for about 10 minutes.

4. Stand the peppers in a casserole. Stuff the peppers with the rice, cover and cook for 5 minutes.

5. Turn the casserole round and cook for 5 minutes.

6. Leave the peppers to stand, covered, for 5 minutes before serving.

Stuffed Marrow

Serves 4

1 medium marrow, about
750 g (1½ lb), halved and
seeds removed
1 medium onion, peeled and
finely chopped
1 small carrot, peeled and
grated
2 tomatoes, skinned and
chopped
1 teaspoon dried mixed herbs
75 g (3 oz) fresh brown
breadcrumbs
350 g (12 oz) minced beef
1 teaspoon Worcestershire
sauce
1 tablespoon tomato purée
salt
freshly ground black pepper
Sauce:
25 g (1 oz) butter
25 g (1 oz) plain flour
300 ml (½ pint) milk
salt
freshly ground black pepper

Preparation time: 20 minutes
Cooking time: about 30½
minutes, plus grilling
Microwave setting: Maximum
(Full)

1. Place the marrow halves in a shallow dish. Cover and cook for 14 minutes.

2. Drain the marrow, cover and set aside.

3. Place the onion, carrot, tomatoes and herbs in a large bowl. Cover and cook for 5 minutes.

4. Stir in the breadcrumbs, meat, Worcestershire sauce, tomato purée, salt and pepper. Cover and cook for 4 minutes. Set aside.

5. To make the sauce, place the butter in a 600 ml (1 pint) jug. Cook for 1 minute or until melted.

6. Blend in the flour, milk, salt and pepper. Cook for 3 minutes, stirring every minute.

7. Fill the marrow halves with the stuffing. Spoon over the sauce, and cook for 3½ minutes.

8. If preferred, brown under a preheated conventional grill before serving.

Stuffed marrow; Stuffed aubergines

Stuffed Aubergines

Serves 4

2 medium aubergines, about
250 g (9 oz) each
salt
oil, for brushing
1 medium onion, peeled and
finely chopped
4 streaky bacon rashers, rinds
removed, diced
50 g (2 oz) mushrooms,
chopped
100 g (4 oz) butter
2 tablespoons tomato purée
1 tablespoon chopped fresh
parsley
2 teaspoons Worcestershire
sauce
dash of Angostura bitters
(optional)
1 garlic clove, peeled and
crushed
freshly ground pepper
75 g (3 oz) brown
breadcrumbs
50 g (2 oz) Cheddar cheese,
finely grated

Preparation time: about 20
minutes, plus salting
Cooking time: about 16¼
minutes
Microwave setting: Maximum
(Full)

1. Cut the aubergines in half lengthways. Sprinkle the cut edges with salt and set aside. After 30 minutes, rinse them with cold water and pat dry.

2. Scoop out the flesh and dice it. Brush shell with oil.

3. Place the onion in a large bowl. Cover and cook for 2½ minutes. Stir in the bacon and diced aubergines. Cover and cook for 4 minutes.
4. Stir in the mushrooms, butter, tomato purée, chopped parsley, Worcestershire sauce, Angostura bitters (if using), garlic, salt and pepper. Cover and cook for 3 minutes. Leave to stand, covered.

5. Place the aubergine shells on a plate or shallow casserole dish, cover and cook for 2 minutes. Turn each shell around, cover and cook for 2 minutes.

6. Stir the breadcrumbs into the stuffing. Spoon the stuffing into the shells. Cook for 2 minutes.

7. Sprinkle the grated cheese on top. Cook for 45 seconds or until the cheese has melted.

Potato Salad

Serves 4
3 tablespoons water
salt
750 g (1½ lb) potatoes, peeled and cut into 1 cm (½ inch) cubes
200 ml (7 fl oz) mayonnaise
1 tablespoon chopped fresh chives, to garnish

Preparation time: about 10 minutes, plus cooling
Cooking time: 9–10 minutes, plus standing
Microwave setting: Maximum (Full)

1. Place the water and salt in a large bowl. Place the potatoes on top. Cover and cook for 9–10 minutes, stirring halfway through cooking.

2. Leave to stand, covered, for 15 minutes. Remove the cover and gently stir with a fork to separate the potato cubes. Leave to stand until cold.

3. Stir in the mayonnaise and sprinkle with chives.

Clockwise: Salami and tomato pizza; Potato salad; Onion and potato bake; Vegetarian curry

Salami and Tomato Pizza

Serves 4
50 ml (2 fl oz) milk
10 g (¼ oz) dried yeast
pinch of caster sugar
25 g (1 oz) butter
1 egg, beaten
175 g (6 oz) plain flour, sifted
   with a pinch of salt
Topping:
1 garlic clove, peeled and
   crushed
1 medium onion, peeled and
   finely chopped
15 g (½ oz) butter
2 tablespoons tomato purée
350 g (12 oz) fresh tomatoes,
   skinned and chopped, or
   350 g (12 oz) canned
   tomatoes
1 tablespoon dried oregano
salt
freshly ground black pepper
75–100 g (3–4 oz) salami,
   thinly sliced
75 g (3 oz) Cheddar cheese,
   grated
6 anchovies, drained
6 stuffed green olives, halved

Preparation time: about 20
minutes, plus rising
Cooking time: about 11
minutes
Microwave setting: Maximum
(Full)

1. Place the milk in 300 ml (½ pint) jug. Cook for 15 seconds. Sprinkle the yeast and sugar over the milk and leave to stand for 10 minutes, or until frothy.

2. Place the butter in a small bowl. Cook for 45 seconds or until melted.

3. Pour the yeast mixture, melted butter and egg into the flour and salt. Knead for 10 minutes or until smooth. Shape into a ball and place in a bowl.

4. Cover and cook for 30 seconds. Leave covered for 10 minutes.

5. Remove the cover and leave dough to rise until it has doubled in size; this will take about 20 minutes.

6. To make the topping, place the garlic, onion and butter in a medium bowl. Cover and cook for 3 minutes. Stir in the tomato purée, tomatoes, oregano, salt and pepper. Cook for 2 minutes. Set aside.

7. Knead the dough and roll it out to make a 23 cm (9 inch) circle. Place on a plate and cook for 2½ minutes.

8. Spread the tomato and onion topping over the pizza base and cover with the salami slices and grated cheese. Arrange the anchovies on top in a lattice pattern. Garnish with halved olives. Cook for 2 minutes and serve straightaway.

Onion and Potato Bake

Serves 4
450 g (1 lb) onions, peeled and
   thinly sliced
600 g (1¼ lb) potatoes, peeled
   and thinly sliced
salt
freshly ground black pepper
2 teaspoons dried mixed herbs
scant 75 ml (3 fl oz) milk
parsley sprigs, to garnish

Preparation time: about 12
minutes
Cooking time: about 14
minutes
Microwave setting: Maximum
(Full)

1. Place the onions in a medium bowl, cover and cook for 5 minutes, stirring halfway through cooking.

2. Layer the potatoes and onions in a 1.2 litre (2 pint) casserole dish. Sprinkle each layer with a little salt, pepper and herbs. Finish with a layer of potatoes. Pour in the milk.

3. Stand the dish on a plate. Cover and cook for 9 minutes, turning round halfway through cooking.

4. Garnish with sprigs of parsley.

Vegetarian Curry

Serves 3–4
1 tablespoon vegetable oil
1 small green pepper, cored,
   seeded and finely chopped
2 carrots, peeled and finely
   sliced
1 celery stick, finely chopped
2 large onions, peeled and
   finely chopped
3 tomatoes, skinned and
   chopped
1 tablespoon lemon juice
1 large eating apple, peeled,
   cored and chopped
25 g (1 oz) dark brown sugar
2 tablespoons curry powder
2 teaspoons turmeric
2 tablespoons desiccated
   coconut
25 g (1 oz) plain flour
300 ml (½ pint) hot vegetable
   stock
2 tablespoons sultanas
25 g (1 oz) peanuts
salt
freshly ground black pepper

Preparation time: about 20
minutes
Cooking time: about 19
minutes
Microwave setting: Maximum
(Full)

1. Place the oil, green pepper, carrots and celery in a bowl. Cover and cook for 5 minutes.

2. Stir in the onions, tomatoes, lemon juice, apple, sugar, curry powder, turmeric and coconut. Cover and cook for 10 minutes, stirring halfway through cooking.

3. Stir in the flour, hot stock, sultanas, peanuts, salt and pepper. Cover and cook for 4 minutes, stirring halfway through cooking.

4. Serve with brown rice.

RICE, PASTA & PULSES

Rice, pasta and pulses can be turned into such a wide variety of dishes, from authentic Italian first courses to simple side dishes and delicious supper-time specials. As well as all the basic cooking instructions that you need, this chapter provides lots of good ideas and a selection of interesting dishes.

Rice

All types of rice cook very well in the microwave. The great saving is not on the timing but on the washing up and on the effort involved. With conventional cooking methods there is always the risk of the rice boiling over or sticking to the base of the pan; in the microwave there is no danger of sticking and, given that you use a large casserole or bowl, the rice will not boil over. The rice should be lightly salted before cooking and, when all the water has been absorbed, it should be allowed to stand briefly after cooking. Before serving the grains are fluffed up with a fork.

Types of rice

Most supermarkets offer a wide variety of rice, from plain unprocessed long-grain white rice to exotic, dark-coloured, wild rice. The cooking times for the types of rice vary as does the quantity of liquid needed to tenderise them.

Dark-grained wild rice requires the longest cooking time and unprocessed brown rice takes longer than the varieties of white rice. Unprocessed white rice cooks quickly and easily, and far more successfully in the microwave than by traditional methods. Easy-cook rice is already partly cooked and when it is ready to serve the grains are all completely separate. Round-grain rice is used for making puddings, or certain types are used for risottos and they are usually sold as 'risotto rice'.

Different types of rice

Delicious ways with rice

Rice, like pasta, comes in various shapes and sizes from round-grain to long-grain and from wild to easy-cook, so you should have little trouble in providing plenty of variety in rice-type meals. Sometimes a meal calls for something a little more than plain boiled rice. Why not try one of the following suggestions.

Chicken or beef-flavoured rice Cook the rice according to the table, but using boiling stock – either beef or chicken.

Herb-flavoured rice Cook the rice according to the table but add a large pinch of dried mixed herbs before cooking.

Peppered rice Place $\frac{1}{2}$ chopped green pepper, $\frac{1}{2}$ chopped red pepper and 4 tablespoons chopped spring onions in a bowl with 25 g (1 oz) butter. Cook on Maximum (Full) for 2 minutes, then add to the rice ingredients before cooking.

Curried rice Place 25 g (1 oz) butter in a bowl with 2 small peeled and chopped onions, a pinch of ground nutmeg and $\frac{1}{2}$– 1 teaspoon curry powder, according to taste. Cook on Maximum (Full) for 3–4 minutes until soft and golden. Add to the cooked rice with 100 ml (4 fl oz) single cream and reheat on Maximum (Full) for 1 minute.

Risotto alla Milanese Place 25 g (1 oz) butter in a bowl with 1 peeled and finely chopped onion and a little powdered saffron or turmeric. Cook on Maximum (Full) for 2 minutes. Add to the rice, substituting an equal quantity of dry white wine for a quarter of the water.

Herbed orange rice Place 50 g (2 oz) butter in a bowl with 2 chopped sticks celery and 2 tablespoons grated onion. Cook on Maximum (Full) for 2 minutes. Add to the rice with 1 tablespoon grated orange rind and substitute an equal quantity of unsweetened orange juice for half of the water. Cook the rice according to the table.

Vegetable rice Cook the rice according to the table, then add 100 g (4 oz) cooked chopped French beans and 100 g (4 oz) cooked peas.

Cooking rice

1. The rice is placed in a large casserole or bowl with the water and seasoning. It is covered during cooking.

2. At the end of the cooking time the water has been absorbed but the rice is still very moist.

3. At the end of the standing time the grains have absorbed all the water and they are fluffed up with a fork before being served.

Pasta

Pasta comes in all shapes and sizes, as well as a variety of colours. The shape and size of the pasta is one of the key factors in determining its suitability for microwave cooking simply because it has to be cooked in a large container with plenty of boiling water. The smaller the shapes, the easier it is to fit them into a suitable cooking dish.

To ensure even cooking do not mix pasta of different sizes. Remember to use boiling water from the kettle and a large mixing bowl or very large casserole dish. The dish should be covered during cooking and a lid or large plate, or microwave-proof cling film can be used for this purpose.

The success with which it cooks in the microwave depends to a certain extent on the shape of the pasta. Lasagne is probably the most difficult pasta to accommodate and second comes spaghetti. These pasta shapes will need plenty of room in the cooking dish – a large oblong dish (if you can fit it on the turntable in the microwave) is ideal for lasagne and a mixing bowl will usually accommodate the spaghetti.

Smaller pasta shapes – shells, bows, spirals and stars – and

Different types of pasta

noodles cook very successfully in a large bowl of boiling water. They should be stirred halfway through cooking to ensure that the pieces do not stick together and the standing times should always be observed since they are important for tenderising the pasta.

Remember to take advantage of the partly cooked lasagne which is available if you are layering the pasta with a moist meat sauce and coating the dish with a cheese sauce.

Lastly, as with any conventional cooking method, it is best to be sensible and recognise the limitations of the microwave oven. If you are cooking a vast quantity of pasta, you are better off using the traditional method of boiling it in a large saucepan on the hob. However, the microwave reheats cooked pasta perfectly.

The pasta can be cooked in advance and drained, then rinsed in cold water to prevent it sticking. When it is thoroughly drained it should be placed in a dish suitable for microwave cooking and covered. Before serving, add butter or oil, and heat the pasta in the microwave on Maximum (Full) for a few minutes. Toss well and it is ready to serve – as good as it was freshly cooked.

Delicious ways with pasta

There is nothing more delicious than pasta tossed with a knob of butter to give a golden buttery glaze, seasoned to taste and topped with freshly grated Parmesan cheese. But here are more ideas to try – simply return the pasta to the oven with one of the following flavourings and cook for 1 minute on Maximum (Full).

Creamy pasta with garlic Add a little chopped garlic and 1–2 tablespoons double cream and toss well.

Herbed pasta Add a few snipped chives or parsley and toss well.

Caraway pasta For a crunchy effect, add a few poppy seeds and caraway seeds and toss well.

Almond pasta Place 25 g (1 oz) flaked almonds in a shallow dish with 15 g ($\frac{1}{2}$ oz) butter. Cook on Maximum (Full) for 2–4 minutes until golden brown. Add to the pasta and toss well.

Peppered pasta Place 1 small chopped green pepper and 1 small peeled and chopped onion in a bowl with 25 g (1 oz) butter and cook on Maximum (Full) for 2 minutes. Add to the pasta and toss well.

Creamed pasta Mix 1 egg yolk with 4 tablespoons double cream and stir into the hot cooked pasta. Do not reheat.

Mushroom and ham pasta Place 50 g (2 oz) sliced mushrooms in a bowl with 15 g ($\frac{1}{2}$ oz) butter. Cover and cook on Maximum (Full) for 2 minutes. Add to the pasta with 50 g (2 oz) shredded cooked ham and toss well. Dress with soured cream for a delicious result.

Pasta with chick peas Cook 1 chopped onion, 3 tablespoons olive oil and 1 chopped red or green chilli on Maximum (Full) for 3 minutes. Toss in a 425 g (15 oz) can chick peas with their liquid. Add the cooked pasta; heat for 2 minutes and serve.

Three-onion pasta Cook 1 small chopped onion in 50 g (2 oz) butter for 3 minutes. Toss into the pasta with 4 finely chopped spring onions and 2 tablespoons snipped chives. Top with soured cream.

Fresh pasta

Fresh pasta cooks very well in the microwave. You will need a large bowl of boiling salted water, with a little oil added. The cooking time depends more on the type of pasta than on the quantity which is cooked, noodles or shapes (usually twists, spirals, bows or shells) cook in about 5 minutes, with a standing time of 5 minutes, before the pasta can be drained and tossed with butter.

Stuffed fresh pasta (such as tortellini) requires longer cooking if the filling is made of raw meat or poultry. Cheese and spinach fillings do not require extra cooking.

GUIDE TO COOKING RICE AND PASTA

Rice	Quantity	Preparation	Cooking time in minutes on Maximum (Full)	Standing time
Brown rice	225 g (8 oz)	Place in a deep, covered container with 600 ml (1 pint) boiling salted water.	20–25	5–10
American easy-cook rice	225 g (8 oz)	Place in a deep, covered container with 600 ml (1 pint) boiling salted water.	12	5–10
Long-grain patna rice	225 g (8 oz)	Place in a deep, covered container with 600 ml (1 pint) boiling salted water and 1 tablespoon oil.	10	5–10

Pasta	Quantity	Preparation	Cooking time in minutes on Maximum (Full)	Standing time
Egg noodles and tagliatelle	225 g (8 oz)	Place in a deep, covered container with 600 ml (1 pint) boiling salted water and 1 tablespoon oil.	6	3
Macaroni	225 g (8 oz)	Place in a deep, covered container with 600 ml (1 pint) boiling salted water and 1 tablespoon oil.	10	3
Pasta shells and shapes	225 g (8 oz)	Place in a deep, covered container with 900 ml (1$\frac{1}{2}$ pints) salted water and 1 tablespoon oil.	12–14	5–10
Spaghetti	225 g (8 oz)	Hold in a deep, covered container with 1 litre (1$\frac{3}{4}$ pints) boiling salted water to soften, then submerge or break in half and add 1 tablespoon oil.	9–10	5–10

Pulses

Dried pulses can be cooked in the microwave without having to pre-soak them. The cooking time is as long as for conventional methods but the advantage is in avoiding the necessity for soaking in advance and in the fact that the pulses will not boil over if they are in a large cooking container.

Boiling is essential

It is essential when cooking red kidney beans to ensure that they come to a full boil and that the boiling is maintained for 5 minutes to ensure that the toxins which are naturally present in the beans are destroyed. You will have to watch the beans closely as they come to the boil and make absolutely sure that all the liquid boils, and that the boiling point is maintained.

Lentils

Lentils cook very well in the microwave and there are two options. they can be cooked in a very large bowl on Maximum (Full) or they can be cooked in an average-sized casserole or basin on a lower power. If you decide to cook them on Maximum (Full), then do make sure that there is plenty of room in the bowl for the water to froth up as the lentils cook. If you do not have a very large casserole, then cook the lentils according to the basic recipe, on Defrost and leave them to stand. This is ideal for lentil stuffings, burgers or pasties.

Canned pulses

Canned pulses are ready cooked and they require heating through – rather than cooking – before serving. They are ideally suited to microwave cooking and they can be added to other ingredients halfway through the cooking time or at the end of the time, depending on the dish.

Alternatively, they can be quickly heated in their canned juice, drained and tossed with butter and chopped parsley or spring onions to be served very simply instead of rice, pasta or potatoes.

Delicious ways with pulses

Plain cooked beans and other pulses can be seasoned or flavoured in a variety of ways. They can be served as a side dish for meat, fish or poultry, or as the main dish for a vegetarian meal.

Beans with tomatoes Cook 1 chopped onion with 1 crushed garlic clove in 4 tablespoons olive oil on Maximum (Full) for 3 minutes. Add cooked butter beans, season and stir in 4 peeled and chopped tomatoes. Heat on Maximum (Full) for 2 minutes, then serve.

Spiced chick peas Cook 1 tablespoon cumin seeds in 25 g (1 oz) butter, then pour over cooked chick peas. Sprinkle with chopped fresh coriander leaves.

Green lentils with nuts Toss a knob of butter, some chopped walnuts and chopped parsley into cooked green lentils.

GUIDE TO COOKING DRIED PULSES

Beans	Quantity	Preparation and cooking time
Kidney, flageolet, butter or haricot beans and chick peas	350 g (12 oz)	Place the beans in a large dish with a little chopped onion, celery and carrot. Cover with 1.4 litres (2½ pints) cold water and cook on Maximum (Full) for 20 minutes. Stir, re-cover and cook on Medium for 1 hour 30 minutes–1 hour 40 minutes, until tender. Top up the water as necessary during cooking, adding boiling water from a kettle.
Split peas	225 g (8 oz)	Place the split peas or lentils in a large dish with a little chopped onion, celery and 1 tablespoon lemon juice. Add a little salt and pepper to taste. Cover with 900 ml (1½ pints) water. Cover and cook on Maximum (Full) for 15 minutes. Stir and cook on Medium for 60–70 minutes, stirring every 30 minutes, until tender. Top up the water as necessary by adding boiling water from a kettle.
Lentils, red	225 g (8 oz)	Place in a large casserole or bowl and pour in 300 ml (½ pint) boiling water. Cover and cook on Maximum (Full) for about 15 minutes, or until all the water has been absorbed and the lentils are tender.
Lentils, green	225 g (8 oz)	Place in a large casserole dish or mixing bowl and pour in 600 ml (1 pint) boiling water. Cover and cook on Maximum (Full) for 35–40 minutes, or until the lentils are tender. Top up the water if necessary during cooking by adding extra boiling water from a kettle.

Risotto

Serves 4
50 g (2 oz) butter
1 large onion, peeled and finely
  chopped
¼ green pepper, cored, seeded
  and finely diced
¼ red pepper, cored, seeded and
  finely diced
1 tablespoon tomato puree
1 garlic clove, peeled and
  crushed
1 teaspoon dried mixed herbs
50 g (2 oz) mushrooms, finely
  chopped
400 g (14 oz) long-grain rice
**900 ml (1½ pints) hot chicken
  stock**
100 g (4 oz) ham, finely
  chopped
¼ teaspoon oil
salt
freshly ground black pepper
1 tablespoon chopped fresh
  parsley, to garnish

Preparation time: about 15
minutes
Cooking time: about 23
minutes, plus standing
Microwave setting: Maximum
(Full)

1. Place the butter, onion,
peppers, tomato puree, garlic,
herbs and mushrooms in a large
bowl. Cover and cook for 8
minutes, stirring halfway
through cooking.

2. Stir in the rice, stock, ham, oil,
salt, pepper, then cover and
cook for 15 minutes, stirring
halfway through cooking.

3. Remove from the cooker and
leave to stand, covered, for 8
minutes.

4. Stir the risotto with a fork,
and sprinkle with chopped
parsley. Hand grated Parmesan
cheese separately.

Kedgeree

Serves 4
750 g (1½ lb) smoked cod or
  haddock fillets
350 g (12 oz) long-grain rice
750 ml (1¼ pints) hot chicken
  stock
salt
¼ teaspoon oil
50 g (2 oz) butter, cubed
1 egg, beaten
2 hard-boiled egg whites,
  chopped
freshly ground black pepper
1 tablespoon single cream
To garnish:
chopped fresh parsley
1 hard-boiled egg white,
  chopped
1 hard-boiled egg yolk, sieved

Preparation time: about 15
minutes
Cooking time: about 23
minutes, plus standing
Microwave setting: Maximum
(Full)

1. Place the cod or haddock in a
shallow dish. Cover and cook
for 3½ minutes. Turn the dish
round and cook for a further 3½
minutes.

2. Flake the fish and set aside.

3. Place the rice, hot stock, salt
and oil into a large bowl. Cover
and cook for 12 minutes.

4. Leave to stand, covered, for 7
minutes.

5. Stir the flaked fish into the
rice with the butter, beaten egg,
chopped egg whites, pepper
and cream. Cover and cook for
4 minutes, stirring halfway
through cooking.

6. Garnish with the chopped
parsley, chopped egg white and
sieved egg yolk, arranged
decoratively over the kedgeree.

Paella

Serves 4
1 onion, peeled and chopped
2 garlic cloves, peeled and
  crushed
350 g (12 oz) long-grain rice
750 ml (1¼ pints) hot stock
few strands of saffron
salt
¼ teaspoon oil
100 g (4 oz) frozen peas
175 g (6 oz) cooked, peeled
  prawns
175 g (6 oz) cooked mussels
175 g (6 oz) cooked cockles
100 g (4 oz) cooked chicken
  meat, diced
2 tomatoes, skinned and
  chopped
cooked prawns in shells

Preparation time: about 15
minutes
Cooking time: about 30
minutes, plus standing
Microwave setting: Maximum
(Full)

1. Place the onion and garlic in a
large bowl, cover and cook for
6½ minutes, stirring halfway
through.

2. Stir the rice, stock, saffron,
salt and oil into the onion.
Cover and cook for 13 minutes,
stirring halfway through
cooking. Set aside, covered, for
13 minutes.

3. Meanwhile place the peas in a
medium bowl, cover and cook
for 3½ minutes. Stir in the
prawns, mussels, cockles,
chicken and tomatoes. Cover
and cook for 7½ minutes, stirring
halfway through cooking. Drain
and stir into the rice.

4. Serve hot, garnished with
prawns.

Curried Rice

Serves 4
1 large onion, peeled and finely
  chopped
1 garlic clove, peeled and
  crushed
50 g (2 oz) sultanas
2 tablespoons tomato purée
1 tablespoon mild curry powder
1 teaspoon mild chilli powder
1 teaspoon dried mixed herbs
salt
¼ teaspoon oil
350 g (12 oz) long-grain rice
750 ml (1¼ pints) boiling beef
  stock
bay leaves, to garnish

Preparation time: about 10
minutes
Cooking time: 18 minutes, plus
standing
Microwave setting: Maximum
(Full)

1. Place the onion in a large
bowl, cover and cook for 5
minutes, stirring halfway
through cooking.

2. Stir in the garlic, sultanas,
tomato purée, curry powder,
chilli powder, herbs, salt, oil,
rice and stock. Cover and cook
for 13 minutes. Leave to stand,
covered, for 10 minutes.

3. Fluff the rice with a fork.
Serve garnished with bay leaves.

*Clockwise: Risotto; Paella; Curried rice;
Kedgeree*

Spaghetti Bolognese

Serves 4

1 quantity cooked spaghetti
    (page 151)
4 streaky bacon rashers, rinds
    removed, chopped
1 medium onion, peeled and
    finely chopped
2 garlic cloves, peeled and
    crushed
1 celery stick, finely chopped
1 small carrot, peeled and
    grated
25 g (1 oz) plain flour
225 g (8 oz) minced beef
450 g (1 lb) tomatoes, skinned
    and chopped, or 1 × 400 g
    (14 oz) can tomatoes
4 tablespoons tomato purée
300 ml (½ pint) hot beef stock
100 g (4 oz) mushrooms,
    chopped
salt
freshly ground black pepper
2 teaspoons dried mixed herbs
1 tablespoon grated Parmesan
    cheese

Preparation time: about 20
minutes
Cooking time: about 20½
minutes
Microwave setting: Maximum
(Full)

1. Place the bacon, onion, garlic,
celery and carrot in a bowl.
Cover and cook for 7½ minutes,
stirring halfway through.

2. Stir in the flour, beef,
tomatoes and tomato purée.
Cover and cook for 3 minutes.

3. Stir in the stock, mushrooms,
salt, pepper and herbs. Cover.
Cook for 10 minutes, stirring
halfway through.

4. Place spaghetti in serving
dish, pour over sauce and
sprinkle cheese on top.

Stuffed Cannelloni

Serves 4
Stuffing:
1 small onion, peeled and finely
    chopped
1 garlic clove, peeled and
    crushed
1 teaspoon dried mixed herbs
225 g (8 oz) minced meat
2 tablespoons tomato purée
salt
freshly ground black pepper
Sauce:
1 small onion, peeled and finely
    chopped
1 garlic clove, peeled and
    crushed
1 teaspoon dried mixed herbs
25 g (1 oz) butter, cut into
    pieces
25 g (1 oz) plain flour
1 × 400 g (14 oz) can tomatoes
2 tablespoons tomato purée
8 cannelloni tubes

Preparation time: about 10
minutes
Cooking time: about 28½
minutes, plus standing
Microwave setting: Maximum
(Full)

1. To make the stuffing, place
the onion, garlic and herbs in a
bowl. Cover and cook for 4
minutes.

2. Stir in the meat, tomato
purée, and salt and pepper.
Cover and cook for 5 minutes,
stirring halfway through. Set
aside, covered.

3. Place the onion, garlic and
herbs in a medium bowl. Cover
and cook for 4 minutes.

4. Stir in the butter until melted.
Stir in the flour. Blend in the

Ham and Chicken Lasagne

Serves 4

1 × 350 g (12 oz) chicken
    portion
175 g (6 oz) green lasagne
½ teaspoon oil
900 ml (1½ pints) boiling water
salt
1 medium onion, peeled and
    finely chopped
1 small green pepper, cored,
    seeded and finely chopped
40 g (1½ oz) butter
40 g (1½ oz) plain flour
300 ml (½ pint) milk
150 ml (¼ pint) hot chicken
    stock
50 g (2 oz) cooked ham, finely
    chopped
freshly ground black pepper
40 g (1½ oz) Cheddar cheese,
    finely grated

Preparation time: about 15
minutes
Cooking time: about 29¼
minutes, plus standing and
grilling
Microwave setting: Maximum
(Full)

tomatoes and their liquid,
tomato purée, and salt and
pepper to taste. Cook,
uncovered, for 3½ minutes,
stirring halfway through
cooking. Purée.

5. Stuff the cannelloni tubes
with the meat stuffing. Place in a
1.2 litre (2 pint) casserole dish.

6. Pour over sauce. Cook,
covered, for 12 minutes.

7. Leave to stand for 3–4
minutes before serving.

1. Place the chicken in a shallow
dish. Cover and cook for 6
minutes. Set aside, covered, for
5 minutes. Discard skin and
bones, chop flesh. Set aside.

2. Place the lasagne in a 5 cm (2
inch) deep oblong casserole
dish. Pour over the oil, boiling
water and salt, completely
covering the lasagne with water.
Cover and cook for 9 minutes.

3. Set aside, covered, for 15
minutes. Drain the lasagne and
place it on a separate plate.

4. Place the onion, green
pepper and butter in a medium
bowl. Cover and cook for 7
minutes.

5. Sprinkle in the flour and
gradually stir in the milk. Cook
for 4 minutes. Blend in the hot
stock. Stir in the chicken, ham,
salt and pepper. Cook for 2
minutes.

6. Place half the drained lasagne
in a layer at the bottom of the
casserole dish. Pour over half
the sauce. Place the remaining
lasagne over the sauce and
cover with the remaining sauce.
Sprinkle the cheese on top and
cook for 1¼ minutes or until the
cheese has melted.

7. Brown under a preheated
conventional grill.

*Clockwise: Spaghetti bolognese;
Macaroni cheese; Stuffed cannelloni;
Ham and chicken lasagne*

Macaroni Cheese

Serves 4

1.2 litres (2 pints) boiling water
¼ teaspoon oil
225 g (8 oz) macaroni
Sauce:
50 g (2 oz) butter
50 g (2 oz) plain flour
600 ml (1 pint) milk
⅓ teaspoon English mustard
salt
freshly ground black pepper
150 g (5 oz) Cheddar cheese,
*   finely grated*

Preparation time: about 10 minutes
Cooking time: about 23–25 minutes, plus grilling
Microwave setting: Maximum (Full)

1. Place the water, oil and macaroni in a large bowl. Cover and cook for 15 minutes. Set aside, covered.

2. Place the butter in a jug. Cook, uncovered, for 1 minute or until the butter has melted. Stir in the flour, then blend in the milk, mustard and salt and pepper to taste. Cook, uncovered, for 5–7 minutes, stirring every minute.

3. Stir in 75 g (3 oz) of the cheese. Drain the macaroni and fold into the cheese sauce. Pour into a casserole.

4. Sprinkle over the remaining cheese. Cook, uncovered, for 2 minutes, or until the cheese has melted. Or, if desired, brown under a preheated conventional grill.

Vegetable and Cashew Rice

Serves 4
50 g (2 oz) butter
1 onion, peeled and chopped
1 garlic clove, peeled and
    crushed
225 g (8 oz) long-grain brown
    rice
600 ml (1 pint) boiling water
½ teaspoon ground turmeric
1 teaspoon sea salt
1 large carrot, peeled and cut
    into thin strips
225 g (8 oz) French beans, cut
    into 5 cm (2 inch) pieces
1 small red pepper, cored,
    seeded and chopped
3 tablespoons water
4 tomatoes, peeled and
    quartered
freshly ground black pepper
175 g (6 oz) toasted cashew
    nuts

Preparation time: about 10 minutes
Cooking time: about 29 minutes, plus standing
Microwave setting: Maximum (Full)

1. Place the butter in a large casserole and cook for 1 minute to melt. Add the onion, garlic, rice, water, turmeric and salt, blending well. Cover and cook for 20 minutes until tender. Leave to stand for 5 minutes, then drain thoroughly if necessary.

2. Meanwhile, place the carrot, beans and red pepper in a bowl with the cold water. Cover and cook for 5 minutes, until tender.

3. Drain the vegetables, then fold into the rice mixture with the tomatoes, pepper to taste and half the cashew nuts.

4. Cook for 3 minutes. Serve sprinkled with the remaining cashew nuts.

Pillau Rice

Serves 4
1 onion, chopped
50 g (2 oz) butter
2 cardamoms
1 bay leaf
1 cinnamon stick
225 g/8 oz basmati rice
salt
600 ml (1 pint) boiling water
1 tablespoon cumin seeds

Preparation time: about 5 minutes
Cooking time: 19–20 minutes
Microwave setting: Maximum (Full)

1. Place the onion and half the butter in a dish. Cover and cook for 3 minutes.

2. Add the cardamoms, bay leaf, cinnamon stick and rice. Sprinkle in a good pinch of salt, then pour in the water. Cover the dish and cook the rice for 15 minutes. Set the rice aside for 5 minutes.

3. Place the remaining butter and cumin seeds in a small basin and cook for 1–2 minutes, until the butter has melted and is sizzling and very hot.

4. Fork up the grains of rice, then pour the hot butter and cumin seeds over them and serve at once. If you prefer, remove the whole spices before serving.

Curried Black-eye Beans

Serves 4
350 g (12 oz) dried black-eye
    beans
1.5 litres (2½ pints) cold chicken
    stock
25 g (1 oz) butter
2 carrots, peeled and cut into
    thin strips
1 onion, peeled and finely
    chopped
1 celery stick, finely chopped
2–3 teaspoons curry powder
2 tablespoons plain flour
4 tablespoons tomato purée
300 ml (½ pint) beef stock
2 tablespoons Worcestershire
    sauce
50 g (2 oz) sultanas
salt
freshly ground black pepper

Preparation time: about 10 minutes
Cooking time: about 1¼–1½ hours
Microwave setting: Medium and Maximum (Full)

1. Place the beans and stock in a large casserole. Cover and cook for 20 minutes.

2. Stir, re-cover and cook on Medium for 45–60 minutes until tender, stirring occasionally. Drain thoroughly.

3. Place the butter in a bowl and cook on Maximum for 1 minute or until melted. Stir in the carrots, onion and celery. Cover and cook for 4 minutes, stirring once.

4. Stir in the curry powder and cook for 1 minute. Blend in the flour. Gradually add the tomato purée, beef stock, Worcestershire sauce, sultanas, salt and pepper to taste. Cook for 5–7 minutes, stirring every 2 minutes until thickened.

5. Stir in the beans. Cook for 2 minutes to heat through. Serve with an Indian meal.

Cook's Tip

Basmati rice should be washed in several changes of cold water before cooking so as to remove as much excess starch as possible. This unprocessed rice has a delicate flavour and fine scent which is characteristic of pillau. Take care not to damage the grains as you wash the rice.

Curried black-eye beans; Vegetable and cashew rice

SAUCES

A good sauce makes a simple meal special and with a microwave there is no excuse for lumpy sauce or gravy. The sauce does not stick to a hot pan and burn, nor does it require the constant attention necessary for traditional cooking. Follow the advice on these pages to adapt your favourite sauces to microwave cooking.

Sauce-making in the microwave is far simpler than by traditional methods and with a greater chance of success. Since the sauce is cooked in a basin or jug it does not stick and burn to the base of a hot saucepan. It is also less likely to form lumps if it is whisked regularly during cooking. Traditional principles can be applied with slight adaptation and one-stage sauces can be cooked with great ease. Even the more difficult sauces which are based on a liaison of eggs and butter, or those thickened with egg, can be cooked in the microwave.

Cooking utensils

Instead of saucepans and wooden spoons, when making a sauce in the microwave you will need a large basin or suitable jug and a whisk. A 600 ml (1 pint) basin is large enough for whisking 300 ml (½ pint) sauce but if you are preparing 600 ml (1 pint) then use a 1.1 litre (2 pint) jug or a basin.

Basins and jugs replace saucepans for microwave-cooked sauces.

One-stage Savoury White Sauce

This is a basic recipe for a one-stage sauce, thickened with flour and enriched with a knob of butter. It can be flavoured with chopped herbs, cheese, onion, eggs or anchovies in the same way as a Béchamel Sauce (see page 162) which is prepared by the roux method.

Makes 600 ml (1 pint)
40 g (1½ oz) plain flour
600 ml (1 pint) milk
salt
freshly ground white or black pepper
25 g (1 oz) butter

Preparation time: 5 minutes
Cooking time: 7–10 minutes
Microwave setting: Maximum (Full)

1. Place the flour in a large basin or jug. Gradually pour in the milk, whisking to make a smooth paste. As the mixture becomes smooth you can add the milk more quickly.

2. Add a little seasoning and the butter. Give the sauce a quick whisk, then cook for 3–4 minutes, or until the edges of the sauce have started to thicken slightly round the basin.

3. Whisk the sauce thoroughly, scraping any set bits of flour from the base and sides of the basin. Remember, do not put a metal whisk in the microwave.

4. Cook for a further 4–6 minutes, until the sauce is boiling and thickened. Whisk at least once during the cooking time.

5. Whisk the cooked sauce thoroughly to make sure that is perfectly smooth. Adjust the seasoning.

Flavourings for One-stage Savoury White Sauce

Onion sauce Finely chop 1 onion and place it in a small basin with a knob of butter. Cover and cook on Maximum (Full) for 3–4 minutes, until softened. Add to the cooked sauce and stir well.

Cheese sauce Stir 75 g (3 oz) grated matured Cheddar cheese into the cooked sauce. Heat for 30 seconds if necessary.

Chive sauce Snip a large bunch of chives into the sauce and add a knob of butter to enrich it. Serve with fish.

Mustard sauce Select a mild mustard – wholegrain is ideal as it gives plenty of flavour, alternatively use a Dijon mustard. Add 3–4 tablespoons of the prepared mustard to the sauce, or to taste. Excellent with boiled ham, with sausages or mackerel.

Mushroom sauce Add 100 g (4 oz) finely sliced button mushrooms to the butter and cover. Cook for 2 minutes before stirring in the flour and milk. Continue as in the main recipe. Serve with fish, chicken or vegetables.

Seasoning

The sauce can be seasoned before cooking but, just as when cooking sauces by traditional methods, this first addition of seasoning should be very light and the cooked sauce should be tasted and the seasoning adjusted to taste just before it is served.

Reheating sauces

The sauce can be prepared well in advance and left until required, then reheated in the microwave just before it is to be served.

It is important to prevent a skin from forming on the surface of the sauce while it is standing. Cover the surface with a piece of buttered greaseproof paper, placing the buttered side downwards, and pressing it gently over the sauce, right up to the edges of the container. Just before reheating the sauce, peel off the paper and lightly scrape away the sauce with a knife, taking care not to break the paper into the sauce.

Alternatively, sweet dessert sauces can be sprinkled with fine caster sugar, in a light, even layer to prevent a skin from forming.

Before reheating, the sauce should be thoroughly whisked and it should be whisked again before serving.

Freezing sauces

Sauces which are thickened with eggs or which contain cream should not be frozen. However, sauces made by the roux method (Béchamel-type sauces) or one stage white sauces which are thickened with flour can be frozen. Pack them in small rigid containers or bags supported in containers until the sauce is frozen.

Defrosting sauces

The sauce should be turned into a suitable basin, then defrosted on a low setting, preferably defrost. When it has softened it should be thoroughly whisked so that it is as smooth as possible before it is reheated on Maximum (Full). Whisk the sauce once during heating, then again before serving. When it has just defrosted the sauce may look slightly separated but it becomes smooth on heating.

Hollandaise Sauce

This rich sauce is one of the mother sauces – it forms the basis for many other well-known sauces which are made by the same method, among them the Sauce Béarnaise (see page 165). The sauce consists of egg yolks which are emulsified with butter in a creamy liaison. It can be served with plain cooked vegetables or fish.

Makes about 250 ml (8 fl oz)
2 tablespoons water
1 teaspoon lemon juice
2 large egg yolks
salt
white pepper (preferably freshly ground)
100 g (4 oz) butter

Preparation time: 5 minutes
Cooking time: $4\frac{1}{2}$–5 minutes
Microwave setting: Maximum (Full)

1. Place the water and lemon juice in a basin and cook for 2 minutes, until boiling. Some of the water should have evaporated. Take care to watch the water all the time in case your microwave is particularly speedy in which case the water may evaporate too rapidly.

2. Add the yolks to the basin immediately it is removed from the microwave and whisk vigorously at once.

3. Place the butter in a suitable jug and heat for 2–$2\frac{1}{2}$ minutes, until melted and very hot.

4. Whisking all the time, pour the hot butter on to the yolks in a very slow trickle. Do not pour the butter in too quickly or the sauce will curdle. The eggs should take up the butter to yield a smooth creamy sauce.

5. Place the sauce in the microwave to heat for about 30 seconds, until thickened. Lightly stir the sauce, then serve at once.

6. The prepared sauce can be set aside to be reheated later. Cover its surface with waxed or buttered greaseproof paper to prevent a skin from forming. Before reheating remove the paper and cook the sauce for 30 seconds at a time until it is hot. Stir gently and serve.

Speedy Hollandaise

Make the Hollandaise in a liquidiser or food processor. Place the yolks and seasoning in the machine, then add the hot water and lemon juice and process until smooth. Heat the butter for an extra 30–60 seconds, so that it is really hot, then pour it very slowly onto the yolks while the machine is running. The emulsified sauce should be hot and ready to serve.

Variations on Hollandaise Sauce

Lemon Hollandaise Stir 1 teaspoon finely grated lemon rind into the sauce just before it is heated for the final 30 seconds. Excellent with fish and seafood, or with chicken.

Mustard Hollandaise Stir 1 teaspoon made Dijon mustard into the Hollandaise sauce just before it is served.

Tomato Hollandaise Add 1 teaspoon concentrated tomato purée to the sauce just before it is heated for the final 30 seconds. Serve with vegetables or seafood.

Hollandaise with capers Stir 1 tablespoon chopped capers into the sauce just before it is served. A good tangy accompaniment for seafood or for grilled veal steaks.

White Sauce

Makes 300 ml (½ pint)
300 ml (½ pint) milk
1 small onion, peeled and stuck
    with 6 cloves
½ carrot, peeled and sliced
½ celery stick, chopped
25 g (1 oz) butter
25 g (1 oz) plain flour
salt
freshly ground black pepper

Preparation time: about 10
minutes, plus infusing
Cooking time: about 6 minutes
Microwave setting: Maximum
(Full)

1. Place the milk, onion, carrot
and celery in a medium bowl
and cook for 3 minutes.

2. Leave to infuse for 10 minutes
before straining.

3. Place the butter in a 600 ml
(1 pint) jug and cook for 30
seconds or until melted.

*From left to right: White sauce; Caper
sauce; Egg sauce; Fish sauce; Parsley
sauce; Cheese sauce*

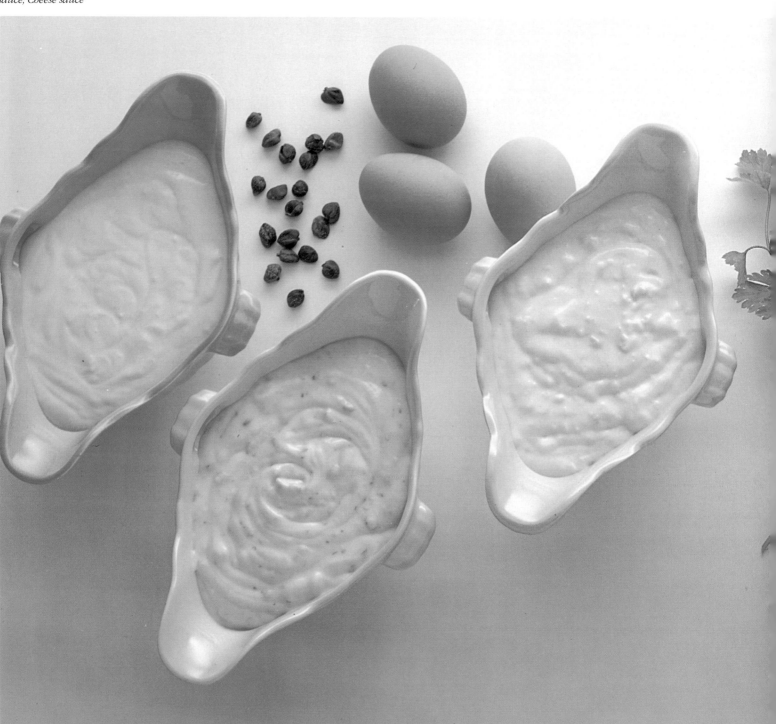

Variations

4. Stir in the flour and gradually blend in the strained milk. Cook for 2½ minutes, stirring every minute, until thick and smooth.

5. Stir in the salt and pepper to taste.

Caper Sauce: Add 1 tablespoon chopped capers and 1 tablespoon caper juice. Serve with boiled chicken, boiled bacon or plain fish.

Egg Sauce: Add 1 finely chopped hard-boiled egg. Add a pinch of paprika, if liked. Serve with vegetables and fish.

Fish Sauce: Add 2 tablespoons cooked peeled prawns, ½ teaspoon lemon juice or ½ teaspoon anchovy essence and a pinch of paprika. Serve with vegetables or fish.

Parsley Sauce: Add 1 tablespoon chopped fresh parsley. Serve with fish.

Cheese Sauce: Stir 25–75 g (1–3 oz) grated Cheddar cheese into the sauce until it melts. Season with 1 teaspoon made English mustard. Serve with vegetables, pasta, and fish. This is also an excellent sauce for making a speedy fish pie, topped with mashed potato.

Cranberry Sauce

Makes about 200 ml
175 g (6 oz) fresh cranberries
100 g (4 oz) caster sugar
grated rind of 1 orange
3 tablespoons orange juice

Preparation time: about 3 minutes, plus chilling
Cooking time: about 14 minutes
Microwave setting: Maximum (Full) and Defrost

1. Place the cranberries, sugar, and orange rind and juice in a small bowl. Cover and cook on Maximum for 4 minutes.

2. Stir the mixture, re-cover and cook on Defrost for 10 minutes, stirring halfway through.

3. Purée in a blender or food processor. Chill. Serve with roast turkey.

Clockwise from top: Sauce Béarnaise; Bread sauce; Tomato sauce; Onion sauce; Curry sauce. Centre: Cranberry sauce

Tomato Sauce

Makes 600 ml (1 pint)
25 g (1 oz) butter
*1 onion, peeled and finely
  chopped*
*1 garlic clove, peeled and
  crushed*
salt
1 teaspoon caster sugar
1 teaspoon dried oregano
2 tablespoons tomato purée
25 g (1 oz) plain flour
*600 g (1¼ lb) tomatoes, skinned
  and chopped*
freshly ground black pepper
*150 ml (¼ pint) hot chicken
  stock*

Preparation time: about 15
minutes, plus cooling
Cooking time: about 13
minutes
Microwave setting: Maximum
(Full)

1. Place the butter, onion, garlic, salt, sugar, oregano and tomato purée in a large bowl. Cover and cook for 5 minutes.

2. Stir in the flour, tomatoes and pepper, then cover and cook for a further 5 minutes.

3. Stir in the hot stock. Cool the sauce slightly.

4. Pour into a liquidizer and blend until smooth.

5. Sieve the sauce. Return to the bowl and reheat for 3 minutes before serving. Serve with hamburgers, chops, sausages and fish.

Curry Sauce

Makes 450 ml (¾ pint)
*1 medium onion, peeled and
  chopped*
*1 garlic clove, peeled and
  crushed*
*1 medium apple, peeled, cored
  and chopped*
1 tablespoon ground coriander
1 teaspoon turmeric
½ teaspoon ground cumin
½ teaspoon chilli powder
¼ teaspoon ground cinnamon
¼ teaspoon ground ginger
¼ teaspoon grated nutmeg
1½ tablespoons plain flour
1 tablespoon tomato purée
1 teaspoon lemon juice
¼ teaspoon meat extract
2 teaspoons curry paste
450 ml (¾ pint) hot stock
salt
freshly ground black pepper

Preparation time: about 10
minutes
Cooking time: about 12½–17½
minutes
Microwave setting: Maximum
(Full)

1. Place the onion, garlic, apple, coriander, turmeric, cumin, chilli powder, cinnamon, ginger and nutmeg in a medium bowl. Cover and cook for 4½ minutes, stirring halfway through cooking.

2. Stir in the flour, tomato purée, lemon juice, meat extract, curry paste, stock, and salt and pepper to taste. Cover and cook for 8–13 minutes, stirring halfway through cooking.

Sauce Béarnaise

Makes 150 ml (¼ pint)
75 g (3 oz) butter
2 tablespoons tarragon vinegar
1 shallot, peeled and chopped
salt
freshly ground black pepper
2 egg yolks (size 1 or 2)

Preparation time: about 5
minutes
Cooking time: about 1½ minutes
Microwave setting: Maximum
(Full)

1. Place the butter in a 600 ml (1 pint) jug and cook for 1 minute or until melted.

2. Whisk the tarragon vinegar, shallot, salt, pepper and egg yolks into the butter. Cook for 30 seconds, whisking the sauce every 15 seconds.

3. As soon as the sauce is ready, place the jug in cold water to prevent further cooking.

Cook's Tip

To prevent curdling, check the sauce frequently during cooking. Serve with grilled steak.

Bread Sauce

Makes 300 ml (½ pint)
*1 medium onion, peeled and
  stuck with 8 cloves*
about 300 ml (½ pint) milk
*75 g (3 oz) fresh white
  breadcrumbs*
*50 g (2 oz) butter, cut into
  pieces*
salt
freshly ground white pepper

Preparation time: about 10
minutes
Cooking time: about 7 minutes,
plus standing
Microwave setting: Maximum
(Full)

1. Place the onion, 300 ml (½ pint) milk, breadcrumbs, butter, and salt and pepper to taste in a medium bowl. Cover and cook for 5 minutes. Leave to stand, covered, for 15 minutes.

2. Remove the onion and add 2 more tablespoons of milk to thin, if necessary. Cook, uncovered, for 2 minutes longer, stirring halfway through.

Onion Sauce

Makes 300 ml (½ pint)
*225 g (8 oz) onions, peeled and
  finely chopped*
15 g (½ oz) butter
10 g (¼ oz) cornflour
150 ml (¼ pint) milk
salt
freshly ground black pepper

Preparation time: about 10
minutes
Cooking time: about 6½ minutes
Microwave setting: Maximum
(Full)

1. Place the onions and butter in a medium bowl, cover and cook for 5 minutes, stirring after 2.

2. Blend the cornflour with a little of the milk. Stir into the remaining milk, and add to the onions. Add the salt and pepper.

3. Cover and cook for 1½ minutes, stirring once.

Orange Sauce

Makes 400 ml (14 fl oz)
75 g (3 oz) butter
175 g (6 oz) icing sugar, sifted
175 ml (6 fl oz) concentrated
*   orange juice*
15 g ($\frac{1}{2}$ oz) cornflour
grated rind of 1 orange
1 egg, separated

Preparation time: about 10
minutes
Cooking time: about 3$\frac{1}{2}$ minutes
Microwave setting: Maximum
(Full)

1. Place the butter in a medium
bowl, and cook for 1 minute or
until melted. Beat the icing
sugar into the melted butter
with a wooden spoon.

2. Blend the orange juice and
cornflour together and stir into
the sugar mixture. Beat in the
orange rind and egg yolk,
incorporating them thoroughly.

3. Cook for 2$\frac{1}{2}$ minutes or until
thickened, stirring every 30
seconds.

4. Whisk the egg white into the
orange sauce. Serve with
marmalade pudding or Ginger
Sponge Pudding.

Gooseberry Sauce

Makes 450 ml ($\frac{3}{4}$ pint)
400 g (14 oz) gooseberries,
*   topped and tailed*
150 ml ($\frac{1}{4}$ pint) water
25 g (1 oz) cornflour
50 g (2 oz) caster sugar

Preparation time: about 10
minutes
Cooking time: about 9 minutes
Microwave setting: Maximum
(Full)

1. Place the gooseberries and
125 ml (4 fl oz) of the water in a
large bowl. Cover and cook for
6 minutes, stirring halfway
through cooking.

2. Rub through a sieve or blend
in a liquidizer until smooth.

3. Blend together the cornflour
and remaining water. Stir into
the gooseberries. Stir in the
sugar and cook, uncovered, for
3 minutes, stirring halfway
through.

4. Serve with grilled
mackerel.

Apple Sauce

Makes 200 ml (7 fl oz)
2 tablespoons water
grated rind of $\frac{1}{2}$ small lemon
1 tablespoon caster sugar
15 g ($\frac{1}{2}$ oz) butter
450 g (1 lb) cooking apples,
*   peeled, cored and finely*
*   sliced*

Preparation time: about 10
minutes
Cooking time: about 5 minutes
Microwave setting: Maximum
(Full)

1. Place all the ingredients in a
large bowl. Cover and cook for
5 minutes, stirring halfway
through cooking. Cool the
sauce slightly.

2. Pour into a liquidizer and
blend until smooth.

3. Return to the bowl and reheat
for 3 minutes.

Melba Sauce

Makes 250 ml (8 fl oz)
350 g (12 oz) raspberries,
*   sieved*
3 tablespoons caster sugar
2 teaspoons cornflour
1 tablespoon water
$\frac{1}{2}$ teaspoon lemon juice

Preparation time: about 10
minutes, plus cooling
Cooking time: about 2$\frac{1}{2}$ minutes
Microwave setting: Maximum
(Full)

1. Place the raspberries and
sugar in a 600 ml (1 pint) jug.

2. Blend the cornflour with the
water and stir into the
raspberries. Cook for 2$\frac{1}{2}$
minutes, stirring every minute.

3. Stir in the lemon juice, and
allow to cool. Serve with ice
cream or cold fruit
pudding.

Chocolate Custard

Makes 300 ml ($\frac{1}{2}$ pint)
15 g ($\frac{1}{2}$ oz) cornflour
15 g ($\frac{1}{2}$ oz) cocoa powder
25 g (1 oz) caster sugar
300 ml ($\frac{1}{2}$ pint) milk
15 g ($\frac{1}{2}$ oz) butter

Preparation time: about 5
minutes
Cooking time: about 2$\frac{1}{2}$ minutes
Microwave setting: Maximum
(Full)

1. Place the cornflour, cocoa
powder and sugar in a 600 ml
(1 pint) jug. Gradually blend in
the milk.

2. Cook the custard for 2$\frac{1}{2}$
minutes, stirring every minute,
until thick and smooth.

3. Beat in the butter and serve
with cold or hot puddings.

Jam Sauce

Makes 175 ml (6 fl oz)
4 tablespoons jam
1 tablespoon lemon juice
4 tablespoons water

Preparation time: about 5
minutes
Cooking time: about 3 minutes
Microwave setting: Maximum
(Full)

1. Place the jam, juice and water
in a 600 ml (1 pint) jug. Cook
for 3 minutes, stirring halfway
through.

2. Sieve the sauce if necessary.
Serve with rice pudding.

Egg Custard

Makes 400 ml (14 fl oz)
300 ml ($\frac{1}{2}$ pint) milk
2 drops vanilla essence
1 egg
1 egg yolk
50 g (2 oz) caster sugar
25 g (1 oz) plain flour

Preparation time: about 10
minutes
Cooking time: about 2 minutes
Microwave setting: Maximum
(Full)

1. Place the milk and vanilla
essence in a 600 ml (1 pint) jug
and cook for 2 minutes.

2. Place the egg, egg yolk and
sugar in a medium bowl and
beat together. Add the flour and
beat until smooth.

3. Gradually stir the milk into
the egg mixture.

4. Cook the custard for 2
minutes, whisking every 30
seconds, until thick and smooth.
Serve with steamed sponge
pudding.

Clockwise from top: Orange sauce;
Gooseberry sauce; Apple sauce; Melba
sauce; Chocolate custard; Jam sauce.
Centre: Egg custard

PUDDINGS AND CAKES

Many old-fashioned puddings that traditionally require hours of steaming can be cooked in minutes in the microwave with excellent results. Fruit can also be cooked with ease and success either to be served simply or as the basis for fools, moulds or ice creams.

The speed of microwave cooking means that traditional steamed puddings can be cooked in minutes rather than hours. The result is delicious – just as expected of old-fashioned methods. If the rise of the pudding is not quite as even as it could be, then it is a small price to pay for the speed and ease of the cooking method.

Fruit

Cut into quarters or slices, or left whole, fruit cooks well in the microwave. The fruit can be poached in syrup to be served hot or cold and various fruits can be combined in a compôte.

Sliced fruits can be cooked until fallen, then sieved or puréed in a liquidiser. The cooled purée can be combined with custard and whipped cream, then chilled to make a delicious fruit fool. Fruit purées also make excellent fillings for pancakes or flan cases.

When cooking whole fruit there are a few points to remember. If the fruit is complete with its peel, then the peel should be scored to prevent bursting. The whole fruits should be positioned as far apart as possible in the cooking dish and they should be rearranged at least once during the cooking time.

Crumbles

Traditionally, the characteristics of a good crumble are the crisp, broken texture and a nice brown top. Crumble toppings can be cooked in the microwave but for a good result the traditional basic recipe requires a little adaptation. Since the microwave does not brown the top of the crumble, then add ingredients to improve the appearance as well as the texture. Try some of the following suggested additions, stirring them into a combination of half fat to flour, sweetened with brown sugar. Remember that you can always brown the top under a grill.

Walnuts and orange Add plenty of chopped walnuts and the grated rind of 1 orange.

Hazelnut and gingernut Add plenty of chopped toasted hazelnuts and some crushed gingernut biscuits.

Almond and mixed peel Add toasted, chopped blanched almonds and some cut peel.

Pastry

Most pastry does not cook well in the microwave (unless the model combines both microwave energy and traditional heat). It is possible to speed up the cooking time of a shortcrust pastry flan case by par-cooking it in the microwave before finishing off in the conventional oven. For puff, flaky or shortcrust pastry it has to be said that traditional or combination cooking methods are by far the best.

However, suet crust pastry cooks very well in the microwave in either savoury or sweet dishes. It can be rolled with a filling and cooked in a roasting bag or covered dish. Alternatively, try the recipe for Apple and Sultana Suet Pudding on page 171.

Cooking whole apples

1. The cored apples have their skin scored all the way round so that they will not burst during cooking. They are arranged as far apart as possible in the cooking dish so that they will cook evenly.

2. Here a simple filling of mincemeat is spooned into the middle of each apple. Do not overfill the apples.

3. Halfway through the cooking time the apples are rotated so that both sides of each piece of fruit cook evenly.

Fillings for apples

Nutty apricot filling Mix a little apricot jam with some chopped toasted nuts (hazelnuts, walnuts or cashews) and stir in some cake or biscuit crumbs.

Orange and raisin Mix some orange marmalade with raisins and a dash of sherry or rum.

Banana and coconut Mix chopped banana with a little lemon juice, desiccated coconut and some orange juice.

GUIDE TO DEFROSTING FRUIT

Quantity of fruit and freezing method	Time in minutes on Maximum (Full)	Time in minutes on Defrost
450 g (1 lb) fruit, dry packed with sugar	4–8	—
450 g (1 lb) fruit, packed with sugar syrup	8–12	—
450 g (1 lb) free-flow fruit (open frozen)	—	4–8

GUIDE TO COOKING FRUIT

Fruit	Preparation	Cooking time in minutes on Maximum (Full)
450 g (1 lb) apricots	Stone and wash, then sprinkle with 100 g (4 oz) sugar	6–8
450 g (1 lb) cooking apples	Peel, core and slice, then sprinkle with 100 g (4 oz) sugar	6–8
450 g (1 lb) gooseberries	Top and tail, then sprinkle with 100 g (4 oz) sugar	4
4 medium-sized peaches	Stone and wash, then sprinkle with 100 g (4 oz) sugar	4–5
6 medium-sized pears	Peel, halve and core. Dissolve 75 g (3 oz) sugar in a little water and pour over the pears.	8–10
450 g (1 lb) plums, cherries, damsons or greengages	Stone and wash. Sprinkle with 100 g (4 oz) sugar and the grated rind of $\frac{1}{2}$ lemon	4–5
450 g (1 lb) soft berry fruits	Top and tail or hull. Wash and add 100 g (4 oz) sugar	3–5
450 g (1 lb) rhubarb	Trim and cut into short lengths. Add 100 g (4 oz) sugar and the grated rind of 1 lemon	8–10

Sweet rich puddings

Rich puddings that are laden with fruit and sugar can be cooked with success in the microwave but they should be watched carefully to make sure that they do not overcook and dry out or burn. Christmas Pudding is a typical example – it cooks, or can be reheated, with success but it is vital to check early on in the suggested cooking time to make sure that the mixture is not overcooking. You should stay near throughout the process of cooking such puddings.

Baking

It has to be said that most traditional baking is best left to the realms of conventional cooking methods for fine results. However the microwave can be used to make a quick cake for tea or some moist gingerbread. There are a few rules to remember.

The shape of the cooking container plays an important role in determining the success of the result. Oblong or square dishes tend to expose the mixture in the corners to overcooking. Round dishes are better and ring dishes are ideal for making cakes. The base of the dish can be lined with a circle of greased greaseproof paper to facilitate easy removal of the cake.

The cooking container should be greased with butter or margarine but it should not be greased and floured as you would a baking tin for a conventional oven, as this results in an unpleasant floury film on the outside of the cooked cake.

The microwave will not brown the cake, so those that are flavoured with chocolate look best. Alternatively, the finished cake can be coated in an icing and decorated, or topped with toasted nuts, or a little jam and coconut to improve its appearance.

Baking utensils

Metal tins should not be used in the microwave. Instead, round dishes, loaf dishes and ring dishes should be employed. Look out for specialist microwave cookware or use dishes like those shown here which are suitable for use in the conventional oven as well as in the microwave.

Note: Defrost fruits in their covered freezer containers, if suitable, for the times given above, or transfer the fruit to a suitable covered dish first. The times given will partially defrost the fruit: it should then be allowed to stand at room temperature to completely thaw. The times given are approximate and will depend upon the freezing method used, the type and shape of the container and the variety of the fruit. During defrosting gently shake or stir the fruit.

Apple and Sultana Suet Pudding

Serves 4–6
150 g (5 oz) shredded suet
½ teaspoon baking powder
250 g (9 oz) self-raising flour
150 ml (¼ pint) water
25 g (1 oz) fresh brown
*   breadcrumbs*
100 g (4 oz) soft dark brown
*   sugar*
2 teaspoons ground cinnamon
100 g (4 oz) sultanas
600 g (1¼ lb) cooking apples,
*   peeled, cored and thinly*
*   sliced*

Preparation time: about 20
minutes
Cooking time: about 11
minutes, plus standing
Microwave setting: Maximum
(Full)

1. Place the suet, baking powder and flour in a bowl. Mix together. Gradually add water to make a soft, not sticky dough.

2. Roll out two thirds of the dough to 3 mm (⅛ inch) thick and line a greased 1.5 litre (2½ pint) basin.

3. Mix together the breadcrumbs, sugar, cinnamon and sultanas.

4. Starting and ending with the apples, make alternate layers with the breadcrumb mixture.

5. Roll out the remaining dough and cover the filling, making sure the lid is well sealed. Make 2 cuts in the lid.

6. Cover with cling film, allowing sufficient room for rising. Cook for 5 minutes. Turn the basin round and cook for a further 6 minutes.

7. Leave to stand, covered, for 5 minutes before turning out and serving.

Apple and Blackberry Crumble

Serves 4–6
600 g (1¼ lb) cooking apples,
*   peeled, cored and thinly*
*   sliced*
350 g (12 oz) blackberries
75 g (3 oz) sugar
175 g (6 oz) plain flour
75 g (3 oz) soft dark brown
*   sugar*
75 g (3 oz) butter

Preparation time: about 20
minutes
Cooking time: about 9 minutes,
plus standing and grilling
Microwave setting: Maximum
(Full)

1. Make alternate layers with the apples, blackberries and sugar in a casserole.

2. Mix the flour and dark brown sugar together, then rub in the butter until the mixture resembles fine breadcrumbs. Sprinkle the mixture over the fruit.

3. Cook for 9 minutes. Leave the crumble to stand for 3 minutes before serving. Brown under a preheated conventional grill.

Apple and sultana suet pudding; Apple and blackberry crumble

Treacle Pudding

Serves 3–4
3 tablespoons golden syrup
100 g (4 oz) self-raising flour
50 g (2 oz) shredded suet
50 g (2 oz) caster sugar
1 egg
2 tablespoons water
4 tablespoons milk
2 drops vanilla essence

Preparation time: about 10 minutes
Cooking time: about 4 minutes, plus standing
Microwave setting: Maximum (Full)

1. Place the golden syrup in the bottom of a lightly greased 900 ml (1½ pint) basin.

2. Mix the flour, suet and sugar together. Beat in the egg, water, milk and vanilla essence. Spoon the mixture on to the syrup in the basin.

3. Cover the basin with cling film and cook for 2 minutes. Remove the cling film and turn the basin round. Cook for a further 2 minutes.

4. Leave the pudding to stand for 2 minutes before turning out and serving.

Cold Strawberry Soufflé

Serves 6
2 tablespoons white wine
4 tablespoons water
2 tablespoons powdered gelatine
300 ml (½ pint) strawberry purée
1½ tablespoons lemon juice
100 g (4 oz) caster sugar
300 ml (½ pint) double cream, stiffly whipped
6 egg whites, stiffly whisked
To decorate:
300 ml (½ pint) double or whipping cream, stiffly whipped
6 strawberries

Preparation time: about 15 minutes, plus setting
Cooking time: about 15 seconds
Microwave setting: Maximum (Full)

1. Place the wine, water and gelatine in a small jug. Stir together well and cook for 30 seconds. Stir to ensure the gelatine has dissolved.

2. Add the strawberry purée, lemon juice and sugar to the gelatine mixture and stir well. Allow to cool, stirring once or twice.

3. Carefully fold the cream into the strawberry mixture, then gently fold in the egg whites.

4. Tie greaseproof paper around the outside of 6 individual ramekin dishes so that it extends 1.5 cm (½ inch) above the rim. Spoon the soufflé mixture into the ramekin dishes.

5. Chill until set, then remove the paper and decorate each soufflé with piped whipped cream and a strawberry.

Treacle pudding; Cold strawberry soufflés

Christmas Pudding

Serves 6–8
75 g (3 oz) plain flour
¼ teaspoon salt
75 g (3 oz) shredded suet
½ teaspoon mixed spice
¼ teaspoon ground cinnamon
*40 g (1½ oz) fresh white
   breadcrumbs*
50 g (2 oz) caster sugar
50 g (2 oz) mixed peel
50 g (2 oz) molasses sugar
*50 g (2 oz) glacé cherries,
   chopped*
75 g (3 oz) currants
75 g (3 oz) sultanas
100 g (4 oz) raisins
*40 g (1½ oz) blanched almonds,
   chopped*
50 g (2 oz) chopped apple
juice of ½ lemon
grated rind of ½ lemon
4 tablespoons brandy
2 eggs
50 ml (2 fl oz) milk
2 teaspoons cane syrup
2 teaspoons gravy browning

Preparation time: about 15
minutes
Cooking time: about 10
minutes, plus standing
Microwave setting: Maximum
(Full)

1. Mix all the dry ingredients
together, then stir in the liquids.

2. Place the mixture in a 1 kg
(2 lb) greased pudding basin.
Cover the basin and cook for 5
minutes.

3. Leave to stand for 5 minutes,
then cook for a further 5
minutes.

4. Allow the pudding to stand
for 5 minutes.

To reheat
Sprinkle 1½ tablespoons water
or brandy over the pudding.
Cover and cook for 1 minutes.
Leave for 4 minutes. Cover and
cook for 3 minutes.

Queen of Puddings

Serves 4
3 egg yolks
50 g (2 oz) caster sugar
600 ml (1 pint) milk
2 drops vanilla essence
*175 g (6 oz) fresh white
   breadcrumbs*
grated rind of ½ lemon
2 tablespoons jam
Topping:
175 g (6 oz) caster sugar
3 egg whites, stiffly whisked

Preparation time: about 15
minutes
Cooking time: about 10½
minutes, plus grilling
Microwave setting: Maximum
(Full)

1. Place the egg yolks, caster
sugar, milk and vanilla essence
in a 1 litre (1¾ pint) jug and
whisk together. Cook for 4
minutes.

2. Place the breadcrumbs and
grated lemon rind in a 1.2 litre
(2 pint) casserole and stir in the
milk mixture. Cook for 5½
minutes, stirring halfway
through cooking. Set aside.

3. Place the jam in a small dish.
Cook for 1 minute.

4. Gently spread the jam over
the cooked breadcrumb and
milk mixture.

5. For the topping, fold the
sugar into the whisked egg
whites. Spread the meringue
over the jam and swirl into
decorative peaks.

6. Brown the pudding under a
preheated conventional grill.

Christmas pudding; Queen of puddings

Fruit Stuffed Pancakes

Serves 4
1 egg
1 egg yolk
300 ml (½ pint) milk
100 g (4 oz) plain flour
pinch of salt
oil, for frying
Filling:
175 g (6 oz) dried apricots
hot water
2 drops almond essence
juice of 1 lemon
50 g (2 oz) ground almonds
2 tablespoons caster sugar
2 tablespoons icing sugar, sifted

Preparation time: about 35 minutes
Cooking time: about 10 minutes, plus standing
Microwave setting: Maximum (Full)

1. Beat together the egg, egg yolk and milk.

2. Sift the flour and salt into a large bowl. Make a well in the centre and gradually incorporate the egg and milk mixture into the flour to make a batter.

3. Using a conventional hob, heat a little of the oil in a 15 cm (6 inch) frying pan. Pour a small amount of batter into the pan, swirling the batter round. Cook until golden; then turn and cook the second side.

4. Make 8 pancakes in this way. Set the pancakes aside while you make the filling.

5. Place the apricots in a bowl and cover with hot water. Cover and cook for 5 minutes. Leave the apricots to stand, covered, for 20 minutes.

6. Drain the apricots, pour into a liquidizer and blend until smooth.

7. Mix together the apricot purée, almond essence, lemon juice, ground almonds and caster sugar. Spread a little of the purée in the centre of each pancake and roll up.

8. Arrange 4 pancakes on a plate and cook for 2½ minutes. Repeat with the remaining pancakes.

9. Sprinkle with icing sugar before serving.

Baked Stuffed Apples

Serves 4
3 tablespoons mincemeat
3 tablespoons strawberry jam
1 teaspoon ground cinnamon
4 large cooking apples, total weight 1.25 kg (2¾ lb), cored, skin scored around middle

Preparation time: about 15 minutes
Cooking time: 14 minutes, plus standing
Microwave setting: Maximum (Full)

1. Mix the mincemeat, jam and cinnamon together.

2. Stand the apples in a shallow dish. Spoon the filling into the cavities in the apples.

3. Cook for 7 minutes. Turn the dish round and cook for a further 7 minutes or until tender.

4. Leave the apples to stand for 4 minutes before serving.

Fruit stuffed pancakes; Baked stuffed apples

Mixed Fruit Sponge Pudding

Serves 4

100 g (4 oz) butter
100 g (4 oz) caster sugar
2 eggs
175 g (6 oz) self-raising flour
2 tablespoons water
50 g (2 oz) mixed dried fruit

Preparation time: about 10 minutes
Cooking time: about 10 minutes, plus standing
Microwave setting: Maximum (Full)

1. Cream the butter and sugar together until light and fluffy.

2. Beat in the eggs one at a time, then carefully fold in the flour. Stir in the water and dried fruit.

3. Place the mixture in a greased 1.2 litre (2 pint) bowl. Cover and cook for 5 minutes. Turn the bowl and cook for a further 5 minutes.

4. Remove the cover and leave the pudding to stand for 2 minutes before turning out. Serve hot.

Honey Cheesecake

Serves 6

1 tablespoon golden syrup
100 g (4 oz) butter
225 g (8 oz) digestive biscuits, crushed
350 g (12 oz) full-fat soft cheese
½ teaspoon ground cinnamon
1 tablespoon lemon juice
2 tablespoons water
1 tablespoon powdered gelatine
4 tablespoons clear honey
150 ml (¼ pint) double cream, whipped

To decorate:
150 ml (¼ pint) double or whipping cream, whipped
walnut halves

Preparation time: about 15 minutes, plus chilling
Cooking time: about 2 minutes
Microwave setting: Maximum (Full)

1. Place the syrup and butter in a medium bowl. Cook for 1¼ minutes.

2. Stir in the crushed biscuits and mix well. Use this mixture to line a 20 cm (8 inch) flan case.

3. Beat the cheese and cinnamon together until smooth.

4. Place lemon juice and water in a 600 ml (1 pint) jug and stir in the gelatine. Cook for 15 seconds. Stir well to make sure the gelatine has dissolved.

5. Place the honey in another 600 ml (1 pint) jug. Cook for 30 seconds. Pour the honey into the first jug containing the gelatine and mix well together. Allow to cool slightly.

6. Beat the honey mixture into the cheese mixture and fold in the whipped cream. Spoon into the flan case and chill until set.

7. Decorate the cheesecake with the whipped cream and walnut halves.

Mixed fruit sponge pudding; Honey cheesecake

Pineapple Upside-down Pudding

Serves 4
165 g (5½ oz) butter
25 g (1 oz) soft dark brown sugar
3 slices canned pineapple
4 glacé cherries
100 g (4 oz) caster sugar
2 eggs
100 g (4 oz) self-raising flour, sifted

Preparation time: about 15 minutes
Cooking time: about 7½ minutes, plus standing
Microwave setting: Maximum (Full)

1. Use 15 g (½ oz) of the butter to grease a 1.2 litre (2 pint) soufflé dish.

2. Place 25 g (1 oz) of the butter and the brown sugar in the dish and cook for 1 minute.

3. Arrange the pineapple slices and cherries in the base of the dish in a decorative pattern.

4. Beat the remaining butter and caster sugar together until light and fluffy.

5. Beat in the eggs and fold in the flour. Gently spread this over the pineapple and cherries.

6. Cook for 3 minutes, turn the dish round and cook for a further 3½ minutes.

7. Leave the pudding to stand for 3 minutes before turning out.

Chocolate Mousse

Serves 6
6 slices jam Swiss roll
4 tablespoons Grand Marnier
225 g (8 oz) milk chocolate broken into pieces
25 g (1 oz) butter
1 tablespoon cold strong black coffee
1 tablespoon brandy
4 egg yolks
4 egg whites, stiffly whisked
To decorate:
150 ml (¼ pint) double or whipping cream, stiffly whipped
1 tablespoon grated chocolate

Preparation time: about 10 minutes, plus setting
Cooking time: about 2 minutes
Microwave setting: Maximum (Full)

Clockwise: Trifle; Chocolate mousse; Pineapple upside-down pudding; Pineapple flan

1. Place 1 slice of Swiss roll into the base of each of 6 small dishes. Sprinkle with the Grand Marnier.

2. Place the chocolate in a medium bowl. Cook for 2 minutes or until it has melted.

3. Beat in the butter, coffee, brandy and egg yolks. Gently fold in the egg whites.

4. Spoon the mousse over the Swiss roll and smooth over the top. Chill until set.

5. Decorate each dish with swirls of cream and grated chocolate.

Trifle

Serves 6
6 trifle sponges, cut into pieces
12 ratafia biscuits, crumbled
150 ml (¼ pint) sweet sherry
50 ml (2 fl oz) orange juice
4 tablespoons strawberry jam
25 g (1 oz) caster sugar
400 ml (14 fl oz) milk
3 eggs
1 egg yolk
150 ml (¼ pint) double or whipping cream, whipped
1 egg white, stiffly whisked
To decorate:
chopped nuts
angelica

Preparation time: about 15 minutes, plus cooling
Cooking time: about 5½ minutes
Microwave setting: Maximum (Full)

1. Divide the sponges between 6 glass dishes or 1 large dish. Sprinkle the ratafia biscuits over the sponge.

2. Mix the sherry and orange juice together and pour over the sponge ratafia base. Spread a little strawberry jam over the soaked base.

3. Place the caster sugar and milk in a small bowl. Cook for 2 minutes.

4. Whisk the eggs and egg yolk together, then pour the heated milk on to the eggs, whisking all the time. Cook for 3½ minutes. Check and whisk the custard every 30 seconds.

5. Whisk and strain the custard before spooning it over the soaked sponge bases. Leave to cool.

6. Fold the cream and egg white together. Gently spread the cream over the custard and decorate the trifle with chopped nuts and angelica.

Pineapple Flan

Serves 4–6
100 g (4 oz) butter
1 tablespoon golden syrup
225 g (8 oz) gingernut biscuits, crushed
4 tablespoons pineapple juice
15 g (½ oz) powdered gelatine
1 × 400 g (14 oz) can crushed pineapple, drained
50 g (2 oz) white marshmallows
300 ml (½ pint) double cream, whipped
To decorate:
glacé cherries
pieces of crystallized angelica

Preparation time: about 20 minutes, plus setting
Cooking time: about 2½ minutes
Microwave setting: Maximum (Full)

1. Place the butter and syrup in a medium bowl. Cook for 1¼ minutes.

2. Stir in the crushed biscuits and mix well. Use this mixture to line a 20 cm (8 inch) flan case.

3. Place the pineapple juice into a 600 ml (1 pint) jug and stir in the gelatine. Cook for 10 seconds, then stir until the gelatine has dissolved.

4. Place the crushed pineapple and marshmallows in a medium bowl. Cook for 1 minute or until the marshmallows have melted.

5. Whisk the pineapple juice and gelatine mixture into the pineapple and marshmallow mixture. Leave until almost set.

6. Fold the cream into the pineapple mixture and then spoon into the flan case, smoothing the top.

7. Decorate the flan with the cherries and angelica. Chill until set. Serve chilled.

Fresh Fruit Salad

Serves 4–6
100 g (4 oz) sugar
150 ml (¼ pint) water
1 tablespoon lemon juice
1 tablespoon Grand Marnier
50 g (2 oz) white grapes, peeled,
  halved and deseeded
50 g (2 oz) black grapes, peeled,
  halved and deseeded
1 dessert apple, peeled, cored,
  quartered and thinly sliced
1 dessert pear, peeled, cored
  and sliced
1 large orange, peeled and
  segmented
1 paw paw, peeled, deseeded
  and diced
¼ honeydew melon, skin
  removed, deseeded and
  diced
1 kiwifruit, peeled and sliced
1 banana, peeled and sliced

Preparation time: about 30
minutes, plus cooling and
standing
Cooking time: about 5 minutes
Microwave setting: Maximum
(Full)

1. Place the sugar and water in a
jug and cover. Heat for 5
minutes, then stir and leave to
cool.

2. When the syrup is cool, stir in
the lemon juice and Grand
Marnier.

3. Place all the prepared fruit
into a large glass bowl. Pour the
syrup over the fruit.

4. Leave for 1 hour to let the
flavours mingle.

Baked Bananas

Serves 4
4 bananas, peeled and sliced
4 tablespoons rum
4 tablespoons orange juice
50 g (2 oz) ginger biscuits,
  crushed
40 g (1½ oz) soft brown sugar
150 ml (¼ pint) double cream

Preparation time: about 10
minutes
Cooking time: about 4 minutes
Microwave setting: Maximum
(Full)

1. Place the sliced bananas in a
glass dish.

2. Mix the rum and orange juice
together and pour over the
bananas.

3. Mix the biscuits and sugar
together and sprinkle over the
bananas.

4. Cover the dish and cook for 2
minutes. Turn the dish round
and cook for a further 2
minutes.

5. Uncover and pour the cream
over the baked bananas. Serve
at once.

Lemon Meringue Pie

Serves 4
175 g (6 oz) prepared
  shortcrust pastry
finely grated rind of 2 lemons
125 ml (4 fl oz) lemon juice
25 g (1 oz) cornflour
200 g (7 oz) caster sugar
2 egg yolks, beaten
2 egg whites, stiffly whisked

Preparation time: about 20 minutes
Cooking time: about 10 minutes, plus browning
Microwave setting: Maximum (Full)

1. Roll out the pastry and use it to line a 15 cm (6 inch) pie dish. Prick the pastry all over with a fork and cook for 5 minutes, or until crisp.

2. Make up the lemon rind and juice with cold water to 300 ml (½ pint).

3. Mix the cornflour in a 600 ml (1 pint) jug with a little of the lemon water, then gradually stir in the remaining liquid. Cook for 3½ minutes or until the mixture thickens, stirring every minute.

4. Whisk 75 g (3 oz) of the sugar with the egg yolks. Beat into the lemon mixture. Pour into the pastry case and leave to cool.

5. Place the whisked egg whites in a bowl and fold in the remaining sugar. Pile over the lemon filling. Cook for 1½ minutes.

6. Place under a preheated conventional grill to lightly brown the meringue.

Ginger Sponge Pudding

Serves 4
100 g (4 oz) butter
100 g (4 oz) caster sugar
2 eggs
100 g (4 oz) self-raising flour,
  sifted
2 teaspoons ground ginger
5 pieces preserved ginger,
  drained and sliced

Preparation time: about 10 minutes
Cooking time: about 6 minutes, plus standing
Microwave setting: Maximum (Full)

1. Cream the butter and sugar together until light and fluffy.

2. Beat in the eggs, one at a time, then fold in the sifted flour and ground ginger.

3. Arrange the sliced ginger over the base of a greased 900 ml (1½ pint) bowl. Spoon the pudding mixture over the ginger in the bowl, smoothing the top.

4. Cover and cook for 3 minutes. Turn the bowl round and cook for a further 3 minutes.

5. Remove the cover and leave the pudding to stand for 2 minutes before turning it out. Serve hot with Egg Custard (page 166) or Orange Sauce (page 166).

From left to right: Fresh fruit salad; Baked bananas; Lemon meringue pie; Ginger sponge pudding

Lemon Sponge Cake

Makes one 18 cm (7 inch) cake
225 g (8 oz) self-raising flour
¼ teaspoon baking powder
100 g (4 oz) butter
100 g (4 oz) soft dark brown sugar
2 eggs
2 teaspoons grated lemon rind
1 tablespoon milk
2 teaspoons lemon juice
3 tablespoons Lemon Curd (page 184)
225 g (8 oz) icing sugar, sifted
2 tablespoons water
yellow food colouring
8 sugared lemon slices, to decorate

Preparation time: about 10 minutes, plus cooling
Cooking time: about 5 minutes, plus standing
Microwave setting: Maximum (Full)

1. Sift the flour and baking powder into a large bowl. Rub in the butter until the mixture resembles breadcrumbs, then stir in the sugar.

2. Beat in the eggs, one at a time, then stir in the lemon rind, milk and lemon juice.

3. Spoon the mixture into a greased and lined 18 cm (7 inch) round, 9 cm (3½ inch) deep container. Stand on an upturned plate and cook for 2 minutes.

4. Turn the container round and cook for a further 2 minutes. Turn round again and cook for 1 minute.

5. Leave the cake to stand for 5 minutes before turning it out upside down on to a serving plate. Leave to cool completely.

6. Split the cake into 2 layers. Spread one layer with the lemon curd and replace the other layer on top.

7. Mix the icing sugar with the water and yellow food colouring. Pour over the cake and decorate with lemon slices.

Gingerbread

Makes one cake
50 g (2 oz) treacle
15 g (½ oz) caster sugar
50 g (2 oz) butter
100 g (4 oz) plain flour, sifted
½ teaspoon bicarbonate of soda
½ teaspoon ground mixed spice
½ teaspoon ground ginger
1 egg (size 1)

Preparation time: about 10 minutes, plus cooling
Cooking time: about 5 minutes, plus standing
Microwave setting: Maximum (Full)

1. Place the treacle, sugar and butter in a medium bowl. Cook for 1½ minutes.

2. Allow the mixture to cool slightly, then stir in the sifted flour, bicarbonate of soda, mixed spice and ginger. Beat in the egg.

3. Pour into a greased 1.5 litre (2½ pint) deep oblong plastic container. Stand on an upturned plate and cook for 1 minute.

4. Turn the container round and cook for 1 minute. Turn it round again and cook for 1½ minutes.

5. Allow the gingerbread to stand for 5 minutes before turning out. Leave to cool completely. Serve cut in slices and buttered.

Chocolate Banana Ring

Makes one cake
2 eggs
4 tablespoons milk
150 g (5 oz) soft brown sugar
100 g (4 oz) soft margarine
450 g (1 lb) bananas, peeled and chopped
225 g (8 oz) self-raising flour
½ teaspoon baking powder
40 g (1½ oz) drinking chocolate powder

Icing:
50 g (2 oz) icing sugar
40 g (1½ oz) drinking chocolate
1 tablespoon water

Preparation time: about 10 minutes, plus cooling
Cooking time: about 15 minutes, plus standing
Microwave setting: Maximum (Full)

1. Place the eggs, milk, sugar, margarine and bananas into a liquidizer and blend until smooth.

2. Sift the flour, baking powder and drinking chocolate into a large bowl. Stir in the banana mixture and mix thoroughly until well combined.

3. Spoon the mixture into a 2.25 litre (4 pint) greased microwave baking ring. Cook for 5 minutes. Turn the ring round and cook for a further 5 minutes.

4. Gently spread any uncooked cake mixture over the surface. Turn round and cook for 5 minutes.

5. Leave the ring to stand for 5 minutes before turning it out. Leave to cool completely.

6. Mix the sifted icing sugar and drinking chocolate together. Quickly stir in the water. Spread the glacé icing over the top and let some drizzle down the sides of the cake.

One-stage Chocolate Cake

Makes one 18 cm (7 inch) cake
175 g (6 oz) soft margarine
175 g (6 oz) caster sugar
40 g (1½ oz) cocoa powder
150 g (5 oz) self-raising flour
1 teaspoon baking powder
2 drops vanilla essence
3 tablespoons milk
3 eggs
2 tablespoons icing sugar, to decorate

Preparation time: about 10 minutes, plus cooling
Cooking time: about 8½ minutes, plus standing
Microwave setting: Maximum (Full)

1. Place all the ingredients, except the icing sugar, in a large bowl. Beat well until the mixture is smooth, but be careful not to overbeat.

2. Spoon the mixture into a greased and bottom-lined 18 cm (7 inch) round, 9 cm (3½ inch) deep container. Stand the container on an upturned plate and cook for 3 minutes.

3. Turn the container round and cook for a further 3 minutes. Turn round again and cook for 2½ minutes.

4. Leave the cake to stand for 5 minutes before turning it out. Leave to cool completely.

5. Turn the cake out upside down on to a serving plate and sift icing sugar over the top to decorate.

Clockwise: Lemon sponge cake; Gingerbread; One-stage chocolate cake; Chocolate banana ring

PRESERVES

The microwave is not a suitable appliance in which to cook vast quantities of preserves but it can be useful for preparing a small quantity of jam or a pot of tasty relish. Try the recipes in this chapter and follow the guidelines below if you want to prepare small quantities of your favourite traditional recipes.

When making jams and other preserves in the microwave follow the usual principles of preserving but it is important to use a large cooking container to make sure that the ingredients do not boil over in the oven cavity.

Jams and preserves cooked by this method have a fine, full flavour and they are usually better in colour than their conventionally cooked counterparts. Do not attempt to cook large quantities of preserves in the microwave – it is difficult to control the boiling and unlikely that you will be able to find a bowl large enough to accommodate all the ingredients with plenty of room for stirring the preserve.

Cooking utensils

Large heatproof glass mixing bowls are best for cooking preserves in the microwave. Glazed earthenware mixing bowls absorb some energy and become hot. If you have a very large casserole dish, then that may also be suitable. If the preserve needs to be covered during cooking use a dinner plate. Do make sure that it is plain and heatproof, and that it does not have any metal decoration.

Evaporation

When cooking in the microwave there can be less evaporation of liquid and this can affect the result when making some chutneys and pickles that require lengthy boiling by traditional methods in order to reduce the liquid content. The balance of sugar and vinegar is important to preserve the chutney or pickle but it can be wavered. Reduce the quantity of liquid slightly and check the progress of the preserve as it cooks – if it is very moist, then remove the lid ahead of the time suggested in the recipe.

Sterilising pots

The microwave is useful for sterilising a small number of pots. Do not put pots with metal clips or attachments in the microwave. Make sure that the pots are free of all metal and that they are thoroughly washed. Using boiling water from the kettle, half fill each pot with water and stand the pots in the microwave. Cook on Maximum (Full) until you can see the water boiling, then continue to cook for 5 minutes. If the pots are to be used immediately, then they should be emptied and dried, then filled with preserve at once. Alternatively, if they are to be left standing for some time, then cover them with microwave-proof cling film and cook for a further 1–2 minutes, then leave to stand and remove the film just before they are to be emptied and used.

Stages in making jams and other set sweet preserves

Extracting the pectin The first stage in making any jam, marmalade or conserve is to soften the fruit and extract the pectin. Pectin is the substance which is naturally present in fruit and which makes a preserve set when cooked.

The pectin combines with the sugar and acid to create a 'jel' or to make the preserve set. Without pectin the preserve will not set. Commercial pectin can be obtained and the manufacturer's instructions should always be followed when it is used.

Selecting the fruit Fruit contains the most pectin when it is slightly under-ripe. Fruit which is ripe contains a certain amount of pectin but fruit which is over-ripe has a very low pectin content. So, for best results select slightly under-ripe fruit and combine it with some which is ripe for flavour.

Softening the fruit The initial step in jam making is softening the fruit. The fruit is prepared according to its type, then cooked with the minimum of liquid – or a measured quantity in the case of marmalades – until very tender. The microwave can be particularly useful for this stage of preparation even if the rest of the preserve is cooked by traditional methods. For example, lemons or oranges can be softened in water in the microwave before they are to be cut up for marmalade.

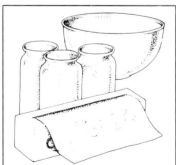

A large mixing bowl or a big casserole dish is essential for allowing preserves to boil in the microwave.

Preparing the pots

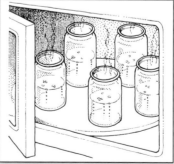

Pots which are free of all metal can be sterilised in the microwave. They should be half filled with boiling water from the

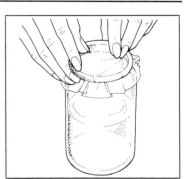

kettle and covered with microwave-proof cling film if they are to be left for any length of time before they are used.

Adding the sugar The sugar is added when the fruit is tender. If the fruit is still slightly tough before the sugar is added, then it will not continue to tenderise after this stage. The sugar should dissolve as quickly as possible and it should lower the temperature of the jam as little as possible. So, for best results, warm the sugar in the microwave for a few minutes before adding it to the fruit. Stir it thoroughly into the fruit, then cook stirring occasionally, until it has dissolved completely.

Boiling This is the process which excludes most types of preserves from being suitable for microwave cooking. You must allow room for the preserve to come to a rolling boil in the bowl. So the quantities that can be cooked successfully are small.

Testing for setting

When the preserve has boiled until the water and sugar concentration is just right it must be tested to determine whether setting point has been reached.

Flake test Take the bowl of preserve from the microwave and use a wooden spoon to give it a stir, then lift the spoon out of the preserve and hold it in the air above the bowl. The preserve should form small set flakes as it drips.

Saucer test Have a very cold saucer ready in the refrigerator. Spoon a small amount of the preserve onto the saucer and leave it for a few minutes. Push the preserve with your finger and there should be a clear skin formed on its surface when the preserve is ready for potting.

If the preserve does not pass the test, then return it to the microwave and continue to cook it for a few minutes before testing it again. Do not leave the preserve to cook for more than 3–4 minutes before re-testing,

and less if it is a second or third re-test. Once the preserve is overcooked it will not set.

Potting

Drain and thoroughly dry the sterilised jars and fill them with the preserve. Cover immediately with waxed discs, placing the

waxed sides down. The discs should come all the way to the sides of the pot and cover the whole surface of the preserve in order to exclude air and moulds or other micro-organisms which will spoil the preserve. The preserve should be covered with an airtight lid either immediately, while it is still very

hot, or when it has cooled completely.

Labelling and storing

When cool, label the pots clearly with the name of the preserve and the date when it was made. Store them in a dark, cook, dry place.

Making strawberry jam

1. The fruit is softened. Here strawberries have lemon juice added to them. The lemon juice provides the acid that is necessary to set the jam.

2. The sugar is added when the fruit has been softened. The mixture is thoroughly stirred at this stage and until the sugar has dissolved.

3. Testing for setting – here the saucer test is used to determine whether the jam is ready for potting. The wrinkles which are obvious when the jam is pushed with a finger mean that it will set, so it is ready for pouring into pots.

Sugar with pectin

The microwave can be used to cook small quantities of unusual preserves or those made from more expensive fruits. One of the disadvantages of this type of produce is that it can have a low pectin content.

Pectin is the substance present in fruit which combines with the correct concentration of sugar and acid to make sweet preserves set. If there is not enough pectin the jam will not set.

Commercial pectin has been available for years but now a special preserving sugar is produced combining the right balance of both

pectin and acid. Once the fruit is softened, this sugar is added to the preserve and it is boiled for a short length of time compared to traditional recipes. This is a distinct advantage when cooking in the microwave.

There is more than one brand of this type of sugar available and information is produced by the manufacturers, in particular Tate and Lyle who offer guidance on using their sugar for making preserves in the microwave. Remember, when in doubt read all the instructions on the packet for information.

Strawberry Jam

Makes about 450 g (1 lb)
450 g (1 lb) strawberries
1 tablespoon lemon juice
350 g (12 oz) sugar

Preparation time: about 5 minutes, plus cooling
Cooking time: about 26 minutes
Microwave setting: Maximum (Full)

1. Place the strawberries and lemon juice in a large bowl. Cover and cook for 6 minutes or until the strawberries are soft.

2. Stir in the sugar. Cook uncovered for a further 20 minutes or until setting point is reached, stirring halfway through cooking.

3. Allow the jam to cool before spooning into clean, dry jars. Seal and label.

Lemon Curd

Makes about 450 g (1 lb)
100 g (4 oz) butter
225 g (8 oz) sugar
175 ml (6 fl oz) lemon juice
grated rind of 3 large lemons
3 eggs

Preparation time: about 10 minutes, plus cooling
Cooking time: about 8 minutes
Microwave setting: Maximum (Full)

1. Place the butter, sugar, lemon juice and rind in a large bowl. Cook, uncovered, for 3 minutes, stirring halfway through cooking.

2. Beat the eggs into the mixture. Cook for 5 minutes or until the lemon curd thickens, checking and stirring every minute.

3. Allow the lemon curd to cool before spooning into clean, dry jars. Seal and label.

From left to right: Strawberry jam; Lemon curd; Gooseberry jam; Tomato chutney

Gooseberry Jam

Makes about 750 g (1½ lb)
200 ml (7 fl oz) water
450 g (1 lb) gooseberries, topped and tailed
450 g (1 lb) sugar

Preparation time: about 10 minutes, plus cooling
Cooking time: about 30 minutes
Microwave setting: Maximum (Full)

1. Place the water and gooseberries in a large bowl. Cover and cook for 5 minutes.

2. Stir, and remove the cover. Cook for a further 5 minutes or until the gooseberries are soft.

3. Stir in the sugar. Cook uncovered for 20 minutes or until setting point is reached, stirring halfway through cooking.

4. Allow the jam to cool before spooning into clean, dry jars. Seal and label.

Tomato Chutney

Makes about 1.5 kg (3 lb)
350 g (12 oz) tomatoes, skinned and chopped
350 g (12 oz) cooking apples, peeled, cored and sliced
1 medium onion, peeled and finely chopped
350 g (12 oz) raisins
2 teaspoons salt
2 teaspoons mixed spice
1 garlic clove, peeled and crushed
225 g (8 oz) molasses sugar
450 ml (¾ pint) malt vinegar

Preparation time: about 10 minutes, plus cooling
Cooking time: about 34 minutes
Microwave setting: Maximum (Full)

1. Place the tomatoes, apples and onion in a large bowl. Cover and cook for 10 minutes, stirring halfway through cooking.

2. Stir in the raisins, salt, mixed spice, garlic, sugar and vinegar. Cook for 24 minutes, stirring the chutney several times during cooking.

3. Allow the chutney to cool before spooning into clean, dry jars. Seal and label.

Sweetcorn Relish

Makes about 1.5 kg (3 lb)

1 large onion, peeled and
  chopped
4 cloves garlic, peeled and
  crushed
225 g (8 oz) carrots, peeled and
  diced
1 green pepper, cored, seeded,
  and chopped
4 tablespoons oil
salt
freshly ground pepper
2 tablespoons cornflour
2 tablespoons water
3 tablespoons made English
  mustard
$\frac{1}{4}$ teaspoon turmeric
300 ml ($\frac{1}{2}$ pint) white wine
  vinegar
100 g (4 oz) sugar
450 g (1 lb) frozen sweetcorn

Preparation time: about 30
minutes, plus cooling
Cooking time: 25 minutes
Microwave setting: Maximum
(Full)

1. Place the onion, garlic,
carrots and green pepper in a
large mixing bowl. Stir in the oil
and salt and pepper. Cook for 5
minutes.

2. Meanwhile, blend the
cornflour with the water,
mustard, turmeric and vinegar.
Add the sugar to the onion
mixture, then pour in the liquid
and stir well. Cook for a further
5 minutes.

3. Stir in the sweetcorn and mix
thoroughly, then cook for 15
minutes, stirring three times
during cooking.

4. Cool slightly before spooning

into clean, dry jars. Cover
immediately and label. Allow the
relish to mature for at least a
week before eating it. It will
keep for up to 3 months.

Cook's Tip

It is possible to scald pots in the
microwave oven. Make sure first
that they have no metal trims,
and that they are thoroughly
cleaned and free from odours.
Pour in water to come halfway
up the pots and cover each with
microwave cling film, then cook
on Maximum (Full) power until
the water in each is boiling. The
time will vary depending on
how many pots you have in the
oven. Do not overdo it in case
the pots break. When the water
has boiled, leave the jars
covered until you are ready to
pot the preserve.
  Protect your hands with an

oven glove or tea-towel, then
remove the cling film (it will
have shrunk into the pots) and
pour away the water. If the jars
have been standing a long time,
then reheat them, this way the
water is very hot and the clean,
hot pots barely need drying.

Sweetcorn relish

Cranberry Relish

Makes about 1 kg (2 lb)
450 g (1 lb) cranberries
*2 onions, peeled and finely
chopped*
*3 cloves garlic, peeled and
crushed*
225 g (8 oz) sugar
*1 tablespoon wholegrain
mustard*
*100 ml (4 fl oz) red wine
vinegar*

Preparation time: 10 minutes
Cooking time: 15 minutes
Microwave setting: Maximum
(Full)

1. Place the cranberries, onions, garlic, sugar, mustard and vinegar in a large bowl and stir well. Cover with cling film, allowing a small gap for the steam to escape, and cook for 10 minutes.

2. Uncover and give the relish a good stir, then cook for a further 5 minutes.

3. Have ready two 450 g (1 lb) jars, clean and thoroughly scalded. Cool slightly. Stir the relish, then spoon into the jars and seal and label. Store in a cool place for up to 3 months. This is a good relish to serve with hamburgers, baked ham and cold roast meats or poultry (particularly turkey!) or it also goes well with full-flavoured farmhouse Cheddar cheese.

Mango Chutney

Makes about 675 g (1½ lb)
*675 g (1½ lb) small green
mangos*
*1 large onion, peeled and
chopped*
*1–2 hot green chillies, seeded
and chopped*
1 tablespoon salt
*2 tablespoons ground
coriander*
*4 cloves garlic, peeled and
crushed*
100 g (4 oz) sugar
150 ml (¼ pint) cider vinegar

Preparation time: 30 minutes
Cooking time: 15 minutes
Microwave setting: Maximum
(Full)

1. Peel the mangos and cut the fruit off the stones in chunks. Place the mango pieces and the onion in a large bowl. Add the chilli(es), salt, coriander, garlic, sugar and vinegar and stir well.

2. Cover the bowl, allowing a small gap for the steam to escape, then cook for 7 minutes.

3. Uncover, and give the chutney a good stir to mix all the ingredients. Continue to cook, without a cover, for a further 8 minutes.

4. Ladle the chutney into clean, dry jars and cover tightly. Allow the chutney to mature for at least a week before serving.

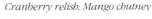

Cranberry relish; Mango chutney

Hot Chocolate

Makes 750 ml (1¼ pints)
50 g (2 oz) plain chocolate,
  broken into pieces
600 ml (1 pint) milk
5 marshmallows, chopped

Preparation time: about 5
minutes
Cooking time: about 8½ minutes
Microwave setting: Maximum
(Full)

1. Place the chocolate in a large
jug. Heat for 3½ minutes or until
the chocolate has melted.

2. Stir in the milk and heat for 4
minutes.

3. Whisk in the marshmallows
until they have melted. Heat for
1 minute, then pour into 4
warmed mugs or glasses.

Hot Whisky Egg Nog

Makes 900 ml (1½ pints)
750 ml (1¼ pints) milk
65 ml (2½ fl oz) whisky
50 g (2 oz) caster sugar
2 eggs, lightly beaten
1 teaspoon grated nutmeg, to
  decorate

Preparation time: about 5
minutes
Cooking time: about 6 minutes
Microwave setting: Maximum
(Full)

1. Place the milk, whisky and
sugar in a large jug. Cook for 6
minutes, stirring halfway
through.

2. Beat the eggs into the hot
milk mixture. Strain into 4
heatproof or warmed tumblers.
Sprinkle grated nutmeg over
each and serve immediately.

Calypso Coffee

Makes 600 ml (1 pint)
600 ml (1 pint) cold, strong
  black coffee
25 g (1 oz) caster sugar
4 tablespoons rum
150 ml (¼ pint) double cream

Preparation time: about 5
minutes
Cooking time: about 4½ minutes
Microwave setting: Maximum
(Full)

1. Place the coffee, sugar and
rum in a large jug. Heat for 4½
minutes, stirring halfway
through.

2. Pour the coffee into 4
warmed glasses or cups.

3. Pour a little cream on the top
of each coffee.

Orange Tea

Makes 850 ml (28 fl oz)
250 ml (8 fl oz) orange juice
600 ml (1 pint) water
1 tablespoon caster sugar
2 tea bags
To decorate:
4 slices orange
4 mint sprigs

Preparation time: about 10
minutes
Cooking time: about 8 minutes,
plus standing
Microwave setting: Maximum
(Full)

1. Place the orange juice, water
and sugar in a large jug. Cook
for 8 minutes, stirring halfway
through cooking.

2. Stir in the tea bags, cover and
leave to stand for 4 minutes.

3. Stir the orange tea, remove
the tea bags, then pour into the
4 glasses and float a slice of
orange on the top. Decorate
each glass with a sprig of mint.

*From left to right: Hot chocolate; Hot
whisky egg nog; Calypso coffee; Orange
tea*

Mulled Red Wine

Makes just over 750 ml (1¼ pints)
450 ml (¾ pint) red wine
150 ml (¼ pint) water
150 ml (¼ pint) orange juice
25 g (1 oz) caster sugar
4 tablespoons brandy
½ teaspoon ground cinnamon
8 orange slices, to decorate

Preparation time: about 5 minutes
Cooking time: about 4 minutes
Microwave setting: Maximum (Full)

1. Place the wine, water, orange juice, sugar, brandy and cinnamon in a jug. Stir well and pour into 4 tumblers.

2. Heat for 4 minutes, stirring halfway through.

3. Decorate with the orange slices.

Mulled Cider

Makes just over 750 ml (1¼ pints)
450 ml (¾ pint) dry cider
150 ml (¼ pint) apple juice
150 ml (¼ pint) orange juice
25 g (1 oz) caster sugar
½ teaspoon ground mixed spice
8 apple slices

Preparation time: about 5 minutes
Cooking time: about 4 minutes
Microwave setting: Maximum (Full)

1. Place the cider, apple juice, orange juice, sugar and mixed spice into a large jug. Stir well and pour into 4 tumblers.

2. Place an apple slice in each tumbler. Heat for 4 minutes, stirring halfway through heating.

3. Decorate with the remaining apple slices.

Hot Rum Punch

Makes 900 ml (1½ pints)
450 ml (¾ pint) water
1 orange
6 cloves
2 Ceylon tea bags
rind of ½ lemon
1 cinnamon stick
150 ml (¼ pint) dark rum
150 ml (¼ pint) white wine
150 ml (¼ pint) orange juice
50 g (2 oz) soft dark brown sugar
To decorate:
4 small slices orange
4 small slices lemon

Preparation time: about 5 minutes
Cooking time: about 10 minutes
Microwave setting: Maximum (Full)

1. Place the water in a large jug and cook for 5 minutes.

2. Stud the orange with the cloves and add to the water with the tea bags, lemon rind and cinnamon stick. Stir and cover, then set aside for 5 minutes, removing the tea bags after 3 minutes.

3. Meanwhile, place the rum, wine, orange juice and sugar in a jug. Cook for 5 minutes, stirring halfway through.

4. Remove the orange and cloves, rind and cinnamon stick. Strain. Mix the tea and rum mixtures together, then pour into 4 heatproof or warmed glasses. Place a small slice of lemon and orange in each glass.

Mulled cider; Hot rum punch; Mulled red wine

FREEZER TO MICROWAVE

The microwave is a cooker in its own right but it is also the perfect partner for your freezer. One of the greatest innovations since the introduction of the freezer for storing food, is the microwave for reducing the defrosting times from hours to minutes.

The microwave cuts defrosting times to a fraction of what they would be if the food were left to stand at room temperature. All microwaves come with a defrost setting, or low settings that are recommended for defrosting. It is important to read the manufacturer's instructions carefully and to follow their guidance when using your microwave to defrost food.

In addition there are certain rules of thumb for defrosting and reheating foods.

Packing for freezer to microwave use

If a little forethought is put into the packing of food before freezing it can save a lot of effort when the food is to be defrosted and reheated.

When freezing foods like vegetables or individual items, it is best to open freeze the items until they are quite hard, then pack them into bags and seal them. Small quantities or single items can be removed with ease if the food is not frozen into a block.

Try to consider the shape of the package that you are freezing. For example, when freezing stews, sauces or other fluid dishes, pack them into containers which can be fitted into a vessel for microwave reheating. Polythene bags can be used to line casserole dishes or basins which can be used to reheat the dish at a later date. The food is ladled into the bag which is then sealed and frozen in the outer container. Once the package is firm the casserole or dish can be removed.

Boilable bags and roasting bags

These are particularly useful as they can be transferred directly from the freezer to the microwave not only to defrost the food but also to reheat it. Remember to use ties which are suitable for use in the microwave or to replace metal ties before transferring the frozen package to the microwave.

Freezer to microwave dishes

These are ideal for cooking food in the microwave, for freezing, then for defrosting and reheating in the microwave at a later date. However, unless you are very well equipped in the kitchen you will probably miss the dishes if they are stored away in the freezer for months. The answer is to line the dish with microwave-proof cling film before putting the food into the dish for freezing. If you cook the food in the dish in the first place, then transfer it to a basin, wash the dish, then line it with the film.

Put the food to be frozen into the lined dish, leave plenty of film overhanging the side of the dish. Make sure that the film covers the whole of the base, overlapping it well where necessary. If in any doubt use two layers of film.

Freeze the food until solid. Gently loosen the frozen food from the dish with a knife, then pull it out in a block, using the overhanging film to help. Wrap the film around the food and pack the whole block in a bag, then label and freeze.

To reheat the food, remove the bag and the film. If the film is stuck to the food, then place the block on a plate and cook on Maximum (Full) for 1 minute, or until the film can be pulled away from the outside of the food. Place the food in the dish in which it was originally moulded and it is ready to be defrosted and reheated.

Removing frozen food from ordinary freezer containers

Whether you are packing food in a dish suitable for heating the food or in a simple storage container, then it is sensible to make sure that it will fit in to the microwave oven cavity. For example, packing soups in very tall containers may mean that the block of frozen soup is too tall to fit into the microwave for reheating.

If the food does not come out of the container easily, then remove the lid and place the container in the microwave for a minute or so. Release the block of food and transfer it to a suitable container for reheating it completely.

Remember, do not heat food in containers which are not designed to stand high temperatures.

Using boilable bags or roasting bags

1. Boil-in-the-bag purchased frozen foods can be reheated successfully in the microwave. The bag should be placed on a plate or suitable shallow dish. Pierce the bag to allow steam to escape during cooking.

2. Home-made dishes or home-frozen foods can be packed in boilable bags or roasting bags ready to be reheated in the microwave. Remember to remove all metal clips and replace them with elastic bands or microwave-proof ties. Loosen the tie to allow the steam to escape and place the packet on a plate or shallow dish to catch any juices which may escape.

Lining dishes before freezing blocks of food

1. Here a lasagne is being prepared for freezing. The dish selected is one that will fit in the microwave. It is lined with microwave-proof cling film. The film is smoothed evenly over the base and up the sides of the dish. There is plenty of overhanging film on all sides for easy removal.

2. The ingredients for the lasagne are layered in the film-lined dish.

3. When the lasagne is layered completely it is frozen until solid, with the ends of film still hanging over the edge of the dish. Here it is removed from the dish, with the help of the film and using a knife to help ease out the block. The lasagne is packed, labelled and frozen.

Selecting the setting

When defrosting raw foods or foods which do not require further cooking before they are served cold, then select a defrost setting.

Defrost setting or the low power setting recommended by the manufacturer is ideal for defrosting all foods, whether they are to be reheated before serving, cooked into other dishes or served cold. However, if you are in a hurry the defrosting time of certain foods (mainly cooked dishes) can be reduced by using a higher setting. This is usually acceptable if the food is reheated following defrosting; the aim is to combine the process of defrosting with reheating. Raw foods begin to cook when defrosted on higher settings.

The higher the setting used, then the more attention needed when preparing the food. A medium setting can be used and only moderate attention has to be paid to the food. Maximum (Full) can also be used but you must stay near and turn, stir and

Defrosting and reheating a block of frozen food

1. The lid is removed from the container and it is heated in the microwave very briefly until the block of food can be released.

2. The food is transferred to a suitable dish as soon as it can be released.

3. As it defrosts, the block of food is carefully broken up, and lumps of food are eased apart.

rearrange the food regularly otherwise some parts will overcook before others are defrosted. The advantage of using the higher setting is, of course, in the speed. It is useful if you are in a hurry to defrost and reheat a casserole for supper, a bolognese sauce or similar foods. To offer some guidance when using a high setting, the charts provide an outline of the timings and brief instructions.

GUIDE TO ONE-STAGE DEFROSTING AND REHEATING

Food	Quantity	Time in minutes on Maximum (Full)	Method
Purchased frozen foods: defrosting time only			
Bread, rolls	2	1	Place on absorbent kitchen paper.
Bread, sliced	2 slices	1	Turn over once.
Cheesecake	2 pieces, 175 g (6 oz)	30 seconds	—
Orange juice, frozen	178 ml (6½ fl oz) can	1	Transfer to suitable jug and stir once.
Purchased frozen foods: defrosting and reheating			
Chips, oven chips	100 g (4 oz)	2	Rearrange once.
Cod in butter sauce, boil-in-the-bag	170 g (6 oz)	5	Pierce bag before cooking to allow steam to escape. Place on plate or dish.
Fish cakes	4, 225 g (8 oz)	4	Turn fish cakes over and round once.
Frozen home-made cooked dishes			
Bread, garlic	½ French loaf, 175 g (6 oz)	1½	Place on a double thickness of kitchen paper
Casserole, beef	4 servings	10–12	Break up the block of casserole as it thaws, then stir as it reheats
Cottage pie	4 servings	15	Remove dish from oven after 10 minutes. Cover with foil and stand for 5 minutes. Remove foil and cook for a further 5 minutes.
Complete meal: meat patties new potatoes peas gravy	2, 100 g (4 oz) 4, 150 g (5 oz) 100 g (4 oz) 4 tablespoons	8	Cover plate with special microwave-proof cover or microwave-proof cling film.
Meat patties (raw)	4, 225 g (8 oz)	6	Turn patties over and round 3 times.
Rice, long-grain, cooked	450 g (1 lb)	8	If in boilable bag, pierce bag to allow steam to escape. Cover dish if rice is not in a bag. Stir once.
Frozen home-made sauces and soups			
Bolognese sauce	4 servings	12–14	Break up the block as it defrosts, then stir once as it reheats

GUIDE TO ONE-STAGE DEFROSTING AND REHEATING

Food	Quantity	Time in minutes on Maximum (Full)	Method
Onion sauce	300 ml ($\frac{1}{2}$ pint)	6–7	Break up the block as it defrosts, then whisk well halfway through reheating and before serving.
Apple sauce	150 ml ($\frac{1}{4}$ pint)	3	Stir once.
Cauliflower soup	1 litre (2 pints)	18	Break up the block of soup as it defrosts, then stir halfway through reheating and again before serving.

Guide to defrosting

Always err on the side of safety and follow the minimum times given in recipes, adding extra if the food is not sufficiently thawed. Special care should be taken with poultry. When completely thawed the wings and legs will be flexible and there will be no ice in the cavity. The following hints will also ensure good results.
● Pierce any skins, membranes or pouches before thawing.
● Turn foods over during thawing.
● If turning is not possible then rotate the dish during thawing.
● Flex any pouches that cannot be broken up or stirred during the thawing time and rotate frequently.
● Place any foods like cakes, bread rolls, sausage rolls and pastry items on a double sheet of paper towel during thawing to absorb any excess moisture.
● Any blocks of frozen food should be broken up with a fork during thawing so that the microwave energy can concentrate on the unfrozen block.
● Separate any blocks of frozen meats like hamburgers, sausages and steaks as they thaw.
● Remove any giblets from the cavity of chickens and other poultry or game birds as they thaw.
● Open all cartons and remove any lids and wrappings before thawing.
● With items like meat joints, whole poultry and whole fish, thaw the items until icy, then leave to thaw completely during the standing time.
● If any parts of the food start to thaw at too fast a rate or become warm, then shield or protect these areas with small strips of aluminium foil, attached with wooden cocktail sticks if necessary.
● Always observe a standing time – foods will continue to thaw with the heat produced via conduction. Allow foods to thaw until just icy for best results.
● Home-frozen food tends to take longer to thaw than commercially frozen food because of the ice crystals.
● When freezing a meal, do not overlap foods and place the thicker, denser items to the edges of the plate.

Guide to reheating

Most foods will reheat in the microwave cooker without loss of quality, flavour, colour and some nutrients. Follow the guidelines below.
● Arrange foods on a plate for reheating so that the thicker, denser and meatier portions are to the outer edge.
● Cover foods when reheating to retain moisture, unless otherwise stated.
● When reheating observe the standing time to maximize use and avoid overcooking.
● When reheating potatoes in their jackets, breads, pastry items and other moist foods, place them on a sheet of paper towel so that it will absorb any moisture.
● Stir foods regularly while reheating. If stirring is not possible then rotate the food or dish or rearrange it.

Smoked Haddock with Noodles

Serves 3–4
1 small onion, peeled
6 cloves
1 bay leaf
6 peppercorns
1 small carrot, peeled
300 ml (½ pint) milk
2 × 198 g (7 oz) packets frozen
    buttered smoked haddock
40 g (1½ oz) butter
40 g (1½ oz) plain flour
2 teaspoons chopped fresh
    parsley
75 g (3 oz) grated cheese
225 g (8 oz) noodles
600 ml (1 pint) boiling water
1 tablespoon oil
To garnish:
lemon slices
tomato slices
parsley sprigs

Preparation time: 10 minutes
Cooking time: 28½–30 minutes,
plus standing
Microwave setting: Defrost and
Maximum (Full)

1. Stud the onion with cloves
and place in a bowl with the bay
leaf, peppercorns, carrot and
milk. Cook on Defrost for 10–11
minutes until hot. Leave to stand
so that the milk is flavoured
while cooking the haddock.

2. Pierce the packets of smoked
haddock and place on a plate.
Cook on Maximum for 10
minutes, shaking the packets
gently after 6 minutes.

3. Place the butter in a jug and
cook on Maximum for 30
seconds to melt. Add the flour,
mixing well. Gradually add the
strained milk and cook on
Maximum for 2–2½ minutes,
stirring every 1 minute until the
sauce is smooth and thickened.
Stir in the parsley and the
cheese until melted.

4. Place the noodles, water and
oil in a deep container. Cover
and cook on Maximum for 6
minutes. Leave to stand for 3
minutes, then drain.

5. Flake the haddock into bite-
sized pieces, removing and
discarding any skin. Stir into the
sauce, tossing gently to mix.

6. To serve immediately, arrange
the noodles round the edge of a
shallow serving dish. Spoon the
haddock mixture into the
centre. Garnish with lemon
slices, tomato slices and parsley
sprigs.

FREEZING DETAILS
1. Prepare the recipe to the end
of step 5.

2. Cool quickly, pack the
noodles and haddock mixture
separately into rigid containers.
Cover, seal, label and freeze for
up to 2 months.

REHEATING DETAILS
Microwave setting: Defrost and
Maximum (Full)
Defrosting and cooking time:
30–31 minutes

1. Remove all wrappings. Cook
the haddock mixture on Defrost
for 8 minutes. Leave to stand for
5 minutes.

2. Cook the noodles on Defrost
for 6 minutes. Leave to stand for
2 minutes.

3. Cook the haddock mixture
on Maximum for 5–6 minutes,
stirring once.

4. Cook the noodles on
Maximum for 4 minutes. Serve
as in step 6 above.

Sweet and Sour Soup

Serves 4
2 tablespoons oil
450 g (1 lb) lean pork, finely
    chopped
25 g (1 oz) plain flour
salt
freshly ground black pepper
1 onion, peeled and chopped
1 green pepper, cored, seeded
    and chopped
1 large carrot, peeled and
    grated
1 × 400 g (14 oz) can tomatoes
300 ml (½ pint) white meat stock
1 tablespoon red wine vinegar
1 garlic clove, peeled and
    crushed
grated rind of 1 orange
1 tablespoon tomato purée
½ teaspoon ground ginger

Preparation time: 20 minutes,
including heating browning dish
Cooking time: 24 minutes
Microwave setting: Maximum
(Full)

1. Preheat a browning dish for 8
minutes (or according to the
manufacturer's instructions).
Brush with the oil and cook for
a further 1 minute.

2. Toss the pork in the flour
with salt and pepper to taste.
Add the pork to the browning
dish and turn quickly on all
sides to brown evenly. Add the
onion, green pepper and carrot,
cover and cook for 8 minutes,
stirring once.

3. Transfer to a large bowl and
stir in the tomatoes with their

Pork Rolls with Cabbage

Serves 4

450 g (1 lb) pork sausagemeat
1 onion, peeled and chopped
100 g (4 oz) button mushrooms,
  chopped
1 tablespoon lemon juice
grated rind of ½ lemon
1 teaspoon mustard powder
2 tablespoons chopped fresh
  parsley
1 egg, beaten
salt
freshly ground black pepper
1 medium cabbage, washed
  and shredded
4 tablespoons water
1 tablespoon soy sauce
1 tablespoon oil
To garnish:
tomato wedges
parsley sprig

Preparation time: 20 minutes,
including heating browning dish
Cooking time: 16–17 minutes
Microwave setting: Maximum
(Full)

1. Mix the sausagemeat with the
onion, mushrooms, lemon
juice, lemon rind, mustard,
parsley, egg and salt and pepper
to taste, blending well. Divide
into 8 portions and shape into
rolls.

2. Place the shredded cabbage
in a bowl with the water and salt
to taste. Cover and cook for 8
minutes, stirring once. Drain
thoroughly and toss with the soy
sauce to coat lightly.

3. If serving immediately, preheat a large browning dish for 8
minutes (or according to the
manufacturer's instructions).
Brush with the oil and cook for
a further 1 minute.

4. Add the pork rolls and turn
quickly on all sides to brown
evenly. Cook for 7–8 minutes,
turning and re-arranging the
rolls once. Serve on a bed of
seasoned cabbage and garnish
with tomato wedges and
parsley.

FREEZING DETAILS

1. Prepare the cabbage mixture
and the uncooked pork rolls to
the end of step 2.

2. Cool quickly, pack the
cooked cabbage mixture in a
rigid container. Cover, seal and
label.

3. Freeze the uncooked pork
rolls interleaved between
freezer film and overwrapped
with aluminium foil. Seal, label
and freeze both for up to 3
months.

REHEATING DETAILS
Microwave setting: Defrost and
Maximum (Full)
Defrosting and cooking time:
28–32 minutes

1. Remove all wrappings. Place
the pork rolls on a plate and
cook on Defrost for 6–7
minutes, turning and re-
arranging once. Leave to stand
while cooking the cabbage.

2. Place the frozen cabbage in a
bowl. Cover and cook on
Maximum for 4–6 minutes,
stirring frequently.

3. Cook the pork rolls as in
steps 3 and 4 above. Reheat the
cabbage on Maximum for 2
minutes if necessary.

4. Serve the pork rolls on the
bed of cooked cabbage and
garnish with tomato wedges and
parsley sprig.

Cook's Tip

If you are freezing this dish you
must not use frozen
sausagemeat to make the rolls,
only fresh ingredients should be
used if the dish is frozen
uncooked.

---

juice, stock, vinegar, garlic,
orange rind, tomato purée and
ginger. Add salt and pepper to
taste. Cover and cook for 15
minutes, stirring twice.

4. Serve hot with crusty bread.

FREEZING DETAILS
1. Prepare the recipe to the end
of step 3.

2. Cool quickly, transfer to a
rigid container, allowing 2.5 cm
(1 inch) headspace. Cover, seal,
label and freeze for up to 2
months.

REHEATING DETAILS
Microwave setting: Defrost and
Maximum (Full)
Defrosting and cooking time:
32 minutes

1. Remove all wrappings and
place the frozen soup in a
suitable serving dish. Cook on
Defrost for 12 minutes,
breaking up and stirring twice.
Leave to stand for 10 minutes.

2. Cover and cook on Maximum
for 10 minutes, stirring twice.

3. Serve hot with crusty bread.

Sweet and sour soup; Pork rolls with cabbage

Pasta Scallops

Serves 3–4
175 g (6 oz) pasta shells
750 ml (1¼ pints) boiling water
1 tablespoon oil
salt
6 rashers streaky bacon, rinds removed
20 g (¾ oz) butter
20 g (¾ oz) plain flour
300 ml (½ pint) milk
freshly ground black pepper
75 g (3 oz) grated cheese
2 hard-boiled eggs, shelled and chopped
To garnish:
parsley sprigs

Preparation time: 10 minutes
Cooking time: 21–24½ minutes
Microwave setting: Maximum (Full)

1. Place the pasta in a deep dish with the water, oil and salt to taste. Cover and cook for 12–14 minutes, stirring once. Leave to stand while cooking the bacon and sauce.

2. Place the rashers on a plate or microwave bacon rack, cover with a paper towel and cook for 3 minutes until crisp.

3. Place the butter in a jug and cook for 30 seconds to melt. Add the flour, blending well. Gradually add the milk and cook for 3½–4 minutes, stirring every 1 minute until smooth and thickened. Add salt and pepper to taste.

4. Stir in two-thirds of the cheese until melted.

5. Mix the eggs with the hot drained pasta and salt and pepper to taste.

6. Arrange the pasta mixture in 4 deep scallop shells. Spoon over the sauce. Crumble the bacon coarsely and sprinkle over the sauce.

7. To serve immediately, cook for 2–3 minutes, re-arranging the shells twice.

8. Brown under a preheated conventional grill if wished. Garnish with parsley sprigs.

FREEZING DETAILS
1. Prepare the recipe to the end of step 6.

2. Cool quickly, cover, seal, label and freeze for up to 3 months.

REHEATING DETAILS
Microwave setting: Defrost and Maximum (Full)
Defrosting and cooking time: 23–24 minutes

1. Remove all wrappings and cook the scallops (in the shells) on Defrost for 10 minutes. Leave them to stand for 10 minutes.

2. Cook on Maximum for 3–4 minutes, re-arranging and turning the uncovered scallop shells twice.

3. Brown under a preheated conventional grill if wished. Garnish with parsley sprigs.

Salami-stuffed Pasta

Serves 4
6 sheets lasagne
2 teaspoons oil
900 ml (1½ pints) boiling water
salt
Filling:
1 large onion, peeled and chopped
100 g (4 oz) mushrooms, sliced
225 g (8 oz) salami, diced
1 × 400 g (14 oz) can tomatoes
1½ tablespoons cornflour
Topping:
50 g (2 oz) butter
50 g (2 oz) plain flour
600 ml (1 pint) milk
175 g (6 oz) grated cheese
bay leaves to garnish

Preparation time: 20 minutes
Cooking time: 27½–29 minutes
Microwave setting: Maximum (Full)

1. Place the lasagne in a deep rectangular dish. Add 1 teaspoon oil, the water and salt to taste. Cover and cook for 9 minutes. Leave to stand for 10 minutes, drain and rinse in cold water.

2. Meanwhile, place the remaining oil and onion in a bowl. Cover and cook for 3 minutes. Add the mushrooms, cover and cook for 2 minutes.

3. Stir in three-quarters of the salami and the tomatoes, blending well. Cover and cook for 3 minutes, stirring twice.

4. Mix the cornflour with a little water and stir into the salami mixture. Cook for 2 minutes, stirring once, until thickened.

5. Cut the cooked lasagne sheets in half. Spoon equal quantities of the salami mixture onto the pieces of pasta, roll up to enclose and place, seam side down, in a large gratin dish.

6. Place the butter in a jug and cook for 1 minute to melt. Add the flour, blending well. Gradually add the milk and cook for 5½–6 minutes, stirring every 1 minute until smooth and thickened. Stir in two-thirds of the cheese until melted.

7. Pour the sauce over the pasta, sprinkle with the remaining cheese and salami.

8. To serve immediately, cook for 2–3 minutes, turning the dish once, or until heated through. Brown under a preheated conventional grill if wished. Garnish with bay leaves.

FREEZING DETAILS
1. Prepare the recipe to the end of step 7.

2. Cool quickly, cover, seal, label and freeze for up to 2 months.

REHEATING DETAILS
Microwave setting: Defrost and Maximum (Full)
Defrosting and cooking time: 29–31 minutes

1. Remove all wrappings and cook the pasta on Defrost for 15 minutes. Leave to stand for 10 minutes.

2. Cook on Maximum for 4–6 minutes, turning the dish twice. Brown under a preheated conventional grill if wished. Garnish with bay leaves.

Leek and Luncheon Sausage Supper

Serves 4

*8 medium leeks, trimmed and
washed*
4 tablespoons water
8 slices luncheon sausage
25 g (1 oz) butter
25 g (1 oz) plain flour
300 ml (½ pint) milk
*100 g (4 oz) Cheddar cheese,
grated*
salt
freshly ground black pepper

Preparation time: 5 minutes
Cooking time: 16–19½ minutes
Microwave setting: Maximum
(Full)

1. Place the leeks in a dish. Add the water, cover and cook for 10–12 minutes until tender, stirring once. Drain thoroughly.

2. Wrap each leek in a slice of the luncheon sausage and place in a flameproof serving dish.

3. Place the butter in a jug and cook for 30 seconds to melt. Add the flour, blending well. Gradually add the milk and cook for 3½–4 minutes, stirring every 1 minute until smooth and thickened.

4. Stir in three-quarters of the cheese until melted. Add salt and pepper to taste. Spoon over the leeks and sprinkle with the remaining cheese.

5. If serving immediately, cook for 2–3 minutes until the cheese is hot and bubbly.

6. Brown under a preheated conventional grill if wished.

FREEZING DETAILS

1. Prepare the recipe to the end of step 4.

2. Cool quickly, cover, seal, label and freeze for up to 3 months.

REHEATING DETAILS

Microwave setting: Defrost and Maximum (Full)
Defrosting and cooking time: 18–21 minutes

1. Remove all wrappings and cook the rolls on Defrost for 8 minutes. Leave to stand for 5 minutes.

2. Cook on Maximum for 5–8 minutes.

3. Brown under a preheated conventional grill if wished.

*Pasta scallops; Salami-stuffed pasta;
Leek and luncheon sausage supper*

Danish Pizza

Serves 2

8 rashers streaky bacon, rinds removed
50 g (2 oz) butter
1 onion, peeled and chopped
1 × 227 g (8 oz) can tomatoes, drained and chopped
1 teaspoon dried mixed herbs
salt
freshly ground black pepper
100 g (4 oz) self-raising flour
water to mix
1 tablespoon oil
100 g (4 oz) Samsoe cheese, sliced
3 stuffed olives, sliced
rosemary sprigs to garnish

Preparation time: 25 minutes, including heating browning dish
Cooking time: 15½ minutes, plus standing
Microwave setting: Maximum (Full)

1. Place the bacon on a plate or microwave bacon rack, cover with a paper towel and cook for 3 minutes until crisp.

2. Place half the butter in a bowl and cook for 30 seconds to melt. Add the onion, cover and cook for 2½ minutes. Add the tomatoes, herbs and salt and pepper to taste. Cover and cook for 4 minutes, stirring twice.

3. To make the dough, rub the remaining butter into the flour and gradually add about 3–4 tablespoons of water to make a soft dough. Knead lightly until smooth and roll out on a lightly floured surface to a square large enough to fit a small browning dish.

4. Preheat the browning dish for 6 minutes (or according to the manufacturer's instructions). Brush with the oil and heat for a further 30 seconds.

5. Place the dough in the browning dish and top with the tomato mixture, spreading it evenly. Arrange the cheese on top and cook for 5½ minutes, turning the dish every 1 minute.

6. Arrange the cooked bacon rashers on top of the pizza to form a lattice. Place the sliced olives in the 'window' of each lattice.

7. To serve immediately, cook for a further 30 seconds. Leave to stand for 5 minutes, then remove from the dish and garnish with rosemary. Serve with a crisp salad if wished.

FREEZING DETAILS
1. Prepare the recipe to the end of step 6.

2. Cool quickly, place in a rigid container, cover, seal, label and freeze for up to 2 months.

REHEATING DETAILS
Microwave setting: Maximum (Full)
Defrosting and cooking time: 6 minutes

1. Remove all wrappings. Place the pizza on a double thickness piece of paper towel. Cook for 6 minutes until the pizza is hot and bubbly.

2. Serve, garnished with rosemary, and with a crisp salad if wished.

Cheese and Ham Toasties

Serves 4

8 small slices thin white bread, crusts removed
1–2 teaspoons wholegrain mustard
4 slices quick-melting processed cheese
4 slices cooked ham
40 g (1½ oz) butter

Preparation time: 15 minutes, including heating browning dish
Cooking time: 4–5 minutes
Microwave setting: Maximum (Full)

1. Spread half the bread slices with mustard to taste. Top each with a slice of cheese and ham. Cover with the remaining bread slices, pressing down well.

2. To serve immediately, place the butter in a bowl and cook for 1 minute to melt.

3. Preheat a large browning dish for 8 minutes (or according to the manufacturer's instructions).

4. Brush one side of each sandwich with half the butter. Place in the browning dish and allow to brown on the underside, about 1–2 minutes.

5. Quickly brush the second side of each sandwich with the remaining butter, turn over with tongs and cook for 2 minutes, turning the dish once.

6. Cut each sandwich in half

diagonally to serve (with napkins).

FREEZING DETAILS
1. Prepare the recipe to the end of step 1.

2. Freeze the uncooked sandwiches, wrapped in aluminium foil, sealed and labelled for up to 3 months.

REHEATING DETAILS
Microwave setting: Defrost and Maximum (Full)
Defrosting and cooking time: 22–23 minutes

1. Remove all wrappings. Place on a plate and cook on Defrost for 5 minutes. Leave to stand for 5 minutes.

2. Cook as in steps 2–6 above. Serve hot with napkins.

Spaghetti Mozzarella

Serves 4

225 g (8 oz) spaghetti
1.2 litres (2 pints) boiling water
1 tablespoon oil
salt
100 g (4 oz) butter
1 garlic clove, peeled and
 crushed
4 tomatoes, peeled, seeded and
 quartered
75 g (3 oz) black olives
175 g (6 oz) Mozzarella cheese,
 cubed
3 tablespoons chopped fresh
 parsley
freshly ground black pepper

Preparation time: 10 minutes
Cooking time: $13\frac{1}{2}$–$14\frac{1}{2}$ minutes,
plus standing
Microwave setting: Maximum
(Full)

1. Wind the spaghetti into a deep dish with the water, oil and salt to taste until softened. Submerge in the water, cover and cook for about 10 minutes. Leave to stand for 5 minutes.

2. To serve immediately, place the butter in a bowl and cook for about 3–4 minutes, until 'nutty'. Add the garlic and cook for 30 seconds.

3. Drain the cooked spaghetti and toss in the hot garlic butter with the tomatoes, olives, cheese, parsley and salt and pepper to taste. Serve at once on warmed plates with a simple green salad.

FREEZING DETAILS
1. Prepare the recipe to the end of step 1.

2. Place in a rigid container, cover, seal, label and freeze for up to 1 month.

REHEATING DETAILS
Microwave setting: Defrost and Maximum (Full)
Defrosting and cooking time: 18–19 minutes

1. Remove all wrappings. Place the pasta in a bowl, cover and cook on Defrost for $6\frac{1}{2}$ minutes. Leave to stand for 2 minutes.

2. Cook on Maximum for 4 minutes. Leave to stand for 2 minutes.

3. Continue from step 2 above.

Danish pizza; Cheese and ham toasties

Ham and Potato Supper

Serves 4–6
50 g (2 oz) butter
2 onions, peeled and chopped
2 teaspoons Meaux mustard
2 teaspoons chopped fresh
tarragon or 1 teaspoon dried
tarragon
3 tablespoons plain flour
300 ml (½ pint) milk
300 ml (½ pint) white meat stock
675 g (1½ lb) cooked ham,
cubed
900 g (2 lb) potatoes, peeled
and cubed
8 tablespoons water
2 tablespoons milk
pinch of ground nutmeg
salt
freshly ground black pepper

Preparation time: 15 minutes
Cooking time: 32–35 minutes
Microwave setting: Maximum
(Full)

1. Place half the butter in a bowl with the onions. Cover and cook for 4 minutes.

2. Stir in the mustard, tarragon and flour, blending well. Gradually add the milk and stock. Cook for 8–9 minutes, stirring every 2 minutes until smooth and thickened. Fold in the cubed ham.

3. Place the potatoes in a bowl with the water. Cover and cook for 16–18 minutes until tender. Drain and mash with the remaining butter, milk, nutmeg and salt and pepper to taste.

4. Spoon the ham mixture into a large dish. Spoon the potato mixture into a piping bag fitted with a large star-shaped nozzle and pipe round the edge to make a border.

5. To serve immediately, cook for 4 minutes, turning the dish every 1 minute.

6. Brown under a preheated conventional grill if wished.

FREEZING DETAILS
1. Prepare the recipe to the end of step 4.

2. Cook quickly, cover, seal, label and freeze for up to 3 months.

REHEATING DETAILS
Microwave setting: Defrost and Maximum (Full)
Defrosting and cooking time: 40–42 minutes

1. Remove all wrappings. Cook on Defrost for 20 minutes. Allow to stand for 10 minutes.

2. Cook on Maximum for 10–12 minutes, turning the dish every 2 minutes.

3. Brown under a preheated conventional grill if wished.

From left to right: Herder's pie; Ham and potato supper; Wholewheat spinach and cheese quiche

Wholewheat Spinach and Cheese Quiche

Serves 4
175 g (6 oz) wholewheat flour
40 g (1½ oz) lard
40 g (1½ oz) margarine
2 tablespoons iced water
Filling:
450 g (1 lb) fresh spinach leaves, washed, or 1 × 225 g (8 oz) packet frozen leaf spinach
100 g (4 oz) cottage cheese
2 eggs, beaten
75 ml (2½ fl oz) single cream
4 tablespoons grated Parmesan cheese
salt
freshly ground black pepper

Preparation time: 20 minutes
Cooking time: 24–29 minutes, plus standing
Microwave setting: Maximum (Full) and Defrost

1. Place the flour in a bowl. Rub in the lard and margarine with the fingertips until the mixture resembles fine breadcrumbs. Add the water and bind together to a firm but pliable dough. Turn on to a lightly floured surface and knead until smooth and free from cracks.

2. Roll out the pastry on a lightly floured surface to a round large enough to line a 20 cm (8 inch) dish. Press in firmly, taking care not to stretch the pastry. Cut the pastry away, leaving a 5 mm (¼ inch) 'collar' above the dish to allow for any shrinkage that may occur. Prick the base and sides well with a fork.

3. Place a double thickness layer of paper towel over the base, easing it into position round the edges.

4. Cook on Maximum for 3½ minutes, giving the dish a quarter turn every 1 minute. Remove the paper and cook on Maximum for a further 1½ minutes.

5. Place the fresh spinach in a bowl, cover and cook on Maximum for 5–7 minutes. Drain thoroughly and chop coarsely. Alternatively, cook the frozen spinach on Maximum for 6–7 minutes, breaking up the spinach after 3 minutes. Drain thoroughly and chop coarsely.

6. Mix together the cottage cheese, eggs, cream, Parmesan cheese and salt and pepper. Stir in the spinach, blending well. Spoon into the flan case and cook on Defrost for 14–16 minutes, giving the dish a quarter turn every 3 minutes. Allow to stand for 10–15 minutes. The flan should set completely during this time.

FREEZING DETAILS
1. Prepare the recipe to the end of step 6.

2. Cool quickly, pack into a rigid container, cover, seal, label and freeze for up to 2 months.

REHEATING DETAILS
Microwave setting: Maximum (Full)
Defrosting and cooking time: 9–10 minutes

1. Remove all wrappings. Cook on Maximum for 4–5 minutes, turning once. Allow to stand for 3 minutes to serve cold.

2. To reheat, cook on Maximum for 2 minutes.

Herder's Pie

Serves 4
50 g (2 oz) butter
1 large onion, peeled and chopped
100 g (4 oz) button mushrooms, quartered
1 × 175 g (6 oz) can pimientos, drained and chopped
1 × 400 g (14 oz) can tomatoes, drained
450 g (1 lb) cooked bacon or ham, coarsely minced or finely chopped
1 tablespoon plain flour
2 tablespoons tomato ketchup
1 tablespoon Worcestershire sauce
½ teaspoon dried rosemary
freshly ground black pepper
675 g (1½ lb) potatoes, peeled and cubed
1 large carrot, peeled and grated
5 tablespoons water
50 g (2 oz) cheese, grated

Preparation time: 5 minutes
Cooking time: 33–35 minutes
Microwave setting: Maximum (Full)

1. Place half the butter in a large bowl with the onion and mushrooms, cover and cook for 5 minutes, stirring once.

2. Add the pimientos, tomatoes, bacon or ham tossed in the flour, tomato ketchup, Worcestershire sauce, rosemary and pepper to taste, blending well. Cover and cook for 10 minutes, stirring twice. Spoon into a large shallow dish.

3. Place the potatoes and carrot in a bowl with the water. Cover and cook for 12–14 minutes until tender. Drain and mash with the remaining butter and cheese. Pipe or spoon over the meat mixture to cover. If piping the mixture, spoon into a piping bag fitted with a large star-shaped nozzle.

4. To serve immediately, cook for 6 minutes, turning the dish every 1½ minutes.

5. Brown under a preheated conventional grill if preferred.

FREEZING DETAILS
1. Prepare the recipe to the end of step 3.

2. Cool quickly, cover, seal, label and freeze for up to 3 months.

REHEATING DETAILS
Microwave setting: Defrost and Maximum (Full)
Defrosting and cooking time: 40 minutes

1. Remove all wrappings. Cook on Defrost for 10 minutes. Allow to stand for 10 minutes. Cook on Defrost for a further 10 minutes.

2. Cook on Maximum for 10 minutes to reheat, turning every 2 minutes.

3. Brown under a preheated conventional grill if wished.

Punchy Hot Pot

Serves 4

1 tablespoon oil
675 g (1½ lb) turkey thigh meat,
* cubed, or turkey casserole*
* meat*
25 g (1 oz) seasoned flour
1 large onion, peeled and sliced
1 garlic clove, peeled and
* crushed*
100 g (4 oz) carrots, peeled and
* sliced*
200 ml (7 fl oz) brown ale
200 ml (7 fl oz) beef stock
1 teaspoon vinegar
1 teaspoon sugar
1½ teaspoons tomato purée
½ teaspoon Worcestershire sauce
1 bay leaf
salt
100 g (4 oz) button mushrooms,
* halved*

Preparation time: 5 minutes
Cooking time: 51 minutes
Microwave setting: Maximum
(Full) and Medium

1. Place the oil in a large
casserole and cook on
Maximum for 1 minute.

2. Toss the turkey in the flour.
Add to the oil with the onion,
garlic and carrots, blending well.
Cover and cook on Maximum
for 10 minutes.

3. Add the brown ale, stock,
vinegar, sugar, tomato purée,
Worcestershire sauce, bay leaf
and salt to taste, blending well.
Cover and cook on Maximum
for 10 minutes.

4. Reduce the setting to Medium
and cook for 20 minutes,
stirring once. Stir in the
mushrooms, cover and cook for
a further 10 minutes. Remove
and discard the bay leaf.

5. Serve with buttered noodles
or boiled rice.

FREEZING DETAILS
1. Prepare the recipe to the end
of step 4.

2. Cool quickly, cover, seal, label
and freeze for up to 3 months.

REHEATING DETAILS
Microwave setting: Defrost and
Maximum (Full)
Defrosting and cooking time:
37 minutes

1. Remove all wrappings. Cover
and cook on Defrost for 25
minutes, stirring twice.

2. Cook on Maximum for 12
minutes, stirring twice.

3. Serve hot with noodles or
boiled rice.

Braised Liver with Vegetables

Serves 4–6

2 tablespoons oil
2 tablespoons plain flour
½ teaspoon salt
¼ teaspoon freshly ground black
* pepper*
550 g (1¼ lb) lamb's liver, thinly
* sliced*
100 g (4 oz) streaky bacon,
* rinds removed and chopped*
2 onions, peeled and sliced
1 turnip, peeled and chopped
3 celery sticks, chopped
50 g (2 oz) carrots, peeled and
* chopped*
300 ml (½ pint) boiling beef
* stock*
1 tablespoon tomato purée
To garnish:
4 rashers streaky bacon, rinds
* removed*

Preparation time: 15 minutes
Cooking time: 54–56 minutes,
plus standing
Microwave setting: Maximum
(Full) and Medium

1. Blend the oil, flour, salt and
pepper in a large casserole.
Cook on Maximum for 2–3
minutes or until the colour of
the mixture is slightly darkened.

2. Add the liver and bacon,
tossing well to coat. Cook on
Maximum for 5 minutes, stirring
once.

3. Add the onions, turnip,
celery, carrots, stock and purée.
Cover and cook on Maximum
for 10 minutes, stirring once.

4. Reduce the setting to Medium
and cook for a further 35
minutes, stirring twice. Leave to
stand for 5 minutes.

5. To serve immediately, pleat
the 4 bacon rashers and thread
on to a wooden skewer or use
cocktail sticks. Cook on

Maximum for 2–3 minutes until
crisp, then use as a garnish.

FREEZING DETAILS
1. Prepare the recipe to the end
of step 4.

2. Cool quickly, cover, seal, label
and freeze for up to 2 months.

REHEATING DETAILS
Microwave setting: Defrost and
Maximum (Full)
Defrosting and cooking time:
42–43 minutes

1. Remove all wrappings. Cook
the casserole, covered, on
Defrost for 25 minutes.

2. Cook on Maximum for 12
minutes, stirring twice. Leave to
stand for 3 minutes while
completing step 5 above.

Cook's Tip

Liver cooks very successfully in
the microwave oven and it can
be topped with croûtons or
served on crisply fried bread to
add interest to the texture.

Punchy hot pot; Braised liver with
vegetables

Roast Chicken with Walnut and Orange Stuffing

Serves 6
1 × 1.75 kg (4 lb) fresh oven-
*   ready chicken*
25 g (1 oz) butter
1 tablespoon plain flour
300 ml (½ pint) chicken stock
Stuffing:
50 g (2 oz) butter
1 small onion, peeled and finely
*   chopped*
100 g (4 oz) fresh white
*   breadcrumbs*
25 g (1 oz) chopped fresh
*   parsley*
grated rind of 1 orange and 2
*   tablespoons orange juice*
50 g (2 oz) walnuts, chopped
salt
freshly ground black pepper
1 egg, beaten
To garnish:
orange slices
parsley sprigs

Preparation time: 15 minutes
Cooking time: 35½–45½ minutes,
plus standing
Microwave setting: Maximum
(Full)

1. To make the stuffing, put the butter in a bowl. Cook for 30 seconds to melt. Add the onion, cover the bowl and cook for 2 minutes.

2. Add the breadcrumbs, three-quarters of the parsley, orange rind and juice, walnuts, and salt and pepper. Add sufficient beaten egg to bind. Use to stuff the neck end of the chicken. Secure with wooden cocktail sticks. Roll the remaining stuffing into balls.

3. To serve immediately, shield the tips of the wings with small pieces of aluminium foil. Place on a roasting rack or upturned saucer in a dish and dot with butter.

4. Cook for 26–34 minutes, giving a half-turn halfway through. Cover with aluminium foil and leave to stand for 15 minutes.

5. Meanwhile, place the stuffing balls in a ring on a plate or roasting rack and cook for 2–3 minutes, turning the plate once. Sprinkle with the remaining parsley.

6. To make the gravy, place 2 tablespoons of the chicken juices in a bowl and stir in the flour. Cook for 3 minutes until the flour turns golden. Gradually add the stock, mixing well. Cook for 2–3 minutes, stirring every 1 minute, until smooth and boiling.

7. Garnish the chicken with orange slices and parsley sprigs.

FREEZING DETAILS
1. Prepare the recipe to the end of step 2.

2. Wrap the chicken and stuffing balls separately in aluminium foil. Seal, label and freeze for up to 3 months.

REHEATING DETAILS
Microwave setting: Defrost and Maximum (Full)
Defrosting and cooking time: about 1¼ hours

1. Remove all wrappings. Cook the chicken on Defrost for 26 minutes, turning it occasionally. Leave to stand for 5 minutes.

2. Meanwhile, cook the stuffing balls on Defrost for 5 minutes. Leave to stand while following steps 3, 4 and 5.

3. To make the gravy cook the frozen juices on Maximum for 2–3 minutes, stirring once. Continue from step 6 above.

Rabbit Casserole with Bacon and Sage Dumplings

Serves 4

1 tablespoon oil
675 g (1½ lb) boneless rabbit or
    4 large rabbit joints
2 tablespoons seasoned flour
1 onion, peeled and sliced
1 garlic clove, peeled and
    crushed
75 g (3 oz) streaky bacon, rinds
    removed and chopped
4 celery sticks, chopped
2 leeks, washed and sliced
2 carrots, peeled and sliced
400 ml (14 fl oz) hot chicken
    stock
1 bouquet garni
salt
freshly ground black pepper
celery leaves to garnish
Dumplings:
25 g (1 oz) streaky bacon, rinds
    removed and chopped
50 g (2 oz) self-raising flour
25 g (1 oz) shredded beef suet
1 tablespoon chopped fresh sage
    or 2 teaspoons dried sage
cold water to mix

Preparation time: 15 minutes
Cooking time: 66 minutes, plus
standing
Microwave setting: Maximum
(Full) and Medium

1. Place the oil in a large
casserole and cook on
Maximum for 1 minute.

2. Toss the rabbit in the flour.
Add to the oil with the onion,
garlic, bacon, celery, leeks and
carrots. Cover and cook on
Maximum for 10 minutes. Add
the stock, bouquet garni, salt
and pepper. Cover and cook on
Maximum for 5 minutes.

3. Reduce the setting to Medium
and cook for 30 minutes,
stirring twice.

4. To serve immediately, place
all the dumpling ingredients in a
bowl and mix to a soft dough.
Turn on to a floured surface and
form into 4 dumplings.

5. Stir the casserole and add the
dumplings. Cover and cook on
Medium for 20 minutes. Allow
to stand for 5 minutes. Remove
and discard the bouquet garni
and garnish with celery leaves.

FREEZING DETAILS
1. Prepare the recipe to the end
of step 3.

2. Cool quickly, remove and
discard the bouquet garni,
cover, seal, label and freeze for
up to 3 months.

REHEATING DETAILS
Microwave setting: Defrost,
Maximum (Full) and Medium
Defrosting and cooking time:
about 1 hour

1. Remove all wrappings. Cover
and cook on Defrost for 25
minutes, stirring twice.

2. Cook on Maximum for 10
minutes, stirring once.

3. Continue from step 4 above.

*Roast chicken with walnut and orange
stuffing; Rabbit casserole with bacon
and sage dumplings*

Slipper Pudding

Serves 4
Suet Pastry:
225 g (8 oz) self-raising flour
salt
100 g (4 oz) shredded beef suet
150 ml ($\frac{1}{4}$ pint) cold water
Filling:
225 g (8 oz) lean cooked bacon, chopped
25 g (1 oz) plain flour
1 teaspoon dried sage
1 onion, peeled and chopped
1 small cooking apple, peeled, cored and grated
100 g (4 oz) button mushrooms, sliced
freshly ground black pepper
150 ml ($\frac{1}{4}$ pint) chicken stock

Preparation time: 20 minutes
Cooking time: 12 minutes, plus standing.
Microwave setting: Maximum (Full)

1. Sift the flour and a pinch of salt into a bowl. Stir in the suet and water and mix quickly, using a round-bladed knife, to form a light elastic dough. Knead lightly until smooth and free from cracks.

2. Roll out the pastry on a lightly floured surface to a round about 5 cm (2 inches) larger than the diameter of a 900 ml ($1\frac{1}{2}$ pint) pudding basin. Cut a quarter section from the pastry round and reserve for a lid.

3. Lift the remaining piece of pastry and ease it into the basin, pinching the 2 cut edges together to seal and moulding the pastry on to the base and round the sides of the basin.

4. Toss the bacon in the flour. Add the sage, onion, apple and mushrooms and pepper to taste. Spoon into the basin and pour over the stock.

5. Roll out the remaining pastry to a round large enough to make a lid. Dampen the pastry edges with water and cover with the lid. Pinch the edges together firmly to seal.

6. Cover with cling film, snipping 2 holes in the top to allow the steam to escape. Cook for 12 minutes, giving the dish a quarter-turn every 3 minutes. Allow to stand for 10 minutes.

7. Serve hot with fresh vegetables in season.

FREEZING DETAILS
1. Prepare the recipe to the end of step 6.

2. Cool quickly, wrap in aluminium foil, seal, label and freeze for up to 1 month.

REHEATING DETAILS
Microwave setting: Defrost and Maximum (Full)
Defrosting and cooking time: 21–23 minutes

1. Remove all wrappings. Cook on Defrost for 6 minutes. Leave to stand for 10 minutes.

2. Cover and cook on Maximum for 5–7 minutes. Serve hot with fresh vegetables in season.

Bean Lasagne

Serves 4
175 g (6 oz) lasagne
1 teaspoon oil
900 ml ($1\frac{1}{2}$ pints) boiling water
salt
Beef and bean sauce:
1 tablespoon oil
1 large onion, peeled and chopped
225 g (8 oz) minced beef
1 × 450 g (1 lb) can baked beans in tomato sauce
2 tablespoons tomato purée
$\frac{1}{2}$ teaspoon ground nutmeg
freshly ground black pepper
100 g (4 oz) Cheddar cheese, grated

Preparation time: 10 minutes
Cooking time: 27–29 minutes
Microwave setting: Maximum (Full)

1. Place the lasagne in a deep rectangular casserole. Add the oil, water and a pinch of salt. Cover and cook for 9 minutes. Leave to stand while preparing the sauce, then drain thoroughly.

2. Place the oil in a bowl with the onion, cover and cook for 3 minutes. Add the beef and cook for 3 minutes, breaking up the beef and stirring twice.

3. Add the beans, tomato purée, nutmeg and salt and pepper to taste, blending well. Cook for 10 minutes, stirring once.

4. Layer the lasagne and beef and bean sauce in the casserole, finishing with a layer of sauce.

Trout with Orange

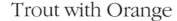

5. To serve immediately, sprinkle with the cheese and cook for 2–4 minutes until heated through. Alternatively, place under a preheated conventional grill until golden if wished.

FREEZING DETAILS
1. Prepare the recipe to the end of step 4.

2. Cool quickly, cover, seal, label and freeze for up to 3 months.

REHEATING DETAILS
Microwave setting: Defrost and Maximum (Full)
Defrosting and cooking time: 40–41 minutes

1. Remove all wrappings. Cook on Defrost for 25 minutes. Leave to stand for 10 minutes.

2. Cook on Maximum for 3–4 minutes to reheat.

3. Sprinkle with the cheese and cook on Maximum for 2 minutes or place under a preheated conventional grill until golden.

Serves 4
4 × 175 g (6 oz) trout, cleaned
Stuffing:
25 g (1 oz) butter
1 small onion, peeled and chopped
50 g (2 oz) mushrooms, wiped and chopped
6 tablespoons fresh white breadcrumbs
2 tablespoons chopped fresh parsley
salt
freshly ground black pepper
1 egg, beaten
Orange sauce:
25 g (1 oz) butter
pinch of caster sugar
1 orange, thinly sliced
8 tablespoons orange juice
1½ tablespoons lemon juice
To garnish:
fresh dill or parsley sprigs

Preparation time: 15 minutes, including heating browning dish
Cooking time: 15½ minutes
Microwave setting: Maximum (Full)

1. Remove the heads from the trout and bone if preferred.

2. Place the butter in a bowl and cook for 30 seconds to melt. Add the onion, cover and cook for 2 minutes. Stir in the mushrooms, cover and cook for 1 minute.

3. Stir in the breadcrumbs, parsley and salt and pepper to taste. Bind together with the beaten egg. Use to stuff the trout and place in a shallow oblong dish, top next to tail and stuffing pockets uppermost.

4. Cover and cook for 5 minutes. Turn the dish and cook for 5 minutes. Leave to stand, covered, while preparing the orange sauce.

5. Preheat a small browning dish for 6 minutes (or according to the manufacturer's instructions). Add the butter and sugar and swirl to coat. Add the orange slices and turn quickly on all sides to brown lightly. Add the orange juice and lemon juice and cook for 2 minutes.

6. To serve immediately, garnish with the orange slices and dill or parsley sprigs and spoon over the orange sauce.

FREEZING DETAILS
1. Prepare the recipe to the end of step 4.

2. Cool quickly, place in a rigid container, cover, seal, label and freeze for up to 2 months.

3. The orange slices are prepared when the dish is reheated.

REHEATING DETAILS
Microwave setting: Defrost and Maximum (Full)
Defrosting and cooking time: 23–25 minutes

1. Remove all wrappings and place on a shallow oblong dish. Cover and cook on Defrost for 20 minutes.

2. Cook on Maximum for 3–5 minutes to reheat.

3. Prepare the sauce. Garnish with the orange slices and dill or parsley sprigs. Spoon over the orange sauce.

Bean lasagne; Slipper pudding; Trout with orange

Pork Spareribs Provençal

Serves 6
6 pork sparerib chops
Marinade:
6 tablespoons oil
3 tablespoons white wine vinegar
1 tablespoon chopped fresh parsley
2 garlic cloves, peeled and crushed
Provençal sauce:
1 tablespoon oil
1 onion, peeled and finely chopped
1 green pepper, cored, seeded and chopped
1 tablespoon tomato purée
1 × 400 g (14 oz) can tomatoes, chopped
1 teaspoon sugar
1 teaspoon Worcestershire sauce
2 teaspoons cornflour
salt
freshly ground black pepper
parsley sprigs to garnish

Preparation time: about 20 minutes including heating browning dish, plus marinating
Cooking time: 37 minutes
Microwave setting: Maximum (Full) and Medium

1. Place the chops in a shallow dish.

2. Mix the oil with the vinegar, parsley and garlic, blending well. Pour over the chops and leave to marinate for 4 hours.

3. To cook, preheat a large browning dish on Maximum for 8 minutes (or according to the manufacturer's instructions).

4. Add the pork chops and turn quickly on all sides to brown evenly. Cook on Medium for 26 minutes. Remove, cover with aluminium foil and leave to stand while preparing the sauce.

5. Place the oil in a bowl and cook on Maximum for 1 minute. Add the onion and pepper, cover and cook on Maximum for 4 minutes. Stir in the tomato purée, tomatoes with their juice, sugar, Worcestershire sauce and cornflour dissolved in a little cold water. Add salt and pepper to taste and cook the sauce on Maximum for 6 minutes, stirring twice.

6. Serve the chops with the sauce and garnish with parsley sprigs.

FREEZING DETAILS
1. Prepare the recipe to the end of step 5.

2. Cool quickly, place the chops and sauce in a rigid freezer container. Cover, seal, label and freeze for up to 3 months.

REHEATING DETAILS
Microwave setting: Defrost and Maximum (Full)
Defrosting and cooking time: 38–40 minutes

1. Remove all wrappings. Place the frozen pork chops and sauce mixture in a serving dish and cook on Defrost for 25 minutes. Allow to stand for 5 minutes.

2. Cook on Maximum for 8–10 minutes.

3. Garnish with parsley.

Sweet and Sour Meatballs

Serves 4
2 tablespoons oil
1 onion, peeled and finely chopped
450 g (1 lb) lean minced beef
50 g (2 oz) fresh white or brown breadcrumbs
1 teaspoon Worcestershire sauce
salt
freshly ground black pepper
1 egg, beaten
Sauce:
1 tablespoon oil
1 red pepper, cored, seeded and chopped
1 green pepper, cored, seeded and chopped
2 tablespoons soft brown sugar
2 teaspoons soy sauce
2 tablespoons vinegar
120 ml (4 fl oz) orange juice
120 ml (4 fl oz) beef stock
2 teaspoons cornflour
parsley sprig to garnish

Preparation time: 15 minutes
Cooking time: 18½ minutes
Microwave setting: Maximum (Full)

1. Heat the oil in a large dish for 30 seconds. Add the onion and cook for 3 minutes, stirring once.

2. Meanwhile, mix the beef, breadcrumbs, Worcestershire sauce, salt and pepper to taste and enough egg to bind the mixture.

3. Divide into 8 portions and roll into balls. Place these in a single layer on top of the onion. Cook for 5 minutes, turning once. Leave to stand while preparing the sauce.

4. Place the oil and peppers in a bowl. Cover and cook for 4 minutes, stirring once. Stir in the sugar, soy sauce, vinegar, orange

juice, beef stock and cornflour, blending well. Cook for 3 minutes, stirring every 1 minute.

5. Pour over the meatballs and cook for 5 minutes.

6. Garnish with parsley sprig and serve with boiled rice or jacket potatoes.

FREEZING DETAILS
1. Prepare the recipe to the end of step 5.

2. Cool quickly, cover, seal, label and freeze for up to 3 months.

REHEATING DETAILS
Microwave setting: Defrost and Maximum (Full)
Defrosting and cooking time: 31–35 minutes

1. Remove all wrappings. Cook on Defrost for 8–10 minutes. Leave to stand for 15 minutes.

2. Cook on Maximum for 8–10 minutes, turning once. Garnish with parsley and serve with boiled rice or jacket potatoes.

Pork spareribs provençal; Sweet and sour meatballs

Celery with Lemon and Almonds

Serves 4

25 g (1 oz) butter
350 g (12 oz) celery, scrubbed
   and cut into 7.5 cm (3 inch)
   lengths
200 ml (7 fl oz) chicken stock or
   water
100 ml (3½ fl oz) lemon juice
1 tablespoon sugar
salt
freshly ground black pepper
50 g (2 oz) flaked almonds
grated rind of 1 small lemon
celery leaves to garnish

Preparation time: 5 minutes
Cooking time: 23½–26½ minutes
Microwave setting: Maximum
(Full)

1. Place the butter in a shallow dish and cook for 30 seconds to melt. Add the celery, tossing well to coat. Cook, uncovered, for 3 minutes.

2. Add the stock or water, lemon juice, sugar and salt and pepper to taste. Cover and cook for 16–18 minutes, turning the dish twice.

3. To serve immediately, leave the celery to stand while preparing the almonds. Place the almonds on a plate and cook for 4–5 minutes, stirring every 1 minute until golden.

4. Serve the celery sprinkled with the lemon rind and toasted almonds. Garnish with celery leaves.

FREEZING DETAILS

1. Prepare the recipe to the end of step 2.

2. Cool quickly, cover, seal, label and freeze for up to 3 months.

REHEATING DETAILS

Microwave setting: Maximum
(Full)
Defrosting and cooking time:
12–14 minutes

1. Remove all wrappings, cover and cook on Maximum for 3–4 minutes, turning the dish twice. Leave to stand for 5 minutes.

2. Meanwhile, toast the almonds as in step 3 above.

3. Serve the celery sprinkled with the lemon rind and almonds. Garnish with celery leaves.

Celery with lemon and almonds;
Spinach terrine (with provençal sauce)

Spinach Terrine

Serves 6–8
20 large fresh spinach leaves
450 g (1 lb) full fat soft cheese
3 egg yolks
100 g (4 oz) cooked ham,
*   minced or finely chopped*
2 teaspoons lemon juice
salt
freshly ground black pepper

Preparation time: 15 minutes,
plus chilling
Cooking time: $9\frac{1}{2}$–$10\frac{1}{2}$ minutes
Microwave setting: Maximum
(Full) and Medium

1. Wash the spinach leaves well, shake thoroughly and place in a bowl. Cover and cook on Maximum for $1\frac{1}{2}$ minutes. Drain and rinse under cold running water.

2. Use about 8 of the spinach leaves to line a 20 cm (8 inch) microwave loaf dish.

3. Mix the cheese with the egg yolks, ham, lemon juice and salt and pepper to taste.

4. Spoon one-third of the ham mixture into the base of the dish and cover with 4 of the spinach leaves. Repeat twice, finishing with a layer of spinach leaves.

5. Cover with cling film, snipping 2 holes in the top to allow the steam to escape. Cook on Medium for 5 minutes.

6. Give the dish a half turn and cook on Maximum for 3–4 minutes or until just set. Allow to cool in the dish.

7. To serve immediately, chill lightly and serve in thin slices with a tomato sauce such as provençal sauce (see Pork spareribs provençal page 212). Serve with crusty bread.

FREEZING DETAILS
1. Prepare the recipe to the end of step 6.

2. Cool quickly in the dish. Cover with aluminium foil, seal, label and freeze for up to 3 months.

DEFROSTING DETAILS
Microwave setting: Defrost
Defrosting time: 40–50 minutes

1. Remove all wrappings. Cook on Defrost for 20 minutes.

2. Leave to stand for 20–30 minutes before serving, cut into thin slices, with a sauce (see left).

Vegetable Rissoles

Serves 4
100 g (4 oz) red lentils
600 ml (1 pint) boiling chicken
*   stock*
1 large onion, peeled and finely
*   chopped*
1 celery stick, finely chopped
2 small carrots, peeled and
*   grated*
50 g (2 oz) cooked green beans,
*   finely chopped*
50 g (2 oz) fresh white
*   breadcrumbs*
3 eggs, beaten
1 teaspoon dried mixed herbs
salt
freshly ground black pepper
75 g (3 oz) dry white
*   breadcrumbs*
2–3 tablespoons oil

Preparation time: about 20 minutes including heating browning dish, plus standing
Cooking time: 27–29 minutes
Microwave setting: Maximum (Full)

1. Place the lentils and stock in a bowl. Cover and cook for 20 minutes, stirring once. Drain if necessary.

2. Mix the lentils with the onion, celery, carrots, beans, fresh breadcrumbs, 2 of the eggs, herbs and salt and pepper to taste. Leave to stand for 30 minutes.

3. Shape the mixture into 8 rissoles. Dip each of these in the remaining beaten egg and then in the dry breadcrumbs to coat.

4. To serve immediately, preheat a large browning dish for 8 minutes (or according to the manufacturer's instructions). Brush with the oil and cook for a further 1 minute.

5. Add the rissoles and allow to brown on the underside, about 2–3 minutes. Turn over and cook for 4–5 minutes, re-arranging them twice. Drain on paper towels and serve hot.

FREEZING DETAILS
1. Prepare the recipe to the end of step 3.

2. Freeze, interleaved with freezer film and wrapped in foil. Cover, seal, label and freeze for up to 3 months.

REHEATING DETAILS
Microwave setting: Maximum (Full)
Defrosting and cooking time: 25–29 minutes

1. Remove all wrappings and place the rissoles on a large plate. Cook on Maximum for 4–6 minutes, re-arranging them frequently. Leave to stand for 5 minutes.

2. Cook as in steps 4 and 5 above.

Broad Beans in Horseradish Cream

Serves 4
450 g (1 lb) shelled broad beans
4 tablespoons water
salt
25 g (1 oz) butter
2 tablespoons plain flour
300 ml (½ pint) milk
4 tablespoons double cream
4 teaspoons horseradish sauce
¼ teaspoon caster sugar
freshly ground black pepper
chopped fresh parsley to garnish

Preparation time: 5 minutes
Cooking time: 11½–15 minutes
Microwave setting: Maximum
(Full)

1. Place the broad beans in a bowl with the water and a little salt. Cover and cook for 6–8 minutes, shaking the dish once. Leave to stand while preparing the sauce.

2. Place the butter in a bowl and cook for 30 seconds to melt. Stir in the flour, blending well. Gradually add the milk and cook for 4–4½ minutes, stirring every 1 minute until smooth and thickened.

3. Add the cream, horseradish sauce, sugar and pepper to taste, blending thoroughly.

4. Fold in the drained cooked beans, tossing well to coat.

5. To serve immediately, cook for 1–2 minutes to reheat. Sprinkle with chopped parsley and serve.

FREEZING DETAILS
1. Prepare the recipe to the end of step 4.

2. Cool quickly, spoon into a rigid container. Cover, seal, label and freeze for up to 3 months.

REHEATING DETAILS
Microwave setting: Maximum
(Full)
Defrosting and cooking time:
15 minutes

1. Remove all wrappings. Place the frozen bean mixture in a bowl, cover and cook on Maximum for 7 minutes, breaking up the beans and stirring twice. Leave to stand for 5 minutes.

2. Cook on Maximum for 3 minutes, stirring once. Serve sprinkled with chopped parsley.

Leeks à la Grecque

Serves 4
1 large onion, peeled and
  chopped
350 g (12 oz) leeks, washed
  and sliced lengthways
100 g (4 oz) button mushrooms,
  halved
1 garlic clove, peeled and
  crushed
2 tablespoons olive oil
100 ml (3½ fl oz) dry white wine
1 × 227 g (8 oz) can peeled
  tomatoes
1 tablespoon tomato purée
¾ teaspoon dried mixed herbs
salt
freshly ground black pepper
chopped fresh basil or parsley to
  garnish

Preparation time: 10 minutes
Cooking time: 14–16 minutes
Microwave setting: Maximum
(Full)

1. Mix the onion, leeks and mushrooms with the garlic and place in a shallow dish.

2. Mix together the oil, wine, tomatoes and their juices, purée, herbs, and salt and pepper to taste, blending well. Spoon over the leek mixture, cover and cook for 14–16 minutes, stirring twice, until tender.

3. To serve, allow to cool, then chill. Garnish with chopped fresh basil or parsley. Serve with lamb or as a starter with crusty bread.

FREEZING DETAILS
1. Prepare the recipe to the end of step 2.

2. Cool quickly, spoon into a rigid container. Cover, seal, label and freeze for up to 3 months.

DEFROSTING DETAILS
Microwave setting: Maximum
(Full)
Defrosting time: 15 minutes

1. Remove all wrappings and place the frozen leek mixture in a bowl. Cover and cook for 5 minutes. Break up and stir well.

2. Leave to stand for 10 minutes until thoroughly thawed but still chilled. Serve garnished as above.

Caponata

Serves 4
4 tablespoons oil
4 celery sticks, finely chopped
2 large onions, peeled and
  sliced
4 small aubergines, diced
4 tablespoons tomato purée
1 tablespoon capers
50 g (2 oz) green olives, stoned
  and chopped
2 tablespoons water
2 tablespoons red wine vinegar
1 teaspoon sugar
salt
freshly ground black pepper

Preparation time: 5 minutes
Cooking time: 14 minutes, plus standing
Microwave setting: Maximum
(Full)

1. Place the oil, celery and onions in a large bowl. Cover and cook for 4 minutes, stirring once.

2. Add the aubergines, blending well. Cover and cook for 4 minutes, stirring once.

3. Stir in the purée, capers, olives, water, vinegar, sugar, and salt and pepper to taste. Cover and cook for 6 minutes, stirring once. Leave to stand for 5 minutes.

4. Serve hot or cold with pork or chicken.

FREEZING DETAILS
1. Prepare the recipe to the end of step 3.

2. Cool quickly, spoon into a rigid container, cover, seal, label and freeze for up to 2 months.

REHEATING DETAILS
Microwave setting: Defrost and Maximum (Full)
Defrosting and cooking time:
24–31 minutes

1. Remove all wrappings and cook on Defrost for 15 minutes. If serving cold, leave to stand for 5–10 minutes.

2. To reheat, cover and cook on Maximum for 4–6 minutes, stirring twice.

Western Baked Potatoes

Serves 4
4 × 250 g (9 oz) potatoes,
*   scrubbed*
100 g (4 oz) corned beef, cubed
1 × 450 g (1 lb) can barbecue
*   beans*
salt
freshly ground black pepper
50 g (2 oz) grated cheese

Preparation time: 10 minutes
Cooking time: 19–21 minutes,
plus standing
Microwave setting: Maximum
(Full)

Broad beans in horseradish cream;
Caponata; Western baked potatoes

1. Prick the potatoes with a fork and arrange on a double thickness of paper towels, spaced well apart. Cook for 10 minutes, turn over and rearrange, then cook for a further 6–7 minutes. Allow to stand for 5 minutes.

2. Split each potato in half and scoop out the flesh. Mix the flesh with the corned beef, beans and salt and pepper to taste, blending well. Return the mixture to the potato skins.

3. If serving immediately, sprinkle with the cheese and cook for 3–4 minutes to reheat.

Serve with barbecued meats, sausages or as a snack.

FREEZING DETAILS
1. Prepare the recipe to the end of step 2.

2. Cool quickly, place in a rigid box, cover, seal, label and freeze for up to 3 months.

REHEATING DETAILS
Microwave setting: Maximum (Full)
Defrosting and cooking time: 33–34 minutes

1. Remove all wrappings. Place the potatoes on a double thickness of paper towels, spaced well apart. Cook on Defrost for 30 minutes, rearranging them twice.

2. Sprinkle with the cheese and cook on Maximum for 3–4 minutes.

Gooseberry and Mint Pudding

Serves 4
Sponge pudding:
100 g (4 oz) butter
100 g (4 oz) caster sugar
2 eggs, beaten
100 g (4 oz) self-raising flour
pinch of salt
1–2 tablespoons hot water
4–5 tablespoons gooseberry jam
½ teaspoon chopped fresh mint
Custard:
300 ml (½ pint) milk
2 eggs
1 tablespoon caster sugar
1 teaspoon cornflour
2–3 drops vanilla essence

Preparation time: 20 minutes
Cooking time: 13–14 minutes,
plus standing
Microwave setting: Maximum
(Full)

1. Line a 900 ml (1½ pint)
pudding basin with cling film or
grease the basin well.

2. Cream the butter with the
sugar until light and fluffy. Add
the eggs, blending well. Sift the
flour with the salt and fold into
the mixture with a metal spoon.
Add enough water to make a
soft dropping consistency.

3. Mix the jam with the mint and
place in the bottom of the
prepared basin. Spoon the
sponge mixture on top. Cover
with cling film, snipping 2 holes
in the top to allow the steam to
escape. Cook for 6–7 minutes,
turning the basin once. Leave to
stand for 5–10 minutes.

4. To serve immediately, place
the milk in a jug and cook for
about 3 minutes or until almost
boiling. Lightly beat the eggs,
sugar, cornflour and vanilla
essence together. Pour the milk
on to this mixture, stir well to
blend and strain back into the
jug.

5. Return to the oven in a deep
dish containing hand-hot water
to come halfway up the sides

and cook for 4 minutes, stirring
every 1 minute to keep the
sauce smooth. The custard is
cooked when it lightly coats the
back of the spoon. Serve with
the turned out sponge pudding.

FREEZING DETAILS
1. Prepare the recipe to the end
of step 3.

2. Cover, seal, label and freeze
for up to 3 months.

REHEATING DETAILS
Microwave setting: Defrost and
Maximum (Full)
Defrosting and cooking time:
13–14 minutes

1. Remove all wrappings. Cook
on Defrost for 1½–2 minutes.
Allow to stand for 10 minutes.

2. Cover and cook on Maximum
for 1½–2 minutes. Leave to stand
while preparing the custard
from step 4 above.

*Gooseberry and mint pudding; Mocha
honey gâteau*

Mocha Honey Gâteau

Makes one 20 cm (8 inch)
cake
Cake:
175 g (6 oz) butter
75 g (3 oz) demerara sugar
2 tablespoons clear honey
3 eggs, beaten
120 g (4½ oz) self-raising flour
10 g (¼ oz) cocoa powder
1 teaspoon instant coffee
granules
4 tablespoons hot water
few drops of vanilla essence
Filling and topping:
40 g (1½ oz) cornflour
450 ml (¾ pint) milk
2 tablespoons instant coffee
granules
215 g (7½ oz) light soft brown
sugar
350 g (12 oz) butter

65 g (2½ oz) walnuts, finely
chopped
To decorate:
chocolate curls or crumbled
chocolate flake

Preparation time: about 40
minutes
Cooking time: 12–14 minutes,
plus standing
Microwave setting: Maximum
(Full)

1. Line a 20 cm (8 inch) cake
dish or soufflé dish with cling
film or lightly grease the dish
and line the base with lightly
greased greaseproof paper.

2. Cream the butter with the
sugar and honey until light and

fluffy. Add the eggs, one at a time, beating well.

3. Sift the flour with the cocoa powder and fold into the butter mixture with a metal spoon.

4. Dissolve the coffee in the water and stir in the vanilla essence. Fold into the cake mixture with a metal spoon. Spoon into the prepared dish and cook for $5\frac{1}{2}$–$6\frac{1}{2}$ minutes, giving the dish a quarter turn every $1\frac{1}{2}$ minutes. Leave to stand for 5–10 minutes before turning out on to a wire tray to cool.

5. To serve immediately, when cold carefully cut the cake horizontally into 3 equal layers.

6. Make the filling and topping by blending the cornflour with a little of the milk in a bowl to form a smooth paste. Place the remaining milk in a jug with the coffee and sugar, cook for $1\frac{1}{2}$ minutes. Add the blended cornflour, stirring well to mix. Cook for 5–6 minutes, stirring twice, until smooth and thick. Cover the surface with greaseproof paper dampened on the top side and leave to cool completely.

7. Beat the butter until creamy. Gradually add the cold coffee sauce, beating well to form a smooth mixture.

8. Mix one-third of the coffee

filling with 25 g (1 oz) of the walnuts. Sandwich the cake layers together with this filling. Spread the top and sides of the cake with about half of the remaining coffee mixture. Press the remaining walnuts on to the sides of the cake.

9. Place the remaining coffee mixture in a piping bag fitted with a large star nozzle and pipe swirls on top of the cake.

10. Decorate with chocolate curls or crumbled chocolate flake. Cut into wedges to serve.

FREEZING DETAILS
1. Prepare the recipe to the end of step 4.

2. Place the undecorated cake in a rigid box. Cover, seal, label and freeze for up to 6 months.

DEFROSTING DETAILS
Microwave setting: Defrost
Defrosting time: 8 minutes

1. Remove all wrappings, and place on plate. Cook on Defrost for 3 minutes. Leave to stand for 5 minutes.

2. To fill and decorate the cake continue from step 5 above.

Honey Crunch Crumble

Serves 4
675 g (1½ lb) cooking apples,
peeled, cored and sliced
6 tablespoons clear honey
75 g (3 oz) butter
175 g (6 oz) muesli-style
breakfast cereal

Preparation time: 10 minutes
Cooking time: 12½–15 minutes
Microwave setting: Maximum
(Full)

1. Put the apples in a serving dish and drizzle over half the honey.

2. Place the butter in a bowl and cook for 1½–2 minutes to melt.

3. Stir in the remaining honey and the cereal, mixing well to coat. Spoon on top of the apples. Cook for 11–13 minutes, giving the dish a quarter turn every 3 minutes.

4. Serve hot with cream or custard (see Gooseberry and mint pudding page 218).

FREEZING DETAILS
1. Prepare the recipe to the end of step 3.

2. Cool quickly, cover, seal, label and freeze for up to 3 months.

REHEATING DETAILS
Microwave setting: Maximum
(Full)
Defrosting and cooking time: 12–13 minutes

1. Remove all wrappings. Cook for 5 minutes, turning the dish once. Allow to stand for 5 minutes.

2. Cook for a further 2–3 minutes. Serve hot with cream or custard (for custard recipe, see Gooseberry and mint pudding page 218).

Black Cherry Cream Pie

Makes one 23 cm (9 inch) pie
Base:
100 g (4 oz) butter
165 g (5½ oz) bran flakes
1½ tablespoons soft brown sugar
Filling:
1 × 425 g (15 oz) can black
cherries in syrup
1 × 135 g (4¾ oz) packet black
cherry jelly tablet
300 ml (½ pint) black cherry
yogurt
300 ml (½ pint) double cream,
whipped

Preparation time: 10 minutes,
plus chilling
Cooking time: 4–5½ minutes
Microwave setting: Maximum
(Full)

1. Place the butter in a large bowl and cook for 1½–2 minutes to melt. Stir in the bran flakes and sugar, tossing well to coat. Press on to the base and sides of a deep 23 cm (9 inch) flan tin with a removable base. Chill to set, for about 30 minutes.

2. Drain the juice from the cherries into a bowl. Add the jelly and cook for 2½–3½ minutes, stirring once to dissolve completely. Chill until just beginning to set.

3. Whisk the jelly with the yogurt until foamy. Fold in half the cream with a metal spoon. Pour into the pie case. Chill to set.

4. Pipe or swirl the remaining cream on top of the pie and decorate with the black cherries. Serve chilled.

FREEZING DETAILS
1. Prepare the recipe to the end of step 3.

2. Place in a rigid container, cover, seal, label and freeze for up to 3 months.

DEFROSTING DETAILS
Microwave setting: Defrost
Defrosting time: 1–2 hours

1. Remove all wrappings. This dessert is best defrosted at room temperature for 6 hours. To speed up this time, however, cook on Defrost for 1 minute. Leave to stand for 1 hour.

Clockwise: Honey crunch crumble;
Black cherry cream pie; Winter
pudding

Winter Pudding

Serves 4
75 g (3 oz) self-raising flour
pinch of salt
½ teaspoon ground mixed spice
75 g (3 oz) fresh wholemeal
breadcrumbs
75 g (3 oz) shredded beef suet
50 g (2 oz) soft light brown
sugar
50 g (2 oz) sultanas
50 g (2 oz) raisins
50 g (2 oz) currants
grated rind of ½ lemon
about 6 tablespoons milk

Preparation time: 10 minutes
Cooking time: 5 minutes, plus
standing
Microwave setting: Maximum
(Full)

1. Sift the flour with the salt and mixed spice. Stir in the breadcrumbs, suet, sugar, sultanas, raisins, currants and lemon rind, blending well. Add sufficient milk to make a soft dropping consistency.

2. Spoon into a greased 900 ml (1½ pint) pudding basin and cover with cling film. Snip 2 holes in the top for steam to escape.

3. Cook for 5 minutes, giving the dish a half-turn twice.

4. Leave to stand for 5 minutes before turning out on to a warmed serving plate. Serve with custard (see Gooseberry and mint pudding page 218).

FREEZING DETAILS
1. Prepare the recipe to the end of step 3.

2. Cool quickly, cover the basin with aluminium foil, seal, label and freeze for up to 3 months.

REHEATING DETAILS
Microwave setting: Maximum
(Full)
Defrosting and cooking time: 13½–14 minutes

1. Remove all wrappings. Cook on Defrost for 2 minutes. Leave to stand for 10 minutes.

2. Cook on Maximum for 1½–2 minutes to reheat. Serve with custard (see Gooseberry and mint pudding page 218).

Sausage and Horseradish Roly-poly

Serves 6
Suet Pastry:
225 g (8 oz) self-raising flour
pinch of salt
100 g (4 oz) shredded suet
150 ml (¼ pint) cold water
Filling:
450 g (1 lb) frozen beef
  sausages
15 g (½ oz) butter
100 g (4 oz) mushrooms, sliced
2 teaspoons creamed
  horseradish
salt
freshly ground black pepper
provençal sauce (see Pork
  spareribs provençal, page
  212)
parsley sprig, to garnish

Preparation time: about 10 minutes
Cooking time: 19–19½ minutes
Microwave setting: Defrost and Maximum (Full)

1. Place the sausages on a plate and cook on Defrost for 5 minutes, turning and re-arranging once. Leave to stand while preparing the mushrooms.

2. Place the butter and mushrooms in a bowl, cook on Maximum for 2 minutes, stirring once. Stir in the creamed horseradish and salt and pepper to taste.

3. Prick the sausages well with a fork. Cook on Maximum for 4–4½ minutes, turning and re-arranging once. Cut into thin slices.

4. Mix the sausages with the mushroom mixture, blending well.

5. Sift the flour and salt into a bowl. Stir in the suet. Add the cold water and mix to a soft but manageable dough. Roll out the dough on a lightly floured surface to a 23 cm (9 inch) square.

6. Spread the sausage mixture evenly over the suet pastry square, leaving a 1 cm (½ inch) border around the edge, and carefully roll up like a Swiss roll.

7. Place, seam side down, on a piece of greaseproof paper and roll the greaseproof up loosely around the pastry roll, allowing plenty of space for the roly-poly to rise. Carefully tie the ends of the paper with string or elastic bands and cover loosely with cling film.

8. Cook for 8 minutes, turning twice, until well risen and cooked through. Test by inserting a skewer into the centre of the roll – the skewer should come out clean and free from dough.

9. Serve very hot, cut into slices, with the provençal sauce. Garnish with parsley.

Cook's Tip

Suet pastry can be made lighter by adding 50 g (2 oz) fresh white breadcrumbs with the suet. Bind together with a little extra water if necessary. Ring the changes and flavour with ½ small grated onion or 1–2 teaspoons chopped fresh herbs.

Turkey Roast with Prune and Mustard Sauce

Serves 4
1 × 600 g (1¼ lb) frozen
  boneless turkey breast roast
25 g (1 oz) butter
2 teaspoons mustard powder
salt
freshly ground black pepper
150 ml (¼ pint) port
175 g (6 oz) stoneless prunes
2 teaspoons cornflour
150 ml (¼ pint) chicken stock

Preparation time: 15 minutes
Cooking time: 27–28 minutes, plus standing
Microwave setting: Defrost and Maximum (Full)

1. Place the turkey roast in a lidded dish and cook on Defrost for 8 minutes. Allow to stand for 5–10 minutes until completely thawed.

2. Spread with the butter and rub with the mustard powder and salt and pepper to taste. Cover and cook on Maximum for 6 minutes.

3. Turn the turkey roast over, baste with the juices, cover and cook on Maximum for a further 5–6 minutes. Remove from the dish, wrap in aluminium foil and leave to stand while preparing the sauce.

4. Add the port and prunes to the dish juices. Cover and cook on Maximum for 4 minutes.

5. Mix the cornflour with the stock and stir into the prune and port mixture. Cover and cook on Maximum for 4 minutes, stirring twice.

6. Carve the turkey roast into slices and place on a dish. Pour over a little of the sauce, garnish with some of the prunes and serve the rest separately.

Potted shrimps; Turkey roast with prune and mustard sauce; Sausage and horseradish roly-poly

Potted Shrimps

Serves 4
350 g (12 oz) frozen peeled
    shrimps or prawns
175 g (6 oz) butter, diced
salt
$\frac{1}{4}$ *teaspoon ground mace*
$\frac{1}{4}$ *teaspoon cayenne pepper*
To garnish:
parsley sprigs
lemon wedges

Preparation time: 5 minutes
Cooking time: $7\frac{1}{2}$–$8\frac{1}{2}$ minutes
Microwave setting: Defrost and
Maximum (Full)

1. Place the frozen shrimps or prawns in a bowl and cook on Defrost for 6–7 minutes, stirring once. Drain and discard any thaw juices.

2. Place the butter in a bowl and cook on Maximum for $1\frac{1}{2}$ minutes, stirring once, to melt. Add the shrimps or prawns, salt, mace and cayenne pepper to taste. Divide equally between 4 small ramekin dishes.

3. Allow to cool, then chill for 30 minutes in the refrigerator.

4. Garnish with parsley sprigs and lemon wedges. Serve with triangles of thin brown bread.

Oriental Chicken with Sweet and Sour Sauce

Serves 4
4 × 225 g (9 oz) frozen chicken
    portions
1 tablespoon oil
1 onion, peeled and thinly
    sliced
1 small green pepper, cored,
    seeded and sliced
1 small red pepper, cored,
    seeded and sliced
1 garlic clove, peeled and
    chopped
pinch of ground ginger
salt
freshly ground black pepper
1½ tablespoons red wine
    vinegar

1 tablespoon brown sugar
150 ml (¼ pint) apple juice
150 ml (¼ pint) unsweetened
    orange juice
1 tablespoon cornflour
1 small carrot, peeled and
    coarsely grated
2 canned pineapple rings,
    coarsely chopped
25 g (1 oz) pine nuts
spring onion tassel to garnish

Preparation time: 15 minutes
Cooking time: 51 minutes, plus
standing
Microwave setting: Defrost and
Maximum (Full)

1. Place the frozen chicken
portions on a microwave
roasting rack and cook on
Defrost for 14 minutes.

2. Cook on Maximum for 20
minutes, turning and re-
arranging the chicken every 5
minutes.

3. Place the oil, onion, peppers
and garlic in a casserole. Cover
and cook on Maximum for 6
minutes, stirring once. Add the
ginger, salt and pepper, vinegar,
sugar, apple and orange juice.
Cover and cook on Maximum
for 4 minutes.

4. Blend the cornflour with a
little water and stir into the
sauce with the carrot and
pineapple pieces, blending well.
Cover and cook for 3 minutes,
stirring once.

5. Add the chicken pieces and
nuts. Cover and cook on
Maximum for 4 minutes. Allow
to stand for 5 minutes. Garnish
with a spring onion tassel.

Haddock Mornay Shells

Serves 4
2 × 198 g (7 oz) packets frozen
    buttered smoked haddock
25 g (1 oz) butter
25 g (1 oz) plain flour
300 ml (½ pint) milk
1 egg yolk, beaten
1 teaspoon made mustard
salt
freshly ground black pepper
75 g (3 oz) Cheddar cheese,
    grated
2 teaspoons chopped capers

Preparation time: 10 minutes
Cooking time: 16–17 minutes,
plus grilling
Microwave setting: Maximum
(Full)

1. Pierce each packet of
haddock and place on a plate.
Cook on Maximum for 10
minutes, shaking the packets
gently after 6 minutes. Leave to
stand while preparing the sauce.

2. Place the butter in a jug and
cook on Maximum for 30
seconds to melt. Add the flour,
mixing well. Gradually add the
milk and cook on Maximum for
3½–4 minutes, stirring every 1
minute until the sauce is smooth
and thickened. Beat in the egg
yolk, mustard, salt and pepper
to taste and half the cheese.

3. Flake the haddock, discarding
any skin. Fold into the sauce
with the capers. Spoon into 4
scallop shells or flameproof
dishes. Sprinkle with the
remaining cheese and cook on
Maximum for 2 minutes, rearranging the dishes after 1
minute.

4. Brown quickly under a
preheated conventional grill.

5. Serve with triangles of hot
toast, if liked.

Light Summer Curry

Serves 4
750 g (1½ lb) frozen firm white
    fish fillets (e.g. cod, rock
    salmon)
1 onion, peeled and chopped
25 g (1 oz) butter
25 g (1 oz) plain flour
2 teaspoons hot Madras curry
    powder
200 ml (7 fl oz) water
1½ tablespoons lemon juice
2 firm tomatoes, peeled, seeded
    and chopped
6 sticks frozen double cream
    (equivalent to 150 ml/¼ pint)
salt

Preparation time: 10 minutes
Cooking time: 25½ minutes
Microwave setting: Defrost and
Maximum (Full)

1. Place the fish fillets in a dish
and cook on Defrost for 12
minutes. Leave to stand while
preparing the sauce.

2. Place the onion and butter in
a bowl. Cover and cook on
Maximum for 2 minutes, stirring
once. Stir in the flour and curry
powder, blending well.
Gradually add the water and
lemon juice. Cover and cook on
Maximum for 2½ minutes,
stirring every 1 minute.

3. Meanwhile, skin the fish fillets
and place in a serving dish. Pour
over the sauce. Cover and cook
on Maximum for 5 minutes,
stirring or re-arranging the fish
fillets twice.

4. Carefully add the tomatoes
and frozen cream sticks with salt
to taste. Cover and cook on
Maximum for 4 minutes, stirring
twice. Serve with boiled rice.

*Oriental chicken with sweet and sour
sauce; Haddock mornay shells*

One-dish Chicken Supper

Serves 4
8 frozen chicken thigh portions
450 g (1 lb) frozen new
*   potatoes*
1 tablespoon oil
1 onion, peeled and chopped
100 g (4 oz) frozen button
*   mushrooms*
1 × 450 g (1 lb) packet frozen
*   stir-fry vegetables with*
*   cauliflower, mushrooms,*
*   peas, onions and carrots*
150 ml (¼ pint) apple juice
salt
freshly ground black pepper
parsley sprig to garnish

Preparation time: 10 minutes,
including heating browning dish
Cooking time: 50 minutes
Microwave setting: Defrost and
Maximum (Full)

1. Place the frozen chicken thigh portions on a plate and cook on Defrost for 12–14 minutes, turning once. Allow to stand while thawing the potatoes.

2. Place the potatoes in a bowl and cook on Defrost for 10 minutes, stirring once.

3. Remove the bone from each chicken thigh portion and cut the meat into slices.

4. Preheat a large browning dish on Maximum for 8 minutes (or according to the manufacturer's instructions). Brush with the oil and cook on Maximum for a further 2 minutes.

5. Stir in the chicken slices and onion and turn quickly on all sides to brown evenly. Cover and cook on Maximum for 6 minutes, stirring once.

6. Add the mushrooms, stir-fry vegetables, potatoes, apple juice and salt and pepper to taste. Cover and cook on Maximum for 12 minutes, stirring twice.

7. Serve hot, garnished with a parsley sprig and accompanied by crusty brown rolls and a mixed salad.

Kipper and Corn Kedgeree

Serves 4
225 g (8 oz) long-grain rice
600 ml (1 pint) boiling water
450 g (1 lb) frozen kipper fillets
50 g (2 oz) butter, diced
175 g (6 oz) frozen sweetcorn
*   kernels*
grated rind of 1 lemon
2 tablespoons chopped fresh
*   parsley*
salt
freshly ground black pepper
¼ teaspoon ground nutmeg
2 tablespoons double cream
To garnish:
1 hard-boiled egg, shelled and
*   quartered*
parsley sprigs

Preparation time: 10 minutes
Cooking time: 28–29 minutes,
plus standing
Microwave setting: Defrost and
Maximum (Full)

1. Place the rice in a deep container with the water. Cover and cook on Maximum for 12 minutes. Leave to stand, covered, while preparing the kipper fillets.

2. Place the kipper fillets in a single layer in a large shallow dish and cook them on Defrost for 3 minutes. Allow to stand for 5 minutes.

3. Cook on Defrost for a further 2–3 minutes, until completely thawed.

4. Cover with microwave cling film, snipping 2 holes in the top to allow any steam to escape and cook on Maximum for 6 minutes, turning the dish once. Remove, discard any skin and bones and flake the flesh into the rice, blending well.

5. Place the butter in a medium bowl and cook on Maximum for 1 minute. Add the sweetcorn and lemon rind. Cover and cook on Maximum for 3 minutes, stirring once. Stir into the rice with the parsley, salt, pepper and nutmeg to taste.

6. Stir in the double cream, cover and cook on Maximum for 1 minute.

7. Serve garnished with hard-boiled egg quarters and parsley sprigs.

Cook's Tip

For even greater speed, use frozen ready-cooked rice in this kedgeree. Turn the frozen rice into a deep dish and cook it on Maximum until it has defrosted and warmed through – about 5 minutes. Stir it at least once during this time, then continue as above.

One-dish chicken supper; Kipper and corn kedgeree

OMBINATION MICROWAVE COOKING

The combination microwave cooker is the most versatile appliance, providing three cooking methods: the food can be cooked by using microwaves only, by traditional methods using the convection mode, or it can be cooked on a combination mode, using the microwaves and convected heat together.

Combination cooking is the method of cooking using microwave energy and conventional heat simultaneously. The majority of ovens offering this facility combine the microwave energy with recirculating hot air, produced by the high-speed fan built into the oven. In addition, some models have a grill built into the oven, in which case a combination of grilling and microwave cooking can be used for certain cooking procedures.

From the range of literature that is available on this cooking process you will find that many terms are used to describe the same cooking process. For example, you may find reference to a *convection microwave oven*, a *microwave-convection oven*, a *multi-micro cooker*, a *microwave plus cooker*, *dual cooking* or *high-speed cooking*.

Whatever the term used, the exciting part of this cooking method is the results that can be achieved. Take all the time-tested standards of traditional cooking and marry them with the speed of cooking with microwaves: the result is the best of good cooking with the advantages of modern technology.

Combination mode

In combination cookers the temperature settings are given in degrees centigrade (C). Throughout the chapter you will find the cooking temperature expressed in this way – if you want to convert back to Fahrenheit (F), then refer to

Useful Facts and Figures on pages 6 and 7. The range of cooking temperatures that can be selected varies; however it is usually in the region of 140–250°C.

The microwave settings that can be used in combination with heat also vary from oven to oven. The majority of ovens allow for the use of Maximum (Full), Medium or Low microwave settings in combination with conventional heat. Some models limit the use of microwave settings to Medium when using the combination cooking mode and other ovens offer Maximum (Full) or Low microwave settings. However, the majority of combination cooking is

carried out on a medium microwave setting.

Some ovens are pre-programmed to provide a selection of different combinations of microwave energy and temperature settings; in this case you are limited in choice of temperature and microwave energy input.

Advantages of combination cooking

By using microwaves the cooking process is speeded up and by using conventional heat the food turns brown and develops a crisp texture, or crust. Cooking by microwaves alone produces food with a steamed flavour – it is fair to say

that microwave cooking is a moist cooking method. However, cooking by the combination method results in food which has a baked flavour.

Pastry, 'roast' meat and batters are a few examples of foods that are inferior or unacceptable when cooked by microwaves only. Cook these items by a combination of microwaves and conventional heat and the results are excellent – pastry becomes crisp, flaked and tasty with a brown crust; meat roasts very well, giving a traditional result in significantly less time than roasting by conventional means; and batters rise, become crisp and turn brown in a fraction of the time normally taken.

A comparison of combination cooking and traditional baking

1. Combination-cooked bread has a brown, crusty top and a good flavour and texture. The sides and base of the loaf are not as brown as expected by traditional baking.

2. Combination-cooked puff pastry is light, well risen and delicious. It does tend to shrink slightly more than pastry cooked by traditional baking and it can rise slightly unevenly.

3. Cakes cooked in a combination microwave are browned on top and they have a good flavour. The sides and base do not brown as well as by traditional methods. Take care not to overcook cakes to darken the crust as this will result in a dry middle

Breads and cakes rise too, cook through and have a crisp, browned crust. The taste is similar to that achieved by conventional methods.

Any recipes that require the food to be thoroughly heated or cooked through, with a crisp coating or browned topping are also particularly successful in the combination oven. While the crisp coating, or pastry pie lid, cooks and browns, the food underneath cooks through without drying out.

Convection cooking

The great advantage of the combination cooker is that you can use it on the convection mode to cook all your own favourite recipes. Convection cooking uses conventional heat that is recirculated in the oven by means of a fan. The movement of the hot air within the oven cavity speeds up the cooking process. The air moves around the food, rapidly displacing the cold air from the uncooked food. The result is not only speedy cooking, but even heat distribution without any 'cold spots'.

The effect of cooking in a fan-assisted oven is equivalent to about 20°C hotter than the actual setting selected. So, if you put something in to cook at 180°C, because of the recirculated air, the cooking time is equivalent to that required at 200°C in a normal oven. If you are cooking something that requires slow cooking, then reduce the setting accordingly; otherwise reduce the cooking time.

If you make soufflés, then you will find that they are best cooked by convection alone, not on combination mode. There are recipes for soufflés cooked on combination; however, even though they are browned and slightly crisp, they do not give the expected rise and are not, strictly speaking, successful. So stick to conventional heat for cooking soufflés!

Choux pastry is another item that is best cooked by convection alone. A gougère (a ring of choux pastry filled with a mixture of bacon, onion, cheese and other savoury ingredients) is just acceptable. If you put choux pastry in to cook on combination you will find that the microwaves cause it to puff up rapidly, then it sinks slightly as the microwave energy pulses off. Even though the conventional heat works hard at browning the pastry, the crust does not form quickly enough to hold a good rise. The result is not disastrous but it is not good enough to include in the combination recipes. So stick to the method you know already.

Combination cookers – features available

There are two sizes of combination cooker: the work-top, plug-in oven that is about the same size as the standard microwave oven, or a full-size built-in combination cooker. The majority of the full-size models are significantly more expensive than the table-top ovens.

Controls The controls can be electronic (touch control) or a push button and dial type. The majority of ovens have electronic controls.

In most cases, the temperature and microwave setting are selected, then the cooking time is selected (the order in which these selections are made varies according to the ovens), then the start or cook control is activated. When the cooking time is complete a bell or bleeper will sound. In some cases the noise will continue until you open the door; other models remind you for a short period, then at intervals until the door is opened.

To use some ovens you have to select the microwave setting, microwave cooking time, oven temperature and oven cooking time, then press the start control. The advantage of this type of control system is that you can select a short period of microwave cooking with a longer period of convection cooking and the convection cooking will automatically continue after the microwave cooking time is complete. The disadvantage of this control system is that the process of selection is fairly lengthy and it is possible to forget to give a cooking time for one part of the cooking operation.

Pre-programmed roasting Some ovens offer a facility for roasting meat or poultry on a pre-programmed setting. In this case you select the roasting function, set the weight of the joint to be cooked and press the start control. The cooking operation has been thoroughly tested by the manufacturer to offer the best possible combination of microwave energy and temperature for roasting the meat. Over the whole of the cooking period the amount of microwave energy and temperature within the oven varies so that the food is cooked to perfection.

Some ovens offer a similar facility for cooking bread, cakes, fruit pies, quiches, casseroles and biscuits. The same technique is also available for defrosting certain foods in some ovens.

Certain ovens only offer a number of cooking categories in the combination mode and in each case a particular temperature is combined with a pre-set microwave setting.

Preheat setting Some ovens offer a preheat control. In this case you select the required oven temperature and the preheat function, then press the start control and the oven will automatically preheat. It will bleep when ready. If you want to preheat without this control (if the facility is not available) then select the temperature and the convection cooking mode, then heat for 10 minutes.

Dual cooking control or two-level cooking In some ovens, if

Preheating the oven for combination cooking

You will find most manufacturers state that it is not necessary to preheat the oven for combination cooking. Moreover, most of them suggest that results are, in fact, better if the oven is not preheated. In some cases this is perfectly correct; however, in some ovens if the cooking time is short (and in many cases this is so) the food does not have time to become crisp and well browned unless the oven is preheated. Results vary significantly from oven to oven – some ovens heat up very quickly, others can take up to 20 minutes. So, when it comes to preheating it really is a case of getting to know your own oven.

The recipes were tested in a preheated oven unless otherwise stated. When roasting meat or poultry, if the size of the food is large enough, there is no need to preheat. Try cooking a few dishes in your oven without preheating it first. If the results are not brown enough or not quite 'baked' enough then you will know it is necessary to preheat for any other recipe with a similar cooking time.

Because of the speed of cooking, preheating is not an essential safety and hygiene factor.

you want to use the rack for two-level cooking, then you have to select this control and the required temperature to ensure even cooking on both levels.

Combination setting In some cases you have to select the combination cooking function by pressing a certain control before you decide on the microwave setting and the cooking temperature.
Note In some ovens the dual cook term is used for the combination cooking mode and not two-level cooking.

Sensor cook Some ovens can be programmed to cook food automatically by the amount of moisture released into the oven cavity.

Combination grilling Some models have a built-in grill and there can be a control to select the combination grilling mode.

Halogen heat An alternative to the convection heat and microwave combination is provided by the use of microwave energy with halogen heat. In this case, heat is provided by halogen filaments located in the top and one side of the oven. The microwave energy can be used in combination with the top halogen element or with both top and side elements.

There are five settings that can be selected:
1 Microwaves with top and side halogen heat for roasting and all-round browning.
2 Microwaves with top halogen heat for top browning.
3 Microwaves only.
4 Top halogen heat only for grilling.
5 Top and side halogen heat.

Accessories and their uses

Most of the work-top combination ovens have turntables. Unlike the standard microwave oven, the combination models come with wire cooking racks. The introduction of metal in the form of a rack into the cooking cavity tends to confuse most people and I cannot offer any scientifically sound explanation for the avoidance or use of metal within a microwave oven!

In addition to a metal rack, a few other accessories come with the oven. The following notes may be of some help in deciding when to use the accessories; remember to read the manufacturer's instructions and follow them closely.

Turntable This can be made of ceramic or metal and it must be in position in order to operate the oven on any cooking mode. In some ovens, the turntable can be stopped when the oven is operated on the convection only setting. This turntable can also be used as a drip pan for roasting.

Splash guard or anti-splash tray This is a perforated metal tray that fits into the turntable, standing slightly above it. When the turntable is used as a drip tray for roasting this splash guard helps to prevent the fat that collects from spitting out during cooking. This tray can be left permanently in position during all cooking operations.

Glass tray or drip tray In ovens that do not have a turntable, there may be a glass tray that slides into the oven. This can be used as a drip tray for roasting or as a shelf for microwave or combination cooking. In other models, a drip tray is provided in addition to the turntable.

Wire racks All combination ovens come with at least one wire rack. This wire rack should be used for combination cooking and for cooking on the convection mode to allow the free flow of hot air beneath the food. In some cases, where two items are to be cooked at once, food in the cooking dish can be placed straight on the turntable, with the second item positioned on the wire rack above. The position of the dishes is usually swopped over during cooking.

In ovens that do not have a turntable, the wire rack slides in as in a normal, full-sized oven. This rack can be used for all cooking modes.

Some models provide a high rack and a low rack. These can be used together for two-level convection cooking (follow the instructions with the oven) and the high one can be used for grilling, where the food should be positioned near the top of the oven.

Insulating mat This accessory is provided with some ovens. It is usually covered with a non-stick coating. It is placed between the wire rack and metal baking tins when cooking using the combination mode. This mat prevents any sparking between the metal of the rack and the baking tin (see cooking utensils for comments on the use of metal). This insulating mat can also be used as a base for cooking certain pastry items like apple turnovers or Cornish pasties. If the food holds its shape well, then it can be placed straight on the insulating mat and it will receive the maximum possible hot air from the base to give best cooking results. The non-stick coating makes for easy cleaning.

Baking tray Some ovens come with a circular tray to fit on the turntable, or with an oblong tray that slides into the oven if there is no turntable. This can be used for cooking individual food items or for making pizza and similar items.

Handle Some manufacturers supply a heavy, detachable metal handle which is useful for lifting the circular tray out of an oven that has a turntable. This is particularly useful when food is being cooked under the grill (where applicable).

Cooking utensils

The same rule applies here as with all other aspects of cooking in microwave ovens – just follow the manufacturer's instructions when it comes to selecting cooking utensils.

The following notes are a general guide; you will probably find that you already have plenty of suitable cookware in the kitchen, so it is not a good idea to rush out and spend a fortune on large quantities of specialist cookware.

Metal Some manufacturers recommend the use of metal on combination cooking mode. Do not use metal baking tins if cooking with microwaves only. In some ovens if you use metal tins when cooking with microwaves and convection mode, then remember to use the insulating mat provided. You can safely and effectively use metal tins when cooking on the convection mode only.

Throughout the recipes, dishes are used instead of tins when using the combination mode. The reason for this is simple: the microwaves do not pass through metal, therefore the food does not receive any microwave energy through the sides or base of a tin, just from the top. This lack of microwave energy to the food can result in an inferior result or lengthy cooking times in some cases. Because of this cooking dishes (made of ovenproof glass, or ceramic) give a better result.

When cooking shallow items, you will find that a dish that allows the microwaves to pass through from the base as well as the sides can give a better result than a tin. So the above comment is true even if the cake or food item is a shallow one.

Ovenproof glassware and ceramic dishes These are ideal for use in the combination oven. Avoid any with metal trims or decorations as they will cause sparking. Remember the

Combination Microwave Cooking/231

combination oven gets very hot so the dishes must withstand the heat.

Specially manufactured plastics There are certain ranges of plastic cookware designed for use in microwave ovens and up to temperatures of 200°C. From testing, I found that many of the recipes cooked quickly and best at temperatures above 200°C. This type of cookware is very expensive and, of course, it is re-useable. However, it does not stand up to really heavy wear over long periods of time. Cake dishes, unusual shaped dishes and items that are not going to be worked to death are good value. For day-to-day cooking for main meals you are probably better off with ovenproof china or sturdy ovenproof glassware.

Roasting bags These are useful to prevent splattering and they can also be used for microwave only cooking.

Pre-programmed settings

Some ovens do not allow you to select the temperature and microwave setting when using the combination mode. Instead they provide numbered settings each of which combines a certain microwave input with a particular temperature. The settings below and charted above are only examples – the instructions' book will tell you exactly what the settings are on your oven if it is pre-programmed. Alternatively the manufacturer may provide all the details you need to know which setting to use for a variety of cooking processes without

Setting	Suggested uses
C1	Rich fruit cakes and light pâtés
C2	Roasting large turkeys or goose, casseroling tougher cuts of meat
C3	Semi-rich fruit cakes, heavy pâtés, steak and kidney stew, lightly cooked fish
C4	Braising steak, pork chops or tender casseroles, cooking whole salmon or gingerbread
C5	Lamb hotpots, mince dishes, pastry-wrapped uncooked

spelling out the precise combinations of temperature and microwave power settings.

To follow the recipes in this book, select the setting that offers the combination nearest to the microwave setting and oven temperature stated in the recipe. You may find that the setting you use has a lower microwave input and slightly cooler oven, in which case you will have to increase the overall cooking time. Remember, it is best to slightly undercook the food, then put it back for a few minutes, than overcook it. If you are unable to select the temperature/microwave setting nearest to the combination given in the recipes, then follow the manufacturer's guidance for using the settings. For example, select a setting suggested for baking bread, cakes or pastry; or a setting used for roasting.

The combination cooking mode is the same even if you

Setting	Suggested uses
	foods (e.g. Cornish pasties), syrup or bakewell tarts or similar shortcrust pastries
C6	Roasting meat and poultry (except large birds), large scones or pizza bases, vegetable casseroles, puff pastry, bread
C7	Chicken casseroles, small whole fish e.g. trout
C8	Roast chicken portions
C9	Combination grilling

vary the power inputs and temperature, so you should find that these recipes work well in a pre programmed oven even if the timing is slightly different. When you do cook a recipe, note the setting and cooking time next to the method for future reference.

Combination grilling

If your appliance offers the facility for grilling in combination with microwave cooking, then maximise the use of it by cooking small cuts of meat or poultry in this way. The following chart outlines some basic cooking methods. Microwave energy combined with the use of a hot grill cooks food very fast and is not suitable for baking cakes or bread, or for roasting joints of meat. Combination grilling can be used for whole fish, for poultry (whole chickens, chicken portions, duck or turkey portions), for steaks, chops or sausages, for gratins and made-up dishes (such as cottage pie or lasagne).

Because the grill browns and crisps the food quickly, a high microwave setting can be used to cook at a similar rate.

Even though the chart gives you some idea of the cooking times remember that as with all grilling you do have to keep a close watch on the food.

PRE-PROGRAMMED SETTINGS

Setting	Microwave input	Temperature
1	Low	160°C
2	Low	180°C
3	Medium-low	180°C
4	Medium-low	200°C

COMBINATION GRILLING SMALL CUTS OF POULTRY

Poultry	Quantity	Microwave setting	Time in minutes	Method
Chicken quarters	2 4	Maximum (Full)	8–10 12–15	Place skin down, turn halfway through.
Boneless chicken breasts	2 4	Maximum (Full)	5–6 10–12	As above.
Drumsticks	4 8	Maximum (Full) Maximum (Full)	7–8 11–14	Arrange drumsticks thick parts outwards. Turn over halfway through.
Duck quarters	2 4	Maximum (Full) Maximum (Full)	12–15 20–22	Place skin down in dish, turn halfway through.

COMBINATION GRILLING SMALL CUTS OF MEAT

Meat	Quantity	Microwave setting	Time in minutes	Method
Steak	2, 225 g (8 oz)			
medium		Medium	5–7	Brush with a little oil or melted butter, then turn over halfway through cooking.
well done		Medium	8–9	
	4, 225 g (8 oz)			
medium		Medium	10–11	As above.
well done		Medium	12–13	
Lamb chops	2	Medium	8–10	Place in dish, brush with a little oil and turn over halfway through cooking.
	4	Medium	10–12	
Pork chops	2	Medium	10–12	As above.
	4	Medium	14–17	

Cooking a complete meal

You can cook a complete meal in the combination microwave oven with great success but do stop and think before you start cooking.
1. Prepare vegetables and sauces cooked by microwaves only in advance, leaving them slightly undercooked so that they can be heated quickly just before serving.

2. Prepare any other recipes that are cooked by microwaves only – for example, a starter or pudding, remembering to slightly undercook if you are going to reheat the dish later.

3. Prepare any dessert that is suitable for cooking in advance and that requires the combination cooking mode.

4. Cook the main dish and make the gravy or any sauce based on the meat juices.

5. Quickly heat the vegetables on microwaves only and serve. By following the above guidelines you should produce a meal that is ready in the right order. The vegetables should be heated for just one or two minutes before serving so that they do not have time to dry out in the residual heat from combination cooking. The main point to emphasise is to avoid cooking by microwaves only in a hot oven if you are cooking food that benefits from a moist cooking method.

Care of the oven

Wipe the oven out frequently to remove any spattering or bits of food before they have time to bake on to the surface. Always follow the manufacturer's instructions when it comes to the cleaning materials to use.

When cooking foods that are likely to spit and splatter, and if it is possible, then cover the dish. When roasting meats or grilling cuts of meat, I find that they produce less mess if cooked in a shallow dish – a quiche dish is ideal. If you do use the rack, then always use the splatter guard provided in the turntable.

It is vitally important to keep the door, its surround and all areas near the opening very clean. Remove the turntable and other items that can be washed (like the cooking racks) and wash them frequently to avoid any build up of baked-on deposits.

Afterthoughts

With a combination microwave oven in your kitchen, dreams of having an oven that cooks significantly faster than normal but still gives the best results come true. I was very excited by the successes I achieved when I first started to cook in a microwave oven – indeed as I experimented, the disasters were just as useful as the winners because they pointed out the direction in which microwave cooking led. Take all those disasters, rethink them slightly and put them in a combination microwave and the chances are most of them will come out tops!

Making pies and cakes, bread and grills or roasting meat really did have me leaping around in the kitchen calling out to my husband to come and look at the latest great results from the combination microwave: I had, of course, anticipated that the combination of heat and microwaves would give good results but I was quite amazed at the quality and speed with which the food cooked.

As I learnt how to use the oven, there were one or two hints that I picked up, usually from my own errors. One thing that I found very difficult at

The temperatures given in the recipes are in degrees centigrade only as the majority of combination microwave cookers use this scale. The maximum temperature in the recipes is 250°C; If the maximum temperature on your appliance is 240°C, then use it instead of 250°C. If your oven has a limited number of temperature settings, then select the one nearest to the temperature given in the recipe. If necessary a lower temperature than that suggested should be used instead of a hotter setting.

All the combination ovens tested were rated at 650 watt microwave power output.

first was to remember that the new appliance was very hot. Having cooked in an ordinary microwave oven for some time, as soon as the timer sounded to let me know that my recipe was ready I rushed over and on many occasions only just stopped myself before I grabbed the red-hot dish with my bare hands! So remember to use oven gloves. Another slight word of warning – the oven cavity itself (in most ovens) is quite small and the position in which the turntable stops can leave the handle of a dish towards the back of the oven, so do take care not to burn yourself on the sides of the oven as you try to remove the food.

As with many tabletop cooking appliances, the ovens do vary according to make, so the old phrase 'get used to your own oven' is relevant yet again. I always feel as though I am cheating slightly when I tell people that they really do have to get to know their own ovens and that this book will not do this for them, but it is true.

SPECIALITIES OF COMBINATION COOKING

The recipes which follow in this chapter provide a variety of different ideas for foods and dishes which can be cooked in the combination microwave cooker. Use them as guidance for adapting your favourite recipes to this method of cooking. The following notes highlight some of the foods which benefit from the speed of microwave cooking and from the conventional heat source. For example jacket potatoes can be cooked by microwaves only very successfully but when they are cooked on combination mode they are crisp outside. Pastry and bread doughs also cook well by this method.

Combination microwave cooking for baked potatoes

Traditional baked potaoes, fluffy inside and crispy-brown outside, are delicious but they require lengthy cooking in the conventional oven. The ordinary microwave cooks potatoes well but it does not turn them crisp and brown. Use the combination cooking mode to give traditional-style results.

The following timings are for potatoes weighing about 275 g (10 oz) each and cooked on a combination of Maximum (Full) and 250°C.

1 potato   –   7 minutes
2 potatoes – 10 minutes
3 potatoes – 18 minutes
4 potatoes – 25 minutes
5 potatoes – 28–30 minutes
6 potatoes – 35 minutes

Combination Microwave Cooking for Pastry

Pastry cooks very well on combination mode, the only exception being choux pastry which does not rise properly and it is not recommended that it is cooked by this method.

The chapter which follows offers recipes which include pastry but the following notes may be useful if you are adapting your own recipes to this type of cooking.

Baking Blind

Pastry can be baked blind on combination mode, using greaseproof paper and dried beans or baking beans. For a 23 cm (9 inch) flan case allow about 5–7 minutes on Medium and using 250°C without preheating the oven first. Alternatively, if you want to cook the pastry very slightly, then chill it well – for at least 45 minutes – and prick it all over, then cook it without the paper and beans for 4–5 minutes. If it is well chilled it should not collapse but it does not cook as well as pastry which is lightly chilled and filled with paper and beans. Sweet pastry should be cooked with paper and beans in place, since it is more likely to fall in.

Cooking an empty flan case

A pastry flan case can be cooked completely on combination mode, ready to be filled with a savoury or sweet filling which is uncooked or which has been cooked separately (for example, fruit-filled flans).

To cook a 23 cm (9 inch) flan case, first line it with greaseproof paper and beans, then cook it on Medium and 250°C for 5 minutes in the preheated oven. Remove the beans and paper, then continue to cook for a further 3 minutes, or until the pastry is cooked and lightly browned. The pastry can be allowed to cool before filling or it can be filled with a savoury sauce mixture and served hot.

Savoury set flans

Whether you bake the pastry case blind before filling it with an egg and milk based filling is largely a matter for personal taste. The dish used also affects the end results – ovenproof glass dishes usually allow enough heat to pass through the bottom to give a well-cooked pastry base; thicker china dishes can promote a soggy pastry base unless the pastry is baked blind first.

For a 23 cm (9 inch) flan allow 3 eggs beaten with 300 ml (½ pint) milk for the filling. Chopped onion, diced bacon and other raw ingredients which require lengthy cooking should be cooked first in a basin using microwaves only.

The filled flan should be cooked using Medium and 200°C for 15–20 minutes, by which time the filling should be set and lightly browned.

Yeasted doughs cooked by combination mode

Bread recipes are included in this chapter but do remember the other applications for this type of mixture, in particular pizza. The combination microwave cooker can be used to make excellent pizza. Make one large one, or try making small, snack-size pizzas.

A pizza base which is folded in half to seal in a savoury filling is known as Calzone and this can also be cooked in the combination microwave cooker.

Basic Pizza Base

Make a basic yeast base using 100 g (4 oz) strong plain flour mixed with a good pinch of salt and 2 teaspoons easy-blend yeast. Mix in about 50 ml (2 fl oz) lukewarm water to make the dough, then knead it thoroughly.

The dough should be allowed to rise in a warm place until doubled in size, then it can be rolled out into a 23–25 cm (9–10 in) pizza.

Use a large shallow dish to hold the pizza, greasing it with a little oil before putting the dough in.

The topping can be made up of ingredients of your choice. Onions and garlic should be cooked first with a little oil or butter for about 3 minutes using microwaves only.

Once the pizza is topped, leave it to stand for 10 minutes in a warm place, then cook it using Medium and 250°C for 10–12 minutes. The edges of the dough should be crisp and browned and the topping should be cooked.

Calzone

Calzone is made by putting the filling on half the circle of pizza dough, then folding over the other half to enclose the filling completely. Pinch the edges together well to seal in the filling. A calzone made from pizza dough based on 100 g (4 oz) flour as above will take about 10–12 minutes to cook on Medium using 250°C. Remember that the exact timing will depend on the ingredients used in the filling – any which need lengthy cooking are best cooked briefly first using microwaves only.

Leek Soup Surprise

Serves 4
350 g (12 oz) leeks, sliced
350 g (12 oz) potatoes, peeled and cubed
25 g (1 oz) butter
2 tablespoons plain flour
450 ml (¾ pint) chicken stock
salt
freshly ground black pepper
150 ml (¼ pint) milk or single cream
1 × 250-g (8¾-oz) packet puff pastry, defrosted if frozen
beaten egg to glaze

Preparation time: 20 minutes
Cooking time: 27–31 minutes
Microwave setting: Maximum (Full) and Medium
Temperature setting: 250°C

1. Put the leeks in a colander and wash them thoroughly, separating the rings and rinsing out any grit. Shake off the excess water.

2. Put the leeks in a large casserole dish or mixing bowl. Add the potatoes and butter. Cover and cook using microwaves only on Maximum for 5 minutes.

3. Stir in the flour, then gradually pour in the stock. Add salt and pepper to taste. Cook on Maximum for 15–18 minutes, or until the vegetables are tender. Stir in the milk or cream. Leave to cool.

4. Heat the oven. Ladle the soup into four individual casserole dishes or ovenproof bowls that are not too wide across the top. Cut the pastry into quarters. Roll out each portion into a circle large enough to cover one of the bowls. Cut shapes from pastry trimmings to decorate the pastry lids and brush with a little beaten egg.

5. Brush the edges of the dishes or bowls with a little beaten egg. Lift a pastry circle over each one and press the edge on to the rims of the dishes, taking care not to press the middle down on to the soup. Brush the tops *very* lightly with beaten egg.

6. Bake at 250°C using Medium for 7–8 minutes, or until the pastry is well puffed and browned. Serve at once.

Cook's Tip

These satisfying soup pots make a delicious, warming lunch or supper dish. Use the same idea for other soups if you like.

Ham Soufflé in Artichokes

Serves 4
4 globe artichokes
225 g/8 oz cooked ham, minced or finely chopped
3 tablespoons plain flour
2 tablespoons chopped chives
salt
freshly ground black pepper
1 tablespoon milk
2 eggs, separated

Preparation time: 15 minutes, plus cooling
Cooking time: 28–30 minutes
Microwave setting: Maximum (Full) and Medium
Temperature setting: 220°C

1. Cut off and discard the artichoke stalks, wash the artichokes thoroughly and place in a large roasting bag. Cook using microwaves only on Maximum for about 20 minutes, or until one of the base leaves comes off easily. Leave until cool enough to handle.

2. Trim off the leaf tips, pull out the centre leaves, then use a small teaspoon to remove the hairy choke in one neat piece.

3. Heat the oven to 220°C. Mix together the ham, flour, chives and salt and pepper to taste, then stir in the milk and egg yolks.

4. Whisk the whites until they are stiff, then use a metal spoon to fold them into the ham mixture.

5. Stand the artichokes on a flan dish and fill with the ham mixture. Bake at 220°C using Medium for 8–10 minutes, or until well risen and browned. Serve immediately with thin bread and butter or melba toast.

Souffléd Avocados

Serves 4
40 g (1½ oz) Cheddar cheese, grated
1 tablespoon grated Parmesan cheese
1 teaspoon prepared mustard
1 tablespoon chopped chives
1 tablespoon plain flour
salt
freshly ground black pepper
1 tablespoon milk
1 large egg, separated
2 ripe avocados
lemon juice

Preparation time: 15 minutes
Cooking time: 5 minutes
Microwave setting: Medium
Temperature setting: 250°C

1. Heat the oven. Mix the cheeses, mustard, chives, flour and salt and pepper to taste in a basin. Beat in the milk and egg yolk.

2. Cut the avocados in half and remove the stones. Sprinkle with a little lemon juice to prevent discoloration. Place the avocado halves on a flan dish, using pieces of crumpled greaseproof paper to support them on the level.

3. Whisk the egg white until stiff, then use a metal spoon to fold it into the cheese mixture.

4. Spoon the cheese mixture into the avocados and bake immediately at 250°C using Medium for 5 minutes, or until the soufflé filling has risen and browned. Serve at once.

Leek soup surprise; Ham soufflé in artichokes

Captain's Cobbler

Serves 4
1 large leek, sliced
2 large carrots, peeled and
*   sliced*
1 tablespoon butter or oil
2 tablespoons plain flour
450 ml (¾ pint) fish stock
bay leaf
salt
freshly ground black pepper
450 g (1 lb) white fish fillet,
*   skinned and cut into chunks*
*   (cod, haddock or coley)*
2 tablespoons chopped fresh
*   parsley*
Cobbler Topping:
225 g (8 oz) self-raising flour
3 teaspoons baking powder
50 g (2 oz) butter or margarine
1 teaspoon dried mixed herbs
50 g (2 oz) cheese, grated
1 egg, beaten
about 5 tablespoons milk, plus
*   extra to glaze*

Preparation time: 15 minutes
Cooking time: 20–22 minutes
Microwave setting: Maximum
(Full)
Temperature setting: 250°C

1. Thoroughly wash the leek, separating the slices into rings to make sure that all grit is removed. Mix the leek with the carrots and butter or oil in a deep casserole dish. Cook using microwaves only on Maximum for 5 minutes.

2. Stir in the flour, then gradually pour in the stock. Add the bay leaf and salt and pepper to taste. Cook for a further 5–7 minutes, or until the stock is almost boiling.

3. Add the fish and parsley and mix well, taking care not to break up the fish. Heat the oven.

4. For the topping sift the flour and baking powder in to a bowl and rub in the fat. Stir in the herbs, cheese, beaten egg and enough milk to make a soft scone dough.

5. Turn the dough out on to a lightly floured surface and knead it until just smooth. Cut the dough into eight equal portions and roll each into a ball, then flatten slightly. Without overlapping them, arrange the scones on top of the fish, round the edge of the dish. Brush with a little milk.

6. Bake at 250°C using Medium for about 10 minutes, or until the cobblers are risen and browned. Serve freshly cooked.

Cook's Tip

You may like to offer an additional green vegetable (peas or French beans, for example) with the cobbler, but the topping is quite filling and will replace potatoes, pasta or rice.

Bacon-wrapped Trout

Serves 4
4 trout, cleaned with heads on
4 bay leaves
4 parsley sprigs
4 strips of lemon rind
4 smoked bacon rashers, rinds
*   removed*
Garnish:
lemon wedges
fresh bay leaves or parsley
*   sprigs*

Preparation time: 5 minutes
Cooking time: 10 minutes
Microwave setting: Medium
Temperature setting: 250°C

1. Heat the oven. Trim the fins off the trout. Place a bay leaf, parsley sprig and strip of lemon rind in each fish. Wrap a rasher of bacon around each trout, then place in two flan dishes.

2. Put one dish on the turntable and the second on the rack above. Cook at 250°C using Medium for 6 minutes. Swop the positions of the dishes, then cook for a further 4 minutes. Serve immediately, garnished with lemon wedges and bay leaves or parsley sprigs.

Cook's Tip

For more squeamish guests, you may prefer to remove the fish heads before cooking. Cut them off cleanly behind the gills using a sharp knife. Use additional parsley sprigs to garnish.

Bacon-wrapped trout; Captain's cobbler

GUIDE TO COMBINATION COOKING POULTRY AND GAME

	Microwave setting	Temperature °C	Time in minutes per 450 g (1 lb)	Method
Chicken, whole	Medium	220	7–9	Preheat oven. Put chicken in dish and dot with a little fat or brush with oil. Turn over twice, ending with breast side uppermost.
Chicken quarters – 2	Medium	240–250	Total cooking time: 10–12 minutes	Preheat oven. Turn joints once, starting skin side down and ending with skin uppermost.
Chicken quarters – 4	Medium	240–250	Total cooking time: 15–16 minutes	As above.
Turkey	Medium	200	6–7	Do not preheat oven. Place turkey in dish. Turn twice, baste several times. Leave to stand 15 minutes before serving.
Duck	Medium	240–250	7–8	Preheat oven. Place duck in dish. Prick skin all over and rub with a little salt. Turn twice, draining off excess fat. Stand 5 minutes before serving.
Duck joints – 2	Maximum (Full)	240–250	5	As above.
	Medium	240–250	Total cooking time: 10–12 minutes	Prick skin, rub with salt. Turn twice, ending with skin side uppermost.
Duck joints – 4	Medium	240–250	Total cooking time: 25–30 minutes	As above.
Pheasant – 2	Medium	220–240	Total cooking time: 18–20 minutes	Preheat oven. Place in dish, breast side up. Place halved bacon rasher on top. Turn over twice, ending breast side up and remove bacon to brown.
Pheasant – 4	Medium	220–240	Total cooking time: 25 minutes	As above.

Marinating poultry or game

Marinating is intended to moisten poultry or game and to infuse it with the flavour of herbs, spices or other ingredients. Although chicken is usually only marinated when the full flavour of spices or wine is required, game birds benefit greatly from being marinated before cooking as their meat tends to be rather dry. Similarly, duck can be marinated in a mixture that will contrast well with its rich tastes and slightly fatty meat.

For marinating put the poultry or game in a suitable dish – it should be deep enough to hold the marinade but not too wide. Pour in the marinade, cover the dish and chill the poultry for several hours or overnight. Ideally, the poultry should be turned at least once or twice during marinating.

The following marinades can be used for all poultry or game.

Walnut oil marinade Walnut oil gives a distinct flavour to foods which are cooked or marinated in it. Mix 8 tablespoons walnut oil with 150 ml ($\frac{1}{4}$ pint) red or white wine. Add a bay leaf, 4 lightly crushed juniper berries and a blade of mace.

Apple marinade Mix 150 ml ($\frac{1}{4}$ pint) unsweetened apple juice with 1 teaspoon finely chopped rosemary, 2 tablespoons sunflower oil and plenty of black pepper. Rub the inside of the dish with a cut clove of garlic before putting the poultry or game and marinade in it.

White wine marinade Mix 300 ml ($\frac{1}{2}$ pint) dry white wine with a slice of onion, a large sprig of parsley and a finely chopped stick of celery.

Roast Chicken with Spicy Rice Stuffing

Serves 4

1 onion, peeled and chopped
¼ teaspoon turmeric
1 teaspoon ground coriander
1 teaspoon cinnamon
75 g (3 oz) long-grain rice
175 ml (6 fl oz) water
25 g (1 oz) sultanas
175 g (6 oz) dessert apples,
   peeled, cored and chopped
salt
freshly ground black pepper
1 × 1.5-kg (3½-lb) oven-ready
   chicken
25 g (1 oz) butter
1 clove garlic, peeled and
   crushed
grated rind of ½ lemon

Preparation time: 10 minutes
Cooking time: 25–40 minutes
Microwave setting: Maximum (Full) and Medium
Temperature setting: 220°C

1. Put the onion in a basin with the spices, rice and water. Cover and cook using microwaves only on Maximum for 10 minutes.

2. Heat the oven. Add the sultanas, apples and salt and pepper to taste to the rice, then use a spoon to press the stuffing into the body cavity of the chicken.

3. Cream the butter with the garlic and lemon rind. Spread this mixture all over the top of the chicken.

4. Place the chicken in a large flan dish and roast at 220°C on Medium for 25–30 minutes, or until the chicken is cooked and browned. To check that the bird is cooked, pierce the meat at the thickest part of the body, near the thigh joints. The juices should be free of blood.

Alternative cooking method
The chicken can be cooked at 220°C using Low for about 35–40 minutes.

Cook's Tip

Take this recipe as a guide to cooking any roast stuffed chicken.

Galantine of Chicken

Serves 4–6

1 small leek, chopped
25 g (1 oz) butter
1 teaspoon rubbed sage
½ teaspoon dried thyme
salt
freshly ground black pepper
175 g (6 oz) fresh breadcrumbs
1 red pepper, cored, seeded and
   chopped
175 g (6 oz) cooked ham, diced
1 × 1.5-kg (3½-lb) chicken,
   boned (see page 61)
oil for brushing

Preparation time: 15 minutes
Cooking time: 23–28 minutes
Microwave setting: Maximum (Full) and Medium
Temperature setting: 220°C

1. Put the leek in a basin with the butter and cook using microwaves only on Maximum for 3 minutes. Mix in the herbs, salt and pepper to taste and half the breadcrumbs.

2. Heat the oven. Mix the remaining breadcrumbs with the red pepper and ham, adding salt and pepper to taste.

3. Open the chicken out flat on a board. Spread half the ham stuffing on it, then put the leek stuffing on top. Top with the remaining ham mixture.

4. Use a trussing needle or large darning needle and strong thread to sew up the chicken into a neat shape. Place in a large flan dish and brush with oil.

5. Roast at 220°C using Medium for 20–25 minutes; turn the chicken over halfway through cooking. Serve hot or cold, sliced.

Tandoori Chicken

Serves 4
4 chicken joints, skinned
1 onion, peeled and grated
5 cloves garlic, peeled and crushed
25 g (1 oz) fresh root ginger, peeled and grated
2 teaspoons ground coriander
1 teaspoon ground cumin
1 teaspoon ground cinnamon
1 teaspoon turmeric
½ teaspoon salt
¼ teaspoon black pepper
150 ml (¼ pint) natural yogurt
juice of 1 lemon
Garnish:
1 lemon, cut into wedges
1 lettuce heart
1 onion, peeled and thinly sliced

Preparation time: 5 minutes, plus marinating for 24 hours
Cooking time 15–17 minutes
Microwave setting: Medium
Temperature setting: 250°C

1. Cut three slits in each piece of chicken, then place in a bowl. Mix all the remaining ingredients and pour over the chicken.

2. Cover and leave in the refrigerator for at least 24 hours. This dish is best left to marinate for a couple of days (make sure the chicken is really fresh before you start).

3. Heat the oven. Put the chicken joints in a flan dish and pour over the marinade. Roast at 250°C using Medium for 10 minutes, turn the joints and continue cooking for a further 5–7 minutes.

4. Serve garnished with lemon wedges, small lettuce leaves and plenty of onion rings. Pillau rice is a traditional accompaniment (see recipe on page 158).

Alternative cooking method
This recipe can be cooked at 250°C using Low setting for about 10–12 minutes. If you prefer follow the instructions for combination grilling on page 231.

Tandoori chicken

Baked Chicken Kiev

Serves 4
50 g (2 oz) butter
2 cloves garlic, peeled and crushed
2 tablespoons chopped parsley
salt
freshly ground black pepper
4 boneless chicken breasts, skinned
1 egg, beaten
2 tablespoons water
100–175 g (4–6 oz) fresh white breadcrumbs
Garnish:
1 red pepper, cored, seeded and chopped
¼ cucumber, sliced
1 lemon, cut into wedges

Preparation time: 15 minutes, plus chilling
Cooking time: 17–20 minutes
Microwave setting: Medium
Temperature setting: 250°C

1. Mix together the butter, garlic, parsley and salt and pepper to taste. Divide into quarters and form each portion into a small pat. Wrap in cling film and chill thoroughly (this can be done in the freezer).

2. Make a small slit in the middle of each chicken breast and press in a pat of the butter mixture. Press the meat back together to enclose the flavoured butter pats completely.

3. Beat the egg and water together. Coat each chicken breast in the mixture, then press on a thick coating of breadcrumbs. Repeat to ensure that the coating is thick and even. Chill for at least 15 minutes.

4. Heat the oven. Arrange the chicken on a well greased flan dish. Bake at 250°C using Medium for 17–20 minutes, or until the coating is well browned. The chicken should be firm and the butter centre will have melted.

5. Serve immediately, garnished with chopped red pepper, cucumber slices and lemon wedges.

Cook's Tip

A very successful way of cooking this well-known recipe – far better than the inconvenience of deep frying.

Baked chicken kiev

Cranberry Pheasant

Serves 4

100 g (4 oz) cranberries
1 onion, peeled and chopped
4 tablespoons sugar
2 tablespoons port
2 firm pears, peeled, cored and
  chopped
50 g (2 oz) fresh breadcrumbs
salt
freshly ground black pepper
2 oven-ready pheasant
2 bay leaves
4 bacon rashers, rinds removed
Sauce:
2 tablespoons plain flour
300 ml (½ pint) red wine
150 ml (¼ pint) boiling water

Preparation time: 15 minutes
Cooking time: 35 minutes
Microwave setting: Maximum
(Full) and Medium
Temperature setting: 200°C

1. Put the cranberries and onion
in a basin. Cover with
microwave cling film or a plate
and cook using microwaves
only on Maximum for 5
minutes. Heat the oven.

2. Mix the sugar, port, pears,
breadcrumbs and salt and
pepper to taste into the
cranberry mixture. Rinse and
dry the pheasant. Spoon the

stuffing into the birds, then
place in a flan dish. Top with
bay leaves and bacon.

4. Roast at 200°C using Medium
for 20 minutes. Remove the
bacon from the top of the birds,
putting it beside them in the
dish. Remove and reserve the
bay leaves for garnish. Roast the
pheasant for a further 5
minutes, or until cooked.

5. Transfer the pheasant to a
warmed serving dish and keep
hot. Crumble the bacon into the
cooking juices and stir in the
flour, wine and boiling water,

then cook using microwaves
only on Maximum for 5
minutes, or until the sauce has
boiled and thickened slightly.
Serve the sauce separately.

Cook's Tip

Use this recipe when
cranberries are in season. For
use throughout the year keep a
packet of the berries in the
freezer; cook from frozen for an
extra minute or so.

*Braised Pheasant; Boned Stuffed
Turkey*

Braised Pheasant

Serves 4
2 oven-ready pheasant
1 orange, quartered
12 cloves
1 onion, peeled and finely chopped
2 bay leaves
300 ml (½ pint) red wine
2 rindless bacon rashers, halved
25 g (1 oz) butter
2 tablespoons plain flour
salt
freshly ground black pepper
Garnish:
1 orange, sliced
parsley sprigs

Preparation time: 15 minutes
Cooking time: 38–45 minutes
Microwave setting: Medium
Temperature setting: 200°C

1. Heat the oven. Rinse and dry the pheasant. Stud the orange quarters with the cloves, then place two pieces in each pheasant.

2. Put the onion in a large casserole dish with the bay leaves. Place the pheasant on top, with the breasts uppermost. Pour the wine over and lay the bacon rashers over on top of the pheasant.

3. Cook at 200°C using Medium for 20 minutes. Turn the pheasant over and cook for a further 10 minutes. Remove the bacon. Turn the birds once more and cook for a final 5–10 minutes.

4. Meanwhile, beat together the butter and flour, and salt and pepper to taste.

5. Transfer the cooked pheasant to a serving platter and keep hot.

6. Whisk the butter and flour mixture into the cooking juices. Cook using microwaves only on Maximum for 3–5 minutes, or until boiling.

7. Garnish the pheasant with orange slices and parsley sprigs. Serve the sauce separately.

Boned Stuffed Turkey

Serves 8
1 × 4.5-kg (10-lb) turkey
175 g (6 oz) cranberries
40 g (1½ oz) sugar
2 tablespoons orange juice
225 g (8 oz) onions, peeled and finely chopped
50 g (2 oz) butter
225 g (8 oz) fresh breadcrumbs
1 tablespoon rubbed sage
150 ml (¼ pint) milk
salt
freshly ground black pepper
450 g (1 lb) pork sausagemeat

Preparation time: 45 minutes
Cooking time: 1 hr 23–28 minutes, plus standing
Microwave setting: Maximum (Full)
Temperature setting: 200°C

1. Trim the leg and wing ends off the turkey. To bone the turkey, place it breast side down and using a sharp, pointed knife, cut straight down the middle of the back, from head to tail. Working on one side, cut off all the meat, as near to the bone as possible. Take great care not to puncture the skin. As you near the ends of the joints, turn the meat and skin inside out to leave the bones completely cleaned. Carefully work underneath the breast meat, cleaning the ribs as far as the main breast bone. Remove the meat from the second side in the same way.

When you reach the breast bone, very carefully cut the finest sliver of bone off to separate the carcass completely from the meat without cutting the skin at all. The bones can be used along with the giblets to make an excellent stock.

2. Prepare the stuffings: put the cranberries in a basin with the sugar and orange juice. Cover and cook using microwaves only on Maximum for 3 minutes. Stir well.

3. Put the onions in a bowl with the butter and cook on Maximum for 5 minutes. Stir in the breadcrumbs, sage and milk, and salt and pepper.

4. Lay the boned turkey, skin side down, flat on the surface. Spread the sausagemeat thinly and evenly over it. Spread the sage and onion stuffing evenly over the sausagemeat to cover the turkey completely. Spread the cranberry sauce down the middle, then carefully lift the sides of the turkey over the cranberry mixture to enclose it completely. Heat the oven.

5. Using a trussing needle or large darning needle and buttonhole thread, sew up the bird, then turn it over so that the breast meat is uppermost. Press it into a neat shape, tucking the wing and leg ends underneath and plumping up the middle. Place in a large flan dish.

6. Roast at 200°C using Medium for 30 minutes. Turn the turkey over, drain off any excess fat and cook for a further 30 minutes. Turn the turkey again so that the breast side is uppermost and cook for a final 15–20 minutes, or until the meat is cooked through. Test whether the turkey is cooked by piercing it at the thickest part – there should be no sign of any pink meat and the juices should run clear.

7. Leave to stand for 15 minutes, then serve hot. Alternatively, the turkey can be served cold.

Cook's Tip

If you have a good butcher, then ask him to bone out the turkey for you. If you are attempting the task yourself just set aside enough time and take it slowly!

If cranberries are not available use bottled cranberry sauce in the stuffing, pepping it up with a dash of brandy if you like.

GUIDE TO COMBINATION COOKING MEAT

Meat	Microwave setting	Temperature °C	Time in minutes per 450 g (1 lb)	Method Note: No need to preheat oven for cooking times over 30 minutes.
Beef				
Rump Steak medium/well done	Medium	240–250	5–6	Preheat oven. Brush steak with a little oil and place on rack or in a large shallow dish. Turn halfway.
Rump Steak well done	Medium	240–250	7–8	As above.
Topside/Sirloin	Medium	180	12–15	Place joint in dish or on rack. Turn and baste twice during cooking.
Rolled Rib	Medium	180	12–15	As above.
Rib on the Bone	Medium	180	10–12	Turn joint and baste once or twice during cooking.
Brisket	Medium	220–180	14–15	Place meat on bed of diced vegetables (onion, carrot and potato). Add 150–300 ml ($\frac{1}{4}$–$\frac{1}{2}$ pint) water and season. Cook at 220 for 15 minutes, then reduce temperature for remaining time. Turn twice during cooking.
Lamb				
Chops	Medium	240–250	7–9	Preheat oven. Arrange chops in dish, sprinkle with herbs. Turn over halfway through cooking.
Steaks (slices off the leg)	Medium	240–250	10–12	As above.
Leg	Medium	190	9–11	Season the joint and place in a dish. Turn and baste two or three times during cooking.
Shoulder	Medium	200	10–12	As above.
Breast, boned and rolled	Medium	220	13–14	As above.
Pork				
Chops	Medium	240–250	7–9	Preheat oven. Arrange in dish, season, turn halfway through.
Loin, boned and rolled	Medium	220–190	14–16	Score rind, rub with salt and place pork in dish. Reduce temperature after 15 minutes. Baste frequently, turn twice, having rind uppermost for 5 minutes at the end of cooking time. Increase temperature again for last 5 minutes. Leave to stand for 5–10 minutes before serving.
Loin, on the bone	Medium	220–190	15–16	Score rind and rub with salt. Place pork in dish, rind uppermost. Cook as above, reducing temperature after 5 minutes. Increase temperature at the end of cooking.
Leg	Medium	220–180	15–16	Rub rind with salt and score well. Place in dish. Reduce temperature after 5 minutes. Baste frequently, turn twice during cooking.
Pork Belly	Medium	240–250	10	Score rind, rub with salt. Place in dish and turn twice during cooking. Have rind uppermost to start, underneath for the majority of cooking, then on top for final 3–5 minutes.
Gammon	Medium	200–180	15–18	Place in deep casserole. Add onion, carrot and bay leaf. Pour in 300–600 ml ($\frac{1}{2}$–1 pint) boiling water. Cover. Turn twice during cooking. Reduce temperature halfway through cooking. Leave to stand for 15 minutes.

Beef Wellington

Serves 4–6
1 kg (2 lb) fillet steak
1 large onion, peeled and finely chopped
1 clove garlic, peeled and crushed (optional)
25 g (1 oz) butter
100 g (4 oz) button mushrooms, chopped
1 tablespoon chopped parsley
salt
freshly ground black pepper
1 × 370-g (13-oz) packet puff pastry, defrosted if frozen
1 egg, beaten

Preparation time: 20 minutes, plus cooling
Cooking time: 20–25 minutes
Microwave setting: Maximum (Full) and Medium
Temperature setting: 250°C

1. Tie the piece of steak firmly in shape so that it does not curve as it cooks.

2. Place the onion and garlic (if used) in a basin with the butter. Cook using microwaves only on Maximum for 3 minutes. Heat the oven.

3. Stir the mushrooms, parsley and salt and pepper to taste, into the onion.

4. Place the meat on a flan dish and cook at 250°C using Medium for 5–10 minutes. The length of time for this initial cooking period depends on how you like your beef: for just red in the middle and quite juicy 5 minutes is enough; for slightly pink in the middle allow 7–8 minutes and for well-done cook for the full 10 minutes. Remove the meat from the oven and set aside to cool.

5. Roll out the pastry on a lightly floured surface into an oblong large enough to enclose the meat completely. It should measure about 30 × 40 cm (12 × 16 in) and be fairly thick. Spread the mushroom mixture in the middle of the pastry.

6. Remove the string from the meat and place the steak on top of the mushroom mixture. Lift the pastry over the meat to ensure that it fits, then trim off square shapes from each corner to avoid thick pastry joins.

7. Brush the edges of the pastry with a little of the beaten egg, then fold the pastry around the meat, pressing the joins firmly together. Turn the package over and place it on a large flan dish. From the trimmings cut a few leaves to decorate the pastry.

8. Glaze the pastry with beaten egg. Bake at 250°C using Medium for about 12 minutes, or until the pastry is well puffed and browned. Serve freshly cooked, cut into slices.

Cook's Tip

This is an expensive dish to prepare but it is truly delicious. If you like, use a neat piece of topside instead of the fillet steak. Other suitable substitutions are a piece of lean boneless lamb, cut from the leg, or a piece of pork, trimmed of all fat. If using pork, then remember to cook it well first.

Stuffed Leg of Lamb

Serves 6
1.75 g (3¾ lb) leg of lamb, boned
225 g (8 oz) ready-to-eat prunes, roughly chopped
4 tablespoons brandy
1 large onion, chopped
25 g (1 oz) butter
100 g (4 oz) fresh breadcrumbs
salt
freshly ground black pepper
100 g (4 oz) button mushrooms, chopped
1 teaspoon dried mixed herbs
Sauce:
2 tablespoons plain flour
300 ml (½ pint) red wine
300 ml (½ pint) boiling water
bay leaf

Preparation time: 30 minutes
Cooking time: 43–53 minutes
Microwave settings: Maximum (Full) and Medium
Temperature setting: 190°C

1. Place the lamb in a large flan dish. Put the prunes in a basin and sprinkle the brandy over them. Set aside.

2. Cook the onion and butter on Maximum (Full) for 3 minutes. Stir in the breadcrumbs, seasoning and mushrooms. Add the herbs, then the prunes and brandy. Mix well.

3. Press the stuffing into the lamb and roast it at 190°C using Medium microwave setting for 35–45 minutes.

4. Turn the joint several times during cooking and baste it frequently with the cooking juices. Pierce it at the thickest part to check that it is cooked.

5. Transfer the lamb to a serving platter and keep hot. Drain off the excess fat from the cooking juices, then stir in the flour. Gradually pour in the wine and water, and add the bay leaf.

6. Cook the sauce using microwaves only on Maximum (Full) for 6–8 minutes, whisking well once during cooking. Taste and adjust the seasoning. Discard the bay leaf.

7. Carve the lamb into thick slices and serve the sauce with it.

Traditional Roast Beef Lunch

Par-cook the potatoes first in an ovenproof dish using microwaves only on Maximum. Add a little fat. Put the meat on the rack above the potatoes and cook for the necessary time. Make a batter using 100 g (4 oz) plain flour to 2 eggs and 300 ml (½ pint) milk. Remove the meat and heat a little of the dripping in a quiche dish. Pour in the batter and cook for 10–15 minutes at 250°C using Medium setting. Make the gravy using microwaves only just before serving.

Minced Beef Pie

Serves 4

*1 large onion, peeled and
   chopped
100 g (4 oz) carrots, peeled and
   diced
1 tablespoon oil
salt
freshly ground black pepper
100 g (4 oz) mushrooms, sliced
450 g (1 lb) minced beef
1 tablespoon tomato purée
½ teaspoon dried or 1 teaspoon
   chopped fresh thyme
2 tablespoons chopped parsley
bay leaf
250 ml (8 fl oz) boiling water
Shortcrust Pastry made with
   175 g (6 oz) plain flour, 75 g
   (3 oz) margarine and 3
   tablespoons water
beaten egg to glaze*

Preparation time: 15 minutes
Cooking time: 20–23 minutes
Microwave setting: Maximum
(Full) and Medium
Temperature setting: 220°C

1. Place the onion, carrots and oil in a pie dish and cover with a plate or with microwave cling film. Cook using microwaves only on Maximum for 5 minutes.

2. Heat the oven. Add a good sprinkling of salt and pepper to the onion mixture, then stir in the mushrooms, beef, tomato purée, herbs and boiling water. Set aside.

3. Roll out the pastry on a lightly floured surface into a piece large enough to cover the top of the pie dish with about 2.5 cm (1 in) all round to spare. Trim a narrow strip from the edge of the pastry, then dampen the dish edge and press the strip of pastry on to it. Dampen it, then lift the pastry lid over the filling, pressing the edges down well. Trim off excess pastry. Re-roll it and cut out decorative leaves.

4. Brush the pie with a little beaten egg and bake at 220°C using Medium for 15–18 minutes or until well browned.

5. Serve immediately with baked potatoes and a crunchy green vegetable to make a satisfying winter's meal.

Cook's Tip

Use this simple recipe for meat pie as a guide for adapting your favourite recipes to combination microwave cooking. Remember that the filling should be at least part cooked before the pastry top is added.

One combination of appliances that is not exploited to the full is the pressure cooker and the microwave. You can always make tasty, tender meat pie fillings in the pressure cooker, using cuts like leg of beef, then top them with pastry and finish the pie by combination cooking to save on both time and fuel.

Beef Lasagne

Serves 4

*1 large onion, peeled and
   chopped
2 cloves garlic, peeled and
   crushed
1 tablespoon oil
salt
freshly ground black pepper
450 g (1 lb) minced beef
1 × 400-g (14-oz) can
   tomatoes, chopped
1 teaspoon dried marjoram
100 g (4 oz) button mushrooms,
   chopped
175 g (6 oz) no precook
   lasagne
450 ml (¾ pint) Cheese Sauce
   (page 163)
50 g (2 oz) cheese, grated
2 tablespoons dry breadcrumbs*

Preparation time: 15 minutes
Cooking time: 33–38 minutes
Microwave setting: Maximum
(Full) and Medium
Temperature setting: 200°C

1. Put the onion in a large basin or casserole dish with the garlic and oil. Cook using microwaves only on Maximum for 3 minutes.

2. Stir in salt and pepper to taste, the beef, tomatoes, marjoram and mushrooms. Cook for a further 5 minutes, then stir well. Heat the oven.

3. For the lasagne you will need a deep casserole dish. If you have a large oven cavity that does not have a turntable then you can use an ordinary, large lasagne dish otherwise a deep round dish will give an excellent result. Layer the pieces of lasagne, breaking them up as necessary, with the meat sauce in the dish.

4. Pour the cheese sauce on top. Mix the cheese with the breadcrumbs and sprinkle over the top.

5. Bake at 200°C using Medium for 25–30 minutes or until well browned on top and cooked through. To check that the lasagne is cooked, pierce the middle with the point of a knife – the pasta should feel softened.

6. Serve freshly baked, with a crisp fresh salad.

Cook's Tip

Minced pork or lamb, or finely chopped cooked chicken are good substitutes for beef in this lasagne.

Ordinary lasagne will require pre-cooking before making layers with the meat sauce in the casserole dish. Bring a large saucepan of lightly salted water to the boil and add a few drops of sunflower or other cooking oil. Cook the lasagne in batches for 7–9 minutes until just tender. Drain thoroughly and pat dry on kitchen paper towels before proceeding with step 3.

Minced beef pie; Beef lasagne

Bread

Makes 1 large or 2 small loaves
450 g (1 lb) strong white or wholemeal flour
1 teaspoon salt
1 teaspoon sugar
50 g (2 oz) margarine
1 sachet easy-blend dried yeast or 3 teaspoons ordinary dried yeast
300 ml (½ pint) lukewarm water

Preparation time: 25 minutes, plus rising
Cooking time: 10–12 minutes
Microwave setting: Medium
Temperature setting: 250°C

1. Line a 1-kg (2-lb) loaf dish with greaseproof paper and grease the paper thoroughly. The paper should stand above the rim of the dish by 2.5 cm (1 in).

2. Place the flour, salt and sugar in a bowl. Rub in the margarine and stir in the easy-blend yeast. If using ordinary dried yeast, then sprinkle it over the lukewarm water and leave in a warm place until the yeast has dissolved and the mixture is frothy. Make a well in the dry ingredients and pour in the water or yeast liquid. Gradually stir in the flour to make a stiff dough.

3. Turn the dough out on to a lightly floured surface and knead it until very smooth and elastic, about 10 minutes.

4. Lightly flour the bowl and put the dough back into it. Cover with a damp cloth or a piece of cling film and leave in a warm place until doubled in size.

5. Turn out on to a lightly floured surface and knead lightly to knock out the gas. Press the dough into the prepared dish and cover with a dampened cloth or a piece of cling film. Leave in a warm place until risen above the rim.

6. Heat the oven. Brush the dough with a little water and bake at 250°C using Medium for 10–12 minutes or until the loaf is cooked and browned on top. Leave in the dish for a few minutes, then turn the bread out on to a wire rack to cool and remove the paper. The base of the bread will not be brown, but the top should be brown and crusty.

Alternative cooking method
Using 200°C and Low setting, cook a 450-g (1-lb) loaf for 9–10 minutes or a 1-kg (2-lb) loaf for about 15 minutes.

Cook's Tip

This recipe gives the basic technique for making dough for breads and buns. If you do not have a suitable 1-kg (2-lb) loaf dish, use an 18–23-cm (7–9-in) deep round dish instead. Alternatively, make 2 × 450-g (1-lb) loaves and bake as in the main recipe but for about 9 minutes. A 15-cm (6-in) soufflé dish can be substituted for a small loaf dish.

Currant Buns

Makes 6
225 g (8 oz) strong white flour
½ teaspoon salt
25 g (1 oz) butter
1 tablespoon sugar
1 sachet easy-blend dried yeast or 3 teaspoons ordinary dried yeast
100 g (4 oz) currants
150 ml (¼ pint) milk
Glaze:
2 tablespoons sugar
2 tablespoons milk

Preparation time: 25 minutes
Cooking time: 10–12½ minutes
Microwave setting: Maximum (Full) and Medium
Temperature setting: 250°C

1. Put the flour in a bowl and add the salt. Rub in the butter, then stir in the sugar, easy-blend yeast and currants.

2. Heat the milk using microwaves only on Maximum for about 30 seconds or until lukewarm. If using ordinary dried yeast, then sprinkle it over the milk and leave in a warm place until dissolved and frothy.

3. Make a well in the dry ingredients, then pour in the milk or yeast liquid. Gradually mix to make a firm dough.

4. On a lightly floured surface, knead the dough, until smooth and elastic, about 10 minutes. Lightly flour the inside of the mixing bowl, put the dough back in and cover with a damp cloth or a piece of cling film. Leave in a warm place until doubled in size.

5. Meanwhile, line the base of a 25-cm (10-in) quiche dish, or large flat dish, with greaseproof paper. Grease well.

6. Turn the risen dough out on to a lightly floured surface and knead lightly. Cut into six pieces. Shape each piece into a neat bun and place on the prepared dish round the edge. As they rise they will touch each other. Cover with a piece of oiled cling film and leave in a warm place until well risen. Heat the oven.

7. Bake the buns at 250°C using Medium for about 8–10 minutes, or until browned.

8. Mix the sugar and milk in a large basin which can go into the hot oven. Cook using microwaves only on Maximum for 1½–2 minutes. Check that the mixture does not boil over. Brush this glaze over the hot buns and transfer them to a wire rack to cool completely.

9. Break apart and serve split and buttered, or toasted and buttered.

Soda Bread

Makes one small loaf
225 g (8 oz) plain flour
1 teaspoon bicarbonate of soda
½ teaspoon salt
150 ml (¼ pint) milk

Preparation time: 10 minutes
Cooking time: 10 minutes
Microwave setting: Medium
Temperature setting: 180°C

1. Heat the oven. Put the flour in a bowl with the bicarbonate of soda and the salt. Make a well in the middle. Stir the milk into the flour to make a soft dough.

2. Turn the dough out on to a lightly floured surface and knead very lightly to make a neat round loaf.

3. Lightly grease a flan dish or similar flat, round dish. Place the loaf on the dish and cut a cross in the top.

4. Bake at 180°C using Medium for 10 minutes, or until the bread is risen and browned. Transfer to a wire rack to cool. The bread tastes best served warm.

Milk Loaf

Makes one 18-cm (7-in) round loaf

450 g (1 lb) strong white flour
1 teaspoon salt
50 g (2 oz) butter or margarine
2 teaspoons sugar
1 sachet easy-blend dried yeast or 3 teaspoons ordinary dried yeast
300 ml (½ pint) milk
1 tablespoon sesame seeds

Preparation time: 25 minutes, plus rising
Cooking time: 11 minutes, plus standing
Microwave setting: Maximum (Full) and Medium
Temperature setting: 220°C

1. Put the flour in a bowl and stir in the salt. Rub in the butter or margarine. Stir in the sugar and easy-blend yeast.

2. Heat the milk using microwaves only on Maximum for 1 minute, or until lukewarm. If using ordinary dried yeast, sprinkle it over the milk and leave in a warm place until dissolved and frothy.

3. Make a well in the dry ingredients. Pour in the milk or yeast liquid, then gradually mix in the flour to make a stiff dough.

4. Turn out on to a lightly floured surface and knead until smooth and elastic, about 10 minutes. Lightly flour the inside of the bowl, put the dough in and cover with a damp cloth or a piece of cling film. Leave in a warm place until doubled in size.

5. Meanwhile, line an 18-cm (7-in) round deep dish with greaseproof paper and grease thoroughly.

6. Turn the risen dough out on to a lightly floured surface and knead lightly to knock out the gas. Press the dough into the prepared dish and cover with cling film or a damp cloth. Leave in a warm place until doubled in size and risen above the rim of the dish.

7. Heat the oven. Brush the loaf with a little water and sprinkle with the sesame seeds. Bake at 220°C using Medium for 10 minutes, or until crisp and very well browned. Leave in the dish for 5 minutes, then turn out on to a wire rack to cool and remove the paper.

Clockwise: Soda bread; Currant buns; Bread, white and wholemeal; Milk loaf

Victoria Sandwich

Makes one 18-cm (7-in) cake
175 g (6 oz) butter or
*   margarine*
175 g (6 oz) sugar
½ teaspoon vanilla essence
3 eggs
175 g (6 oz) self-raising flour
225 g (8 oz) jam
caster sugar to dust

Preparation time: 15 minutes
Cooking time: 11–13 minutes
Microwave setting: Medium
Temperature setting: 200°C

1. Grease two 18-cm (7-in) round shallow dishes (cake, soufflé, or fairly deep flan dishes). Line each with a circle of greaseproof paper and grease the paper. Heat the oven.

2. Beat the butter or margarine with the sugar and vanilla essence until very pale and soft. Gradually beat in the eggs, adding a little of the flour if the mixture begins to curdle. Use a metal spoon to fold in the remaining flour.

3. Turn the mixture into the prepared dishes, dividing it equally between them. Smooth the surface. Put one dish on the turntable, and the second on the rack above. If the oven shelf is wide enough put both cakes on the same level. Bake at 200°C using Medium.

4. Cook for 8–9 minutes, then remove the top cake from the oven and move the cake below up on to the rack to finish cooking. Cook for a further 3–4 minutes. The cooked cakes should be lightly browned and firm to the touch.

5. Turn both cakes out on to a wire rack to cool and remove the lining paper.

6. Sandwich the cakes together with jam and sprinkle the top with a little caster sugar.

Alternative cooking method
Cook using 200°C and Low for 10 minutes. Remove top cake, move bottom cake up and cook for a further 1–2 minutes.

Variations

Chocolate Cake Substitute 25 g (1 oz) cocoa powder for an equal quantity of the flour. Sandwich the cakes together with whipped cream or chocolate butter icing. To make a chocolate butter icing, beat 50 g (2 oz) butter with 75 g (3 oz) sifted icing sugar until smooth and soft. Dissolve 1 tablespoon cocoa powder in 2 tablespoons boiling water, cool slightly and beat into the icing. Top the cake with melted chocolate and sprinkle with a little icing sugar.

Lemon Cake Add the grated rind of 1 lemon to the creamed mixture instead of the vanilla essence. Sandwich the cooled cakes together with lemon curd and top the cake with a lemon glacé icing. To make the icing, sift 100 g (4 oz) icing sugar into a bowl and beat in 1–2 tablespoons lemon juice.

Cherry and Almond Cake

Makes one 18-cm (7-in) cake
225 g (8 oz) glacé cherries
175 g (6 oz) butter or
*   margarine*
175 g (6 oz) sugar
3 eggs
¼ teaspoon almond essence
200 g (7 oz) self-raising flour
100 g (4 oz) blanched almonds,
*   chopped*
2 tablespoons milk

Preparation time: 15 minutes
Cooking time: 13–15 minutes
Microwave setting: Medium
Temperature setting: 220°C

1. Heat the oven. Line an 18-cm (7-in) deep, round dish with greaseproof paper and grease the paper thoroughly. Halve the cherries, put them in a sieve, wash under warm water, drain and dry on paper towels.

2. Beat the butter or margarine and sugar together until very pale and creamy. Beat in the eggs and almond essence, adding a little of the flour if the mixture begins to curdle. Toss the cherries in a little flour. Fold the remaining flour into the cake mixture using a metal spoon. Fold in the cherries, then the almonds and milk.

3. Turn the mixture into the prepared dish and lightly smooth the top.

4. Bake at 220°C using Medium for 13–15 minutes, or until the cake has risen and lightly browned. Leave the cake in the dish for a few minutes, then turn it out on to a wire rack to cool. Remove the paper when cold.

Madeira Cake

Makes one 18-cm (7-in) cake
175 g (6 oz) butter
175 g (6 oz) sugar
grated rind of 1 lemon
3 eggs
200 g (7 oz) self-raising flour
2 tablespoons milk
strip of candied citron peel

Preparation time: 15 minutes
Cooking time: 13–15 minutes
Microwave setting: Medium
Temperature setting: 220°C

1. Heat the oven. Line an 18-cm (7-in) deep round dish with greaseproof paper and grease the paper thoroughly. The paper should stand about 2.5 cm (1 in) above the rim.

2. Beat the butter, sugar and lemon rind together until pale and very creamy. Beat in the eggs, adding a spoonful of the flour if the mixture begins to curdle. Use a metal spoon to fold in the flour. Lastly fold in the milk. Turn the mixture into the prepared dish, smooth the surface. Lay the peel on top.

3. Bake the cake at 220°C using Medium for 13–15 minutes, or until the cake is well risen and lightly browned. Leave the cake in the dish for a few minutes, then turn it out on to a rack. Remove the paper when cold.

Variation

Light Fruit Cake Add 100 g (4 oz) mixed dried fruit to cake mixture and omit the peel.

Mocha Cake

Makes one 18-cm (7-in) cake
175 g (6 oz) butter or
*   margarine*
175 g (6 oz) sugar
3 eggs
175 g (6 oz) self-raising flour
2 tablespoons instant coffee
2 tablespoons boiling water
Filling and Icing:
75 g (3 oz) butter
175 g (6 oz) icing sugar, sifted
2 tablespoons cocoa powder
1 tablespoon boiling water
2 tablespoons rum or brandy
Decoration:
175 g (6 oz) walnut halves

Preparation time: 25 minutes
Cooking time: 9½–10½ minutes
Microwave setting: Medium
Temperature setting: 200°C

1. Base-line and grease two 18-cm (7-in) round sandwich cake dishes. Heat the oven.

2. Beat the butter or margarine with the sugar until very pale and soft. Beat in the eggs, adding a little of the flour if the mixture begins to curdle. Dissolve the coffee in the boiling water and leave to cool slightly. Use a metal spoon to fold the flour into the creamed mixture. Lastly fold in the coffee.

3. Turn the mixture into the prepared dishes, dividing it equally between them. Smooth the top.

4. Bake the cakes, one on the turntable and the second on the wire rack, at 200°C using Medium for 7–7½ minutes, or until the top cake is golden and springy to the touch. Remove the top cake from the oven and transfer the cake from the turntable to the rack. Cook for a further 2½–3 minutes, or until cooked.

5. Leave the cakes in the dishes for a few minutes, then turn out on to a wire rack to cool. Remove the greaseproof paper.

6. To make the filling and icing, beat the butter with the icing sugar until pale and very soft. Mix the cocoa powder with the boiling water, then gradually stir in the rum or brandy. Beat this into the butter icing.

7. Reserve a few of the walnut halves and chop the remainder.

8. Sandwich the cakes together with a little butter icing. Spread a little round the sides of the cake. Put the chopped walnuts on a sheet of greaseproof paper and roll the sides of the cake in them. Spread a thin layer of butter icing over the top. Put the remaining butter icing in a piping bag fitted with a star nozzle and pipe a border round the top edge of the cake. Decorate with the reserved walnut halves.

Cherry and almond cake; Light fruit cake; Mocha Cake

INDEX

Allspice 18
Almond(s)
    and cherry cake 250
    and orange butter 136
    and potato soup 23
    browning 14
    celery with lemon and 214
    buttered 61
    pasta 152
Anchovy(ies)
    butter 47
    cod with 52
Aniseed 18
Apple(s) 169
    and blackberry crumble 171
    and sultana suet pudding 171
    baked stuffed 174
    drink 189
    fillings for 168
    marinade 238
    pork chops with 116
    sauce 166
        defrosting 197
    whole cooked 168
Apricots(s) 169
    filling, nutty 168
Artichoke see globe; Jerusalem
Asafoetida 18
Asparagus 137–8
    cooking 134
Aubergines 138
    stuffed 147
Avocado
    souffléd 234
    stuffed baked, with shrimps 41

Baby food and milk: heating 15
Bacon
    and broccoli soup 24
    and liver casserole 105
    and sage dumplings 209
    and vegetable casserole 121
    cooking 113–14
    courgette shells with 146
    crisping 14
    frankfurters wrapped in 124
    herder's pie 205
    joint, glazed 118
    scrambled eggs with 127
    slipper pudding 210
    sticks, garlic 118
    -wrapped trout 237
Banana(s)
    and coconut filling 168
    baked 178
ring, chocolate 180
Barbecue
    beans: Western baked potatoes
        217
    sauce 122
Basil 16
    and garlic butter 136

tomato soup with rice and 26
Bass 46
Bay 16
Beans 137–8
    lasagne 210–11
    see also barbecue; black-eye;
        broad; butter; green
Béarnaise sauce 165
Beef
    bourguignon 91
    casserole, defrosting 196
    Chinese-style 92
    cooling 82, 83, 244
    defrosting 83
    garlic roast 86
    goulash 89
    in beer 88
    in cider 88
    marinating 82
    Mexican 92
    olives 86
    roast 99, 245
    stock 21
    Stroganoff 89
    tarragon 87
    tomato cottage pie 97
    tournados with pâté 84
    Wellington 245
    see also minced beef; steak
Beefburger and onion rolls 96
Beer, beef in 88
Beetroot 138
Benedict, eggs 130
Berry fruits 169
Biscuits, drying 14
Black cherry cream pie 221
Blackberry and apple crumble 171
Black-eye beans, curried 158
Blanching vegetables 135, 137
Bolognese sauce, defrosting 196
Bourguignon, beef 91
Brandy sauce 38
Bread 248
    combination cooked 228–9
    defrosting 196
    milk loaf 249
    quick jug 31
    sauce 76, 165
    soda 248
    warming 15
Breadcrumbs
    buttered 47
    drying 14
Broad beans 137–8
    in horseradish cream 216
Broccoli 137–8
    and bacon soup 24
    cooking 134
    reheating 135
    serving 137
    with cheese sauce 144
Browning food 14
Brussels sprouts 137–8
Buns, currant 248
Butter
    defrosting 14
    melting 14

Butter beans 153
    with tomatoes 153
Butters
    for vegetables 136
    savoury 47, 64

Cabbage 137–8
    parcels 144
    pork rolls with 199
    with caraway 140
Cakes 180, 218–19
    combination cooked 228–8
    ingredients, warming 19
Calypso coffee 191
Campden tablets, dissolving 14
Cannelloni, stuffed 156
Caper(s)
    in Hollandaise sauce 161
    sauce 50
Caponata 216
Captain's cobbler 237
Caraway seeds 18
    cabbage with 140
    pasta 152
Cardamom 18
Carrot(s) 137–8
    haddock steaks with 54
    soup, cream of 25
    Vichy 140
Cachew and vegetable rice 158
Casseroles
    bacon and vegetable 121
    defrosting 196
    lamb chop 105
    lambs' kidney 104
    liver and bacon 105
    pork 116
    rabbit, with bacon and sage
        dumplings 209
    turkey 71, 74
Cauliflower 137–8
    cheese 143
    cooking 134
    soup, defrosting 197
Cayenne 10
Celery 139
    braised 140
    with lemon and almonds 214
Chaudfroid chicken 72
Cheese
    and ham pudding 131
    and ham stuffing 41
    and herb toasties 202
    and salami flan 132
    and spinach quiche, wholewheat
        205
    cooking 127
    Mozzarella, lamb with 106
    Parmesan herb butter 136
    sauce 50, 93, 143, 144, 157, 161,
        163
    scrambled eggs with 127
    spaghetti Mozzarella 203
    stuffed jacket potatoes 145
    turkey breasts cordon bleu 67
    warming 15
    Welsh rarebit 131

Cheesecake
    defrosting 196
    honey 175
Cheesy smoked haddock 50
Cherry(ies) 169
    and almond cake 250
    lamb with 106
    see also black cherry
Chervil 16
Chestnuts: steak 94
Chick peas
    pasta with 152
    spiced 153
Chicken
    à la King 73
    and ham, jellied 37
    and ham lasagne 156
    and vegetable soup 28
    boning 61
    chaudfroid 72
    combination cooking 231, 238
    cooking 64
    defrosting 65
    drumsticks, devilled 67
    galantine 239
    in vermouth 75
    in wine 68
    marengo 68
    roast, with spicy rice stuffing 239
    with walnut and orange
        stuffing 208
    sherry 70
    stock 21
    supper, one-dish 226
    with sweet and sour sauce 224
Chicory 139
Chilli 18
    con carne 91
Chinese-style beef 92
Chips, defrosting 196
Chive(s) 16
    and tomato topping 47
    sauce 161
Chocolate
    banana ring 180
    cake, one-stage 180
    custard 166
    hot 190
    melting 14–15
    mousse 177
Chutney
    mango 187
    tomato 185
Christmas pudding 173
Cider
    beef in 88
    gammon in 120
    lamb in cream and 109
    mulled 192
Cinnamon 18
Cloves 18
Cobbler topping 236
Cocoa 188
Coconut and banana filling 168
Cod 46
    in butter sauce, defrosting 196
    in tomato and onion sauce 55

risotto 57
  with anchovies 52
  with herbs 48
Coffee
  calypso 191
  heating 188
Combination microwave
    cooking 228–51
Containers
  for combination cooking
    230–1
  for microwave cooking 11–12
Convection cooking 229
Coq au vin 68
Coquilles St Jacques 34
Coriander 16, 19
Corned beef: Western baked
    potatoes 217
Corn-on-the-cob 137, 139
  cooking 30
  with parsley butter 37
  see also sweetcorn
Cottage pie
  defrosting 196
  tomato 97
Country vegetable soup 26
Courgettes 137, 139
  shells with bacon 146
Crab, hot 34
Cranberry(ies)
  pork with orange and 119
  relish 187
  sauce 164
Croquette potatoes 142
Croûtons 14, 15, 28
Crown roast of lamb 108
Crumbles 168
  apple and blackberry 171
  honey crunch 221
Crumbs, buttered 136
Cumberland sauce 114
Cumin 18
Currant buns 248
Curried black-eye beans 158
  pork, cold 123
  rice 150, 154
Curry
  lamb 109
  light summer 224
  sauce 165
  vegetarian 149
Custard 218
  chocolate 166
  egg 166

Damsons 169
Danish pizza 202
Defrosting 11, 195–7
  beef 83
  lamb 101
  meat 81
  poultry and game 65
  spinach 136
Devilled chicken drumsticks 67
Dill 16, 19
Dough, pizza 149
Dressing, French 33

Dried fruit
  Christmas pudding 173
  sponge pudding 175
  winter pudding 221
Drinks 188–2
Duck
  combination cooking 231, 238
  cooking 63, 64
  defrosting 65
  roast 78
  spiced 18
  with red wine sauce 76
Dumplings, bacon and sage 209

Egg(s)
  baked 128
  Benedict 130
  boiled 129
    for topping 136
  cooking 126–7
  custard 166
  Florentine 130
  fried 128
  nog, hot whisky 190
  noodles 152
  omelette 129
  poached 129
  sauce 132
  scrambled 126–7

Fennel 16, 19
Fenugreek 19
Fish
  as convenience food 45
  boning 44
  cakes, defrosting 196
  captain's cobbler 236
  cooking techniques 42, 43, 46
  curry 224
  defrosting 47
  gutting 47
  pie 57
  portioning 45
  preparation 45
  reheating 46
  risotto 57
  rolls 44
  sauce 163
  sauces for 47
  scaling 45
  skinning 44
  smoked, kedgeree 154
  soup 27
  steamed 48
  stock 21
  toppings for 47
  see also seafood *and specific fish*
Flageolet beans 153
Flan
  pineapple 177
  salami and cheese 132
Florentine, eggs 130
Frankfurters wrapped in bacon 124
Freezing soups 22
French beans 137–8
French dressing 33
French-style lamb 103

Frozen food for microwaving 194–7
Fruit
  cooking 168–9
  defrosting 169
  drinks 189
  heating before squeezing 14
  preparation for preserve 182
  salad, fresh 178
  starters 30
  -stuffed pancakes 174

Galantine of chicken 239
Game
  cooking 60, 61, 64
  defrosting 65
  marinating 238
  see also duck; pheasant; pigeon;
    rabbit
Gammon
  cooking 113–14, 244
  in cider 120
  steaks with pineapple 120
Garlic 16
  and basil butter 136
  bacon sticks 118
  butter 33
  roast beef 86
Gâteau, mocha honey 218–19
Gelatine, dissolving 14
Ginger 19
  sponge pudding 179
Gingerbread 180
Globe artichokes 138
  ham soufflé in 234
  with French dressing 33
Gooseberry(ies) 169
  and mint puddings 218
  jam 185
  sauce 166
Goulash, beef 89
Grape(s)
  Chicken livers and 68
  sauce 50
Grapefruit and orange, honeyed 36
Gravy 99
Green beans 140
Greengages 169
Grilling, combination 231
Guard of honour 111

Haddock 46
  baked, with capers 50
  cheesy smoked 50
  Mornay shells 224
  mousse 58
  smoked 46
    pie 57
    with egg sauce 132
    with noodles 198
    spiced 53
  steaks with carrots 54
Halibut 46
Ham
  and cheese pudding 131
  and cheese stuffings 41
  and cheese toasties 202
  and chicken, jellied 37

and chicken lasagne 156
and mushroom pasta 152
and potato supper 204
herder's pie 205
omelette 129
pâté, picnic 124
risotto 154
soufflé in artichokes 234
stuffing 239
turkey breasts cordon bleu 67
with scrambled eggs 127
Hamburgers, cooking 83
Haricot beans 153
Herb(s) 16–17
  and lemon marinated lamb
    chops 103
  and walnut stuffing 64
  butter 47, 64
  drying 16
  flavoured rice 150
  orange rice 150
  Parmesan butter 136
  pasta 152
  scrambled eggs with 127
  stuffing 48, 49
Herder's pie 205
Herrings
  rollmops 34
  with mustard sauce 50
Hollandaise sauce 161
Honey
  cheesecake 175
  crunch crumble 221
  grapefruit and orange 36
  mocha gâteau 218–19
Horseradish 17
  and sausage roly-poly 222
  cream 216
Hot pot, punchy 207

Jam 182–3
  gooseberry 185
  sauce 166
  strawberry 183, 184
Jars, heating up 182, 186
Jellied ham and chicken 37
Jelly, dissolving 14
Jerusalem artichokes, buttered 142
Juniper berries 19

Kebabs, pork 122
Kedgeree 154
  kipper and corn 226
Kidney *see under* lamb
Kidney beans 153
Kipper(s) 46
  and corn kedgeree 226
  pâté 40

Lamb
  accompaniments 103
  boned 100
  chops: casserole 105
    combination cooked 114, 244
    lemon and herb marinated 103
    with spicy sauce 107
  cooking 100–1, 244

crown roast of 108
curry 109
cutlets 100
defrosting 101
French-style 103
guard of honour 111
in cream and cider 109
kidney casserole 104
liver and bacon casserole 105
 with vegetables, braised 207
marinating 101
moussaka 108
noisettes 104
roast leg 103
stuffed breast of 110
stuffed leg of 110, 245
sweet and sour 106
with cherries 106
with Mozzarella cheese 106
Lasagne
 bean 210–11
 beef 246
 ham and chicken 156
Leeks 137, 139
 à la greque 216
 and luncheon sausage
  supper 201
 soup surprise 234
Lemon
 and herb marinated lamb
  chops 103
 butter 47
 celery with almonds and 214
 curd 184
 Hollandaise sauce 161
 meringue pie 179
 parsley butter 136
 sponge cake 180
 tea 188
Lemon balm 17
Lemon trout 54
Lemonade 189
Lentils 153
 and orange soup 25
 green, with nuts 153
 vegetable rissoles 215
Lettuce soup with croûtons 28
Liver
 and bacon casserole 105
 pâté 40
 see also chicken; lamb
Lobster 46
Lovage 17
Luncheon sausage supper, leek
 and 201

Macaroni 152
 cheese 157
Mace 19
Mackerel
 in a bag 35
 roll-ups 49
Madeira cake 250
Maître d'hôtel butter 47
Mango chutney 187
Marinades
 for beef 82

for lamb 101, 103
 for poultry and game 238
 for spareribs 212
 red wine 82
Marjoram 17
Marrow 137, 139
 stuffed 147
Meals: combination cooking 232
 defrosting 196
Meat 80–81
 combination cooking 232, 244–5
 see also specific meats
Meatballs
 in mushroom and tomato
  sauce 96
 sweet and sour 212
Melba sauce 166
Microwave technology 10–13
Milk
 drinks 188
 heating 188
  baby's bottle 15
 loaf 249
Minced beef
 bean lasagne 210–11
 beefburger and onion rolls 96
 chilli con carne 91
 cooking 82
 lasagne 246
 meat loaf 98
 meatballs in mushroom and
  tomato sauce 95
 mushroom and onion suet
  pudding 90
 pie 246
 savoury, with mixed
  vegetables 97
 shepherd's pie 98
 spaghetti bolognese 156
 stuffed cannelloni 156
  marrow 147
 sweet and sour meatballs 212
 with cheese sauce 93
Minced lamb moussaka 108
Mint 17
 and gooseberry pudding 218
 and pea soup 27
 cream 103
 sauce 103
Minted peas 140
Mixed fruit sponge pudding 175
Mocha
 cake 251
 honey gâteau 218–19
Mornay sauce 224
Moussaka 108
Mousse
 chocolate 177
 haddock 58
 tuna 58
Mozzarella cheese
 lamb with 106
 spaghetti and 203
Mulligatawny soup 25
Mushroom(s) 139
 and ham pasta 152
 and ham sauce 96

and onion stuffing 86
 in garlic butter 33
 onion and beef suet pudding 90
 sauce 81, 95
 soup 29
Mussels 43
Mustard 19
 and prune sauce 222
 cream 114
 Hollandaise sauce 161
 sauce 50
Noisettes of lamb 104
Noodles 152
 smoked haddock with 198
Nutmeg 19
Nuts, green lentils with 153
 see also specific nuts
Nutty
 apricot filling 168
 topping 47
Omelette 129
Onion(s) 137, 139
 and almond butter 136
 and mushroom stuffing 86
 and potato bake 149
 and potato soup 24
 and sage dumplings 209
 and tomato sauce 55
 mushroom and beef suet
  pudding 90
 pasta with 152
 rolls, beefburger and 96
 sauce 161, 165
  defrosting 197
 stuffed 145
Orange(s)
 and grapefruit, honeyed 36
 and lentil soup 25
 and raisin filling 168
 and walnut butter 47
 and walnut stuffing 208
 juice, defrosting 196
 pork with cranberries and 119
 rind, shredded 22
 sauce 166, 211
 tea 191
 turkey with almonds and 70
Oregano 17
 and tomato sauce 117
Oriental chicken with sweet and
 sour sauce 224

Paella 154
Pancakes
 fruit-stuffed 174
 prawn and lemon 39
Paprika 19
 pork chops 122
Parmesan herb butter 136
Parsley 17
 and thyme stuffing 64
 butter 37
 lemon butter 136
 parsnips with 140
 sauce 163

Parsnips 137, 139
 with parsley 140
Pasta 151, 156–7
 additions to 152
 bows, tomato 39
 cooking 152
 fresh 152
 salami-stuffed 200
 scallops, 200
Pastry 168
 choux 229
 puff 228
Pâté 30
 beef tournadon with 84
 kipper 40
 liver 40
 picnic ham 124
Patties, defrosting 196
Peach(es) 169
 garnish 64
Peanut sauce, spicy 64
Pears 169
Peas 137, 139
 and mint soup 27
 dried 153
 minted 140
Pectin in sugar 183
Pepper(ed) 19
 pasta 152
 rice 150
 sauce 94
Peppers with savoury rice 146
Pheasant
 combination cooked 238
 roast, with bread sauce 76
Picnic ham pâté 124
Pie
 black cherry cream 221
 cottage 97
 fish 57
 herder's 205
 lemon meringue 179
 minced beef 246
Pigeons, braised 77
Pillau rice 158
Pineapple
 flan 177
 gammon steaks in 120
 upside down pudding 177
Pizza
 Danish 202
 tomato and salami 149
Plaice
 fillets in white wine 50
 with sweetcorn 52
Plums 169
Poppy seeds 19
Pork
 casserole 112, 116
 chops: combination cooked 232,
  244
 paprika 122
 with apple 116
 with oregano and tomato
  sauce 117
 cold curried 123
 cooking 112–13, 244

crackling 112
defrosting 113
fillets in wine sauce 119
kebabs 122
loin, stuffed 125
roast 114
rolls with cabbage 199
seasoning 112
spareribs with barbecue
    sauce 122
    Provençal 212
stuffing 112
sweet and sour soup 198 9
with orange and cranberries
    119
see also bacon; gammon; ham
Potato(es) 139
    and almond soup, puréed 23
    and ham supper 204
    and onion bake 149
    and onion soup 24
    and sweetcorn soup 25
    boiled 140
    cooking 135
    croquette 142
    salad 148
    serving 137
    shepherd's pie 98
    slices, crisp 75
    stuffed jacket 145
    tomato cottage pie 97
    Western baked 217
Poultry
    accompaniments 64
    boning 60–61
    breasts 62
    browning 61
    casseroles 62–63
    combination cooked 231,
        238
    cooking 60–64
        times 64
    defrosting 65
    joints 62
    marinating 238
    portioning 62–63
    stuffing 64
    trussing 60
    see also chicken; poussins; turkey
Poussins 74
Prawn(s) 46
    and lemon pancakes 39
    defrosting 47
    peeling 45
    scrambled eggs with 127
    stuffing 41, 49
    with garlic and tomatoes 38
Preserves 182–3, 184–7
Provençal sauce 212
Prune
    and mushroom sauce 222
    stuffing 71
Puddings 168–9, 171–9, 218–21
Pulses 153, 158
Punches 189
    hot rum 192
Punchy hot pot 207

Queen of puddings 173
Quiche, wholewheat spinach and
    cheese 205

Rabbit
    casserole with bacon and sage
        dumplings 209
    in white wine 76
Raisin and orange filling 168
Ratatouille 36
Red mullet 46
Red snapper 46
Red wine
    chicken in 68
    duck in 76
    marinade 82
    mulled 192
    pigeons in 77
Redcurrant cream, rich 103
Reheating food 196–7
Relish
    cranberry 187
    sweetcorn 186
Rhubarb 169
Rice
    additions to 150–1
    cooking 151–2
    curried 154
    defrosting 196
    kedgeree 154
        kipper and corn 226
    paella 154
    pillau 156
    risotto 154
        alla Milanese 150
        fish 57
    savoury 148
    stuffing, spicy 239
    tomato soup with basil and 26
    types 150
    vegetable and cashew 158
Rissoles, vegetable 215
Rissoto 154
    alla Milanese 150
    fish 57
Rollmops 84
Roly poly, sausage and
    horseradish 222
Rosé wine sauce 119
Rosemary 17
Rum punch, hot 192
Runner beans 137–8

Saffron 19
Sage 17
    and onion dumplings 209
Salad
    fresh fruit 178
    potato 148
Salami
    and cheese flan 132
    and tomato pizza 149
    -stuffed pasta 200
Salmon 46
    cooking 42
    poached 59
    smoked, with scrambled egg 127

Salmon trout 46
Sauces 160–6
    apple 166
    barbecue 122
    Béarnaise 165
    brandy 38
    bread 76, 165
    caper 50
    cheese 50, 93, 143, 144, 157, 161,
        163
    chive 161
    cranberry 164
    Cumberland 114
    curry 165
    defrosting 161, 196–7
    egg 132
    fish 163
    for fish 47
    for vegetables 136
    freezing 161
    gooseberry 166
    grape 50
    Hollandaise 161
    jam 166
    meat 82
    Melba 166
    mint 103
    Mornay 224
    mushroom 81, 95, 161
        and tomato 96
    mustard 50, 161
        prune and 222
    onion 161, 165
    orange 166, 211
    oregano and tomato 117
    parsley 163
    pepper 94
    Provençal 212
    red wine 76
    reheating 161
    rosé wine 119
    seasoning 161
    spicy 107
        peanut 64
    sweet and sour 73, 224
    tomato 39, 165
        and onion 55
    white 160, 162–3
Sausage(s) 113–14
    and horseradish roly-poly 222
Scallops 46
    cleaning 45
    coquilles St Jacques 34
    defrosting 47
Scampi 46
    defrosting 47
    in brandy sauce 38
Seafood
    as convenience food 45
    cocktail, hot 34
    cooking 43
    paella 154
    portioning 45
    starters 30
    see also crab; prawns; scallops;
        scampi; shrimps
Sesame seeds 19

Shellfish see seafood
Shepherd's pie 98
Sherry chicken 70
Shrimps 46
    and sole rolls 53
    defrosting 47
    potted 223
    stuffed baked avocado with 41
Slipper pudding 210
Smoked haddock see haddock
Soda bread 248
Sole and shrimp rolls 53
Soufflé
    avocado 234
    cold strawberry 172
    combination cooked 229
    ham, in artichokes 234
Soups
    broccoli and bacon 24
    chicken and vegetable 28
    convenience 22
    cooking 22, 23
    country vegetable 26
    cream of carrot 25
    defrosting 23, 196–7
    fish 27
    freezing 22
    lettuce, with croûtons 28
    leek surprise 234
    lentil and orange 25
    mulligatawny 25
    mushroom 29
    pea and mint 27
    potato and onion 24
    puréed potato and almond 24
    serving 22
    sweet and sour 198–9
    sweetcorn and potato 25
    thickening 22
    tomato with rice and basil 26
    vegetable 23
    vichysoisse 29
Spaghetti 152
    bolognese 156
    Mozzarella 203
Spareribs
    Provençal 212
    with barbecue sauce 122
Spices 18–19
Spinach 137, 139
    and cheese quiche,
        wholewheat 205
    defrosting 136
    eggs florentine 130
    terrine 215
Split peas 153
Sponge cakes 250–1
    lemon 80
Sponge pudding
    ginger 179
    mixed fruit 175
Star anise 19
Steak
    cooking 83, 232, 244
    in pepper sauce 94
    tournados with pâté 84
    whisky 95

with chestnuts 94
with mushroom sauce 95
Stock 20
  beef 21
  chicken 21
  fish 21
  vegetable 21
Strawberry(ies)
  jam 183, 184
  soufflé, cold 172
Stroganoff, beef 89
Stuffed
  aubergines 147
  baked avocado with shrimps 11
  cabbage 144
  cannelloni 156
  chicken 71
  jacket potatoes 145
  lamb 110, 111
  marrow 147
  onions 145
  pork loin 125
  poultry 64
  roast chicken 71
  tomatoes 41
  trout 49
  turkey 79
  vegetables 144–7
Stuffings
  bacon 146
  cheese and ham 41
  fruit 174
  ham 239
  herb 48, 49
  mushroom and onion 86
  orange and walnut 208
  prawn 41, 49
  rice 146
    spicy 239
  salami 200
Suet puddings
  apple and sultana 171

beef, mushroom and onion 90
sausage and horseradish 222
slipper 210
winter 221
Sugar
  for preserving 183
  warming 15
Sultana and apple suet pudding 171
Summer savory 17
Swedes 137
Sweet and sour
  lamb 106
  meatballs 212
  sauce 73, 224
  soup 198
Sweetcorn 141
  and kipper kedgeree 226
  and potato soup 25
  plaice fillets with 52
  relish 186
  see also corn-on-the-cob

Tagliatelle 152
Tarragon 17
  beef 87
Tea 188
  lemon 188
  orange 191
Terrine, spinach 215
Thickeners 22
Thyme 17
  and parsley stuffing 64
Toasties, cheese and ham 202
Tomato(es) 139
  and chive topping 47
  and mushroom sauce 96
  and onion sauce 55
  and oregano sauce 117
  and salami pizza 149
  chutney 185
  cottage pie 97
  Hollandaise sauce 161

pasta bows 39
prawns with garlic and 38
relish, quick 103
sauce 39, 165
soup with rice and basil 26
stuffed 41
with beans 153
with scrambled eggs 127
Toppings
  for fish 47
  for vegetables 136
Treacle pudding 172
Trifle 177
Trout 46
  bacon-wrapped 237
  lemon 54
  stuffed 49
  with orange 211
Tuna mousse 58
Turkey
  breasts cordon bleu 67
  casserole 74
  combination cooked 238
  cooking 64
  defrosting 65
  legs casserole 71
  punchy hot pot 207
  roast, with prune and mustard
    sauce 222
  stuffed roast 79
  with orange and almonds 70
Turmeric 19
Turnips 137, 139

Vegetable(s)
  and cashew rice 158
  and chicken soup 28
  blanching 135, 137
  braised liver with 207
  buttered 136
  caponata 216
  casserole, bacon and 121

cooking 134–8
cutting 134
defrosting 136
mixed, savoury mince with 97
ratatouille 36
reheating 135
rice 151
rissoles 215
sauced 136
soup 23
  country 26
  starters 30
  stock 21
Vegetarian curry 149
Vermouth, chicken in 75
Vichy carrots 140
Vichysoisse soup 29
Victoria sandwich 250

Walnut
  and herb stuffing 64
  and orange butter 47
  and orange stuffing 208
  cream 64
  oil marinade 238
Welsh rarebit 131
Western baked potatoes 217
Whisky
  egg nog, hot 190
  steak 95
White sauce 162–3
  one-stage 160
White wine
  marinade 238
  plaice fillets in 50
  rabbit in 76
Wholewheat spinach and cheese
    quiche 205
Wine
  warming mulled 15
  see red, rosé, or white wine
Winter pudding 221

ACKNOWLEDGEMENTS

Photographers: Howard Allman 1; James Jackson 159, 186, 187, 198/9, 201, 203, 204, 206, 208/9, 210/11, 213, 214, 217, 218/19, 220, 223, 225, 227; David Jordan 12, 13, 14, 15, 20, 23, 30, 31, 42, 43, 44, 61, 62, 63, 81, 82, 127, 134, 136 150, 151, 160, 168, 183, 189, 194, 195, 228; James Murphy 2/3, 4/5, 6/7, 8/9, 235, 236/7, 240, 241, 242, 247, 249, 251; Peter Myers 24, 26, 27, 28, 29, 32/3, 35, 36, 37, 39, 40, 41, 48, 49, 51, 52, 53, 54, 55, 56/7, 58, 59, 66/7, 69, 70/1, 72/3, 74/5, 77, 78, 79, 84/5, 86, 87, 88, 91, 92, 93, 94, 95, 96, 97, 98, 99, 102, 104, 105, 107, 108, 109, 110, 111, 115, 116/17, 18, 119, 120, 121, 123, 124, 125, 128, 129, 130, 132, 141, 142/3, 144, 145, 146, 147, 148, 155, 157, 162/3, 164, 167, 170/1, 172, 173, 174, 175, 176, 178/9, 181, 184/5, 190/1, 192/3; Charlie Stebbings 38, 89, 90, 133.

Illustrator: Patricia Capon; Joan Farmer Artists.